A HUNDRED YEARS OF CHINA METHODISM

A HUNDRED YEARS
OF CHINA METHODISM

WALTER N. LACY

ABINGDON-COKESBURY PRESS
New York • *Nashville*

A HUNDRED YEARS OF CHINA METHODISM

x

Printed in the United States of America

TO MY FATHER *and* MOTHER
who, from 1887 to 1925, labored for the building of the
church in China
whose mortal remains lie buried in Chinese soil
in that sacred cemetery in
Foochow
and whose influence led their five children
also to have a share in the development of
The Methodist Church in China

FOREWORD

"CONSIDER THE PAST AND YOU WILL KNOW THE FUTURE," SAYS A CHINESE proverb. "The past must live or else the future dies," R. P. Shuler once wrote in *The Upper Room*. "The fountains are in the yesterdays. The streams root back into the mists and clouds. They flow today, but the showers fell in the other days."

In September, 1947, the Methodist Church in China marked its centennial. Its fountains were in the yesterdays, the showers that brought it to the fruitage of today fell in days now gone; its healing and life-giving streams which are flowing today root back into mists and clouds. We dare not forget these; they must be made known to our children and our children's children.

Perhaps they are right who say we should look forward rather than backward. It is just as true today as it was when Frank D. Gamewell penned these words in China twenty-seven years ago: "Prospect, not retrospect, is the demand of present world conditions, and yet in all our planning there must be the backward as well as the forward look." The Methodist Church in China had to live a century before it could face the problems and developments of its second century. If any other excuse is necessary before I tell this story of my church in the land that was so long my home, it is that

> For her my tears shall fall,
>   For her my prayers ascend,
> To her my cares and toils be given,
>   Till toils and cares shall end.

I have not written this book to be stacked on the shelves of historical libraries. I have written it to preserve for the church of the coming centuries some of the significant facts and records of the first century of China Methodism. I have written it for those Chinese and Americans and other Methodists and other churchmen who want the inspiration of what has been done in order to do what remains to be done. I want the reader to see that the church that was brought from the United States to China in sections is now a united church at home in China, a church which is Chinese, though a part of a world-wide church.

John W. Bricker once said: "Only about one tenth of one per cent of what happens ever gets into the history books." Doubtless he is right, for many things must have happened through this century that are not even mentioned in my unused material. I have not tried to make this a factual compendium but rather to select the significant and typical in order to give an impression of the general movement. Burton J. Hendrick, in the prologue to *Bulwark of the Republic*, says: "Anyone who embarks on a survey of one hundred and fifty years finds an abundance of material." And so I have found it. To keep the story within the limits of this volume I have had to deprive my readers of many a fascinating incident and many an item, for the omission of which I may be criticized by those who have shared in the events. So many missionaries and so many Chinese, whose names are not mentioned, have had a part in the building of this church. They are as immortal as any, and I wish it had been possible to include a complete roster of the noble roll.

R. S. Maclay, that great Methodist pioneer builder in China, said in an address which he made in New York when the Methodist Episcopal Church had been in China just twenty-five years:

I am not here to tell the story of our struggles and victories in China, but I may be allowed to state that when the history of our China mission is written, it will constitute one of the brightest pages in the glorious records of our church, a page over which the good of all lands and ages will linger with delight.

The seventy-five years that have passed since these words were spoken have so fully borne out this prediction that I believe this book is justified.

I have not solved one problem that has perplexed me throughout the preparation of this work: the orthography of proper names, personal and geographical. The Chinese whose names appear in the story of the earlier years have disappeared from the later pages, and hence their names as then spelled have outlived them. The national language spelling, as used in later years, has commonly been used in the names of men and women now living. Exceptions even to this occur, as, for example, in the names of Bishop Z. T. Kaung and James Ding, who are known to many in the United States by the local spelling of their names. One matter of uniformity has, however, been followed in the spelling of personal names: the given names are all spelled with capitalization of both names, separated by a hyphen—thus altering, to that extent at least, the quoted orthography.

Geographical locations, on the other hand, have outlived the spelling of their names, sometimes two or three times. The present official postal spelling would mean nothing to the hosts of people who have through the decades given to and prayed for the work, for example, at Lekdu, now spelled Lutu, or at Nanping, more familiarly and widely known as Yenping—city and conference—and before that as the Iong-bing field of the Foochow Conference. It has seemed best, therefore, to follow the line of least resistance, and in general to use the contemporary spelling. A cross index to alternative spelling of geographical names has therefore been provided at the end of the book.

It is a source of real regret that I could not find certain records of the Board of Missions of the Methodist Episcopal Church, South, covering quite a period of years. Many apparent omissions in the story of the China Mission and Conference are due to that loss.

Of the many people who have helped me with this book, all too few can be named here.

I owe a very great deal of gratitude to my wife for the many times her memory of events and persons served to supplement or check facts and data before I dared to write them down. But to an even larger degree I appreciate her willingness over the past ten years to devote our vacations to this purpose, making the best of her time while I explored library stacks, or copying extracts for me from dusty volumes, and then during those days when I was putting on paper those findings amid the quiet surroundings of our vacation spots. And she has borne with me through these years while I have devoted most of my Sunday evenings to typing, editing, and revising what had been written.

Miss Myrtle Cline, research librarian at the Board of Missions library, and later at Union Theological Seminary, New York, has given most valuable aid. Again and again I have had to ask her to get information on some point or check conflicting statements on my cards. In every case she has not only dug out the material, if it was to be had at all, sweating sometimes in attic stacks in the heat of summer, but always anxious to have me call on her again and again, and never failing in her encouragement. The accuracy of many an item in this book is due to Miss Cline.

My special thanks must be expressed to the librarians and their assistants at Baldwin-Wallace University; Mount Union College; Ohio Wesleyan University; the Methodist Historical Library, Boston; the Missionary Research Library, New York; the former Library of the Board of Missions of the Methodist Episcopal Church, South, Nashville; the former Library of the Board of Foreign Missions of The Methodist Episcopal Church, New York; the Library of the Division of Foreign Missions of The Methodist Church, New York; the Burton Historical Library of the Detroit Public Library; and the Cleveland Public Library. Their willingness and co-operation have been a very great help in finding the wealth of material that they made available.

My thanks are also expressed to the following persons who have generously loaned precious manuscripts in their possession: the late Mrs. Spencer Lewis; the Rev. Lloyd F. Worley; and the librarian of the former Board of Missions of the Methodist Episcopal Church. Also to Mrs. C. F. S. White, for the gift of the diary and considerable personal correspondence belonging to her father-in-law, Moses White, from which I have quoted in spite of his statement written nearly a year before he sailed for Foochow, and after several weeks had passed without any entry in his diary: "Another reason why I have neglected writing is that I have a great horror of the book-making mania of the present age and I am unwilling to have anything I may write printed after I am dead for the sake of making another book."

The following persons have read much or all of the manuscript while it has been in preparation; and without their continued encouragement, their frank criticisms, and their valued suggestions, I would hardly have dared offer it to the publishers: The Revs. Frank T. Cartwright, J. W. Cline, C. B. Rappe, Hubert L. Sone, E. M. Stowe, Louis C. Wright; Bishops John Gowdy, Paul B. Kern, Carleton Lacy, Ralph A. Ward; and Dr. C. V. Thomas.

To the following persons for reviewing and criticizing certain sections on which I needed their help I am also extremely grateful: The Revs. Perry O. Hanson, J. C. Hawk, C. S. Heininger, F. P. Jones, F. Olin Stockwell; and Mr. Paul P. Wiant.

Mrs. George F. Fitch wrote the section on the Epworth League, and Mrs. John Gowdy the section on Bishop Bashford, both at my request; both graciously permitted me to edit, abbreviate, and supplement what they wrote. To them both my appreciation is greater than I have been able to express to them personally.

Having expressed my inadequate thanks to many and valued critics and assistants, I am willing to let the book convey as best it may the story of three missions from the United States which in a hundred years have become a church at home in China. This panorama of achievement, which I have seen while I have been writing it, is presented in the following pages

Lest we forget, lest we forget!

WALTER N. LACY

CONTENTS

INTRODUCTION

IN THE CHANCEL OF A METHODIST CHURCH IN CLEVELAND IS A BEAUTIFUL rose window in shades of blue. Another window in the same church is varicolored, and depicts six scenes, each different but each forming a unit in the symbolism. The glass of this window has been colored with pigments externally applied, rich in shading and harmony, but varying in intensity and permanency. In contrast, the rich blue of the rose window has been fused into the glass. The rare beauty of this window results from the fact that the coloring is not an externally applied stain, but is equally innate throughout all sections; the pigment which was introduced into the molten flux was extraneous to it but became an inherent part of the glass.

For the past century China has been at the mercy of foreign nations. The Opium War, the Boxer attack, with the treaties which resulted, and the invasion by Japan were only more notable manifestations of these impacts from outside. Japan, the United States, and the European powers have been for a hundred years using diplomacy and force, commerce and intrigue, to secure for themselves something which they have coveted and which they felt they could get from China.

To a nation which had a history, a literature, and the beginnings of democratic government when Jesus was telling his people to seek first the kingdom of God, there came younger nations which had grown faster, seeking gain for themselves. Whether Anglo-Saxon or Muscovite, Nipponese or Latin, the nations of the world during the past century have looked to China as a field for acquisition.

But simultaneously most of these nations have had something to offer to this race which had always been so rich. Opium was already being supplied to China when the war of 1840-42 took Hong Kong away from China, and the narcoticization of the country has continued to this day. And the land that had invented gunpowder was given firearms, grenades, and airplanes with which to defend itself against the aggression of those nations which had outstripped it in the means and the will to warfare.

Fortunately, however, the Western nations offered with the other hand the roots of peace and good will. The greedy merchant and the covetous statesman were accompanied by the missionary who came to China to preach good will and to share with the Chinese the blessings which the Christian church had brought to those who lived on either side of the Atlantic Ocean. The people of Europe and North America have, for nearly a hundred and fifty years, been giving to the people of the Orient the best that they have, sometimes, it is true, tainted with their own faults and idiosyncrasies, and flavored with their creeds and rituals, but nevertheless given with the sincere belief that the church of Christ, as it had been built in the so-called Christian countries, was needed and would be welcome in those lands in the life of which it could become a part.

During the past century China has gone through fire. But for a hundred years now American Methodism has been pouring into this changing nation the rich blue of its life; the molten flux which the century has produced has had the spirit of the Wesleys fused into it.

From the landing of American Methodist missionaries in Foochow and Shanghai, with the spread of the church through Kiangsi and Anhwei to Chengtu and beyond, through Shantung, radiating from Peking, and on to Kalgan—

From missions whose policies and detailed programs were prescribed by board offices in New York and Nashville, to the election by the Chinese of Chinese to be bishops and administrators of the ten conferences of the church in China—

From the founding of a little day school in Foochow through schools for boys and girls to the colleges and professional schools, and on to its inter-denominational co-operation in great universities—

From the handling out of pills and salve by the missionaries, to the self-supporting, well-equipped hospitals, where surgery, ophthalmology and dental care could be combined with the healing of the soul—

From the private publication of three hundred copies of Matthew's Gospel and the purchase of a font of double pica Chinese type, through the local printing presses in nearly every conference to the establishment of a great Publishing House, the publication of a *Christian Advocate,* and a share in the translation of the Bible—

From the renunciation by Sia Sek-Ong of any financial support from American sources, through contributions of water chestnuts and sacks of beans to help support the institutions of the church, to the day when a Chinese layman could say, "Now the people give to the Lord"—

From the day that Isabel Atwater White gave her life for the women of China, and every one on the streets of Nanchang knew the name and spirit of Dr. Ida Kahn, to the time when the women of East China sent a woman missionary to the prewar frontier of Yunnan—

From the renting of a fifteen-by-fifty-foot room for a chapel to the $325,000 church with its neon-lighted cross where two thousand people found help and comfort daily—

From the time when churches had Epworth Leagues before they had young people to the great student conferences on the surf-beaten island of Pootoo—

INTRODUCTION

From three separate missions in Foochow, Shanghai, and Kalgan to one Methodist Church at home in China—

That is a part of the story that unfolds in the following chapters, the story of the growth of The Methodist Church in China, a very part of the Christian China that is to be.

I
THE DAY OF MARCH HAS COME

Lead on O King Eternal,
The day of march has come.

1. *Methodism Ready for China*

THAT METHODISM SHOULD ENTER CHINA WAS INEVITABLE. JOHN WESLEY'S immortal words—"The world is my parish"—will forever describe the church that has grown from his spiritual awakening. In these words he stated a fundamental principle, gave his followers a campaign slogan, and uttered a prophecy of divine purpose as true as that of any of Hebrew writ. What the Wesleyan Movement would have been had it not been built on the faith that it was meant for all people and that all men everywhere could be warmed with that strange inner glow, no optimist can imagine. Had Wesley's followers not taken him at his word, crossed the ocean, climbed continental mountain ranges, penetrated primeval forests, and still pressed on to the university centers of Europe's culture and the crowded villages of Oriental farmers, had they not thought that he meant that they should carry the gospel into all the world as Jesus had directed his disciples to do, Wesley would today be remembered only as a brilliant light that had flashed as a meteor across England's sky and left only a cold stone to show where his flight ended. But whether or not he saw with the eye of an Isaiah or a Malachi the world-wide result of his preaching, his utterance has been fulfilled, and China, like Poland and Argentina, Rhodesia and India, has become the home of that movement which is claiming the world for Wesley's Master.

That Methodism must enter China was directly the result of the spirit which pervaded the Protestant church, and, therefore, the Methodist churches in the United States during the first half of the nineteenth century. That half-century in the United States was an era of great territorial growth and expansion. In that span the nation which had included merely the Atlantic seaboard became a nation which reached from ocean to ocean across a continent of mountain ranges and prairie expanses. A people which had so recently turned its back upon its mother country and now found itself face to face with a continent in which to develop, must be restless. Henry Kalloch Rowe pictures this restless epic in these words: "America had been vitalized by the swift life currents of the frontier."

But economic and social changes no less significant were taking place among its people. The desire to extend the right to hold slaves in the territory west of the Mississippi was heading the country towards the greatest crisis which has existed in North America since the Declaration of Independence. Repeatedly from the days of Jefferson's administration to Lincoln's inauguration the enlarging nation was being threatened with secession and consequent division. The industrial development of New England and the North Atlantic states; the trade partiality between the South Atlantic states and Great Britain; the invention of the cotton gin and other laborsaving devices; the construction of the Erie, Ohio, and other canals; puffing locomotives pulling cars over steel rails; the westward drift of commerce and population inevitable with these means of travel and the topography west of the Alleghenies, especially with the American flag now flying over all parts of the Mississippi basin, all these shared in producing labor problems and commercial readjustments which further increased the restlessness of the American people during a period when new land, new opportunities, new production methods, and growing racial agitations were jarring them out of their routine.

Said Daniel Dorchester: "For a period of fifty years—from 1815 to the end of the Civil War—the vibrant deep-toned theme of the West ran through the orchestration of American events," and permeated its religious life as well, compelling it to grow and expand its activity. The closing years of the eighteenth century, said Leonard Woolsey Bacon, had seen the "lowest low-water mark of the lowest ebb-tide of spiritual life in the history of the American church." But the opening years of the nineteenth century witnessed a period of revival which seems to have been extensive enough and genuine enough to have made the church keep pace with the nation in its expansion and development. During that fifty years the membership of the Protestant church increased 1,000 per cent with a "glow of renewed fervor" that, Bacon said, "girded it for stupendous tasks that were about to be devolved upon it." Tract societies, denominational periodicals and publishing houses organized between 1814 and 1836 resulted from this revival of church life; seventeen theological schools were established between 1808 and 1827; eighty-seven colleges were founded in the thirty years before 1850, including Mount Holyoke, the first women's college, in 1837; the organization of a temperance society in 1826, followed by local-option victories (1833-45), brought about the best temperance habits in this country since the introduction of distilled liquors as a beverage. The antislavery campaign grew steadily more vigorous after 1830; the ten-hour day for labor was an achievement of 1835, and the 1840-50 decade witnessed a special stressing of Sabbath observance.

With the "decline of infidelity" during the first quarter of the century and the social advances paralleling or resulting from the revival of religious life during the second quarter, it was a normal expression of Christian faith that the influences from without and within the church should result in a new zeal and enthusiasm for missionary activity. The Presbyterian General Assembly as early as 1803 "observed with great pleasure" that an interest, even a desire, to spread the gospel among the Negroes and the Indian tribes on our borders had rapidly increased during the previous year. The American Board of Commissioners for Foreign Missions had been organized in 1810; the Episcopalians had commenced their foreign mission work in 1819. The westward expansion of settlement prompted the churches in the East to carry their religion to the frontier towns and along the trails as log cabins, sod houses, and covered wagons more and more dotted the Western prairies and mountainsides.

The Methodist Episcopal Church had no organized missionary society until 1819. But, as Luccock and Hutchinson, in *The Story of Methodism*, say: "Before the form or organization of foreign missions comes the spirit." And Bishop Coke, who has been called "the Foreign Minister of Methodism," had injected that missionary spirit into the church as early as the Christmas Conference of 1784, when he took a collection "toward assisting our brethren who were going to Nova Scotia," and secured £50 as the first foreign missionary donation from the Methodist Episcopal Church. In 1786 Bishop Coke went to the West Indies and began missionary work there, and in 1814 he was on his way to India with a group of missionaries who hoped to start the Methodist Episcopal Church in that land, when he died at sea and was buried in the Indian Ocean. Of this burial, Luccock and Hutchinson say: "That sunset scene marked the end of a life. But it marked also the beginning of a movement. It was a sunrise hour as well as sunset."

But American Methodism was still too fully occupied in meeting the needs of those western-moving pioneers and frontiersmen in their isloated settlements to be ready for a foreign field. In 1819 the Ohio Conference took a collection from its preachers—it amounted to seventy dollars—to send James Montgomery as a missionary to the Wyandotte Indians, and the Methodist Episcopal Church was actually launched on its missionary career.

The Missionary Society of the Methodist Episcopal Church was organized the same year, and was adopted and endorsed by the General Conference of 1820, which declared: "Methodism itself is a missionary system. Yield the missionary spirit and you yield the very life-blood of the cause." Yet at that time foreign work was not projected and the first missionary sent out by the society was sent to the French settlers in Louisiana. Nevertheless,

many suspicious souls feared that it would soon branch out into foreign lands. Well founded fears! "Bitter enders" railed against such "foreign entanglements"

of the church. Several of the managers tendered their resignations. . . . The movement, however, was too inevitable an expression of the genius of Methodism and
of the growing missionary temper of the times to be long retarded.[1]

In 1832 Melville Cox, going to Liberia, became the first foreign missionary
sent out by the Methodist Episcopal Church.

The stage was set. American Methodism was evangelical, it was awake
to new opportunities and enlarging responsibilities, and it had committed
itself to a foreign as well as a domestic field for the gospel. Sooner or
later it must set foot in China. But before that day had come the church
had been rent, and its entrance into China was under three Chinese names
that indicated no relationship, and that conveyed to the Chinese people
no conception of that unity which had been, and which again in the distant
future would be, one Methodism.

Two years before Cox had sailed for Liberia, a group in the Methodist
Episcopal Church had become so dissatisfied with its episcopal form of government and the exclusion of the laity from the legislative councils of the
church, that it seceded from the church and organized the Methodist
Protestant Church. The next fifteen years witnessed within the church a
growing consciousness of the slavery question. Charging that the Methodist Episcopal Church was not only a slave-holding but a slavery-defend-
ing church, and that her principles were subversive to the rights of both
ministers and laymen, three ministers withdrew from the Methodist Episcopal Church in 1842, and the following year formed the Wesleyan Methodist Church, which they considered free from episcopacy and slavery.

At the General Conference of 1844 the slavery feeling, which had been
growing and repeatedly smothered within the church, burst into flame.
In the same year that the Southern Baptist Church became a separate
body because of the question whether slaveowners might be sent out as
missionaries, among Methodists the episcopal address of Bishop Soule stressed
missions to the colored people and avoided any reference to the touchy
question of slavery, "as much as to say," comments William W. Sweet: "Let
us occupy ourselves with converting the colored people and cease concerning ourselves regarding their enlsavement." But during the preceding
quadrennium Bishop Andrew, through his second marriage, had become
technically an owner of slaves and the Northern delegates in the General
Conference felt that a slave-owning bishop should not be permitted to
travel at large through the connection in the North where abolition sentiment was rising. Luccock and Hutchinson tell the result in these words:

When, however, the Southern delegates saw that the Northerners were determined to push through the resolution which should call on Bishop Andrew to
cease to travel as a bishop, they felt that there was only one course to take. . . .

So, quietly, perhaps somewhat grimly, but with every evidence of deep sorrow, the Southern delegates, led by stern old Bishop Soule, went home to form their own church.[2]

Leonard Woolsey Bacon refers to this culmination, "not in the rupture of the church, but in the well-considered, deliberate division of it between North and South," and Bishop Hoss mentions the organizing general conference of the Methodist Episcopal Church, South, of 1846, as one which "proceeded to business as regularly as if nothing had happened. A Board of Missions was organized," he adds, "and a mission projected to China," as though foreign mission work, to which the whole church had committed itself fourteen years earlier, was taken for granted in this new church.

All Methodism now knew that it must plant itself in the non-Christian lands—nothing less could come from the church of John Wesley. Liberia and South America had already been entered; the church was ready for China.

2. China Challenges the Church

China, serene in its old age and satisfied with its development, was, in the early part of the nineteenth century, closed against the youthful and restless activity of the Western nations, including the benefits which the Christian church wished to offer.

The Chaldean breviary of the Malabar Church declares: "By St. Thomas were the Chinese and the Ethiopians converted to the truth. . . . By St. Thomas hath the kingdom of heaven taken unto itself wings and passed even unto China." Subsequently the Nestorians in the seventh century, the Franciscans in the thirteenth, and the Jesuits in the sixteenth, had attempted to plant Christianity in Cathay. Grover Clark said:

Had Christianity been presented in China entirely by such men as [Ricci and the Jesuits who followed him] quite possibly it would long since have become as much the religion of the Chinese as the other faith which came from the outside: Buddhism. But even while Ricci and his associates were at work, Western traders and adventurers were blackening by their outrageous conduct the name of Christian.[3]

Early in the sixteenth century Portuguese traders had arrived in South China, but were truculent fellows who created considerable trouble; in 1639 the Spanish had massacred some 22,000 Chinese in the Philippine Islands; and in 1689 the British (to cite but one more of many cases) were ousted from Canton partly because of a brawl in which a Chinese was killed. In 1682 Emperor K'ang-Hsi had removed all restrictions against the preaching of Christianity in his empire, but twenty-five years later, because of the acts of the missionaries, he had again closed the doors which were not even ajar when Robert Morrison knocked on them in 1807 at Canton.

After three centuries, the Westerners remained, in the eyes of Chinese law, and to a considerable extent of Chinese practice, simply upstart, bumptious, unwanted, troublesome barbarians. Quite properly, therefore, according to the Chinese way of thinking, they were allowed to trade at only one port far removed from the capital.[4]

At Canton, Morrison had commenced the fourth and present Christian advance into China, under restrictions, some of which had been in force since 1757 when an imperial edict permitted foreign trade at, but not in, Canton, and which included, among other regulations, that

women must not be brought to the factories: nor could guns, spears, or other arms. . . . . Foreign traders must not engage Chinese servants. . . . Foreigners must not use sedan chairs—walking was the only mode of progression suitable for such folk as the foreign traders, and not too much of that. Foreigners must not row for pleasure on the river. Three days in the month they may take the air at Fati, the flower gardens across the river, in small parties, under the escort of an interpreter, who was held literally and personally responsible for all their misdeeds.[5]

The avarice of the foreign trader and the haughtiness of the British official, however, led to the forced removal of barriers against the entrance of the Christian church. The opium poppy was known in China fully as long ago as the T'ang dynasty (A.D. 618-906), and opium has been produced there for more than four hundred years, although it was not smoked much, if at all, before 1800. But by that time China was importing 4,000 chests annually, by 1821-28 the yearly importation was averaging 9,708 chests, by 1828-35 this average had increased to 18,712 chests, and in the year 1838-39 the amount was 40,445 chests. Chinese officials, fearful of the effects on their people, had forbidden the importation of opium. Though the word "bootlegging" was not coined until nearly a century later, the practice in opium was as profitable as that in whiskey in the United States during the latter part of the prohibition era. That the Chinese officers who were not bribed or who were not bribed enough should clash with the foreign merchants was inevitable.

War might have been avoided, however, had the European nations had the right of diplomatic intercourse with China. A few foreign traders were suffered to live outside the gates of Canton, but the representative of the king of England had been refused an audience with the emperor or his officials in Peking, and Lord Napier's letter had been returned through the brokers at Canton because it was not inscribed as a "humble petition." The restrictions on foreigners, the lack of adequate guarantees of safety of life and trade, and the arrogant refusal to deal with the British except as "low inferiors, without rights of any kind," were more than the official protectors of the opium traffic could brook.

In 1839 the viceroy in Canton seized and destroyed, in his efforts to enforce the law, a cargo of opium, repeating, but with somewhat different motives and materials, the famous Boston Tea Party of 1773. The war, which all parties had feared for some time, was thus precipitated, and in June, 1840, an English fleet appeared off Macao and two weeks later captured the island of Chusan, opposite Hangchow Bay. For two years British cannon bellowed along the Chinese coast, until at length the Chinese, thoroughly beaten, and amazed at the British power, capitulated after the capture of Chinkiang, and accepted the demands of the British.

S. Wells Williams, himself a missionary at Canton at the time, declares that the war was an unjust and immoral contest, but he felt, on the other hand, as did other well-wishers of China, that force was necessary to secure recognition by China that other nations were its equal, and that Christianity and science, then forbidden to the people of China "by their supercilious rulers," could be made available to the Chinese. "The conviction," he added, "that it was unjust, unfounded and foolish in itself, could safely be left to the gradual influence of true religion, profitable commerce, and sound knowledge." [6]

W. A. P. Martyn, later and for many years one of the best-known and honored missionaries to China, says he had his attention "first turned to China as a mission field by the boom of British cannon in the Opium War. China was not opened; but five gates were set ajar against her will." The gates that were pried ajar by the treaty which closed this war were pushed still wider open by others which followed in its wake, and the barriers which for a hundred and thirty-five years had kept Christian missionaries out of China (except the few who were at Canton's city gates) were lowered. Great Britain and China signed the Treaty of Nanking in 1842, followed by a supplementary treaty a year later; France and the United States secured similar treaties in 1844. Kenneth S. Latourette has summarized the effects of these treaties on missions: The cession of the island of Hong Kong to Great Britain, and the opening to foreign trade and residence of five ports: Canton, Amoy, Foochow, Ningpo, and Shanghai; the inauguration of extraterritoriality; the granting of permission to foreigners to study the Chinese language; a most-favored nation clause; provision for the arrest of foreigners who might attempt to travel outside the ports, and their delivery to the nearest consul; and permission for foreigners to build houses, hospitals, schools, and places of worship in the ports then opened. [7]

"This mysterious land" which had been considered "a jewel of priceless value" and which had been "earnestly coveted by faithful hearts to deck the crown of the world's Redeemer," was open to the churches of America and Europe. Whether the end justified the means and whether there was any incongruity or malfeasance in the followers of Jesus Christ availing themselves of doors opened by a war precipitated by the smuggling of opium into the country seems to have weighed little, if even it were considered, in those missionary societies which "were waiting at the threshold."

While the political portcullis was being raised, the dialect drawbridge was being lowered. William Milne, colleague of Robert Morrison, though possessing a remarkable gift for language, wrote in 1814: "To acquire the Chinese is a work for men with bodies of brass, lungs of steel, heads of oak, hands of spring steel, eyes of eagles, hearts of apostles, memories of angels, and lives of Methuseleh." [8] Morrison's translation of the New Testament had been completed in 1813, and the whole Bible in 1819. The hostility of Chinese officials, coupled with the restrictions under which these missionaries lived and worked, had made the publication of the Scriptures exceedingly difficult. Chinese who assisted in the preparation of the manuscript or printing of Christian books were hunted down by the authorities and some of them imprisoned, and by 1838 the distribution of Christian literature had been all but abandoned. Nevertheless the little band of missionary pioneers continued their literary labors, laying foundations on which many successors, through years to come and in every province, were to build.

In 1821 Morrison completed his *Dictionary of the Chinese Language*, in six quarto volumes of 4,595 pages, containing 40,000 characters, a work which cost £12,000 to print. Almost a cyclopedia of information on matters Chinese, it was to be a monumental aid to those hundreds of missionaries yet to come to China. S. Wells Williams had, in 1842, the very year of the Nanking Treaty, published a little volume of some three hundred octavo pages entitled *Easy Lessons in Chinese*, designed to assist foreigners in the prodigious task of acquiring the Chinese language. A writer in the *North American Review* commented on Williams' book: "It surely demanded a more cheerful faith and elastic confidence than those of the mere linguist, to coin the title of *Easy Lessons in Chinese*." And in January, 1844, Williams' *An English and Chinese Vocabulary in the Court Dialect*, a convenient manual of 528 octavo pages, was published.

In his message to the angel of the church in Philadelphia, John was bidden to write: "Behold, I have set before thee a door opened, which none can shut." Likewise, before the Methodists of the United States, as before all Protestants and Catholics of Europe and the United States, the mailed fist of a Christian nation had smashed open five gates to an empire which knew not God as they knew him. And while his messengers had been unable to get within the great wall with which China had surrounded herself, they had prepared a way and begun to level a highway for those voices which could soon be heard in the land. Four hundred million people to whom John Wesley could not have preached, but whom he included in his parish, could now be reached by his followers when the Methodist Episcopal Church should be ready to respond to the urge. China now challenged the church!

3. The Methodist Episcopal Church Accepts the Challenge

To Wesleyan University belongs the credit for first seeing the vision and listening to China's challenge. In fact the doors had not yet been pried ajar when, on April 28, 1835, the Missionary Lyceum of that University unanimously passed the following resolution, as reported in the *Christian Advocate and Journal* of May 15, 1835:

Resolved, that in the opinion of this Lyceum it is the duty of the Methodist Episcopal Church to extend her missionary operations.
Resolved, That it is expedient for her to send forth immediately missionaries and a printing press to some favorable location in China.

This action of the Missionary Lyceum was the outgrowth of a conference earlier in the year on the propriety of establishing a mission in Africa, and of a spirited discussion which had taken place when, a few weeks later, it had been learned that the church had already sent missionaries to Liberia. Now that the propriety of an African mission was hardly an appropriate topic for debate, the lyceum had discussed the question, "What country now presents the most promising field for missionary exertions?" The immediate results were the unanimous opinion quoted above, and the appointment of B. F. Tiffin, D. P. Kidder, and Erastus Wentworth as a committee to present this matter to the church.

The reasons which had inspired this action of the lyceum are summarized in the address of this committee to the church as summarized from the *Christian Advocate and Journal:* "The Chinese Empire, as a field for missions, is at this time interesting in probably more particulars, and to a greater extent, than any other nation upon the globe"; its population is given as 367,000,000; it has a common written language which is not as difficult as is generally supposed; many Christian books have already been issued in Chinese; "in no nation hitherto have more sweeping changes been wrought by the mere influence of books as in this"; other churches have commenced work there; the government is more tolerant of religion and foreigners than it pretends to be; the moral conditions present a strong appeal; the Methodist Episcopal Church is able to send the gospel to China; "how insignificant the labors which Christian ministers are ordinarily contented to perform when compared with what they might do in a sphere like this."

Two weeks after the Missionary Lyceum had passed the foregoing resolutions, President Fisk of Wesleyan was one of the speakers at the sixteenth anniversary of the Missionary Society, and offered an extemporaneous resolution proposing a mission to China, and that a subscription should at once be taken for the purpose. This was undertaken, and Dr. Bangs announced that one man had offered to be one of ten to subscribe $100 each, and very quickly the sum of $1,450 was subscribed. Thereupon, on May 20, 1835, on motion of the corresponding secretary, the Missionary Board adopted a resolution requesting and recommending the bishops to secure missionaries to open a mission in China, and authorizing the transmittal of said resolution to Bishops Hedding and Emory. (See Appendix A, item 1.)

Speaking of the ten years that then elapsed before this resolution became effective, Frank Mason North, that master missionary-statesman of nearly a century later, said:

The delay is not easy to explain. . . . Then, as now, however, there were devoted people whose minds moved in small circles and, accepting the motive of a world task for the church, deemed it sufficient to interpret it wholly in terms of America. Methodism was poor. The church was apathetic.

That ten years saw stupendous and dramatic changes in American Methodism and in China. Five doors had been opened into China, and spontaneous combustion was warming the church to the response which had been so nearly dormant for a decade. Note the scattered sparks which were almost simultaneously stirring the church to action. In 1845, Judson Dwight Collins, who was scarcely twenty-two years of age, but who "loved souls and was an unwearied laborer in every possible field of usefulness," was graduating from the University of Michigan. He had been passionately interested in China, "and the chief desire of his soul seems to have been to carry the Gospel to its unsaved and unconverted multitudes." He applied to Dr. Durbin, Secretary of the Missionary Society, to be sent to China, only to be told that the Methodist Church had no mission there. At the Michigan Conference in the fall of the same year he wrote begging Bishop Janes to appoint him to China, and when the bishop replied, as had the corresponding secretary of the Missionary Society, Collins said: "Bishop, engage me a place before the mast, and my own strong arm will pull me to China and support me while there."

On January 5, 1846, S. P. Williams of the Vermont Conference, had touched off another spark in a letter to the editor of the *Missionary Advo-cate*, in which he wrote that the North District of that conference "had resolved upon a mission to China," and would contribute $300 "for that object." (See Appendix A, item 2.)

In March, 1846, another enthusiast contributed this call through the *Missionary Advocate*:

We are glad to perceive that the subject of a mission in China is agitating the M. E. Church, South, as well as our own. . . . Rev. Wm. M'Mahon. . . . writes in the *Southern Christian Advocate* as follows: "I want the South to be before the North in this thing!" Good, very good! ! . . . There is room in China for 300,000 such missions as we shall be able to sustain. . . . We have missionaries ready to go, and China is ready to receive them. . . . Shall the "South" be allowed to "be before the North in this thing?"

And the *Zion's Herald and Missionary Journal* of July 29, 1846, published from the pen of H. C. Wood a plea for no further delay in taking the gospel to China, when the New England conferences could send five mis-sionaries and the rest of the church could supply "a glorious little army . . . that would plant the blood-dyed banner of Prince Emmanuel on that soil." (See Appendix A, item 3.)

But before this letter had appeared, the board had taken action. On May 27, 1846, the board met, with Bishop Hedding in the chair. Dr. Pittman presented the report of the joint committee for the annual appropriations, which included the following resolutions, which were thereupon adopted by the board:

Resolved, That the sum of $66,000 be appropriated for missions for the ensuing year; and that $28,000 of this sum shall be used in support of foreign and $38,000 for domestic missions.

Resolved, That Western Africa, Oregon, South America and China shall be in-cluded in the list of our Foreign Missions in the ensuing year. . . .

Resolved, That the number of persons to be employed in said missions be as fol-lows: . . . . In China, two missionaries, married men being preferred. . . .

The following estimates were made: . . . . For the China Mission, $3,000, $1,500 of which is to be applied to the salaries of the two missionaries, and $1,500 to their outfit, passage, and travelling expenses. . . . After adoption by the Board of the foregoing Resolutions, Bishop Hedding being present, signed a concurrence in the report in the following words, viz: "I hereby concur in the above report." Signed, "E. Hedding." [9]

The challenge to a ready church had been accepted by its officials. Eleven years of hope and prayer, of agitation and effort, had resulted in the authoritative decision and financial provision for Methodism to commence its part in making China Christian.

That was late in May. In July, on recommendation of the corresponding secretary, Dr. Peck was instructed to purchase, while in London, two copies of Dr. Morrison's dictionary for the use of the intended mission in China.

Candidates for the China Mission were not lacking. On July 30, 1846, the board was called together to consider a letter from Bishop Hedding, stating that he had appointed Brother Adams as a missionary to China and asking as to whether he should be sent during the approaching fall or the following spring. To this the board unanimously replied that "it is very desirable that the brethren who shall be appointed to the China Mission should embark for their place of destination during all the approaching autumn, provided a suitable opportunity occur." [10] But to venture forth on a six-month's sea journey, to establish a home in a crowded foreign city, where the physical and moral environment was unknown, would at best mean hardship to any newcomers. Rather than permit a man with six children to undertake the risks that were inevitable, it was wisely decided that younger men should be permitted the honor and given the responsibility of being the first Methodist Episcopal missionaries to "double the Cape of Good Hope."

Judson Dwight Collins seems to have been born with a missionary passion. His eagerness to go had been evidenced by his offer to "pull himself to China and support himself while there." In youth, vigor, and consecration, no man could have been better qualified for the terrific difficulties which such an offer and the present opportunity presented. But his appointment was still delayed because Bishop Janes hesitated, in view of the resolution which the board had passed, to appoint a single man rather than a married preacher. It is interesting to read alongside of this the following from the records of the board for February 17, 1847:

Bishop Janes mentioned that it is probable Bro. White will enter the matrimonial state before he leaves for China, provided the Board gives their sanction. It was resolved that the Bishop having charge of foreign missions be informed that they do not object to the proposed marriage of Br. White, previous to his leaving the United States for China.

In view, however, of the fact that Bishop Janes recommended the appointment, the board, on October 21, 1846, approved the appointment of J. D. Collins, "should Bishop Hedding deem it expedient to appoint him," and Bishop Hedding appears to have confirmed the appointment at about the same time (January 24, 1847) as he wrote Moses C. White:

MOSES C. WHITE, PREACHER OF THE GOSPEL
DEAR BROTHER.
You are hereby appointed Missionary to China.

Affectionately yours,
ELIJAH HEDDING [11]

As early as December 1, 1845, Moses White had written in his journal:

I went to the home of Mr. James Babcock on Ohio St. to see Mr. Williams who has recently returned from China where he has been for nearly twelve years. . . . I told him it was likely I might some day go to China as a missionary. He asked if I would go under the American Board? When I told him no! but that it was likely that the Methodists would send missionaries there in the course of a few years, he replied, "I would advise them to wait till the country is more open." I called this a rather cold hearted reception from one who has had an opportunity to see the wants of the perishing heathen.

And on May 30, 1846, three days after the board had resolved to open the China Mission, he had written:

Bro. Osborn returned from Conference and announced that Rev. H. Bangs, Sup., was to have charge of the St. John's M. E. Church, New York, and that I was appointed his colleague. . . . I presume, however, that the appointment is little more than a nominal one designed to prepare the way for my ordination previous to going to China. I am told that the councils of the church have resolved on sending two men to China and suppose it is quite likely that I shall be selected as one of those two and that Br. Collins, a graduate of Michigan University, will be my colleague.

White, we are told,

had been highly recommended, but the appointment of Mr. Collins led the bishop to prefer an older and more experienced man than Mr. White, who should become the superintendent of the mission. . . . By a singular train of providence Mr. White was unexpectedly substituted at the last minute for the man originally designated for this work. [12]

Two weeks after Bishop Hedding's letter was written, White, then pastor at Milford, New York, "bade that church and people farewell not expecting to see them again till the graves give up their dead." [13] and went to Rochester, where, on March 13, 1847, he was married to Isabel Atwater.

With two young men ready, but technically not yet appointed, the board on December 16, 1846, took another definite step in preparation for its new mission, when it

31

Resolved, That the Board recommend to the Bishop in charge of Foreign Missions the appointment of two young brethren as missionaries to China, giving to one of them if he think proper the office of superintendent, in case the office be vacant, temporarily, and reserving the future appointment of a superintendent of more mature age, if that shall be recommended by the General Missionary Committee.

Resolved, That a Committee on China be appointed with instructions to collect from reliable sources such information as may be useful in view of our commencing missionary operations in that field.[14]

This committee, by an interesting coincidence, included in its membership D. P. Kidder, who had been a member of the Wesleyan University Lyceum committee which had prepared the address to the church more than eleven years previous, and who was afterwards for many years chairman of the China Committee of the board. After considering the question as fully as it seemed possible, this committee recommended that the China Mission be established at Foochow (then spelled Fuh Chau), and on March 26, 1847, at a special meeting of the Board of Managers, this recommendation was adopted.

Here I must digress from the direct history of the mission long enough to point out the reasons for the selection of Foochow, which occupied a prominence inferior only to Canton among the newly opened ports of China, as the site of the new mission.

As early as 1668 an agent of the English East Indies Company reported to the directors of that company:

Hokchue [now Foochow] . . . will be a place of great resort affording all China commodities, as tutanag, silk, raw and wrought, gold, china-root, tea, etc.; for which must be carried broadcloth, lead, amber, pepper, coral, sandal-wood, incense, cacha [cassia], putchuk, etc." [15]

In 1681 the company took preliminary steps to make Foochow one of its trade centers. The Rev. G. Smith, representing the Church Missionary Society, had reported several factors favorable to Foochow as a mission station—living quarters were obtainable; it was the capital of the province; it was accessible to the interior; it was free from the deteriorating influences of foreign commerce (it was not till 1853 that foreign commerce was fully opened at Fuhchau); there was "no city in which he [Smith] would cherish greater confidence in the absence of persecution and immunity from interruption"; and, what "gives to Fuchau its highest and paramount claim," wrote Smith, "was the fact that while every system of superstition has here its living representatives, Protestant Christianity is alone unrepresented in this vast city; and while every point along the coast, accessible to foreigners, has been occupied by missionary laborers, the populous

capital of Fukien is destitute of a single evangelist of the pure and un-
adulterated faith of the gospel." [16] While this last argument from Smith
seems to have been a strong one in influencing the decision of the committee, yet nearly a year before their recommendation was made and
adopted, but still unknown to them, the first missionary had arrived at
Foochow—the Rev. Stephen Johnson of the American Board, who had
been sent from Bangkok, and arrived on January 2, 1847. And finally,
since the first missionaries were to sail on the same ship with the Rev. Mr.
Doty of the American Board, who was going to Amoy, it was thought that
Amoy was near enough to Foochow so that Doty could help them with the
language en route (evidently not realizing the dialect variations in this
province) and make an opening for them to settle in Amoy if Foochow
should prove to be impossible. Smith, in his report, had pointed out three
very serious obstacles to Foochow as an opening for mission work: the
unfamiliarity with and distrust of foreigners, "the obvious disadvantage
of its present inaccessibility," and the "local dialect, partaking of all the
difficulties of the Fukien dialect in other parts, is here considered to be
doubly barbarous and difficult of acquirement." [17] These, however, seemed
not to outweigh the reasons for choosing this port as the entry for the
Methodist Episcopal Church, but to give added stimulus to the heroes who
were soon to undertake the task.

The decision for the missionaries to open work at Foochow was taken
on March 26, 1847, two months after the two men had received their
appointments, two weeks after Moses and Isabel White had been married,
and within three weeks of their sailing. At the time the location of the
mission was determined the board adopted certain policies and gave definite
instructions to the missionaries which can best be expressed in excerpts from
the minutes of this special meeting of the board:

Resolved, That our missionaries now about to sail, be instructed to remain as
long at Amoy, as their judgment, aided by the best advice they can secure on the
spot, may dictate to them as desirable, in view of their ultimate destination.

Resolved, That in case their way should be permanently hedged up at Fuhchau,
they be instructed to return and remain at Amoy until they shall have communicat-
ed with the Board.

Resolved, That said missionaries be instructed to purchase Scriptures and Tracts
at Canton for their future use, and so make arrangements, if practicable, for regular
supplies of printed matter, so long as they may find it best to procure them in that
manner.

Resolved, That Brother White be instructed to give such portion of his time
to the distribution of medicines, and healing the sick, as may seem calculated to
promote the best interests of the mission.

Resolved, That our missionaries be instructed, as early as practicable, to open a school for each sex, upon the most approved plan of missionary teaching now known among the Protestant missionaries in China.

Resolved, That this Board recommend to the General Missionary Committee at its meeting in May next, the subject of providing for the appointment of two additional missionaries for China, as early as practicable.[18]

If eagerness to preach the gospel in China could surmount the inevitable difficulties and lay the foundations of Methodism in that land, no better qualified missionaries have been sent to the field by the Methodist churches in the one hundred years since. Judson Collins' zeal has already been mentioned; no one could have been as bitterly disappointed as Moses White would have been had he not been assigned the task; and no woman has been more wholly desirous of giving her all—both during her months of preparation and her few months of devoted life in Foochow—to the women of China, than Isabel Atwater White. If it was necessary to wait until 1847 for such missionaries to start the work, perhaps the delay was providential. The church had at last accepted the challenge, and its representatives were impatient to go forward.

4. *The Methodist Episcopal Church, South, Prepares*

The leaven which the Wesleyan University Missionary Lyceum had put into the Methodist Episcopal Church continued to work through both the loaves which had been molded by the New York General Conference and the Louisville Convention. The subject of a mission to China was early discussed in the *Southern Christian Advocate,* and was taken up by the rest of the Southern press, prominent speakers, and missionary societies.

Even before this, Charles Taylor, a first-year member of the South Carolina Conference, had suggested to his presiding elder the formation of a mission to China, and volunteered to go. Some of the conference missionary societies had backed the project to the extent of donations and subscriptions to make possible a China mission, and the Committee on Foreign Missions had recommended to the board of managers of the Missionary Society in March, 1846, "the establishment of a mission in the Chinese empire," at the same time suggesting "the propriety of commencing a mission in France, at as early a period as may be practicable, as a wide and effectual door appears to be opening in that kingdom." [19]

At the General Conference in Petersburg, Virginia, in 1846, Charles Taylor's presiding elder, William Capers, who was before the close of the conference elected a bishop, was chairman of the Missionary Committee, which reported that there was considerable demand for a mission to China, that funds had already been contributed for the purpose, and that two men of rare qualifications were then available for such a mission; it then called upon the bishops and the Board of Missions to appoint two missionaries to China as soon as possible. (See Appendix A, item 4.) On this resolution the Board unanimously concurred, and recommended that the Missionary Society open new work in China, Africa, and among the Jews in America.

The Northern church had been twelve years getting ready to send missionaries to China, but in spite of the Rev. William McMahon's wish, "I want the South to be before the North in this thing," and that "two excellent men of rare qualifications" were available at the time of the 1846 General Conference, the program could not be immediately effected. The Rev. Charles Taylor, like Moses White, was studying medicine along with his ministerial responsibilities, and at the sesssion of his conference in January, 1847, he was left without appointment to permit him to complete these studies. The other man whom the Missionary Committee had reported could "be immediately obtained for this service," had, through circumstances over which he had no control, reluctantly been forced to withdraw his acceptance. Of the consequences of this change the Annual Report of the Board of Missions in 1889 said:

Charles Taylor was appointed missionary. The Board deemed it desirable that, considering the distance from home, together with the uncertainties and hazards of that far-off empire, another should be found to accompany him. This caused an unlooked-for delay of over a year and a half, when B. Jenkins offered, was licensed to preach, and was appointed his colleague. This unexpected interval was employed by young Taylor in the study of medicine and attending two courses of lectures in Philadelphia, where he graduated in February, 1848.

Of the two men finally appointed and ready to go to China, the following appreciation appeared in the *Southern Christian Advocate* of February 4, 1848:

Happily for us God's providence has put at our disposal two men, each of them admirably adapted in point of qualification for the field to which they devote themselves. The Rev. Charles Taylor, a graduate of the New York University, is just completing his studies in the Philadelphia College of Medicine, under the immediate instruction of Dr. James McClintock whose special attentions to Mr. Taylor, as one of the missionaries of the Methodist Episcopal Church, South, have laid us under great obligations. The Rev. Mr. Jenkins, his colleague, is one of the best linguists in the country. To a knowledge of Hebrew, Greek, and Latin, he adds a familiar acquaintance with the French, German and Spanish languages. He is, besides, a practical printer, and will be able on that account, to command respect and enlarge materially his field of operations in the Celestial Empire. Both of these brethren are married men, with small families, and engage to remain in China at least ten years. They are both in the vigor of life, not too young to be novices, not too old to acquire a difficult language, and adapt themselves to the novel manners and habits of the Chinese people. They both belong to the South Carolina Conference, the old Missionary Conference.

The Methodists were the last of the larger American Protestant denominations to commence work in China. One of the factors, however, that determined Foochow as the destination of Collins and White was the statement that no other church had yet entered that port, the decision having been made before it was known that it was no longer true. Hence none of the five ports was strictly unoccupied territory when Taylor and Jenkins were given their appointments, and while the location of the Southern Methodist station may have been left entirely to Dr. Taylor's judgment (as has been stated) it seems more probable that Shanghai was definitely their destination—perhaps "subject to change without notice" when they arrived. Although there were at the time six Protestant missions already located in Shanghai, the report of the Rev. George Smith had largely influenced the Southern Methodist Missionary Society in its decision to commence work there, and for the following reasons: "Its situation is good and salubrious"; its population was over 200,000 and in a province whose population was some 35,000,000; it was the seaport for Nanking, erstwhile capital of China, and of Soochow, the "metropolis of fashion and literature"; it was the "emporium for the European and American trade in the north of China," as contrasted with Canton in the south; it is located near the crossroads of the two mighty highways, the Yangtze with its source in Tibet, and the Imperial Canal from north to south—"thus giving Shanghai the commercial control, as it were, of half the empire"; the people were friendly, having little "exasperation of feeling or disaffection to the British . . . [and] we suppose there is less toward America"; and finally,

already have Christian books, like so many leaves from the tree of life, found their way to Nanking, Soo-chow, Chin-kiang, and other important localities, and excited a desire to know more of the doctrines they reveal. Already 14,500 cases of medical relief have tended to mitigate the sufferings of our fellow-heirs of sin, and helped to diffuse among the native community a respect for the religion of the benevolent foreigner.[20]

Northern Methodism was facing a southern door, and Southern Methodism was looking towards the most northerly door that had been opened in China. Never again did Methodist missionaries look ahead to greater uncertainties and graver responsibilities; never again, unless it was in 1937-41, have new missionaries needed greater courage to accept their appointment to China. Cost what it might, the day of hesitation was past; American Methodists were ready to enter China.

II
A FOUNDATION IS LAID

How firm a foundation, ye saints of the Lord,
Is laid for your faith.

1. *The Methodist Missionaries Arrive*

WHO COULD DESCRIBE THE SCENE IN BOSTON HARBOR ON THE FIFTEENTH
day of April 1847, when the good ship *Heber* sailed? Emotion runs too
strongly. The sailing of the first Methodist Episcopal missionaries sent to lay
the foundations of their church in Asia must have sent thrills through the
crowds of church friends who gathered at the dock and watched the hawsers
thrown off and the sails raised. It must have meant hymns of praise on the
lips of those who, through twelve long years, had been working and praying for this day.

But what it meant to Judson Collins and Moses and Isabel White, as
they faced the future, we can never fully imagine. Their heroism calls to
fresh consecration every new missionary and every missionary returning
from furlough as his ship leaves the dock. For was not Mrs. White sailing
without the box containing most of her wearing apparel and other valu-
ables, which she was not to receive until it arrived in Hong Kong over four
months later? Were they not setting out on a 144-day journey before
reaching their field? Were they not going to a city whose climate, whose
language, whose accommodations for their comfort were both crude and
unknown? Were they not the fulfillment of many hopes and prayers through
many years? Were they not going to plant the Methodist Episcopal Church
in Foochow, in China, yea, in Asia, and make possible the gospel of Christ
to millions who were not being reached at the time?

The events of that day, which was both a culmination and an inception,
were tremendous in import. This whole story bears witness thereto. As a
part of this great story, the personal happenings and worries of the depart-
ing missionaries might seem out of place; but as long as it is human personality, in its details as much as in its mass influence, which has made the
church, these bits from the diary of Moses White should be preserved:

Monday, April 12, 1847. Received from Rev. G. Lane two thousand five hundred Mexican dollars, packed them up in papers of $50 each, and gave $1100 to
Br. Collins. Mrs. White & myself took charge of the rest. . . . My own goods arrived
in due season in the P.M. except one box, and as a kind Providence ordered, that

37

was the box which I could afford to leave behind better than any other. Finding that the ship is actually to sail at noon tomorrow and that Isabel's goods cannot possibly be here in season unless they come by express tomorrow morning I went this evening and told Bishop Janes that perhaps I should be obliged to stay behind if Mrs. W's things did not arrive. He said that if they did not come we must buy others in their stead and that he would see to have assistance rendered us in procuring what was necessary, that we must keep our minds calm and try the strength of prayer and see what the morning would bring.

Tuesday, April 13—Went to the wharf at 9 A.M. to look for Mrs. White's goods which had come from Albany in the tow boat *Globe*. Found that the boat had but just come to the wharf and that there was no prospect of getting the things till the next day—rather trying as we must leave for Boston at 5 P.M. Bro. Isaac Atwater is to see to forwarding the goods tomorrow. . . . At 11 A.M. I met Mr. S. Wells Williams in Broadway. . . . Mr. Williams advised us to take a woolen carpet and to make a floor to our house high enough to allow our servants to get under it and keep the space clean.

Ship *Heber*. Boston Bay, Thursday Eve, April 15, '47. Rose at 4 this morning— was at the Rail Road Office at 5 and spent the time till 8 A.M. at the R. R. and Express offices waiting for the cars to learn whether I were to receive my goods. At length the cars arrived and I learned that our goods had been left at Norwich because the Express crates were full. No alternative was left but to purchase new outfits and get on board ship within three or 4 hours or be left behind. . . . [Our goods] are to be sent on by the next vessel which is expected to sail Apr. 25. . . . At 11½ A.M. the attention of the missionaries and friends who had assembled on the vessel was called to the parting religious exercises. Bp. Janes read a hymn which having been sung he addressed the throne of Grace in an appropriate prayer commending us to the God of Missions.

In 1887, in an address at Boston, White told of the sailing:

The ship had started on her voyage as the shades of evening hovered near. At 4:30 P.M. land disappeared—sea and sky—God overhead, in the ship, in our hearts. We are off on our long desired voyage to tell the glad story of Jesus and his love.

And although the sand dunes of Cape Cod were sinking below the horizon while the afternoon sun too was sinking, there was no sinking of the spirits of the missionaries on the *Heber*. Of that afternoon Mrs. White some time later wrote a friend: "That blue line of native land is engraven indelibly on my memory; I would not have it effaced; but I saw the last dim outline without any regret."

One hundred and twenty-one days later this sailing vessel had rounded the Cape of Good Hope and crossed the Indian Ocean, and with its ten passengers arrived at Hong Kong. A week's stay there was necessary before the chartered lorcha—shipping connections with Foochow seem always to have been deficient—was ready to leave. It was also fortunate, for before they sailed the "truant chattels" had arrived.

It was nearly two weeks later, after a stop at Amoy, that the missionaries passed "The White Dogs"—an island—marking the mouth of the Min River, and dropped anchor at the lower anchorage on a Saturday afternoon. There they remained Sunday morning and celebrated the Lord's Supper, proceeding to an anchorage above the Pagoda Sunday afternoon. Monday they sailed up the river, anchoring near the Foochow Custom House in the evening and went ashore with their fellow passenger L. B. Peet to meet his predecessor, Stephen Johnson. They returned to spend a hot night on the lorcha, and on Tuesday, September 7, 1847, they landed with their goods at Lo-ah-ong on the little island between the two bridges.

It was fortunate for them that they could reach Foochow on the same ship from Amoy with the Rev. L. B. Peet of the American Board Mission, and were met by the only missionary then in Foochow. A house had recently been secured which was to be occupied by Peet and his family, but they "kindly agreed to live with Brother Johnson until our missionaries could procure another house," and Brother Collins "took up his abode with Brother White having a part of the house appropriated for his special use." Thus began that harmony within the mission and with our sister missions which R. S. Maclay referred to in the *Missionary Advocate* of August, 1850, when he wrote: "There is no port in China where the missionaries live together in such harmony and love. May this delightful feeling ever last." And it has, for a hundred years.

While these early missionaries were securing a home of their own and commencing the task of learning the language and adjusting themselves to their new environment, the board at home was preparing to reinforce them. (See Appendix A, item 5.) Scarcely more than a month after Collins and the Whites set foot in Foochow, the Rev. and Mrs. H. Hickok and the Rev. R. S. Maclay sailed from New York, arriving in Foochow April 15, 1848, Hickok under commission to be temporary superintendent of the mission. (See Appendix A, item 6.)

A little more than a year after the *Heber* sailed the story repeats itself. The same port of departure, the same Christian joy, the same prospect of moldly bread and stale drinking water, the same long voyage through southern oceans, the same uncertainties and glorious calling at the end.

Arrangements had been made for these missionaries to sail from Norfolk, Virginia, late in February. Benjamin Jenkins may give the story in his own words as he wrote it from Boston:

Boston, Mass. April 13, 1848. . . . I think that the Hon. Judge Mason, Secretary of the Navy, and likewise Capt. Gedney, would gladly have made the necessary arrangements for our accommodations by that vessel, if the gentleman who first made the application for us had stated definitely the size of our families. As it was, Capt. Gedney got ready two berths for *single* gentlemen, in his own cabin, which he politely offered us; but as we both designed taking our families, we could not accept them.

After spending nearly four weeks in Virginia, during which time I served the people at Norfolk, Portsmouth and Gosport, as often as practicable (for the change of climate affected us all to some extent) I availed myself of the first opportunity to get off to New York, where I arrived on the twenty-second of March. I remained there two weeks serving the congregation at Vestry Street Chapel on the morning of Sunday, April second, and in the afternoon, the congregation at Greene Street. Finding no vessel up for China at New York, I left on Wednesday, April fifth for Boston. . . . We have found a vessel bound for our port of destination, the ship *Cleone*, for Shanghai, touching at Hongkong; and we expect, *Deo volente*, to sail from Boston on the 27th inst. I trust this will reach you in time to enable you to give us a final word of counsel before our departure from America. I feel that a work of transcendent importance lies before me.

On board Ship Cleone
3 o'clock, Monday, 24th April, [1848]

MY DEAR BRO.:

Religious services are just over. Our *Northern* brethren have, with one consent, met us *cordially* on board, barring the little they have against us for not making ourselves known before. Nearly one hundred of the Boston sisters have also attended, and united with the brethren in wishing "good luck" to us, in the name of the Lord. . . . We are all in good health. The ladies, tho somewhat affected, are now becoming cheerful; and with a delightfully fair breeze—and a glad heart— *I am off for China.* . . . In great haste,

B. JENKINS [1]

There were two staterooms on the *Cleone*, six by four feet in size, with two two-foot berths along one side and two-foot space for washing and dressing. The Taylor family occupied one of these staterooms, with the six-months old baby sleeping on the floor. Jenkins, "with his wife and two children stowed themselves away in the room opposite," with the two older boys in a room adjoining the dining-cabin on the deck.

Counting it all joy because of the honor that was theirs to take Christ to China, these families occupied the cramped quarters until they reached Hong Kong 110 days later. The *Cleone* was bound for Shanghai, and Dr. Taylor and his family remained aboard, arriving at their destination September 20, 1848. Mrs. Jenkins' health made it necessary for her to remain for a time in Hong Kong; twice after she was able to continue her journey they had attempted to proceed but were prevented by heavy typhoons, and narrowly escaped shipwreck. Finally in May, 1849, Jenkins and his family joined the Taylors in the "salubrious city" of Shanghai, fifteen months after leaving South Carolina.

No recruits came within a year to strengthen their hands as had been the happy experience in Foochow. But by the time Benjamin Jenkins had commenced his labors in Shanghai, the two Methodist Episcopal Churches were represented by ten missionaires in two of the major cities of China. Methodism had arrived. It had come to stay and to fuse itself into the life of the country, though it required a faith greater than that needed to remove mountains to enable the church to believe this during the next decade.

2. *The First Ten Years in Foochow*

Those first ten years in Foochow were heartbreaking, or would have been to less courageous and less farsighted men and women. To those who have come as missionaries to China in more recent years, finding comfortable dwelling-places ready to occupy, people who sometimes call them "foreign devils" but never throw stones at them, fellow missionaries with experience and sympathy to guide and encourage, language schools developed on modern pedagogical methods able to make the acquiring of tones and characters as painless and pleasant as possible, a Rockefeller institution to provide the medical care that may be required beyond that which competent doctors in every port can provide—to missionaries of this later day, even to those who came to the tune of the air raid siren and to the comforts of a bombproof dugout, the experiences of these pioneers can never be fully realized. Listen to some of their experiences and thoughts as they themselves expressed them:

It has been our endeavor, first of all, to acquire a knowledge of the language of every day life. . . . In that dialect we are now able to converse on all ordinary subjects, and I believe express intelligently the saving truths of our holy religion. . . .

Here too is a new world of thoughts as well as of the expressions of thought; we are to make acquaintance with this. When we reflect how ridiculous those ideas appear to us which seem natural to the Chinese, we may be sure that ours, on corresponding subjects, are equally as ridiculous to them. We must become acquainted with the shape and complexion of their ideas and feelings, if we would have our thoughts find entrance and exert influence over them. The world of things no less demands our study. Commonplace objects of daily use and daily observation. . . . present much that is new to us, and with which we must become familiar, before we shall be thought by the Chinese to have attained the accomplishment—common sense. We shall not then for a long time be able to discard our books, our studies, and our teachers. Some part of the day should be spent with them; the morning is usually chosen, in the afternoon we preach, converse, or distribute books.[2]

And this from a letter by the Rev. H. Hickok:

If the missionary will give his chief attention, the first four years at least, to the *colloquial* he will soon have the priceless advantage of being able to address these heathen, so that through the ear, they shall learn the great truths of the gospel. . . . In a few months, if the missionary have health, he may be able to use the colloquial, quite freely and safely.[3]

After four and a half months in the residence prepared for Peet, the Methodist missionaries moved into one "repaired and rebuilt" for them near the southwest corner of Dong-ciu, very damp in the rainy season which was then commencing, with windows of gauze smeared with glue which were so open that the wind would often blow out the lamps. Later when more space was required, White's diary contains these three entries on three successive days:

Spent the day in writing and overseeing some mason work we are having done to make our house accommodate our large family for the winter.

So many men are employed about the house I can do nothing but look after them and see that the work is properly performed.

Domestic duties and superintending chimney building have occupied the whole day. I am heartily tired of fixing and repairing houses.

When it was possible to secure property on Mirror Hill (now Tieng Ang Hill), which was higher and drier than the Middle Island location, and where a residence was built amid the olive trees for Mr. and Mrs. Colder, who joined the mission in 1851, Maclay wrote in the *Missionary Advocate* of March, 1852:

We are now trying to procure a situation for Brother Colder's residence. I know of nothing so trying to one's patience as business negotiations with this people. They resort to all kinds of means to accomplish their object. We cannot depend on anything in the way of a contract until the bargain is actually closed. Even when the Chinese party has made up his mind to accept your offer, he will frequently continue his chaffing for several days. . . . Were it not for the felt approval and support of my Heavenly Father I could not endure the mental excitement and irritation produced by such business. One coming as a missionary little expects to have much of his precious time occupied with matters of this kind. Yet those things are necessary; they constitute part of our work as missionaries to this people. This experience suggests to us that a talent for business is no unimportant part of a missionary's qualifications. We bring with us to the heathen a human body with all its wants, and for these provision must be made. . . . After all, much of a missionary's work is of a plain matter-of-fact character, and if he is not furnished with a sound judgment to guide his conduct in such matters, he will make but a sorry business of living among the Chinese.

In 1855 the corresponding secretary laid before the China Committee of the board a letter from Maclay, stating that the British Consul at Foochow had secured permission from the local government for foreigners to hold real estate by perpetual lease; he advised the board to avail itself of this privilege so that the mission premises could be held in this way. After due consideration, the following resolution was adopted:

That we deem it expedient to obtain permanent leases for the Mission premises we have or may acquire in Fuh Chau, provided the price of the lease and the conditions of tenure shall be satisfactory to the Board upon report made specifically and in detail by the Mission at Fuh Chau." [4]

At this time, and ever afterwards, foreign exchange and the procurement of funds were a constant problem. On November 28, 1848, Moses White had written in his journal:

Today a council has been held and it has been concluded that our financial prospects are so desperate as to render it necessary to send orders on New York to Canton to be sold at almost any price to procure supplies for us. It is unaccountable that our necessities should be so long disregarded. Yesterday I dismissed my Chinese teacher on account of our straitened circumstances. It was a painful duty to part with him as he has served me faithfully for more than a year.

But the following day he added:

The darkest time is just before day appears. Thanks to our kind Heavenly Father a letter from our Missionary Treasurer has arrived bringing us a letter of credit on a house in Liverpool for eight hundred pounds sterling and as we can get money for it when we choose at the mouth of the river Min our embarrassment is relieved. I have written to Br. Loomis at Canton that he may return the drafts sent yesterday if not convenient to sell them.

This necessity for the missionaries to visit the opium ships off the mouth of the river was, in the opinion of H. W. Worley, partly responsible for the ten year's delay in securing members for the church, as he says:

Foochow, perhaps more than some other centers, felt the moral incongruity of the message of the missionary who came in the wake of the opium ships. This was still more augmented by the fact that in the early days of the mission in Foochow no satisfactory means of forwarding money to the missionaries had been found. The only way of getting local currency, without taking a trip all the way to Hongkong was to go to the opium ship which anchored off the mouth of the river and there exchange drafts on New York for Mexican silver dollars. No missionary could make a trip from Foochow, thirty miles down to the mouth of the river, visit an opium ship, and come back again with a bag of silver dollars, without the fact being known to a very wide circle of Chinese. In view of this circumstance and connection it is not so surprising that the mission grew so slowly, but that it grew at all.[5]

A similar difficulty, though apparently lacking the reflex effect which had occurred at Foochow, beset the missionaries at Peking nearly a quarter century later, when Wheeler wrote Maclay: "We are responsible for all our silver after it leaves Tientsin. We will have to go after it ourselves, or have it consigned to the care of friends who may be coming from Tientsin to Peking." To which Maclay replied:

For some years after the Foochow Mission was established, we were compelled to bring all our funds from the Opium Receiving Ships which lay near Sharp Peak. . . . . The transportation of the money was at the expense and risk of the mission, but we never lost a cent in this way; and I trust you may be as highly favored in getting your money from Tientsin.[6]

But while there was no loss between ship and mission house, foreign exchange was taking a toll of from 20 to 30 per cent, and the story continued through the decades ahead, not always, it is fortunately true, so expensively, and at least once during the century at a premium, but reaching its most frantic and desperate nadir after the inevitable inflation due to conditions resulting from World War II.

When preparing to send Collins and White to China, the China Committee specified the desirability of establishing, as soon as possible, schools for boys and girls, since, as the committee said, "little can be done toward a permanent establishment of Christianity anywhere, without training up the young in the fear of God." Following these instructions, Collins opened a school for boys on February 28, 1848, and on December 30, 1850, the first school for girls was opened by Mrs. Maclay, "who, like the wife of Isaac, was chosen by proxy, and has proved a God-send" from the day of her arrival, August 14, 1850.

Sunday, March 5, 1848, is the day of another "first"—this time the first Methodist Sunday school. Collins' own account of that signal event should be preserved:

I had appointed half-past nine as the time for the children to come, but most of them were present by eight o'clock. I observed that the day was a new era in their lives, and that they had no correct notions of its sanctity; they were far more boisterous and noisy than was proper. By gently rebuking them and placing a trusty person over them, they were in good degree kept in order. At the time appointed I went, in company with Brother White, to the school room. All were quiet. We sung in Chinese the long meter doxology, to the tune of "Old Hundred." The Lord's Prayer was then read in Chinese, and explained, and, all kneeling down, Brother White led our devotions in the use of the Lord's Prayer in English. The second chapter of St. Matthew's Gospel was then read and explained, the boys being frequently questioned individually in regard to their understanding of it. We closed at eleven o'clock with singing and the Lord's Prayer.[7]

While Collins was starting school and Sunday-school work, Dr. White was dispensing medicines, and both were distributing Christian literature on the streets in the afternoons. But the medicines which Dr. White had brought with him on the *Heber* appear to have been but a six-to-eight-months' supply, after which he had for many months to confine his practice to a "few very simple cases" which could be treated with little or no medicine.

About a year after their arrival in Foochow a class was started, composed of all the servants connected with the mission and the four personal language teachers. Dr. White wrote:

This class assembles in my rooms in the forenoon of the Sabbath, and we spend about an hour reading the Scriptures, with explanation in the colloquial by the teachers, and a few occasional explanatory remarks by myself. This exercise, it is hoped, will grow into a regular and more efficient Bible Class and from that to expository preaching as acquaintance with the language enables me to enlarge.[8]

And Maclay wrote in the *Missionary Advocate* of April, 1851:

Within the last two months I have observed with joy a decided interest in the subject of the gospel, manifested by some who have, for the last two years, been studying its doctrines. Four persons express desires for admission into the church by baptism. . . . I have formed a class of five persons, which meets twice a week at my house for religious instruction. *Four* of these give me much satisfaction.

Among other things started during that first ten years was the argument which continued through many decades as to the relative merits of the colloquial and the classical style language for the scriptures. Of this beginning, Dr. White, in an address at Boston in 1887, said:

In 1851 M. C. White proposed to publish a colloquial version of the Gospel of Matthew. Rev. J. D. Collins, Supt., said that no such version should be published at the expense of the Mission, as that was a low form of literature not approved by Chinese scholars. . . . Brother White was allowed to publish at his own expense 300 copies of Matthew's Gospel, but forbidden to publish any more even at his own expense. The cost of this first colloquial edition was . . . . $23.47. This was a tentative translation. . . . These colloquial books were so eagerly sought and read by the people that in a few weeks all the missionaries, English and American, Methodists and members of the A.B.F.M. Mission, to a man, gave their unanimous approval of this form of presenting the Scriptures to the common people of Fuhchao. . . . Incidentally, this transaction shows the nature of the arbitrary authority once supposed to belong to a missionary Superintendent.[9]

This last sentence refers to a situation which unfortunately was not confined to the single question here mentioned nor to the Foochow Mission; but since the office has long since been abolished there is no occasion to dwell upon it further.

In the early part of 1855 the mission rented a small room, 15 by 50 feet, in the Chong Seng ward, to be used as a chapel. A. B. Hyde, in his *Story of Methodism Throughout the World*, tells us that "one day, a fine-looking, well-spoken man offered the missionaries his services on salary to master and present their themes for them. He was a talker by profession." Before this, as early as 1851, the erection of a church in Foochow had been approved by the board and $4,000 authorized to be raised "for this important and special object." (Was this the first "special gift" authorized?) In May of the same year, at the annual meeting of the Missionary Society,

Mr. A. Cummings [on behalf of a number of laymen, offered] the following resolution:

Resolved, That the churches in Philadelphia will answer, at the end of the Missionary year, for the balance necessary to build the first Methodist Episcopal Church in Germany, provided the churches in New York will do the same in reference to the proposed church in China. . . . the resolution was carried heartily and unanimously.[10]

A year later, $2,200 was in hand, and the China Mission was authorized to proceed with the building, not to cost more than $2,500, and the church, when completed, was to "be the property of the Board." The building was erected at Iong-tau, and a bell weighing 333½ pounds, cast for the purpose in Foochow, was hung in the cupola, and Cing-Sing-Dong (The Church of the True Spirit) was dedicated on August 3, 1856. This was soon followed by another church on Mirror Hill (now commonly known as "The Hill before the Warehouses") on the south bank of the river, towards the erection of which the foreign community of the port contributed generously, in consideration of its containing a chapel in which English services could be held. This church was dedicated October 18, 1856, Dr. Maclay officiating. The English part of the church was dedicated December 28, 1856, Dr. Wentworth preaching from I Kings, 9:3.

Less than nine months after her arrival in Foochow, and less than six weeks after the arrival of the first re-enforcements, Mrs. White passed away.

She had too fervently taxed her strength in preparation for the long voyage and the new experiences; her spirit, longing for the conversion of the Chinese, pressed her frail body too fast amid those novel duties in a trying environment. "Sad mistake, too often made, but hard to avoid by the young, enthusiastic missionary," commented Dr. I. W. Wiley. But she had written a friend: "I had much rather lay my body here in China than in America," and her wish was granted all too soon. Her body was laid "in what has since become the Mission Cemetery . . . under a wide-spreading olive-tree, deep in the soil of the land she loved so well." [11] Her life will live forever in the womanhood of China for which she gave it.

Early the following year, Hickok, who had been taken sick on the voyage to China and had never recovered, had to leave the field, never to return. Judson Collins was another who never spared his body when anything could be done to further the Kingdom; perhaps his zeal overcame prudence, and wearied and exposed to the Foochow summer heat, symptoms of diarrhea and dysentery developed within two months after his arrival, from which he never fully recovered. Depressed and disappointed in the matter of a house to live in, "cynical at what he called the double dealing of the race," the strain was too great, and bitterly disappointed at having to leave his beloved China, Collins was compelled to return to America, where he died in 1852. Meanwhile, on April 25, 1851, Ellen Henrietta Maclay was born, the first of that glorious army of boys and girls who have been born in Methodist missionary homes in China.

Both at Foochow and at New York, on the field and at the home base, there were many times when the clouds hung low and dark. The annual report of the Missionary Society for 1853 even expressed this:

China Mission. We are unable to report favorably of this mission. It seems to have suffered from ill-health and from death, and from other adverse causes, more than missions in China usually suffer. For two years the local authorities at Fuh Chau refused to authorize the mission to build a new church, and dwelling and hospital, which they had projected and they had authorized. While the mission was thus embarrassed in regard to its extension, the movements of the revolutionists threatened the city; and such was the delicate state of the health of Mrs. Maclay and Mrs. Colder, that their husbands judged it necessary to retire to Hongkong. Rev. M. White had, with consent of the mission, returned home with his wife on account of the total loss of her health. [Mary Seeley had come to China and married White in 1851.] Thus the mission was reduced to Rev. Dr. Wiley and family; and we regret to learn by last letters that his health was quite impaired. But we are not advised that he has been obliged to leave the mission, except to take an excursion down the river Min. We trust God will spare his life and health. . . .

The statistics of the mission at the close of the year 1853 stand thus: R. S.

Maclay, Superintendent; J. W. Wiley, Missionary physician; M. White, returned home; James Colder, withdrawn.

Well, then, this looks rather unpromising. But we remember that the missionary work is a work of faith, and while we regret that the revolution and sickness have scattered our band of missionaries in China to some extent; and one has felt it his duty to withdraw; our building has been interrupted, and our schools scattered; yet we will trust in God, and will believe that there are yet men among the sons of prophets who will rise up and proceed to reinforce our China mission, so that we may be on the spot in force, and ready to do our part in the work which it now seems God will call the Protestant Church to do in China, when all the results of the strange revolution now in progress there shall have been developed. Let us hold fast our faith in the China Mission, and trust in God.[12]

But this mission had been called "pre-eminently a mission of faith," and as the curtain drops just before the close of the tenth year of the mission, we listen to the following clarion call of faith from Dr. Wentworth—he who, twenty-two years earlier, had been a member of that Wesleyan Lyceum committee and who was now one of the China missionaries—as he wrote in the *Missionary Advocate* of September, 1857:

It appears not a little singular to me that out of the ten or eleven thousand travelling preachers of the Methodist Episcopal Church, not one suitable man can be found willing to come to China. I wish there were any mode, besides actual inspection, of dispelling the thick ignorance and direful apathy that prevail in reference to this extensive and interesting field. Because converts from a foul heathenism to the purest form of Christianity are not at once forthcoming, in a community where, fifteen years ago, a white face had never been seen, and where the difficult barriers to communication are not yet broken down, the heads of the church flag, ministers of the Gospel call to halt, and young men, the forlorn hope of the cause, retire to other fields in despair. Could the two extremes, the work as it existed ten years ago, and as it exists now, be brought before the mind of the church, there is not a man in it with perceptions so dull as not to perceive that the cause in 1857 is almost infinitely in advance of what it was in 1847. It has progressed astonishingly before my own eyes. . . . It is a great thing that the people are no longer afraid of us; that they listen to our broken brogue; that they no longer stone us; no longer refuse to take the Gospels and other books when offered them; nay, that they have commenced to *buy* Christian books with their own hard-earned cash; and thus contribute a trifle, heathen though they yet are, to make the mission self-supporting. Instead of hunting the church all over, from Dan to Beersheba, to find men willing to come to China, if brethren could only know what we know, they would find it difficult to keep them back. God send that someone may be found to reinforce us soon.

Faith was the substance of a China Methodism hoped for, the evidence of a glorious church not then seen, but very soon to become evident beyond faith.

3. *The First Years in Shanghai*

The wish that the South should be before the North in the establishment of a China mission had not been fulfilled literally. But the Southern tree planted in Chinese soil was the first to bear fruit. Four years of seed-sowing and cultivation without visible results could hardly tax the faith of the Shanghai mission as ten years did in Foochow. But as in Foochow, those were years of learning the language, procuring property, dispensing medicine, distributing Christian literature.

Dr. Taylor had been responding to calls for medical aid as they came to him daily, but he seems to have considered such service as purely incidental to "what I conceive to be the more special and important end of my mission to this heathen people." But to acquire the ability to preach to the people took time, and it was hard to wait patiently for it; M. L. Wood, one of the later reinforcements, expressed this in these significant sentences:

They cannot understand me, and I cannot understand them. And when will it be otherwise? Not soon, I fear. As light increases, mysteries increase, and difficulties multiply. And it will require months and years to surmount the difficulties and pry into the mysteries.[13]

But Jenkins was undaunted as he wrote:

As to preaching to the people, I still think, after nearly five months study of the *Shanghai dialect*, that I shall need the balance of a year, and good health to continue my labors unabatedly, before I can venture formally to do the thing,[14]

Here [in the grounds of the city temples] amidst the vanities and follies of the present life, and there, before the idol-gods to whom they bow down and worship, I have tried to declare to man his responsibility to that God, of whose very existence they are nearly all totally ignorant.[15]

Nor were his efforts in vain. In January, 1850, Dr. Taylor had held their first formal religious service in a small chapel erected in the yard of his own residence in Shanghai, and which was used for the same purpose until the chapel was destroyed by the Taiping rebels. In this chapel, on January 4, 1852, the first Chinese to become members of a Methodist Church, were baptised by Jenkins. Liew Tsoh-Sung, a native of Nanking, and his wife, a native of Chang-chau, had been associated with Jenkins and Taylor for about two years; Liew had been on trial for a year, and had been enthusiastic as an exhorter; fearlessly he broke with Buddhism and became a Christian, and courageously he preached the gospel for fourteen years. (See Appendix A, item 7.) But in the nearly nine years that followed, the growth of the church was slow enough to test the faith of these missionaries.

The early years showed gains and losses to the missionary staff, paralleling those during the first decade in Foochow. Early in 1852 Mrs. Jenkin's health having failed to such a degree that it was not wise for her to remain in China, the family sailed for home, and Mrs. Jenkins died at sea. Jenkins married again and returned in 1854 to his beloved work but eight years later resigned, and a year later passed away, and his body was laid to rest in Shanghai in 1863. Mrs. Taylor, too, had failed in health and, having seen the foundations of the church substantially laid, Taylor withdrew from the field and returned to the United States in 1853. Meanwhile one of the missionaries had made the "well-timed remark" that "a half-million of Christians abounding in means, send two men as their share to help convert three hundred and sixty million of idolaters." Fortunate was it, therefore, that the Rev. and Mrs. W. G. E. Cunnyngham had arrived about a fortnight before the Jenkins family had left, and were able to carry on, with the help of Liew Tsoh-Sung, when left alone by Dr. Taylor's departure until Mr. Jenkin's return in 1854, accompanied by the Rev. D. C. Kelly from the Tennessee Conference, the Rev. James L. Belton from the Alabama Conference, and the Rev. J. W. Lambuth from the Mississippi Conference. Thus both missions, those at Foochow and Shanghai, were reduced in 1853, for the first time, to a single missionary family each—and not again for another ninety years.

But the life of the church never did and never will show mathematical correlation with the number of its missionaries or pastors. Belton had to leave the next year because of his health, and Kelly after only a year and a half because of that of his wife, and until that stalwart Young J. Allen, who must ever be recognized as one of the dozen outstanding Methodist missionaries to China, and his colleague the Rev. M. L. Wood, arrived in July 1860, after a 175-day voyage, the missionary force was again reduced to three. Those were disheartening days, for they were days in which the field could have been extended, and in which the church at home was finding it difficult to support the mission; but they were heartening days as well, for new members were being brought into the church, and from two members in 1852 the church had grown to eleven in 1859. (See Appendix A, item 8.)

The first Quarterly Conference of the Methodist Episcopal Church, South, in China—or to use its Chinese designation, the Chien Li Huei, which is the equavilent of the "Episcopally Governed Church"—was held in October, 1855. This conference commenced on Friday and "embraced the first Sabbath of the month." I. G. John, in *Handbook of Methodist Missions* reported: "Bro. Cunnyngham preached on Friday, Saturday, and on Sunday morning. In the afternoon he baptised a woman who had long been a servant in his family, and in whose sincerity he had implicit faith."

This woman—Mrs. Kwei—became the first Methodist Bible woman, a woman whose "subsequent life was a consistent and beautiful illustration of the virtues and graces of the Gospel."

As early as 1850 a place for public worship and instruction in the Christian religion had been

considered by all an object of the first importance. Besides this, a printing press, type, fixtures, etc., will be required at an early day. And here it may not be improper to remark that, but for the unexpectedly heavy demands of the California Mission, these interests could have been provided for at this time without embarrassment to the Society.[16]

Yet in 1852 funds for the erection of a church had not been secured, and the missionaries were pleading that now "there is scarce an eligible location to be had" within the walls of Shanghai, that five other mission boards had purchased and built on most of the "best places," and that "the trade of Shanghai is increasing so rapidly that native merchants are constantly buying wherever they can find a spot for sale on any frequented street." Four years later, however, there is a note of triumph in a report from J. W. Lambuth, who says that, in addition to his preaching and medical practice,

I have been building a small chapel for preaching. It is situated on quite a thorofare in the city. It is now just about completed. The whole will cost me, together with the land, about $800 Mex. I do this with part of the school funds, part of my own salary, and part I have borrowed from one of God's children. The whole length is 38 ft., and width 26 ft. The room for preaching is about 22 ft. square.[17]

Elementary education work was started early, and while it seemed to progress, at times that progress seemed backward (etymology notwithstanding to the contrary).

Foreign exchange had, as with their Northern brethren, become a problem. In 1851 a draft for $1,000 on the home board had netted only $750 in Shanghai, and in 1856, $300 had been lost on $900 in three months. Then Cunnyngham aptly and significantly said:

Our Board must look this ugly thing of exchange full in the face, and decide the question whether they are prepared to set the example of breaking up the station because too expensive or whether they will maintain the ground at any cost.[18]

And in 1859 he wrote:

All our male schools were dismissed in the early part of the year for want of funds to keep them going. We have not money enough now to re-open. The two

female schools have been kept going, chiefly through private contributions. . . .
Our supply of books (for distribution) is small and we have not one dollar with
which to enlarge it. . . . We want funds to buy Bibles very much.[19]

The appropriation for 1860, however, enabled the Mission "to carry on
without embarrassment." By 1860, also, Cunnyngham was rejoicing at the
advance which the church was making:

Our native church is prospering, and there are nine candidates for baptism, or,
in Methodist phraseology, nine probationers. We observe now the good old rule of
six months' trial before admission to full membership. It works well, as does every
other regulation of Methodist economy, when properly administered among the
Chinese. "Christianity in earnest" with its class-meetings, love-feasts, itinerancy,
etc., is the very thing for China; and if Methodism fails to maintain itself in the
front rank here, it will be the fault of your missionaries.[20]

In that year Soochow had been selected as a new station which Young J.
Allen and M. L. Wood were expected to occupy. But the unsettled condition of the country made this step inadvisable, and, since a native could
live and preach there without molestation, Liew Tsoh-Sung was assigned
to start the work in that city. Later, Hangchow, which was "attracting
the attenion of all the Boards and Committees having missionaries in this
part of China," and was "the only point as yet selected for an interior
station by any Mission Board" was "fixed upon" as the field for these new
missionaries. But Allen was unable to secure a teacher of the Hangchow
dialect and therefore concluded to devote his attention to the dialect of
Shanghai. That chance forfeited, Hangchow never did, it seems, become a
station of Southern Methodism, and Soochow ultimately equalled or surpassed Shanghai as the center of this mission field.

The situation twenty years later has been summarized by James Cannon
III, in his *History of Southern Methodist Missions*:

When the General Conference of 1866 met there were in the China Mission only
Dr. Young J. Allen and J. W. Lambuth, with their families, and one native preacher,
Liew, who received his support then and thereafter from the Church of the
Strangers in New York City. Dr. Allen was in the employ of the government and
Dr. Lambuth earned his support partly from that source. Mrs. Lambuth by teach-
ing and other efforts supplemented the family income. In 1870 a report prepared
by Dr. Cunnyngham, who has conducted the correspondence of the Board of
Foreign Missions for a period, contained the following summary:

"The China Mission has been in existence twenty-one years. During this time
eight missionaries, with their families, have been sent out. Two female members
of the mission have died and one of the missionaries. One has withdrawn from the
work, four have returned, and two remain in the field. Between fifty and sixty

natives have been baptized and admitted into full membership in the Methodist Episcopal Church, South; of these, six have died in the faith. Two native preachers of great gifts and usefulness have finished their course with joy. The mission now occupies three stations, Shanghai, Soochow and Nantziang. . . . The mission is now out of debt with its property intact. It is financially in as sound a condition as before the war—thanks to the energy, fidelity and good management of our missionaries." [21]

The Civil War in the United States had seriously handicapped this infant church in China. Recruits to the mission staff could not be provided, the missionaries on the field were forced to seek their support outside of the church, and what funds were secured from home had sometimes to be drawn in drafts on, and negotiated through, the board of the northern Methodist Episcopal Church. But the fusing of Methodism into the life of China had begun, and neither war on either side of the Pacific, nor official or unofficial freezing of assets, could ever prevent its continued advance.

4. Members Received and Ministers Ordained

June 14, 1857, was a red-letter day in Foochow. No day in the history of the Methodist Episcopal Church in China, not even that on which the first missionaries sailed from Boston, brought deeper emotion and thanksgiving to those who were interested in this work. Ten weary years had come to an end, the faith which had inspired Kidder and Wentworth and Bishop Hedding, that had kept Collins and White and Maclay triumphant over difficulties and delays, had won. On that day, in Tieng-Ang-Dong, the first Chinese to be baptised in the Methodist Episcopal Church made those who witnessed the scene feel that the ten years had been worth while, in spite of their awful cost, and that a new day was beginning for these workers. Neither the church at home nor the missionaries on the field could understand why their brethren in Shanghai had baptised their first convert more than six years earlier, while they must see results only through the eye of faith. History was searched to find analogies of tardy growth of the church and to draw therefrom a promise of ultimate success. All that was forgotten on that hot June Sunday. Had the "Missions Code" been in existence, the joyful news would have been in the New York office the next morning.

Ting Ang, a tradesman, forty-seven years of age, who had a wife and five children and "respectable connections," had been baptised and made a member of the Methodist Episcopal Church. For two years he had been an attendant at services held in Cing Sing Dong, had obtained and read literature which the missionaries had been distributing, had made their acquaintance when the day-school teacher had brought him to a morning service at Tieng-Ang-Dong, and under their careful instruction he had commenced private and family prayer. Messrs. Maclay and Gibson visited him, and found his home stripped of idols, and blessed with religious books, and their examination of him was scrutinizing and very satisfactory. His family were also consenting to his course. The men of God closed their visit by reading the fifth chapter of Matthew and praying with the family. This was the first time they had offered prayer within a Chinese house within the walls of the city, and this house was almost under the shadow of the viceroy's mansion. The deed could not be done without emotion.[22]

As the first crocus to burst into bloom after a winter's snow is followed in quick succession by other blooms, and as the sky becomes a canopy of jewels soon after the evening star becomes visible following a day of scorching heat, so others soon acknowledged their belief in Christ the Saviour, and publicly professed this belief through baptism in the Methodist Episcopal Church. Ten years had seen but one convert, the next six years recorded a hundred; from 1863 to 1866 the membership doubled, and in 1867, 139 members were added to the church.

By October 9, 1858, the membership of the Methodist Episcopal Church had advanced sufficiently for the organization of a quarterly conference. The significance of that occasion justifies quoting the words of R. S. Maclay, one of the participants:

The exercises were conducted in our Iong-tau Church. Saturday forenoon, at eleven o'clock, Brother Gibson preached, and was followed by discourses from our three native helpers. The congregation was large and very attentive to the word preached. Sunday morning we held our love-feast, which was attended by all our church members, and a few others friendly to the cause. It was a gracious season. Our members well improved the time for speaking, by appropriate remarks, and a profoundly religious feeling seemed to prevail in the meeting. It reminded us of other days in our native land, and we praised the Lord for His goodness and for His wonderful works. The furnishings of the feast were somewhat peculiar. Wishing to train our converts to self-reliance in such matters, we instructed the brethren to provide the symbols of brotherly love for the feast. They were unanimously of the opinion that *tea* should take the place of cold water, and as bread, such as foreigners use it, is not used here by the Chinese they proposed a small kind of [seasmine seed] cake as a substitute for it. We approved of the arrangement, and accordingly the stewards served the meeting with cakes and tea instead of bread and water.

At eleven o'clock A.M. we opened the doors for public preaching, and three discourses were delivered to large and attentive congregations. At two o'clock P.M., the usual session of the Sunday school was held, and immediately after our regular hearers and church members assembled for the celebration of the Lord's Supper. Before proceeding to administer the ordinance, the quarterly collection for the support of the Gospel was taken from our native members. Their contributions amounted to 7,500 paper cash, or sixty-four cents of our currency. This is the first public collection we have taken up for the support of the Gospel, and the sum received will appear very small to our friends at home; still the occasion was one of much interest to us all, and the amount of the collection surpassed my anticipations.

On Monday, at twelve o'clock, M., we held our Quarterly Conference for the Iong-tau appointment. There were present the members of our mission, the stewards, and Brother Hu Bo-Mi, whom Brother Gibson has licensed to exhort. We improved the opportunity by trying to lead the minds of our Chinese brethren to an apprehension of our church polity, and we were gratified with the judgment and spirit which they manifested. We transacted the business of the meeting in harmony, and separated with faith greatly strengthened. Thus closed our first quarterly meeting in Foochow. The occasion was one of very humble incidents; and yet who knows but it may hereafter be classed with those meetings in the old "rigging loft" in New York, or even with the gatherings of the disciples in that "upper room?" God grant it may be so.[23]

The Methodist Episcopal Church in China could now qualify as the Mi-I-Mi Huei. Of this name, H. W. Worley says:

The Chinese name for the Methodist Episcopal Church in China . . . goes back to the days when the missionary was struggling with an unfamiliar language. There was no Methodist *Church* in China then, only a mission of the M. E. Church. They took the initials of the Methodist Episcopal Mission, M. E. M., and tried to find three characters having good meanings and with similar sounds. . . . M. E. M. became . . . "Mee Ee Mee" and translated "Good, yet good." [24]

On the first Sunday in January, 1859, an adopted child of preacher Liew was presented for baptism in Shanghai. "Our brethren at Foochow have baptised several children," wrote Cunnyngham, adding, "This is the first application we have had."

From the very first the mission had felt it advisable for one of its number to reside within the walled city of Foochow, and maintain a chapel there. Collins had attempted to secure accommodations and a house was secured at a rental of four dollars a month, but neighbors objected; a month's rent was paid for rooms in a temple, but official threats to the priests thwarted that arrangement. In 1861 Wentworth wrote that other missions were taking advantage of a new treaty which permitted residence within the walled city, but that the Methodists were then unable to do so because of a shortage of men and money. But in spite of the new treaty all opposition was not yet removed. Hence, by November, 1862, when Maclay felt that they could sell two of the houses they then occupied in order to purchase "a very excellent building site in the north part of the city," which the owners were willing to sell, he added, "But the gentry of the ward have threatened to punish any Chinese who sell us land in that part of the city, so that at present our progress in the matter is arrested." [25]

However, by the first of the following April, "a convenient house had been rented from the Church of England Mission" within the city, and Martin and his family moved into it. A chapel room had been rented in the western part of the city in 1869, and now another building on East Street was secured for a chapel. "The city was at last ours," wrote one, "but what was one minister to more than 300,000 people?" Nor was this victory long-lived, for the following year a riot compelled C. R. Martin to move out and the chapel had to be temporarily abandoned. Native workers of our own church and missionaries of other denominations were able soon again to live within the walls, but not again till 1923 did another missionary of the Board of Foreign Missions reside within the city of Foochow.

The seed had from the first been sown broadcast by preaching. In 1851 one of the missionaries wrote: "In the afternoon we preach, converse, or distribute books." In a later year Maclay wrote: "It is the policy of the mission to open Cing Sing Dong every day of the year for the public preaching of the Gospel, each missionary in turn taking his day for conducting the exercises. . . . I itinerate more extensively than the others, and all the brethren are anxious to go abroad among the people just as fast as possible." S. L. Baldwin voiced the feeling: "Since the recent lamented death of Brother Martin, it has become more than ever necessary that the mission should have its full force of ministers engaged directly in preaching the Gospel."

While the missionaries were healing the sick, preaching the doctrine, and introducing Irish potatoes and tomatoes into Chinese soil, while schools and presses were being established and growing in usefulness, and while the first rootlets were being sent out into the city of Foochow, other rootlets were reaching out elsewhere. During 1859 preaching places in A-do and Guang-ing-cang had been transferred to the Methodist Mission by the American Board Mission, and To-cheng, fifteen miles northwest of Foochow, had been opened as a preaching place. Westward the course of empire is said to take its way, and likewise the early growth of the Methodist Church in Foochow took its way westward. By 1861 Gang-cia had been reached, and chapels dedicated at Goi-hung and Ngu-kang. Thus, wrote Maclay with faith: "Our way is gradually opening to the western portions of this province, and thence to the central and western provinces of China." In 1862 Mr. and Mrs. Nathan Sites had "the honor of leading the van of this western movement of our mission families towards the interior of this vast empire," and took up their residence at Ngu-kang, twelve miles from Foochow. From this time on the story is one of rapid growth, so that by October 1, 1863, the "Plan of the Work" for the year embraced six circuits extending from Foochow to such distant points as Lo-nguong on the northeast, Hok-chiang at the southeast, Iong-bing in the far northwest, and Ing-hok to be opened in the southwest. (See Appendix A, item 9.)

When Liew Tsoh-Sung and Kwe Tsang-zz in Shanghai and Hu Bo-Mi and Iek Ing-Guang in Foochow became members of the Methodist churches, they also became apostles that insured the permanence and inherence of the church in China. Of these Chinese Methodists, Maclay, in one of his annual reports, wrote:

Another trait in the character of our converts is their boldness in confessing Christ before the world. This under God, we attribute partly to the character of the Foochow Chinese, who all seem to be naturally eloquent, but mainly to our system of training. Our entire operations are *public*, our enquiries are *public*, our baptisms are *public*, and we aim at training every one of the converts to do something toward the spread of the Gospel here.[26]

Having demonstrated his faith and his eloquence, Hu Bo-Mi was deemed worthy of admission on trial into the basic organization of the Methodist Episcopal Church—the annual conference. Two quarterly conferences were in existence in China, but as yet no annual conference, and the Wyoming Conference honored itself and honored Chinese Methodism by admitting Hu Bo-Mi to its membership on trial in 1860. The minutes of the Vermont Annual Conference of 1864 recording the admission of Hu Yong-Mi on trial in 1864, state: "At the instance of D. P. Hurlburd, as an expression of gratitude to God for the privilege of receiving this brother into the Conference, the Conference rose and sung the Doxology."

In 1867 Sia Sek-Ong was admitted to the North Ohio Conference on trial. On this action the *Missionary Advocate* commented editorially:

It gives us pleasure to say that half a dozen or more of native Chinese brethren have been admitted to the annual conferences at home. . . . They will increase from year to year, until in a generation at most, the ministry in our work in China will be entirely native.

But who were these half-dozen men and to what conferences were they admitted? Every effort to locate such records has so far been in vain.

It was to be expected that these early Chinese Christians and preachers should be jeered at, spit upon, ostracized by relatives and neighbors, and deprived of their share of the family income. The coming of Christianity has always found opposition and China was no exception. Stories of heroic suffering for the name of Christ are almost numberless. Of the early persecution of Chinese Methodists, Cartwright's *Notes on Early Foochow History* recounts a couple of typical experiences. The success of the work at To-cheng in 1859 spread alarm through all the valley, and consultations were held to devise some effectual method of preventing the spread of Christianity. Some proposed criminal prosecution of all who became Christians, a plan that in former years had succeeded with the Roman Catholics. On applying to the courts, however, it was found that things had changed, and that the old methods could not now be tolerated. Personal violence was then proposed, but the better class of the people discountenanced this, and nothing remained but to create, as far as they could, public sentiment against these enemies of their ancestral idolatries.

The heathen members of the Li family declared that when the missionary entered their house the spirits of the idols all ran away. Hence when the missionary had left they would go to the mountain in the rear of their house, and beg the departed spirits to return, and to this, as they imagined, the spirits yielded. After one very powerful meeting, they called in vain, for the spirits refused to return. A famous exorcist then tried his incantations, but found Jesus too powerful for them, and the spirits did not again enter the house. The exorcist and two others, heathen members of the family, were conquered by Christ and became his devout servants. On March 13, 1859, seven were baptised at this place, and five more on August 21st, following. The glorious gospel of the risen Redeemer had fairly begun its march westward.

Some years later the report was broadcast that the foreigners and their Chinese associates poisoned wells. This was a common charge for a good many years. The Rev. Ling Mi-Lai, at Deng-diong, was cruelly beaten by a mob and nearly killed, being accused of having given foreign poison to the dog of one of the villagers. When he was nearly dead he was asked to sign a written confession that the foreigners had influenced him to do this. He said: "God knows I am innocent. I am thankful to be accounted worthy to come near dying for the blessed Saviour." Volumes could be filled with such stories of the faith and stability of Chinese Christians, Methodists and all others.

An early, if not the first, instance of the testing in the hour of death of God's grace in the hearts of Chinese Methodists may well be mentioned, not so much because of the triumph—though that would justify it—with which Father Hu went to his Master, but because of the legacy he left to the church: Six sons, four of them adult members of our church in Foochow, two of them in the boys' school, and one girl in the girls' school, and three of them later to be numbered among the first seven Chinese to be ordained to the Methodist ministry.

The year 1869 is not less significant for Chinese Methodism than 1847 and 1852. By 1864 the Mi-I-Mi Huei in Fukien had been recognized as a part of the Methodist Episcopal Church to the extent that the Board of Bishops felt one of its number should visit this local organization. Bishop Edward Thompson was given the privilege of making the first official episcopal tour to those parts of the church in the Far East, and spent the last days of February, 1865, in Foochow, where he presided at the annual meeting and greatly stimulated and heartened both missionaries and Chinese members. But it was the visit of Bishop Kingsley that made 1869 a significant year, for he came, assigned by his brother bishops to ordain into the ministry of the Methodist Episcopal Church those Chinese who had served acceptably as ministers-in-absentia of several annual conferences in the United States. The Methodist Episcopal Church had been brought to China, it had secured a Chinese membership, it was now ready to commence its own development, following the ordination of three deacons and four elders—"The Seven Golden Candlesticks," as Mrs. S. L. Baldwin called them. Her sketch of these seven men appeared in the *Missionary Advocate* of September, 1870:

Li Yu-Mi was converted about twelve years ago. He has been called the learned blacksmith, as that was his occupation, and after his conversion he was in the habit of putting his Bible by the side of his anvil, and studying it between his strokes. He is a humble, faithful man, physically weak, yet strong in faith. He is especially distinguished for being very apt in original and beautiful metaphors.

Hu Sing-Mi is the youngest of the three brothers of the Hu family that are preachers in our church. He was converted about twelve years ago. In 1862 he went to New York with Dr. Wentworth, for the purpose of seeking an education. . . . He returned to China stronger in his faith, and ready to give himself up to the work of the ministry, to which he felt called.

Iek Ing-Guang is a graduate of our boys' boarding school in which Brother Gibson took such an interest. . . . One day a poor, wretched-looking boy, without friends, and almost a beggar, came to Brother Gibson and asked to be admitted as a student in the school. The number of scholars had to be limited, and Brother Gibson had tried to secure bright, promising boys. This poor beggar boy made so unfavorable an impression upon his mind that he told him he did not think he could admit him. Just then, Mrs. Gibson said, "Look at the boy's eyes; there is something in that boy; don't turn him away." . . . He went through the usual course of study at the school. He expressed his wish to preach, and after leaving the school was numbered among our helpers. He is regarded as an eloquent preacher of the Truth, and today he is pastor of our city church.

The three already mentioned were ordained deacons; the four following, elders:

Sia Sek-Ong was a literary man, and was employed by Brother Sites as his personal teacher. When Li Yu-Mi preached at Ngu-kang . . . . this teacher would go off to the room most distant from the chapel, because, as he says, the words of the preacher made him feel that he was a sinner. He, a proud, literary man, was unwilling to acknowledge this, so he tried to hide himself from the truth, and day and night, for months, endeavored to stifle the voice in his heart that was ever crying, "The preacher's words are true." They followed him from place to place, and finally he yielded, became convinced of sin, of his need of a Saviour, believed, and was saved, and he is today one of our most earnest and successful preachers.

Hu Yong-Mi and Hu Bo-Mi are older brothers of Hu Sing-Mi, already spoken of.

Hu Yong-Mi has suffered more than tongue can express for his Christianity. He was pastor of our East Street Church, in the city of Foochow in 1864, when the great heathen mob tore down that church, beat this one helper, insulted his wife and sister, drove Brother Martin and family out of their house, destroyed all their furniture, and acted like madmen for hours. His sermons, especially since his ordination, when he seemed to receive a fresh baptism of the Spirit, have been full of power.

Ling Ching-Ting is perhaps the *remarkable* man among the seven ordained. One of the last to receive the truth and preach it, he has, like Paul, been apparently more successful than all the others. He is from the southern part of our work, and speaks a different dialect from ours at Foochow. Before he heard of Christ he was a wretched opium-smoker, and a partaker in every kind of sin, as he himself says. He heard the truth, embraced it, and became an examplar and preacher of Christ to his people. Bold, eloquent, and full of zeal, yet hasty, impulsive and determined, we have been wont to call him our Peter, as we have termed Hu Yong-Mi and Sia Sek-Ong our beloved Johns. Ling Ching-Ting has borne several persecutions for Christ's sake. *At one time he received one thousand stripes on his bare back.* He has, indeed, endured much, but his faith has not failed, and today he is a *power* for good among his people. He is esteemed and honored, yea, and feared by his heathen countrymen around him.

Neither cablegrams nor headlines were fitting recognition of this event. Could the "Hallelujah Chorus" have been sung then, as it was sung in Foochow fifty years later, it would have been a worthy portrayal of the thanksgiving of all who, in the United States, in China, and in heaven, had hoped and worked that what John Wesley preached should be a reality amidst the people of China.

III
IT SPREADS AND GROWS

When He first the work begun,
Small and feeble was His day:
Now the word doth swiftly run;
Now it wins its widening way:
More and more it spreads and grows
Ever mighty to prevail.

1. *Kiukiang and Peking Entered*

As METHODISM COULD NOT BE CONFINED TO GREAT BRITAIN NOR TO THE
Atlantic seaboard of the United States, neither could it be confined to frac-
tional parts of the Fukien and Kiangsu provinces. Wrote R. S. Maclay in
1861:

Taking the Fukien province, then, as the starting point for our operations, if we
grow at all we are shut up to a western development. The field thus indicated contains the provinces of Fukien, Kiangsi, Hunan, and Szechuen, and forms a belt
some three hundred miles wide, stretching through the central portion of China
from its eastern seaboard to Tibet.[1]

The beginnings of the western growth have already been seen. By the end
of 1866 the "Hoking Tong Circuit" comprised Hok-ing-Dong, Yekiong,
Deng-iong, Mingchiang, Lek-du, Iu-ka, and Iong-bing, and at
the annual meeting the next year Hu Bo-Mi was appointed as pastor to
Iongbing City. By April, 1871, the Iongbing work had grown so that the
mission decided to occupy as soon as practicable the following ten points
in the Iongbing prefecture, all of which were then open to the Methodist
Church: Iong-kau, Song-chiong, Sa-gaing, Ciong-lok, Ing-ang, Kau-tu,
Iong-kang, Yong-fan, Sek-se-du, and Hu-pe-sang. At the next session
of the conference Nathan Sites was appointed presiding elder of the Iong-
bing District, which included all of the present Yenping Conference and
the cities of Ciong-lok and Tatien.

Almost simultaneously with this westward growth a southward extension
was taking place. At the annual meeting of 1867, Maclay and H. H. Lowry
were appointed missionaries for the Tieng-ang Dong Circuit, which included Haitang and Hinghwa, with Ling Ching-ting and Sia Ching-Chung
assigned. Here the work grew with equal rapidity during these early years,
so that by the end of 1871 Maclay was appointed presiding elder of the
Hinghwa district. Though he appears never to have administered the dis-

61

trict, its growth was unchecked, and by the next year Taik-hwa and Ing-chung had been successfully occupied; the latter, where a chapel had been rented, being made a regular appointment for 1872.

The westward expansion, which in 1861 had justified the inclusion of Iongbing in one of the circuits of the mission, meant that the next step would be into Kiangsi. This was more easily reached via the Yangtze River than over the mountains, and Kiukiang, as a base from which to work towards Foochow, seemed better than attempting operations further westward from Foochow. Kiukiang, Hankow, and Chinkiang on the Yanktze River, and Tientsin on the Chihli coast, had, by the treaty of 1858 and the "convention" of 1860, been opened to foreign trade and missionary residence. "Now," says Latourette in his *History of Christian Missions in China*,

it was the central and northern regions that were the heart of the country, and here, if China were ever to be profoundly influenced by Christianity, the church must be well-established; the nation could never be adequately reached from ports on the south coast.[2]

Accordingly the arrival of reinforcements impelled the mission to send two of these recent arrivals to open up work in Kiukiang, and on December 1, 1867, the Rev. Vergil C. Hart and the Rev. E. S. Todd entered upon the occupancy of Kiukiang, being the first Protestant missionaries to reside in that city. On their arrival they found three or four Christian Chinese, whom Hart invited to meet in his room the following Sunday, and after reading the Scripture and offering prayer organized them into the first Methodist class in Central China. The records make no mention of the differences between the Kiukiang and the Foochow dialects, nor how Hart was able to read and pray so soon after his arrival.

As had been the case in Foochow and in Shanghai, so in Kiukiang the first five years saw losses from the missionary personnel, and rejoicings in the arrival of reinforcements. By 1872 there was no less doubt in the minds of this mission group than there had been in the farsighted vision of Maclay, of the significance of the "Kiukiang Circuit." Some years later, Bishop James W. Bashford explained the choice of Kiukiang in these words: "Kiukiang was regarded as the northern gateway to the Kiangsi Province, as the eastern gateway to the Hupeh Province, and as the western gateway to the Anhwei Province, and so was considered an exceedingly important doorway to 85,000,000 people." And then he added, from his viewpoint as a master statesman:

Probably it would have been better had our missionaries gone a hundred and fifty miles further up the Yangtze and settled at Hankow, which is proving to be the Chicago of China, and which, with the cities of Hanyang and Wuchang . . . now numbers 2,000,000 people as compared with 80,000 in Kiukiang. But our missionaries could not forsee the relative growth of these cities . . . and Kiukiang has proved to be a good location with unlimited possibilities of work.[3]

But this would seem to overlook the fundamental reason for the selection of Kiukiang as stated at the time by Superintendent Maclay, and as confirmed after five years of work in Kiukiang, by H. H. Hall, writing from the field in the *Missionary Advocate* of October 15, 1872:

No more important mission has ever been opened by the church than this, which has been for five long years seeking to root itself firmly in the heart of this vast valley of the Yangtze-kiang. We purpose pressing forward toward our brethren in Foochow, who are already within a few miles of the Kiangsi border, nearly, if not quite, half way from Foochow on the south to Kiukiang on the north, with a cordon of stations from the Yangtze to the Min. In a few years the first conference in China may be formed—a conference which, in occupying the provinces of Fukien and Kiangsi, will form the nucleus of other conferences, through which the Gospel shall reach the millions who people these valleys, lakes and rivers.

And also:

When the last link is added to the chain connecting the Yangtze at Kiukiang with the seaboard at Foochow, and a line of mission stations extends unbroken through these great provinces then may we talk of conferences and bishops for China.[4]

The plan that the Methodist Episcopal Church was to be confined to a belt three hundred miles wide from Foochow to Tibet was forgotten when developments so opened Peking for missionary occupation that the China Mission felt constrained to enter the capital. The sending of men to open the work there was decided upon in Foochow on June 30, 1868, and at the next annual meeting Maclay and Lowry were appointed to the Peking Circuit. However, owing to the failure of L. N. Wheeler's health, making it inadvisable to remain in Foochow, he was substituted for Maclay, and with his family left Foochow January 30, 1869, going by mule cart from Tientsin to Peking, where they arrived March 12, were "hospitably received by the missionaries of the American Board" (as had been the case in Foochow in 1847), and soon secured a temporary residence. On April 10, Mr. and Mrs. Lowry joined them, and there began one of the great Methodist missionary careers in China.

While the work was younger and less developed than that in Kiukiang —in fact, while the first spadeful of earth had scarcely been turned—Bishop Kingsley felt justified in making this a separate mission at the same time that Kiukiang was separated (1869), and Wheeler was made superintendent, thus relieving Maclay of all official care over the Peking and Kiukiang missions.

Although the New Connection Brethren at Tientsin "very generously loaned" these Methodist brethren "one of their most efficient native preachers" for six months, it appears that no public service was possible until June 5, 1871, and during that same year mission and chapel properties were secured, and the first probationer—a man fifty-nine years of age—was received into the church.

During that same year, the General Executive of the Woman's Foreign Missionary Society (which had been organized two years before the Peking Mission) acting in response to a resolution adopted by the Peking Mission while Bishop Kingsley was present, "authorized the New England Branch to send to Peking Miss Maria Brown of Melrose, Mass., and the Western Branch to send Miss Mary Porter of Davenport, Iowa. They were accordingly appointed and instructed to go to work under the direction of the married women of the mission, Mrs. L. N. Wheeler and Mrs. H. H. Lowry." [5] Reaching China when winter had forced the closing of navigation to the north, the Misses Brown and Porter spent several months with the Woolston sisters in Foochow, and it will be worth while to quote two passages from a letter of reminiscence written some time later by Miss Brown:

... There was a postive conviction that she [Mary Porter] was called to the foreign field, which did not yield to the repeated expression of opinion from three veteran missionaries, that our Mission Board has made a grave mistake in appointing us to Peking, as there was absolutely no work that a young woman could do there."

Although we did not learn much Chinese, we did learn very many lessons while in Foochow. We saw the work as it then was, and heard many stories of the early years, when faith, not sight, held the workers to the task they had undertaken, and we came north prepared not to "despise the day of small things." [6]

On September 12, 1872 Wheeler reported the close of their first regular annual meeting

on the first of the present month. . . . The Sacrament of the Lord's Supper was, on this occasion, administered for the first time among us in Chinese; six native Christians and more than that number of foreigners, were participants, kneeling together around our common altar. . . . Women's work is fairly inaugurated. [7]

. . . .

One important result of this meeting was the division of our field in Chihli Province into eight circuits or districts, for which we shall need as many missionaries within the next year or two. [8]

Bishop Kingsley had visited China in 1869 after the Methodist Episcopal Church had barely set foot in Peking, when a class with several members and probationers was in existence in Kiukiang, and when he could ordain seven to the ministry in Foochow. The *Missionary Advocate* of March 15, 1870, reported his impressions:

Peking, Kiukiang and Foochow are three great centers, one in the north, one in the middle, and the other in the south of the Empire. These points, if properly worked, will soon be the centers of three annual conferences, and I here predict that in less than one hundred years from this time there will be more than a hundred annual conferences of the "Methodist Episcopal Church in China."

Maclay returned to the United States in 1871 on furlough. For twenty-three years his faith, his wisdom, his practical sense, his broad vision, had been the guidance and the inspiration of the Methodist Episcopal Church in China. No missionary had given so many years to the cause, none had traveled so many miles of Chinese roads, none had been more indefatigable in preaching. To him had been given the responsibility of leadership, and the condition of the Mi-I-Mi Huei at the time of this furlough testifies to his faithful and able fulfillment of this responsibility. He was not a leader in material growth alone; his was a spiritual leadership that was reflected in the great Christian lives of Hu Yong-Mi, Sia Sek-Ong, Iek Ing-Guang, and their many colleagues and successors. His was the vision that saw Methodism grow in Kiangsi and Szechuen and the influential city of Peking, and his was the creative mind that made that vision a reality. Few men, if any, have had a larger share in making Methodism an inherent reality in Chinese life, or that of any other country, than Robert S. Maclay.

But on December 16, 1870, Maclay had written to Dr. Harris, Board Secretary, urging that the Methodist Episcopal Church open work in Japan, which, he said, cannot be begun too soon, since, he added, "Japan is just entering the portals of modern civilization." (See Appendix A, item 10.) His prayer, like many prayers, was answered, but in a way he had not expected, for, while he was on his furlough, "the bishops determined to avail themselves of Dr. Maclay's ripe experience to lay the corner-stone" of a mission in Japan, and China gave to Japan a noble missionary organizer and a great Christian leader.

A quarter century had passed since Collins and White had entered the Min River. Nathan Sites, that indomitable pioneer into openings, wrote in the *Missionary Advocate* of November 16, 1869:

The whole church will rejoice in the three stations she now has in China. The station at Foochow, among the hills, has already shown how missionary work ought and can be done, and the two new stations, Kiukiang and Peking, show where it must be done. The greatness of the work now in hand by our Zion is worthy of the noblest efforts of our American Methodism.

Had he not been writing with the shadow of civil war across that American Methodism, he might have seen the day when Southern Methodism, as then realistically rooted in Shanghai and Soochow, and the Northern Methodism that he knew, would be united in one world-wide Methodism at home in China.

2. *The West China Mission*

Twenty-five years after Maclay's eyes had been lifted up to the hills, seeing the Methodist Episcopal Church standing foursquare to the heavens over Tibet, it was already moving definitely in that direction. Kiukiang and Peking had been direct offsprings of Foochow; but the West China Mission was conceived by the Missionary Society in New York, and brought to its birth by the offer of financial support for two or three years by Dr. John F. Goucher, of Baltimore. Dr. Goucher's interest in and aid to China had already been evident in Foochow and Tientsin, but those were but the forerunners of generous contributions, especially to West China, and of masterly stimulation to the church, especially through its educational work, particularly in its participation in union enterprises. No story of Methodism in China, or throughout the world, could be complete without more than the mere honorable mention of Goucher. He cannot be named as one of this or that group which has made China Methodism possible, for he stands alone—small in stature but mighty in influence.

Feeling that the call to enter West China was "a more than human call," the society included $5,000 in its appropriations for 1881, the use of which was "made dependent upon the proposed donation," and the Rev. and Mrs. Spencer Lewis were appointed to accompany the Rev. L. N. Wheeler and family, then on furlough from Peking, to found the new mission that year. While Mr. and Mrs. Lewis remained in Chinkiang to study the language, the Rev. B. Bagnall, "an experienced missionary of the Central China Mission" accompanied Wheeler "on a tour of exploration," during which Chungking was selected as the location of the mission headquarters, thus completing "a line of Methodist missions across the entire empire from east to west."

Chinese buildings with mud walls and tiny rooms were rented in Chungking, adaptable for use as chapel, school, and missionary residence. On December 3, 1882, Mr. and Mrs. Wheeler and their daughter Frances, who had been appointed to open the work of the Woman's Foreign Missionary Society in Chungking, and Mr. and Mrs. Lewis arrived to establish the mission. Within a very short time Wheeler was able to report success:

An application now comes to me for baptism from a literary gentleman, who evidently possesses unusual talent for public speaking, and who, if found consistent and faithful in his profession of Christianity, may be very useful as an evangelist. We could, indeed, organize at once a class of seven to nine probationers; but, while admitting a few, we prefer to deliberately consider the case of other candidates. Numerous applications to enter the prospective girls' school are received, and we see no difficulty in organizing as many schools for boys as may be desired, when we can get to that part of the work. When we are able to open a domestic chapel to the public we shall doubtless have full congregations.[9]

The first preaching service was held in February, 1884, and on the second Sabbath a crowd of several hundred "overwhelmed" the chapel, necessitating services in several places at one time. Wrote Lewis:

For several months there was not a Sunday when we could seat all the women. In deference to the Chinese notions of propriety, a partition was put through the center of the chapel, and the women's side was always more than full . . . they constituted by far the larger part of our Sabbath congregations; . . . an exceptional experience in mission work in China, as far as I knew.[10]

And Wheeler was writing the Woman's Foreign Missionary Society at home; "There has been no such opening of our work in any other part of China as we have already seen in this frontier province." In 1883 the mission had been reinforced by the arrival of Dr. and Mrs. Crews to undertake medical work, and Miss Gertrude Howe, who had resigned from the mission in Kiukiang; but it soon lost the leadership of Wheeler, who was compelled by his loss of health to withdraw. As superintendent of the mission, the Rev. F. D. Gamewell, with his wife, the former Mary Porter, arrived on December 14, 1884, having been transferred from Peking.

The mission so auspiciously commenced was not long to be maintained without interruption. Chapels had been attacked, missionaries had been stoned, property-holding and residence within the cities of Foochow and Soochow had been prevented, but not until the West China Mission was four years old had the Methodist churches been forced to withdraw entirely from any of their China missions. By 1886 a fine piece of property had been purchased three miles from Chungking on the road to Chengtu, on which it was proposed to erect the entire plant of the mission station—residence, schools, church, hospital. The Methodist Mission was the last of the foreign property at Chungking to be attacked, but it was thoroughly looted and destroyed, and the missionaries were compelled to seek refuge in the magistrate's yamen for fourteen sweltering days, until safe passage and the state of the river made it possible for them to leave Chungking for Kiukiang, Shanghai, and points beyond. Superstition, antiforeignism, tales of outrages on Chinese in the United States, the high price of rice, and other causes, were all given at the time as possible or partial reasons for this riot;

perhaps the best explanation can be found in an entry in Mary Porter Gamewell's diary:

> Any of these forces or all combined have set us adrift without houses or goods or work. However the riot may have been stirred up, it is certain the only object of the mob was to loot and get gain. At this time, rice is very high, and the people are, many of them, desperate.[11]

The missionary secretaries, in their annual report for 1886, stated:

> At the moment of this writing we have no mission in West China. Our property has been destroyed, and our missionaries, through great anxiety and peril, have escaped with their lives, but nothing else. . . . Of the suffering native church and preachers we at the "Rooms" know but little. But we know that times of persecution in the Church of God have often been times of the greatest enlargement.[12]

But the following spring Vergil C. Hart, who had opened the Kiukiang Mission, was assigned the task of re-opening that in West China. The story is best told in the words of his son:

> In the spring of 1887, after four years of absence from his wife and family, Mr. Hart was granted a well-earned furlough by the Missionary Board. In twenty-one years he had only been in America twice. After a farewell dinner and a generous testimonial given by his fellow missionaries in Chinkiang, which greatly touched him, he proceeded to Shanghai. He purchased a ticket for San Francisco, had his baggage put on board, when just as the vessel was about to leave and he was looking forward with boyish glee to seeing his dear ones soon, a message came from Bishop C. H. Fowler informing him of his appointment to the superintendency of the West China Mission, and asking him to go at once to Chungking and re-establish the work which had been so tragically brought to a close recently by antiforeign riots.[13]

Hart's own explanation of why he was selected for this delicate and difficult task was that "Mr. Gamewell, who was at the head of that mission, is on bad terms with native officials and the Catholics, who threaten his life if he returns to that field." [14] Thus, for Hart, whom Kenneth Latourette has called "the outstanding pioneer for his board in the Middle Kingdom," began his service in his third field—Szechuen, after Central China and Foochow; Szechuen, first for the Methodist Episcopal Church, and later for the Methodist Church of Canada, entitling this missionary statesman to a place among Methodism's dozen great missionary names in China.

If West China calls to mind Hart, it even more calls to mind the name of Spencer Lewis, who, continuously from 1881 to 1939, lived for West China, and in whom West China lived. In 1889, as superintendent of the mission, Lewis was feeling the inadequacy of the Methodist impact in Szechuen.

"The report of the West China Mission," he said, "continues to be the report of a single station, Chunking. We have not even an out-station. Our limited force forbids expansion of our work" [15] But the mission statistics showed: "Foreign Missionaries, 4; native unordained preachers, 2; native teachers, 4; other helpers, 1; members, 18; probationers, 27; . . . number of halls and other rented places of worship, 2." [16]

In 1891 H. Olin Cady, who had come to Chungking with Hart in 1887, was able to open work in Chengtu, the political and literary center of the province, which "should be the chief educational center of our mission," as indeed it has become. The following year Hart, who had resigned in 1889 on the advice of his physician, and whose health had been restored by three years in northern New York, and who had been born and raised in Canada, returned to Chengtu to open the mission work for the Canadian Methodist Church.

Not until 1893 did the Woman's Foreign Missionary Society feel again that it had a duty in West China. Then a sum of money "sufficient to provide a home for the missionaries," was tendered to the society through W. E. Blackstone, "providing that the missionaries should be deaconesses." Missionary deaconesses were thereupon sent to the field and the work for women and girls, which had been carried on through the years by the married women of the general society, was resumed by the Woman's Foreign Missioanry Society.

The first annual meeting of the mission was held in Chungking in June, 1890, of which Spencer Lewis said: "The love-feast, especially, will be ever memorable in the spiritual history of our work here. . . . The Holy Spirit has put his seal upon our work" Seven years later the annual meeting was presided over by the first bishop to visit West China, Bishop Isaac W. Joyce.

The West China Mission was "on the map." The two chief cities of China's largest province were definitely and permanently occupied by the Methodist Episcopal Church. Westward the course of Methodism had taken its way where a half century later it should be in a position to minister in one of the greatest needs the country ever had, at the time of one of the greatest opportunities ever offered the Christian church.

3. *Further Extensions of the Methodist Episcopal Church*

Although South, East, Central, North, and West China had, within fifty years, seen Methodism established and begun to feel its influence, geographical extension had not yet reached its limits. The Central China Mission had, in 1898, spread north into Hupeh and Anhwei provinces, and in Kiangsi south to the Fukien border and towards the Hunan province; and, as we shall see, the Stewart Fund enabled it to develop in southern

Anhwei. Everywhere around the borders the church was pushing into the regions beyond.

But sometimes this expansion had been too rapid. By 1910 the city of Yangchow, north of the Yangtze, had been turned over to the Episcopalians. "There is far more work south of the river than our church can possibly do," said one missionary. Elsewhere too during the ten or fifteen years that followed the Boxer outburst, the church made a number of "strategic withdrawals" from territory which it had occupied, as it had done at other times in the interest of comity and for other reasons. The Yenshan District of the North China Conference, with its property and membership, was, in 1900, turned over to the London Mission, which had missionaries living within ten miles of this Methodist outpost. Tung-chow was never reoccupied after the 1900 evacuation. North China and West China were very definitely dividing territory with the other churches working in these fields, so that thereafter they need not cross each other's fields of labor. In West China Bishop Bashford judged this had given the Methodists a "superior location," superior, he thought, because it had given Methodists "more Chinese workers than all the other Protestant missions combined," and also superior geographically because it had given the Methodists the rhomboidal heart of Szechuen, based on the two roads between Chungking and Chengtu through Tzechow and Suining. In 1914 a part of this territory, Linshui County, was transferred to the China Inland Mission, a county in which Methodists had only two small chapels and which required two weeks of hard travel to visit it, while it was easily reached from a China Inland station. As early as 1901 the transfer of Methodist work in South Fukien to the Presbyterians was also being seriously discussed.

A few withdrawals had taken place—wisely. But read through the list of strategic cities which were occupied during these years and it will be evident that "strategic withdrawals" do not indicate defeat. There were added Wusih and Sung-kiang in East China, Tze-chow and Sui-ning in West China. Miss Ogborn opened Nanchang when Bishop David C. Moore appointed her to start a school there, though she "reversed the usual order" and "built first, then opened the school." Yenping, another future conference center, was opened as a mission station in 1902, but the gospel had been carried into nearly every township throughout the vast extent of the district before that time.

Bishop Moore wrote: "After careful consideration, covering all features of the situation, it has been decided to maintain a strong native station at Tsun-hua, and build the hospitals, schools, etc., at Chang-li, on the railroad between Lan-chow and Shan-hai-Kuan," [17] and the mission plant there was begun in 1903. "A circumstance at Changli, and our determination to live somewhere on the district," explained G. W. Verity in 1914, "led to our moving to Shanhaikuan. We now see that what looked like disappointment has proved his appointment and a glorious victory," for Shanhaikuan "offers the greatest opportunity on the district for both evangelistic and medical work." [18]

Yungan in Fukien and Fuchow in Kiangsi are examples of cities which became missionary residences during these years—Yungan in 1906, Fuchow in 1916—only to be abandoned after one short term of residence, though they have continued to be important church centers.

One other city, not a mission center, must be mentioned because it had been the home of the great sage Confucius, and for years the church had been seeking to plant its banner there. In 1910 the magistrate had declared that the church "could neither buy any land nor establish any church in the district of Chu-fuh-hsien," and the American consul at Chefoo, whose assistance had been solicited, felt "that Chu-fuh-hsien ought to be respected, because it was the birthplace of Confucius," and land which had been purchased in the east suburb had to be given up. A colporteur was kept there in rented quarters, and later a small school was started. Eventually the victory was won, very desirable property was secured in the west suburb, and in 1919 H. S. Leitzel was able to report:

The new Chufu church is a reality. A fine building in Chinese architectural style is about finished. It will seat about four hundred people with room for several hundred more in case of need. In connection with the church we will have tea-rooms, library, reading and recreation rooms, with boys' and girls' day schools all fully equipped for real service.[19]

"Instead of the hostility of the Duke and the city Fathers," wrote Perry O. Hanson, "we have their good-will. When we moved into our new place, the Duke and many of the officials offered to loan us furniture for our reception. Some was borrowed." [20]

In 1898 and 1899 the problem, said D. W. Nichols, "is no longer how to get the masses into the church, but how to keep them out." Older missionaries in all parts of the country were expressing the idea "that nearly all who were seeking entry into the Church had a lawsuit or some other matter on hand. Brother Chen, our assistant pastor," wrote J. F. Peat, "estimated that nine out of ten who applied for church connection, upon being pressed, would acknowledge that there was an ulterior motive in the case." [21] The growth of the Sienyu District, said its district superintendent in 1911,

is very similar to that of the moon, which reaches "full moon" and then wanes the next evening. Circuits in the northwest were formerly good ground for gospel seed;

now they are become stony ground in which no seeds sprout. The majority of old members are neither cold nor hot in spirit. Last year the evangelists did their best to arouse them, but they are indifferent.[22]

His statement is quoted here, not alone for its Chinese picturesqueness, but because the picture could be put in the frame of many a church between the Himalayas and the Pacific. After an absence of sixteen years from the Tsunghwa District, George Davis had noted a shift of strength from Tsunghwa, where the largest membership had been, to "the borders of the great plain, south of the hills, along the great road from Peking to Mukden, about Fengjun, Shaliuho and Yutien."

Kiangsi had had its downs as well as its ups. Edward James commented on

a terrible collapse in the fabric of our church organization. . . . The appointments on this district had been reduced to five, and in not one of these is there a real church organization or quarterly conference, for in none of these places is there anyone recognized as a full member of the church. The chaotic condition of the membership, and the suspended conditions of the property question, made all functions of church oraganization undisciplinary, and reduced us, so far as concerns evangelistic work, to the one line of calling sinners to repentence.[23]

Was it cynicism when he added: "Two helpers have retired from this district this year, but the force is not weakened by their retirement"? And had he been unduly pessimistic when he had referred to the Chingkiang District, after years of occupation of the city itself, as a "forlorn hope" saying that it had "held an uncertain tenure in our Mission polity"? And W. S. Bissonnette, who for a quarter century tramped the stone roads and escaped death in the small villages of Kutien, that early outpost of the Foochow Conference, was analyzing the causes of less than a 2 per cent growth in the Kutien District in the ten years before he went there, as emigration to Borneo and Malaysia, regions which were taking much of the enterprising population of this section: the nonstrategic positions of many of the stations which had been opened in small, remote villages, rather than in the large towns on the main road; and the seemingly too large use of missionary funds to support the Chinese church, instead of a vigorous effort to develop its indigenous resources.

Lack of strategy, lack of competent pastoral leadership, lack of continuity in missionary supervision, lack of a genuine conversion of the membership, all had had their effect, as they had in every land which the church had entered. But they were not fatal. The church of John Wesley still had the virility of its founder. It was still ready to follow the wider call of its statesman-bishop, J. W. Bashford, who, in 1906, was confiding to his diary:

Spencer Lewis thinks my plans too large, viz: to strengthen present work; 2. expand Shantung District into a conference; 3. enter Manchuria; 4. enter Shanghai. I am prepared to go as far towards realizing these plans as funds will permit or justify, but to raise the cry and ask largely. He wishes I would favor entering Thibet.

Shantung later became a conference, Manchuria and Tibet were to become Chinese missionary fields, work was being done by northern Methodists in Shanghai and Canton, though not according to the rules of Methodist organization.

Although Bishop Bashford would not "favor entering Thibet," the West China Mission in 1907 would undertake this missionary project, and accepted the volunteer enlistment of two of its preachers, appointed them as missionaries to Tibet, and sent them to Batang, a thirty-day journey west of Chengtu, the first foreign missionary project of China Methodism.

Foochow Conference, or rather the Woman's Missionary Society which had been organized within the districts of the conference during the ten years following 1913, had the honor of sending the first woman as a home missionary. The pennies which these auxiliaries had collected sacrificially and sacredly sent Miss Ethel Li in 1923 to open a school in Yungan, in the mountains of far western Fukien, and the work that she began has continued uninterruptedly ever since for the women and girls of that city which, undreamed of then, was to become the wartime capital of the province.

In October, 1920, W. G. Cram and J. S. Ryang were assigned by Bishop Lambuth to go from the Korea Mission to open Methodist work in Siberia and Manchuria. Because Manchuria was then a part of the Chinese republic, my readers will accept the propriety of including this item in this chronicle, although it was then, and even since has been, connected with the Korea organization of Methodism. The Chien-Li-Huei also felt the call to foreign mission work, and the China Annual Conference raised $12,000 in 1922 to open a mission to Chinese in Manchuria.

When the Methodist Publishing House was opened in Shanghai, many of the employees of the Mission Press in Foochow were taken to Shanghai. Their needs and those of an increasing number of the graduates of the Anglo-Chinese College in Foochow, entering business in Shanghai, soon raised the question of a church home in that city for people who spoke the Foochow dialect. Here was a different problem: the agreement between the two branches of episcopal Methodism in the United States prevented the Northern church from opening work in Shanghai, while the use of the Foochow dialect made it impossible for the Southern church to supply a pastor for such a church. The Central Conference of 1903 asked the China

Conference to undertake this work, and the rest of the story comes from Bishop Bashford's diary:

Oct. 18, 1911. I met the pastor of our Fuhkien-speaking church in Shanghai who is a local elder in Fuhkien and advised with him in regard to maintaining that church. At the Conference I urged the Southern Methodists to maintain this work and told them that while I greatly desired to establish our church in Shanghai, I would not do so without an invitation from them. At a mission meeting Bishop Murrah urged them to keep the church. But on account of lack of funds or inability to do the work the mission voted by a majority of all save one or two to invite our church to come to Shanghai and take this work. The majority was so small as I have heard and they were so clearly inviting us under financial stress that I pledged them $100 gold the coming year towards support of the work if they themselves would keep it. They were very grateful over this solution of the question. Later the Southern Methodists were compelled to give up the work and after another conference with the Foochow Conference, owing to the Revolution and the uncertainty as to income and new life, the Foochow bretheren decided that at least for the present they could not raise the $200 more to put with my $100 and support the work. Hence we have been reluctantly compelled to suspend the work for the present.

But the church continued, an orphan church, never very strong, but there, where it could render a service to the Foochow people of that metropolis, ultimately uniting with the Church of Christ in China and the Sheng-Kung-Huei (Anglicans) to become a union community church for Foochow-speaking residents and visitors in Shanghai.

Another orphan church was that at Canton. The Rev. Otis Gibson, who had been a missionary in Foochow, had proposed to the Missionary Society in 1872 that $10,000 be appropriated to start a mission in Canton, and the motion was adopted without opposition. But the appropriation was not used, and was continued for 1874, but never used. Some years later, Chinese returning from California, where the Methodist Church had provided them a church home such as they wanted for themselves in their native heath, started a Methodist Church in Canton. In 1911 they had purchased for $7,500 a plot of land in Canton, on which they later built a church with a seating capacity of five hundred. A church at Hong Kong and churches at several intermediate points had also grown up, and at one time they maintained four schools for girls. The churches in the United States, whose influence had given birth to these churches in Canton and its vicinity, had a "missionary society through which they help to support the infant churches in the Kwangtung Province." Although these churches had no connection with the Methodist Episcopal Church organization anywhere in China, Bishops Bashford and Lewis had visited them and Bishop Bashford ordained their first preacher who became superintendent.

The bishops in their Episcopal Address in 1915 said: "We invite your earnest attention to this problem, and ask you to consider what our responsibilities are in this case, and what should be our policy concerning the propagation of the Gospel in the Kwang-tung Province." [24] Again referring to the question in 1920, Bishop Bashford not being present to share in the wording of the address, the reference was brief: "The Board has referred the question to its own executive committee and doubtless would be glad to know the judgment of those nearest to the work in question." [25] The Central Conference, however, asked the bishops to give the problem some firsthand study and recommend action, but at Foochow in 1923, the Committee on Boundaries and Extensions expressed itself in this brief paragraph:

We are informed that the bishops have not been able, collectively, to visit this work or to give it direct consideration, and that therefore they have no specific recommendations to present. We are also informed that the work is flourishing under its present auspices, fostered by Chinese Methodists in California. We therefore, recommend no action by the Conference at this time.[26]

This recommendation was accepted and no action was taken.

In 1928 Bishop Birney presented to the Foochow Conference a request from Canton "for fraternal relationship with one of the China Conferences," and during the next two years Foochow received and sent fraternal represntatives. In 1933 Lo Daik-Kieng of Canton was present at the Foochow Conference, was received into the conference on trial, placed in studies of the first year, "granted Deacon's and Elder's Orders under the Missionary Rule," and ordained accordingly by Bishop Wang. Not having visited Foochow again, and no word having been received from him, Lo Daik-Kieng was, in 1938, "discontinued as a Probationer in the Conference," but continued "as a Local Preacher with Elder's Orders." [27]

With these geographical expansions, the everyday task of evangelism, of carrying the gospel to those who had not heard it, deepening the warming at the heart, was going on. Methodism was continuing to grip the businessmen of Shanghai, Tientsin, and Canton, the farmers and artisans of the Szechuen plains and the Kiangsi mountain-valleys, the women and girls of stylish Soochow and remote Yungan.

4. The Methodist Protestant Church Enters Kalgan

The growth in area and spiritual life, the lights of new mission stations, the increase in church membership, which had been taking place elsewhere, had also been taking place in the Methodist Protestant Mission in Kalgan. This slightly different tint—small in quantity, but rich in tone—had been added in 1909 to the Methodism that had for sixty-two years been coloring the life of China.

The Woman's Foreign Missionary Society of the Methodist Protestant Church had opened work in Hunan Province in 1899 by sending two women missionaries, one of whom, Miss Annie Lawrence, had been serving the society in Japan. But the Boxer uprising, which followed so soon after the commencement of their work, the marriage of Miss Grace Hill to a missionary of another church, and the breakdown of Miss Lawrence's health, caused that undertaking to die in its infancy. "But ladies of the Missionary Society carried China on their hearts, and certain funds for China in their treasury, and in 1909 made a new start," wrote the Rev. C. S. Heininger, and he was accepted by the Woman's Foreign Missionary Society for this venture, which was to be in northern China, starting on September 23, 1909, for this new field. The field was new only to the Methodists, however, for the Congregationalists had worked in Chahar Province, had owned property in Kalgan, which was immediately available for occupancy, and in fact had agreed to co-operate in the work for a time with financial assistance.

During the Boxer uprising this station had suffered severely, a number of Christians had been killed, the buildings of the mission were all destroyed, and the missionaries had been forced to flee through Mongolia to Siberia. No rehabilitation had been undertaken as the Congregational board had decided to centralize their work elsewhere; consequently the Chinese Christians were considerably discouraged but quickly rallied to the new leadership.

This venture lacked much of the pioneering difficulties with which Foochow and Shanghai had surrounded and sometimes almost engulfed the pioneer missionaries. Into Kalgan, with pioneering problems, it is true, came Heininger, but with the privilege of entering into the labors of others, of building upon a foundation which others had already partially laid. The following year Miss Lulu McKinney was appointed to China and on her arrival at Tientsin was married to Heininger. With the arrival of Mrs. Heininger, who was a graduate nurse, more work for women and more medical work were both possible, and a Chinese graduate of the Union Medical College in Peking was soon secured to take charge of the medical work.

During these early years, two facts were used in the American church to disparage this work, according to Heininger: "First of all, the right of the Woman's Society to send a man as a missionary was questioned, and, second, some said that the field could not be a hopeful one or the much stronger church would have continued the work." [28]

On January 1, 1913, the Congregationalists discontinued their financial assistance to the new church, and in the same year the Woman's Foreign Missionary Society made the initial payment on the American Board property which they had been occupying and which was to be henceforth the center of the Methodist Protestant Church in China. On September 18, 1918, by joint agreement, the Board of Foreign Missions accepted the responsibility for all the work for men and boys, and the Woman's Foreign Missionary Society, which had thus far carried the full responsibility for this mission, continued with the work for women and girls only.

In September, 1912, Heininger had been joined by the Rev. P. W. Dierberger, but health conditions made it necessary for him to withdraw within a couple of years, and in 1914, the Rev. and Mrs. Carl G. Soderbom, who had already had twenty-five years experience as Swedish missionaries in northern China, joined the mission. The war in Europe created financial difficulties, and for three years Soderbom served in the employ of an American commercial firm as their Mongolia agent, returning to this mission in 1922, after the death of his wife. Other reinforcements came yearly from 1919 to 1922, but sickness and marriages made inroads, and the year 1923 left the mission staffed with the two men, Mrs. Heininger, and three single women.

In 1919 the Board of Foreign Missions had sent the Rev. Fred C. Klein and the Rev. J. C. Broomfield to visit its foreign mission fields, and for the China visit they were joined by Miss Olive Hodges of the Woman's Foreign Missionary Society mission in Japan. They reported from China:

The China Mission Conference was duly organized in Kalgan, in the chapel of the Society's compound, on Friday, December 12, 1919.

The action of the Board of Foreign Missions authorizing its formation, and appointing Dr. Heininger President, was read, and he took the chair. Pastor Yao Shu-Te was elected Secretary, and Pastor Ts'ui Shik-Hai Assistant Secretary and Conference Steward.

The membership roll consisted of two ministers, nine preachers, and nine delegates, total twenty. Ten stations and circuits were represented.

On Sunday, December 14th, Brother Kao Yueh was ordained, under authority conferred by the Board of Missions (Foreign), in the chapel of the Center in Kalgan. He is the first Chinese brother to be ordained in our denomination.

. . . .

The field has been well covered, the strategic places are occupied, the outlying points are connected up, and results are proving the efficiency of the general plans followed, but there is much territory to be entered by our forces.[29]

Dr. Roberta Fleagle and Dr. and Mrs. Harold Hammett arrived in 1920 to open more extensive medical work than the dispensaries had been able to do since 1911, with Chinese helpers in attendance. None of these missionaries, however, was able to remain long enough to see the opening of the hospital, but the dispensary work was continued by Dr. Ts'ui and his three native helpers.

To Heininger and Soderbom, with their vision and their loyalty, to their efforts and their faith, is due much of the success that the Methodist Protestant Church attained. Never large in numbers, nor extensive in its operations, it had at least a spiritual foothold in Kalgan, where its schools for boys and girls flourished and twenty Chinese pastors met their responsibilities in this part of the "world parish." The conditions in the years to follow might hold the work in check, but winter does that to vegetation, and the spring which follows is enriched with its beauty. The life was there for hearts had been warmed, and Methodism had come to Kalgan to stay.

IV
UPWARD AND ONWARD

They must upward still and onward,
Who would keep abreast of truth.

1. Conferences Organized

TWENTY-SIX YEARS HAD PASSED SINCE THE FIRST COLORING OF METHODISM
had been dripped into China's life. It had made its impression, and the
church which had commenced when Ting Ang was baptised was ready for
another significant phase in its development. Bishop Harris was present and
presided at the annual meeting in Foochow in 1873, and appointed four Chinese as presiding elders. The Mi-I-Mi Huei was able to tell the world that as
soon as capable spiritual leaders had been found and trained, the Methodist
system of church administration was able and ready to give these native
leaders their rightful place in the administration of that church. That these
"preachers are thorough Methodists and strongly attached to our system"
which "is unquestionably the true system for missionary aggression in
China," was the testimony of the secretary of the Missionary Society a
few years later.[1]

Another advance was soon to follow. One of that Wesleyan University
committee, which had first proposed the China Mission, and who, since
before the first convert had been baptised, had been a member of that mission, Erastus Wentworth, wrote in *Zion's Herald* (July 25, 1878) under
the title "Foochow Conference":

I feel like appending to the above heading an exclamation point. An annual
conference of the Methodist Episcopal Church in China! on the other side of the
globe! in the midst of the most populous and densest heathenism on the globe!
It would almost exhaust a printer's case of exclamation points—the very
idea! Think of it, reader; think of it, patient missionary contributor, in connection
with its past history and its dawning promise! . . . Dec. 20, 1877, the Foochow
Mission was organized into the Foochow Annual Conference of the Methodist
Episcopal Church by Bishop I. W. Wiley, who went to the mission as physician
in 1851.

At the opening of this conference Bishop Wiley announced the following transfers from the conferences named:

S. L. Baldwin, from the Newark Conference; N. Sites, N. J. Plumb, Sia Sek-Ong,
and Li Yu-Mi, from the North Ohio Conference; F. Ohlinger, from the Central

German Conference; David W. Chandler, from the East Ohio Conference; Hu Bo-Mi, from the Wyoming Conference; Hu Yong-Mi, from the Vermont Conference; Yek Ing-Kwang and Hu Sing-Mi, from the California Conference; Li Cha-Mi, Chiong Taik-Liong, Sia Lieng-Li, Pang Ting-Hie, Ting Neng-Chiek, Ngoi Ki-Lang, Ting Shing-Kwang, Ngu Ing-Siong, and Taing Kwang-Ing, from the East Maine Conference.[2]

The bishop then declared the Foochow Annual Conference organized. The name of Ling Ching-Ting, one of the seven who had been ordained in 1869, is noticeably missing from this list; he would have been transferred from the Indiana Conference had he not passed away the previous May while on his circuit at Deng-diong.

"When a foreign mission is organized as an Annual Conference, it takes on a new measure of autonomy. The Foochow Mission was now to be given this permanent structural form." Thus wrote J. M. Reid of the year 1877, when, acting under authorization of the General Conference, the Foochow Annual Conference was organized, again demonstrating that Methodism, brought to China, did not have to remain American Methodism. Nor was it to be a nationalistic or isolated Methodism. The Foochow Lay Electoral Conference two years later elected a lay delegate to the General Conference, "not with any purpose that their candidate should actually make the journey to Cincinnati, but in grateful recognition of the standing accorded them in the councils of the church." [3]

Under the annual conference organization the passing of the character of its ministers, which appears not to have been done under the mission organization, was a requirement. Reid describes an "affecting scene" when this examination began:

The name of S. L. Baldwin stood first on the list, and by the new order of things Hu Bo-Mi became his presiding elder, and was called upon to "represent" him. Brother Hu quite broke down and said the like was never seen in China. "These foreign teachers have come here to teach us of Jesus, and now we are an annual conference, and I am called upon to 'represent' the teacher. I can think of nothing like it but when the Saviour insisted upon washing the disciples' feet." The whole conference was moved to tears on witnessing the feeling of this grand old man.[4]

The statistics of this first annual conference showed thirty-five members of the conference, sixty local preachers, and a membership of 1,235—and the first ten years of the thirty leading to this had not produced one member! "The work of making appointments proceeded as systematically and carefully as in any conference at home," and they were "read by Sia Sek-Ong, and with the doxology and benediction the first session of the Foochow Conference was closed." [5] These appointments covered five districts, with five Chinese presiding elders, and five "Missionaries" (not "Missionaries-in-charge" as appeared in later conference appointments for so many years). And this was just eight years after Bishop Kingsley had ordained the first Chinese Methodist preachers.

A year before this, 1876, Bishop E. M. Marvin, representing his colleagues and the General Conference of the Methodist Episcopal Church, South, made an official visit to China, and in Shanghai ordained four deacons and two elders in the Chien-Li-Huei. Hence it is not surprising that at the annual meeting of the China Mission in 1880, the conviction was expressed that "the time is near when the preachers of this mission, foreign and native, should be organized and set apart as an annual conference . . . not later than the autumn of 1882." [6]

But the church was not ready to move so fast. The Episcopal Address to the General Conference of the Methodist Episcopal Church, South, in 1882, contained the following paragraph:

> The evangelization of heathen lands must be, under God, carried on mainly by converted and trained natives. America cannot send enough laborers to China, now or hereafter, for the harvest; but by such schools as have lately been inaugurated there we see the promise of the possible occupation of that field at no great distance of time. A providential preparation seems to have been completed, and our church is about to see fruit where faith has waited long. Let us be equal to the full measure of the opportunity and the undertaking. It would be well, in view of the native helpers already engaged and preparing, and the encouraging outlook, for you to make provision for organizing the Shanghai Annual Conference, within the four years next following.

The quadrennium was well advanced before this was done, for it was not till 1886, with Bishop A. W. Wilson visiting China for the purpose, that the China Annual Conference of the Methodist Episcopal Church, South, was organized. At that time the conference numbered three ordained Chinese preachers, six unordained members, and a church membership of only 146; and seven missionaries were transferred from their home conferences to membership in the China Conference, thus sundering another link that bound them to their old homes. One of the charter members of this conference was C. J. Soong, who, as a nine-year old lad had shipped from Canton to India, and then turned up in an uncle's tea and silk shop in Boston, and who, years later, was the father of China's future financier and statesman, T. V. Soong, and the three famous Soong sisters. He had been introduced to Mrs. Tom Ramsey of Wilmington, North Carolina, by an officer on a Coast Guard ship on which he ran away from Boston, was converted under the preaching of the Rev. Thomas Page Ricaud, then pastor of the Fifth Street Methodist Episcopal Church, South, in Wilmington, and later lived in the home of General Julian S. Carr, of Durham, who put him through Trinity College (now Duke University). He was admitted to the North Carolina Annual Conference on trial in 1885, ordained deacon, and appointed "Missionary to China," for which he sailed within a few weeks. "When the China Conference was organized and held its first session in November, 1886, Soong became one of its original members—'on trial' but already ordained—and was appointed to the Kwan-san Circuit in the Soochow District." [7] The following month, probably without knowing of the organization of the China Mission Conference, the North Carolina Conference, "without examination by the committee," passed Soong's character, advanced him "to the class of the second year," and reappointed him a "Missionary," located at Quinsan, China. [8]

Ten years later the conference minutes show the appointment of C. F. Reid as "Presiding Elder of the Korea District," and until 1907 Korea remained a part of the China Conference. There was still room for Methodism to expand in China, but as Maclay felt that Japan should be entered, so Reid heard the call from the Hermit Kingdom. As "China herself was in the past the mother of civilization and literature" in the Orient, so China Methodism became the mother of the Methodism of the Far East.

While the Foochow and the China Annual Conferences were being organized, the North China Mission (which until 1873 had been the Peking Mission) was pushing ahead toward that day in 1893 when it could be organized as the North China Annual Conference. On April 7, 1877, Chen Ta-Yung and Te Jui were admitted to the North Indiana Conference on trial, and, under the "missionary rule," elected to deacon's orders. On November 12, 1877, a Methodist society was organized in Tientsin with stewards and a leader, and a quarterly conference was held under the presidency of George R. Davis, presiding elder. From the very first, as soon as the mission staff was large enough, the work had been developed by the Methodist system of itinerating, using every local means of travel, but these "journeys, though sometimes performed in Chinese carts, or mule-litters, are, for the most part, undertaken on horse-back, with saddle-bags, after the manner of primitive Methodism." [9] Thus as far distant as four hundred miles north of Peking preaching places had been opened and workers appointed. When the conference was formally organized it included the "provinces of Shantung and Honan and all China north of them."

In 1890, Nathan Sites who, "in journeyings often," including most of the "perils" listed by Paul, and "in labors abundant," had been carrying Christianity throughout that portion of Fukien which eventually embraced four conferences, had said in his report of the Hinghwa District, that "in six years time we hope for an episcopal visitation and the organization of the Hinghwa Annual Conference of the Methodist Episcopal Church, as authorized 'by the General Conference of 1896.' "

An enabling act for the formation of a Mission Conference was requested, but the General Conference of 1896 had gone one step farther than requested, and constituted the Hinghwa Mission Conference outright, and Bishop Joyce called the conference into being on November 26 of the same year, at which time the church membership within this new conference was reported as 5,628.

The year of jubilee was one of rejoicing for all who were interested in China Methodism, for within fifty years the church had grown until it had a membership of over twenty thousand (about half of whom were listed as probationers), and had spread into three annual conferences, one mission conference, and two missions. More than this, the eye of faith could see in the future the shape of other conferences to be. Iong-bing had been recognized as a part of the Nantai Circuit in 1863; there was an Iong-bing District when the Foochow Conference was organized in 1877, and Iong-bing city became a mission station in 1901. Yung-chun appears as a "new appointment" in 1873; by action of the cabinet in 1878 it was separated from the Hinghwa District and, with Teh-wha and the Yuki-hsien of the Iong-bing District, made the Yung-chun District; in 1894 it became a mission station when the Rev. and Mrs. R. L. McNabb moved there from Hinghwa.

Wang Jui-Fu, "a literary gentleman" from Shantung, heard the gospel preached in Methodist chapels in Peking during one of the triennial examinations, asked for, and was given Christian baptism. This was in 1873. From the time he returned home, he never ceased to make known "the dear Saviour he had found," and

after a few weeks he sent his son Wang Chen-Pei to Peking with a report of the work done and a list of eighteen names of persons anxious to become Christians. The son wheeled a wheel-barrow the four hundred miles from An-chia-chuang to Peking. He remained a few weeks for further instruction, and returned with his wheel-barrow loaded with books and tracts.[10]

In 1874, when Lowry and Walker visited An-chia-chuang, Wang Cheng-Pei was baptized and he and his father were received into the church. At the same time their wives, Wang's daughter, nephew, and cousin were all received on probation and the Lord's Supper administered. A quarterly conference was organized on November 5, 1880; the Shantung District had an enrollment of 506 members and probationers when North China became an annual conference; and the Rev. W. C. Longden, and Miss

Steere and Miss Barrow, of the Woman's Foreign Missionary Society, opened Taianfu as a mission station in 1898.

Probably the historian is not called upon to be a diagnostician. Why the Methodist Episcopal Church, with its prompt start at Kiukiang and its able leadership was not ready to become even a mission conference in the Yangtze Valley by this time, it is difficult to say. One could hardly attribute it to lack of unity in policies and harmony between missionaries, though Central China seems to have suffered from this malady during this period more than any of the other China missions. Nor can we attribute it too largely to the policy of expansion and the desire to occupy the commercial ports between Shanghai and Kiukiang—Chinkiang, which was first occupied in 1881, Wuhu, where the "finest plot for building purposes at that growing port" was purchased the same year, and Nanking, which Hart had said, "ought, by its geographical position, become the future capital of a rejuvenated people." Other reasons in part or in whole may have contributed to this relatively slow advancement, but for many years the missionaries were feeling the need of their own trained preachers, who were not forthcoming in the number needed, and these few who were eligible for conference membership were being admitted as members of the Foochow Conference. Nevertheless, as early as 1881—a year mentioned frequently for its several significant events—the Central China Mission decided to divide its work into five districts: Kiukiang, Wuhu, Nanking, Chinkiang, and Nanchang, thus preparing for that day when Kiukiang and Nanchang should be the foci of another conference.

Before leaving the roll of the conferences and prospective conferences in China as of 1897, reference must be made to the Central Conference, which met in that year for the first time in the office of the American Bible Society in Shanghai. The history of this organization has been so ably portrayed by H. W. Worley in *The Central Conference of the Methodist Episcopal Church* that only such account of it will be made in these chapters as is necessary to complete the story.

With two annual conferences, a mission conference, and two missions, the Methodist Episcopal Church, as it existed in China in 1897, was feeling the need for some centralizing and co-ordinating agency, and the success of a central conference in India pointed to that as the probable solution. It is more than possible that the missionaries who promoted the conference did not foresee the significance of their idea as it developed during the decades that were to follow. The organization then had no legal standing in the church, but official recognition was given to it by the presence of Bishop Joyce as its presiding officer. That it was still an organization of the Methodist Episcopal Church and not of the Mi-I-Mi Huei was attested by its membership, for the North China Conference was the only one which was represented by Chinese delegates, its delegation consisting of H. H. Lowry, M. L. Taft, Y. K. Tsau, and Chen Ta-Yung. It showed its purpose in developing a church which was not to be controlled by American Methodism by initiating the preparation of a uniform course of study for traveling and local preachers, and by calling into being the *China Christian Advocate*. Furthermore, it took the first step of united Northern Methodism in China in shaping or controlling administration of China Methodism through the episcopacy when it approved of the policy, then in force, of a bishop remaining two years on the field, and expressed the hope that four-year assignments would be made.

Those who were children in the Methodist compound in Foochow in 1897, and who were old enough to remember, still recall the excitement of the days of celebration and the house guests which marked the jubilee. It was an event of significance both to the members of the Foochow Conference and to their visitors from North China and the Yangtze Valley. Fifty years before, three persons had stepped from a chartered lorcha, the only Methodists in all China, and they were just arriving. Now scores of Methodists had come from the north and the west, representing thousands of Chinese Methodists; they had come by coastal steamer and river launch to rejoice with their mother, and to learn of her; they were celebrating fifty years of achievement, but they were looking forward to centuries of vital Methodism in China. A half century had seen the Methodist Church well-rooted with its Chinese pastors and presiding elders functioning through conference organizations, and a central, co-ordinating and unifying conference for those of the Methodist Episcopal Church. The jubilee of 1897 was not, as the centennial of 1947 was not, any more than a landing point along a road that winds up a mountainside, from which to view the road that has been traversed, so as to take fresh courage for the further road ahead.

2. *Further Development of Conferences*

And so during the next quarter century the development of conference organizations and the growth of self-government moved forward. There was no sign that the conferences comprising the three branches of Methodism would number the one hundred which Bishop Kingsley had predicted would be organized within a century, but the increase in membership and the geographical expansion which have already been noted, were tending in the direction of an ultimate fulfillment of that prediction as surely as scattered showers over the mountains cause the reservoir to overflow its dam.

In spite of the slow growth of the Central China work, which had more than once caused concern to bishops and missionaries, and in spite of the fact that, following his first visit to the area in 1904, Bishop Bashford had expressed his view that "the Central China Mission is not large enough to organize as an annual conference," the Central Conference of 1903 had considered dividing it. This proposal was to create a Mid-China Mission, extending westward to the boundary of the West China Mission, and an East China Mission to "include all the territory between the Mid-China Mission and the sea, excepting Fukien province." Lacking the faith that could see forty years ahead, this disregarded the place, geographical and ecclesiastical, of the China Conference of the Methodist Episcopal Church, South.

Bishop Bashford had been presenting diplomas to college gradutes for many years, and he must therefore have felt at home when, on his first tour of the conferences in China, he was able to present a diploma to a conference. As T. B. Owen expressed it, the Hinghwa Conference was, in November, 1904, "relieved of the adjective 'Mission' in our name," and was graduated, by authority conferred by the General Conference of 1904, into the rights and privileges of an annual conference.

That same General Conference, which was about to send James W. Bashford to China to administer its missions and conferences, had also passed an act enabling the Central China Mission to become a mission conference. The Hinghwa Mission Conference had, as we have seen, immediately availed itself of its new privilege, but Central China was either discouraged by its new bishop or realized its own insufficiency, and it was not till three years later that the Central China Mission Conference was organized with a membership of twelve ordained and unordained ministers.

The General Conference of 1904 evidently felt that the church in China was ripe for great advance, or that under the leadership of Bishop Bashford, existing organization procedures would soon be outmoded. At any rate an enabling act was also granted to the West China Mission, in its case to skip a grade, and organize into an annual conference. No promotion was made, however, until January, 1908, when Bishop Bashford's diary shows that he "consented to the organization of the West China Mission Conference," noting that he "did this under the authority granted by the General Conference . . . assuming that the grant of power to organize an annual conference carried with it the lesser power to organize a mission conference."

Central China had considered division in 1903. It had become a mission conference in 1907; in 1908 "Bishop Bashford announced that when this conference meets again it will meet as an annual conference," which it did on October 7, 1909. In 1911 the China Central Conference adopted a memorial to the General Conference praying that "that portion of the Central China Conference embracing the province of Kiangsi, together with such portions of Anhwei and Hupeh as are at present included in the present Kiukiang District," might, when properly approved by the authorities on the field, "become a mission conference with such name as it may adopt." [11] The following year, proper authority having been given, the Kiangsi Mission Conference was created, with Kiukiang and Nanchang as the two foci; in September, 1917, the first and organizing session of the Kiangsi Annual Conference evidenced the success of this division.

Four years earlier, nine hundred miles to the west, with Chungking and Chengtu as its two centers, the West China Mission Conference, after an existence of five years in that status, had become the West China Annual Conference. Of the area between these two conferences, the 1915 Annual Report of the Board of Foreign Missions said:

In all this area we have not a single missionary of our church, neither have we at the present moment any plan for opening work in the magnificent cities which bear convincing evidence of the enormous populations living in this region. The other great denominations have neglected this area and the multitudes wait in vain for the Gospel message.

Again the General Conference created an enabling act for China. The greatest advance in the Foochow Conference had been in its western districts, and in that field dialect conditions and difficulty of access from Foochow had argued for another division of the Foochow Conference. Hence, in 1916, with but three dissenting votes the entire conference stood for the separation, and the six districts at the western end of the conference were constituted the Yenping Annual Conference with thirty members.

In the customary legal phraseology the Eastern Asia Central Conference was again in 1920 memorializing the General Conference, as the Hinghwa Conference had done twelve years earlier, to "enable" the division of the Hingwha Annual Conference and the formation of a mission conference embracing the counties of Yungchun, Tehwa, and Tatien. Here again it was language and travel that argued for the separation; a considerable mountain range served as a barrier between these two sections of the conference, and the use of the Amoy dialect by the people southwest of this range formed a no less barrier to the training of preachers in Hinghwa and their exchange between the various districts. Of the consummation of this desire, Bishop L. J. Birney, who administered the Fukien Conferences in 1922, wrote in *Zion's Herald* of March 14, 1923:

The crowning hour of all these Fukien Conferences was the hour when the new Yungchun Mission Conference was born by the unanimous vote of the Hinghwa Conference and the telegraphed approval of Bishop F. T. Keeney. Here was an Act of the Apostles which for sheer daring of faith was worthy to be made a twenty-ninth chapter.

To complete this record up to the close of the Eastern Asia Central Conference of 1923, three actions by that conference should be noted here: First, "that that part of the North China Conference within the province of Shantung be set off as a separate annual conference"; second, that the West China Annual Conference be divided into the Chengtu West China Conference and the Chungking West China Conference, each embracing ten counties; and third, that the South Fukien Mission Conference—at first called the Yungchun Mission Conference—"become an annual conference on attaining the membership prescribed by the *Discipline*." [12]

One is almost surprised as he looks back through the years to see these South Fukien districts climbing, steadily climbing towards that goal of ecclesiastical organization which to every Methodist preacher means what statehood meant to the inhabitants of Ohio and Kentucky in the early days of the nineteenth century and to the citizens of the Territory of Hawaii, now that Pearl Harbor has made it feel its maturity. Those missionary evangelists of the early days, Nathan Sites and others, had "gone everywhere preaching the Word," and finding in the mountains beyond Hinghwa men and women who "believed and turned to the Lord." After Hinghwa Mission Conference was organized, T. B. Owen and W. W. Williams, soon tied closely the bands that bound Yungchun, Tehwa, Tatien, and Yungan to that organization. An attempt to withdraw from this field was made in 1901, only to result in "the most marked progress," so marked that W. N. Brewster felt another year like that would "put our evangelistic work upon an entirely self-supporting basis." It was doubtless Bishop David H. Moore's visit to this field which had resulted in that "attempt to withdraw," for he had "expressed his judgement, according with that of the missionaries there," that the vast extent of the territory, the small force of workers, and the remoteness of these mountain valleys warranted the transfer of these districts and their churches "to the care of the English Presbyterians, occupying an adjoining field." But the church members "refused to be given away," affirming that, "having been born anew as Methodists, Methodists they would remain. If the mother church could not provide for them, they would put up for themselves." [13]

Missionary families were sent in 1904 to live in Yungchun in an effort to support and build up that end of the conference. But when, in 1909, at the Hinghwa Conference, a delegation called on Bishop Bashford, he told them that he could not see his way clear to recommend a division, not until there were "at least fifteen Yungchun speaking members of the conference or probationers."

In 1910, J. E. Skinner, residing at Yenping, was appointed district missionary for the Tatien District to see whether that portion of the field could be administered from Yenping as a base. His "candid judgement" after a year was that Yenping was not a practical base, "that Yungchun has proven especially unsatisfactory," and that, therefore, the Tatien District "should be worked from Yungan City, and that missionaries should be sent there as soon as practicable and Yungan be developed into a strong missionary station." The next fall Bishop Bashford was confiding the problem to his diary:

I made clear to the cabinet the following: . . . Bishop Moore's judgement after visiting the field. . . . On coming to this conference in 1904 and learning that the conference had rejected Bishop Moore's advice, I accepted their decision to hold the work for Methodism and worked earnestly at home to get men and money to develop it, but failed. . . . On petition of Hinghwa Conference the General Conference of 1908 authorized the separation . . . [and the] formation of a mission conference. In 1909 I made another tour . . . of three weeks and I was obliged to reach the same judgement as Bishop Moore had reached . . . but again to a large extent I failed. In 1910 Bishop Lewis made a tour of the whole region spending a month . . . and he reached a stronger conviction than I that all the Amoy speaking work should be given to the Presbyterians.

But the bishops were not anxious to force the issue and Si I-Seng, district superintendent, in his report to the Hinghwa Conference in 1915, describes the most recent phases of the situation at that time:

There have been reports that our church was about to withdraw from this section of the conference. The members prayed earnestly over the matter and are grateful to Dr. North . . . who came to our conference and examined into the matter, with the result that the Society decided to grant our request and recalled Mr. Hawley to his work among us.[14]

Seven years later, as we have seen, these districts were organized into a mission conference, and annual conference status was asked the next year.

On October 8, 1925, the South Fukien Mission Conference met to admit eight worthy candidates into full membership, record its membership as twenty-five, and adjourn sine-die, to reassemble, call the roll of twenty-five charter members, and with Bishop Wallace E. Brown presiding, organize the South Fukien Annual Conference. This conference had twenty-five preachers, it had all the schools customary in a conference, and in spite of the fact that presses had come and gone in Foochow, Hinghwa, Kiukiang, Shanghai, and elsewhere, its remoteness in the mountains of Fukien seemed to warrant the installation that same year of a new and modern printing press with Chinese type.

But then came 1927, and the arguments of Bishops Moore, Bashford, and Lewis were reappraised in New York, and then one missionary family was transferred to Malaysia, and another which started to return to Yungchun was stopped at the Pacific coast. At the conference session of 1931, the Rev. and Mrs. Harry C. Jett were the only missionaries on the field. At that session, as Mrs. Jett tells the story in the *China Christian Advocate* of February, 1937, "it was voted by a majority of only one to unite with the Church of Christ in China," becoming "an organic part of the Amoy group, that is, a Presbytery of the Amoy Synod."

Even after the official vote was taken, difficulties loomed large. Many felt that a church organization without a Bishop would be next to impossible. The ordained ministers feared very much the plan of a called ministry instead of the old system of appointments. Many of the members simply did not want their name and organization changed, without being able to give any good reasons.

This was the third attempt to unite the work of this region. It is and has been desirable because the people of this region are connected with the people of Amoy by dialect (the tongues are very closely related, at least) and by business relations —especially since the opening of bus roads practically all connnection is with Amoy and Chuanchow instead of with either of the city centers of the three Methodist conferences of the Province. The South Fukien Conference was too small a group to do effective work alone. Leaders were of necessity few, and there was not the helpful contact with larger Methodist centers nor the possibility of interchange of workers, with the broadening influence that both these bring.

Yet on May 1, 1934, Bishop Gowdy was able to inform the Central Conference only that "the South Fukien Conference had voted to unite with the Church of Christ in China," and it was voted "to send a message of greeting to Mrs. Harry Jett, . . . delegate elect to this session." But before the end of that year the union of the South Fukien Conference with the Amoy Synod of the Church of Christ in China was accomplished.

Turning the pages back to the diamond Jubilee of the 1923 session of the Central Conference, the statistics for the Methodist churches in China stand at eight annual conferences and two mission conferences, the division of two conferences asked, and the advance requested for one mission conference (South Fukien) to become an annual conference.

Little need be said at this point regarding the Central Conference, although it continued and grew in power as the central control of the Methodist Episcopal Church from Yungchun to Shanhaikwan and Chengtu. "Probably the most important single effect of the Central Conference in China," in the opinion of H. W. Worley, "was to keep the Chinese Methodist Church from organic union with the Church of Christ in China. The development, the powers, and the actions of that conference have been so adequately discussed elsewhere, and quotations from its official minutes appear so frequently in these pages, that no narrative is here called for beyond the record of a few facts or trends.

One of these is its name. The conference was organized in 1897 as the Central Conference of the Methodist Episcopal Church in China—commonly spoken of as the China Central Conference. The sixth session of the Central Conference in China, held in Nanking November 9-15, 1915, became the first session of the Central Conference of Eastern Asia, since the conference at Foochow in 1911 had made provision for the Methodists of Korea, Japan, and the Philippines to share in its organization and cooperate in its sessions. But although the conferences of 1919 and 1923 met as the second and third sessions of the Eastern Asia Central Conference, and although Korea was well represented in all three sessions, the number of delegates from China, and the conference actions applicable to the China conferences only, so far outnumbered those in the rest of the field that it is doubtful that the name truly represented the facts or that the representatives from Korea and Japan ever felt thoroughly at home in its sessions.

A second aspect that should be mentioned is its membership. The first session, as already noted, included only two Chinese members, though numbering eleven missionaries; the second session was composed of twenty-six delegates, half of whom were Chinese, and that session, on November 18, 1899, adopted an amendment to its constitution providing that "the conference shall be composed of ministerial and lay delegates. . . . It shall always be provided that at least one-half of the ministerial delegates shall be foreign missionaries." [15] The arrangements made for the election of lay delegates were such as to make it more than possible that the lay delegates would have a large number, if not be chosen entirely, from the missionaries of the Board of Foreign Missions and the Woman's Foreign Missionary Society. In the third session, 45 per cent of its ministerial and 18 per cent of its lay delegates were Chinese, each conference represented having at least one Chinese delegate. In 1907 fourteen of the fifty-one delegates were Chinese. The 1911 conference was held at relatively remote and inaccessible Foochow, and for the first time North China was not represented by Chinese delegates, and Central China by only one; but the Fukien conferences were largely represented, and of the total membership, 40 per cent was Chinese. In 1915, 1920, and 1923 the Chinese members composed 47, 48 and 66 per cent respectively, of the elected delegates from the China conferences, thus showing a steady rise.

Then there was the increasing acquisition of power which Worley has so well portrayed. Of this, but one item is mentioned here because it was a policy that had been used openly and repeatedly and generally with the desired results. In 1907 Bishop Bashford wrote in his diary that he advised the conference

to ask the Chinese conferences and missions to give to the China Central Conference the same powers for China which our Methodist churches give to the General Conference subject to the restrictions imposed upon the China Central Conference by the *Discipline*, and by future acts of the General Conference, [and to] ask the Methodist Episcopal Church, South, to send delegates to the Central Conference to participate with us in our next conference with the same rights which we enjoy.

Commenting on this advice, the bishop further wrote:

A pound of possession is worth a ton of petition, and I believe it is better to exercise these rights and in case we find it a mistake our respective general conferences can say we have exceeded our powers; in case it succeeds, as I believe it will, the home [?] General Conferences will ratify it.

And finally we note the difficult problem of financing the Central Conference. Obviously to require the delegates to pay their own expenses or for local organizations to defray the expenses of its own delegates, as had been done with some of the China-wide missionary conferences, would result in an entirely unrepresentative conference. To ask the Chinese membership to meet the entire cost would be too much of a burden when so large a proportion of the delegates were Americans and steamship fares and American habits of living made the expenses of each missionary several times that of his Chinese fellow delegate. Hence the result, which Worley describes in and following the conference of 1899:

The Committee on Finance, faced with the problem of providing travelling expenses of twenty-six delegates suggested that the Missionary Society pay the expenses of the missionaries who were delegates, and that collections be taken in all the local churches to pay that of the Chinese delegates. This last suggestion was eventually followed, but it took a long time to get it into operation. The first amount reported under this division was $13 collected during the whole quadrennium 1907-1911 by the Foochow Conference. No other conference took up a collection until after that time.[16]

In the main this method was followed and made more effective through successive quadrenniums, with the final modification in 1920: each conference assigned a quota of eight cents per member, each missionary (man, wife, or single woman) was requested to pay $4.00 and the remainder, estimated at $8.00 per capita for each foreign missionary, was to be raised by such methods as the several Finance and Field Reference Committees might determine. The Committee on Conference Finances in 1923 expressed itself satisfied that the plan in effect had been quite successful, although one conference, and only one, had failed to follow the plan. While the plan had not been generally acceptable, no better plan for raising the funds necessary to meet the expenses of this gathering and for publishing the *Minutes* and the bishop's address had presented itself, and hence its continuance was recommended for another quadrennium.

In seventy-five years Methodism in China had developed an orthodox Methodist organization that the General Conference could and did accept with pride. This organization was already handling its affairs in a way which indicated its maturity and foretold its ability to look after itself in whatever degree of independence it might ultimately achieve or be assigned. Furthermore the organization was actually suggesting to the conferences which dominate the General Conferences certain lines of development and advancement which would work towards the wholesomeness of a church that was to become a world-wide church.

To be allowed to formulate its own courses of study, and even its own ritual, were not steps towards separation but were rather the recognition that the annual conferences—and their co-operation in the Central Conference—could be trusted to make decisions for themselves and to plan the details of their own daily life. No longer was it necessary for mother to prescribe the diet or specify the hat and coat to be worn or even the company to be kept. Soon the church in China would be ready to "enable" its own conferences to organize; soon it would choose its own episcopal leadership.

3. *Annual Conferences Come and Go*

The weather-wise had been detecting in the atmosphere increasing electrical tension as the accumulating nationalism was soon to precipitate an anti-Christian storm. But the advances in conference organization in the Methodist Episcopal sections of the country, as described in the foregoing pages, not only served as further steps towards autonomy but might be thought of as preparations for cyclone cellars.

Glancing back at the previews thrown on the screen, as of 1923, we recall that the West China Annual Conference was to be divided, Shantung was to become a separate annual conference, and the South Fukien Mission Conference was given permission, on attaining the required membership, to become an annual conference.

The West China Conference in 1923 had 63 full members, with 23 members on trial; 100 local preachers; 89 churches and chapels; 90 rented places of worship; and 1100 members, a membership which had quadrupled during the past four years. The leaders felt that, considering its size, growth, extent, and inadequate facilities for communication, it could function more efficiently as two bodies rather than one. Hence in 1924 it split itself into the Chengtu West China Conference and the Chungking West China Conference. For thirteen years these two conferences carried on, as friendly rivals if there were any spirit of rivalry, and as loyal partners for the church in Szechuen. This experience taught them, however, that "in union there is strength," and that the changing conditions favored a reunion. A decrease in the number of pastors had come simultaneously with improved travel facilities which made Chengtu and Chungking now only two instead of ten days apart; hence the two conferences were rewed, and 1937 marked the reappearance of the West China Annual Conference.

The Central Conference of 1923 had approved, and the General Conference of 1924 had "enabled," the organization of a Shantung Conference. The Taian and Yenchow District Conferences in August, 1924, decided to ask that this be done in 1925. October 22-26 were the dates arranged for the setting up of the new conference, but by that time one of those war-lord contests which had cursed China for years was on, and

grey columns threaded the open fields, pack mules jammed the city gates with mortars and machine guns, parks were full of artillery, while endless trains of soldiers moved at the behest of powers sublimely remote from the needs of the travelling public,[17]

and Bishop Grose was unable to reach Taian. The Rev. Ting Li-Mei, however, worked his way up from Teng-hsien, and

held meetings on Saturday night, Sunday, Monday, and Tuesday. His subject was "With Christ." He was a great inspiration to all, and the men received a great blessing. Business meetings were also held, the general plan for the work of the new conference formulated, committees appointed and the work arranged, so that it could be carried on this year.[18]

Thus was the Shantung Annual Conference organized in 1925 with four missionaries supplementing the twenty-one ordained Chinese to make up the required number. Writing of the organization in the absence of the bishop, with true Methodist loyalty, Miss Effie Young, who was present, added: "But of course there may be changes later, as the plans did not have the sanction of the bishop, and he may not approve."

The events of 1927-28 had hurt the working force in the Shantung Conference. In 1932 the work was further threatened by the influence of an ultraemotional religious sect which was affecting some of the churches, and which, by 1935, contributed to a feeling by the Woman's Foreign Missionary Society that its work in Shantung should not be continued. Therefore in December the society withdrew its activity from the Shantung Annual Conference, except for its share in the Cheeloo University, which it then aligned with its North China Conference organization. The General Board workers have, however, with some financial help from the Woman's Foreign Missionary Society, continued the work among women and children through the years since that time, using and maintaining the society's property, continuing and increasing the staff of workers, conducting one co-educational institution, and using Chinese women evangelistic workers in the conference.

As Brewster, almost singlehanded, had built the Hinghwa Conference, as West China cannot be mentioned without thinking of Spencer Lewis, as Bankhardt has been the lifelong inspiration of the Yenping mission station and the Yenping Conference, so Perry O. Hanson and Shantung cannot be separated in thought. By 1940 this general, whom nothing could force to surrender, was saying in the *China Christian Advocate* of March 1940:

Fifteen years ago there were fifteen American missionaries in Taian, including five of the W. M. S. *Now* there is one man and his wife from overseas working in the Shantung Conference. However, the growth in National workers more than makes up for this loss; after all, it is a *Chinese* church.

For in these fifteen years, he added,

the 21 Chines preachers then had become 39 when roll was called last November. The membership of 5,039 has reached 9,141. The present program calls for the addition of a hundred new preachers during the next ten years.

Had the church been left undisturbed, this program probably would have been realized!

The work for women and girls, which was suddenly dropped into the lap of the Board of Foreign Missions workers in Shantung in 1935, was a forced step towards a general unified administration of all the work. It had been the policy of the China Mission and Conference of the Southern church from the very beginning, a policy which had been so successful that it was adopted by the Yungchun Conference at its organization. When E. C. Parlin later expressed his satisfaction with the working of such a unified policy, he was expressing also the almost unanimous sentiment of both men and women in Shanghai and Soochow and throughout the China Mission Conference: "It more closely unites all phases of the work, makes possible more thorough co-operation, and tends to richer fellowship, giving a feeling of oneness of tasks and joys impossible with work separated under two administrations." [19]

In 1923 China Methodism had eight annual Conferences and two mission conferences. In 1931 these statistics were eleven annual conferences and one mission conference. By 1937, when the great crash came that stabilized the figures for the duration, the statistics were nine annual conferences, and one provisional annual conference, the latter term being the new terminology of the united church as later applied to the former Kalgan "Mission Conference." With these organizations the three branches of Methodism in China became, in 1941, the one Methodist Church extending from Kalgan and Chengtu to Shanghai and Yenping.

V

MEN OF GOOD STANDING IN CHARGE

You, brothers, must pick out from your number . . . men of good standing, who are wise and full of the Spirit, and we will put them in charge of this matter.

—Acts 6:3 (Goodspeed)

1. *Episcopal Administration from the United States*

THE QUESTION OF EPISCOPAL LEADERSHIP AND ADMINISTRATION FOR those sections of the church now established in China first appeared in China when the Foochow Conference sent the first delegate to the General Conference of the Methodist Episcopal Church in 1880. S. L. Baldwin, sitting as a member of that General Conference, had presented a memorial from the Chinese missionaries against the election of a missionary bishop, perhaps feeling, as H. W. Worley suggests had been the case in Liberia, that they would miss "the stimulus of cross-fertilization provided by the Methodist itinerancy, the freshening of periodical visits to the home base, and the opportunity so afforded for presenting the need of the field in the home churches." [1]

At first general superintendents had been assigned to occasional globe-circling tours. They had come, seen and administered, and took back to the home churches glowing reports of the churches abroad. Then for a number of years annual tours of inspection, administration, and inspiration (to the church in China as well as to the bishops) were the program, and some of the great men, who in the eighties and the nineties were bishops consecrated to "travel throughout the connection," strengthened the church and its sense of unity. It was on one of these visits that Bishop I. W. Wiley died in Foochow during the conference of 1884 without having been able to ordain the candidates for the ministry who had been awaiting ordination at his hands, and was laid to rest by the side of Isabelle White and others who had been his colleagues in the Foochow Mission during 1851-54.

Bishops Isaac W. Joyce and Earl Cranston came during the 1896-1900 quadrennium, assigned to hold the conferences in two successive years, spending the intervening months with the Methodists of eastern Asia. This made possible, for the first time, that arduous trip of an episcopal visit to West China, and probably gave better administration to the conferences the second year than had been possible the first, though John C. Ferguson wrote some time later in *Zion's Herald:* "The two-year bishops, as a result of further observation, were inclined to undo the second year, what they had deemed wise the first."

During most of those years, on both sides of the Pacific, Methodists had expressed their feeling that closer and more permanent episcopal supervision would strengthen the church in China, intensify American interest in its work, and knit the Asiatic and American parts of the church more closely together. It is an interesting coincidence that the year the empress dowager tried to break the ties that had been drawn between China and the Western nations, the General Conference of the Methodist Episcopal Church tried to strengthen the connections between its China conferences and the rest of the world. The biennial administrations of Bishops Joyce and Cranston had proved so far superior to the occasional, and then the annual, episcopal visits that the Central Conference in China and the General Conference of the church were convinced that a general superintendent assigned to a foreign residence for a quadrennium could do a still better job. Hence, in 1900, episcopal residences were created in Shanghai and Zurich, with Bishop David H. Moore assigned to the former, and Bishop John H. Vincent to the latter for a quadrennium. This began the second stage in the development of episcopal supervision in China. But was a general superintendent resident in Shanghai for four years the final and satisfactory solution of the problem, or was it another experiment towards some final solution? Bishop Moore expressed his opinion at the end of the quadrennium, when, writing in the *Methodist Review,* he stated his belief that some man in China should be elected as missionary bishop for that field. Of course he recognized certain disadvantages in this solution, and *Zion's Herald* pointed out on March 9, 1904:

But in the tabulation of the two sides which closes his article he gives as the figure of net results, when all things are taken into fair consideration, 87 for a missionary bishop chosen from the field, 70 for a missionary bishop chosen from some other missionary field, 63 for a missionary bishop chosen from home, and 58 for a General Superintendent—out of 100 total points.

Commenting on Bishop Moore's article, *Zion's Herald* continued:

The work of the missionary bishop would be supplemented, as it is now in India, by a visit once in a quadrennium, from a General Superintendent, who could hold a Bishop's Conference and be arbitrator or referee in case of any differences, and bring inspiration in many ways. . . . The Board of Bishops were in favor of it four years ago, but some of the China missionaries so strongly opposed that it failed to carry. We hope they will be able to agree this time upon some one of their number to take the post. This seems to be the only difficulty.

But was it? Episcopal aspirations of certain missionaries may have influenced some to oppose a plan which might result in their election; but episcopal aspirations of men in the United States may also have influenced to an equally small degree the consideration of General Conference policies. The majority of missionaries in China were in agreement with the memorial adopted by the Central Conference in Nanking in November, 1903, and the Chinese members of the several annual conferences were at that time still forming their opinions on such matters pretty largely on those of their missionary brethren with whom they were most intimately associated. So the memorial that went to the General Conference of 1904, from which the following is quoted, represented, in general, the views of the conferences in China:

> One quadrennium is not sufficient time to fully test the merits of this new movement, and we beg that it may be given full opportunity to demonstrate its superiority over anything heretofore proposed in the supervision of Missions. The only change our experience would suggest is that China be separated from Japan and Korea, as Eastern Asia is too large a field for the superintendance of one Bishop.
>
> [This will] demand the statesmanship, the consecration, the wisdom, and the experience of men accustomed to a world view of the Kingdom of Christ, and we beg that this work shall be left to the godly wisdom and administration of our General Superintendents.
>
> And we do hereby request and instruct our delegates to the General Conference... to oppose the election of a Missionary Bishop for China.[2]

Legally the only changes which the General Conference made in 1904 were, first, the separation of Japan and Korea from the supervision of the bishop assigned to China; and, second, the man assigned to China. Shanghai was continued as a General Superintendent's residence for the next quadrennium. But, as H. W. Worley says:

> The Board of Bishops initiated an experiment in 1896 which was to eventuate after eight years in the most important single contribution the Methodist Church in America ever made to China. The experiment was consecutive supervision by the same general superintendent; the contribution was Bishop James W. Bashford, [who] started the custom of a general superintendent taking a certain part of the foreign missions of the church as his lifework.[3]

In three years Bishop Bashford, by his Christlike spirit and administrative perspicacity, captivated the hearts of missionaries and Chinese, ministers and laymen, Methodists and those of other denominations. The bigness of his heart and the breadth of his statesmanship had already justified his assignment by the General Conference; any other than the memorial adopted at the Central Conference in May, 1907, would have been unthinkable.

That conference prayed the General Conference "that there shall be no change during the next quadrennium, as in our opinion to remove Bishop Bashford from the field at this time would be an irretrievable calamity." But the field was too big and the burdens too heavy for even a giant Bashford, and the Central Conference expressed its judgment to the "Dear Fathers and Brethren" who were to meet in Baltimore the next May, that an additional general superintendent should be assigned to China in 1908 in view of the vastness of the field, the great awakening then taking place, and the great forward movements contemplated as a result of the great Centenary Missionary Conference. And then, although there was still a pro-missionary-bishop miniority, added this resolution. "That in view of any possible contingencies which may arise at the next General Conference, we hereby request the General Conference of 1908 not to elect a Missionary Bishop for China, nor a Bishop for the Chinese race or language." [4] Bishop Wilson Seeley Lewis was the General Conference's answer to this resolution.

From the day in 1904 that James W. Bashford accepted election as bishop and assignment to China, to that in 1921, when Wilson S. Lewis was transferred from earth to heaven, these two men gave the finest spiritual and constructive leadership and dominated the programs and policies of the Methodist Episcopal Church in China, guiding it through difficulties and strengthening it for the future as skillful pilots and master engineers. What the church in China is, and ever will be, is due in large measure to the General Conference actions of 1904 and the following sessions and their choice of men for continuous residential supervision. In 1920, with this program of administration a settled policy, and with the enthusiasm of strengthening the church which the centenary had inspired, a third general superintendent was provided for China, and Lauress J. Birney and Frederick T. Keeney came as stalwart, consecrated, forward-looking leaders to take Bishop Bashford's place in association with Bishop Lewis.

We must pause here to look at the secret of the power and influence of this college president and bishop, this man of great physique, genial smile, and sympathetic handclasp, Wilson Seeley Lewis. His daughter says that when he reached the Custom's Jetty at Shanghai,

before the ropes were tied or the gang-plank fixed, a multitude of half-clad, yelling, smelling, scrambling coolies jumped on the decks of the launch. . . . But Bishop Lewis stood quietly in the midst of that mob of the neediest on earth. . . . Said he, "I loved them all. From that day to this, I never saw a Chinese whom I did not love and I never doubted that God called me to China!" [5]

And F. D. Gamewell quoted Bishop Bashford as saying one day, after Bishop Lewis had been in China for some time: "I have it. I know the secret of

Bishop Lewis' power. Bishop Lewis knows God. Bishop Lewis walks with God." A man like that could not but make his church a real influence in the country.

In 1900 Shanghai, although not within the bounds of any annual conference of the Methodist Episcopal Church, and purely on geographical considerations, had been made the episcopal residential city. In 1908, when a second general superintendent was to be sent to China, Peking in the north and Foochow in the south were designated as their bases of operations. In 1915, with the members of the Fukien conferences opposing the petition, the Central Conference voted a memorial that Shanghai again be made an episcopal residence instead of Foochow, for the following reasons:

1. Shanghai is the center for all of the general offices of the church in China; the Editors, Publishers, Treasurer, Educational and Medical Secretaries having their offices in Shanghai. 2. For administrative purposes Shanghai is the most central and satisfactory place for the episcopal residence in southern China.[6]

The vote was fifty for and thirty-four against; the Fukien conferences had thirty-five members in the conference. For the administration of the Yangtze Valley conferences, the attitude of that conference in session in Nanking was fundamentally right; but with 48 per cent of the total church membership and 35 per cent of all the conference members located in the two Fukien conferences, the action of the Central Conference might well have been questioned, but was nevertheless granted by the General Conference at Saratoga Springs. Right or wrong, the question did not have to be reconsidered in 1920, for the addition of a third bishop re-established Foochow as an area center.

Meanwhile episcopal supervision of the Methodist Episcopal Church, South, in China was proceeding along lines similar to those in the sister church; but with a smaller, more intensive, and more compact work, the need for similar advances in episcopal administration was years behind that of the Methodist Episcopal Church. In the early nineties a missionary expressed the view of the Southern Church, not different from the Northern view, on the matter of episcopal supervision, when he said:

Instead of holding the operations of its missions under the sole control of a company of men on the other side of the globe, our church extends its government into the mission field, and secures to the missionary the same conference rights, and the same episcopal supervision that is enjoyed by the church at home. The mission field is not dealt with as a mere appendage of the home church, but is considered as part of the church, and entitled to all its rights and privileges. Its work being arranged, and its appointments being made by the same authorities that supervise the home administration, we escape, in a large measure, the friction and conflict that has disturbed the work of some of our sister organizations. . . . Our missions in China . . . furnish abundant illustrations of the advantages which have followed faithful episcopal supervision.[7]

The occasional and annual episcopal visits had come to an end in 1910 when Bishop Murrah had been assigned to administer the conferences in eastern Asia for the quadrennium. After three years of his continuous, wise, and sympathetic administration, a Joint Mission Meeting of the China Mission expressed itself as satisfied that his three years of continuous episcopal supervision had made possible continuity of policy, growth, and a spirit of unity "not hitherto possessed," and asked the Board of Missions to memorialize the General Conference of 1914 for "the episcopal supervision of one bishop for a quadrennium," adding that

We desire to record that we do not favor the election of a "missionary bishop," but prefer . . . some law directing our College of Bishops to assign one of their number for the full quadrennium to our Conference or by a law assigning to our bishops residential districts for the quadrennium in which latter case we should desire . . . China and . . . Japan (including Chosen) to be created into one episcopal residential district.[8]

But another four years passed, and while quadrennial supervision had been afforded, residential supervision had not. A missionary episcopacy was no more desirable than it had been to the Methodist Episcopal conferences, which, since the Bashford-Lewis administration, had ceased to talk of it. In anticipation of the General Conference of 1918, therefore, the China Mission Conference asked for a resident bishop for the Orient, adding, "we would deprecate the election of a missionary bishop for the Orient, and believe that the interests of the Church would be served by a continuance of episcopal supervision as at present than by such resident bishop." [9]

The system and the seers that the General Conferences had furnished for China were giving that land a Methodism that was well-organized and spiritual. As long as men would consecrate their lives to this leadership the question of a missionary episcopacy lost some of its appeal. But still the almost negligible number of votes which the China delegates had in the selection of these leaders made the church feel that it was yet subject to the American churches. The General Conferences were not yet ready to grant the Central Conferences the right to elect their own bishops; the Central Conference of Eastern Asia was not yet ready to do so, though in 1923 it did ask for the privilege of nominating those from whom the General Conference would elect. But the nomination of general superintendents was never made Methodist procedure. The time would come, however, when

China would lead the church, electing its own general superintendents and assigning them to areas and residential cities.

2. Bishop James W. Bashford

To begin one's career as a foreign missionary at the age of fifty-five might seem a doubtful undertaking even for a superman. Yet no young missionary ever came to China more gladly or threw himself into the work with more wholehearted enthusiasm than did James Whitford Bashford in 1904, on his appointment as the first resident bishop of the Methodist Episcopal Church in China. Frank D. Gamewell, one of Bishop Bashford's closest friends and co-workers in China, relates that this appointment was by no means an accident:

For years the name of Bashford had been of frequent mention as one who would bring to China the leadership that this difficult field demanded. . . .His election to the episcopacy practically meant his assignment to China, and for this task he had unique qualifications and unique preparation having been for a life-time an eager student of world-movements, and more particularly of world-movements centering in the Pacific Basin.[10]

As a university student, James Bashford had felt the urge to devote his life to China but the way did not open until many years later. In his own words: "When at Los Angeles I was elected bishop I knew that it was God's way to get me to China, and I have always been thankful that I kept up my preparation and study and was ready for the work when the opportunity came." Hence, stalwart and symmetrical as the cedars of Lebanon, this general, statesman, and seer led the church for fifteen years ever forward. Henry Clyde Hubbart, in *Ohio Wesleyan's First Hundred Years,* says: "It might well be said that the Bashford period was the most important in our whole history." With almost equal accuracy the same thing can be said of the Methodist Episcopal Church in China during its first hundred years.

A student of things Chinese, especially if he is a writer, not infrequently becomes so absorbed in some particular phase of Chinese life that he loses touch with ordinary Chinese people. Like his Master, James Bashford loved commonplace men and women. The flame of his fervor for evangelism never grew dim, yet his concern for a man's soul included a genuine personal interest in everything pertaining to the welfare of that man. During one of his last annual conferences, the bishop was far from well, and was being awakened very early every morning by violent paroxysms of a bronchial cough that had wracked his frame for more than twenty years. Wishing to spare her distinguished guest, his hostess said: "Bishop Bashford, you know that during conference we usually invite a different group of preachers each day to share the noon meal with us. We were planning to begin by asking a number of our country pastors to dinner with us tomorrow. But in view of your crowded schedule it might be better for you if we did not invite any guests this year. I'm sure everyone would understand." The bishop replied: "Oh, no indeed. Please follow your usual custom. I always enjoy getting better acquainted with our preachers." On that particular occasion the guest of honor took the lead in conversation by asking each of those rural pastors to mention as many different Chinese plants used for food as they could think of. This opened up a lively and informing discussion in which the bishop shared, through an interpreter, almost as freely as if he had been able to understand the local dialect. After jotting down a few notes, he himself told of many unusual articles of food that he had come across in other provinces. The results of the bishop's numerous enlightening table talks may be seen in Bashford's monumental volume *China, An Interpretation*.

The stories with which Bishop Bashford illustrated the points in his sermons will linger, together with the points themselves, for many a decade. Who among his hearers has not chuckled again and again with the good bishop over his boyhood experience with the dignified deacon who came to their farm looking for his runaway horse? The deacon had spent a long morning in fruitless search, his small stock of patience had been completely exhausted, and he had relieved his feelings in a stream of profanity quite blistering to the unaccustomed ears of James and his brother. As it was nearly noon, the deacon was invited to stay for dinner. When the family had gathered around the table, the host said to his guest: "Deacon, will you say grace?" "You'll have to excuse me, brother," faltered the lips that had just taken the name of the Lord in vain, "I'm sorry—my eyes are sore." The Bashford boys kicked each other under the table as their father returned thanks for the meal. "My eyes are sore" was ever afterwards a byword in that family whenever a flimsy excuse was given. The delicious sense of humor with which the story was told was characteristic of this great bishop. Combined as it was with the almost childlike innocence that looked out of those kindly blue eyes, it added a most endearing touch to the personality of a man whose whole life showed the simplicity of true greatness.

The itinerary of a bishop in China involved long, tedious journeys by sedan chair, river trips on crowded launches, temper-testing delays, countless emergencies, and now and again a really hazardous experience. Yet in spite of his years added to a serious health disability, Bishop Bashford marvelously adapted himself to so rigorous a life. By habitually carrying a good lantern with him, he even managed to keep up with his reading at the close of a long day's journey. Frank D. Gamewell, who so frequently accompanied him on his travels, gives the following intimate sketch of one travel episode:

We were in a collision in one of the wildest stretches of the Yangtze, where there was a very swift current. The captain said we might sink. It was a cold night in December. The bishop was coughing badly. I told him to go to bed, saying that I would watch all night, and at the first sign of sinking would call him. He went to bed. A few days later I said, "Bishop, you have a good conscience. Any man who could sleep through the night under the conditions in which we were placed has a good conscience." "No," he replied, "it was not a question of good conscience, but of lack of imagination. I didn't realize our danger until I got ashore, and then I spent most of the night thanking God for saving us." [11]

Many great speakers who have visited China have felt irked by the necessity of presenting their thoughts to an audience through an interpreter. Quite characteristically Bishop Bashford turned this necessity into an opportunity. During an annual conference he took time every afternoon to go over with his interpreter the address for the devotional hour next morning, always closing with a prayer that the Holy Spirit would inspire both the interpreter and the original speaker. One of the bishop's finest interpreters often said that his training in interpreting Bishop Bashford's addresses year after year had been one of the best preparations he could have had in the art of preaching.

Any estimate of James Bashford's life and work in China must also take into account the valuable contributions made by his brilliant and deeply consecrated wife Jane Field Bashford, whose life was so completely merged with her husband's in their lifework. At first Mrs. Bashford accompanied the bishop on his itinerating trips but this soon proved too difficult for one so frail. Yet in spite of long periods of separation, the Bashfords were still one in spirit. Mrs. Bashford's influence and deep sympathetic interest in the work were felt by missionaries more than a thousand miles from her residence in Peking.

As an administrator, Bishop Bashford endeavored never to allow personal considerations to bias his judgment as to what was for the best interests of the Kingdom. When a decision had been reached the bishop stated it kindly but firmly. It was a matter of principle with him that if such decision tended to arouse personal resentment on the part of the man involved, the odium this incurred should be borne by the administrator. "My shoulders are broad, brethren," he would say to a committee of missionaries and Chinese leaders, "let me be the scapegoat. I am going away. You have to stay here and live with that brother."

Bishop Bashford was really a great Christian statesman—an ambassador for Christ. One mark of this statesmanship is the way in which he constantly worked toward union and co-operation among Protestant forces in China, especially in higher educational institutions and in medical work. One of Bishop Bashford's greatest services to China Methodism was rendered in giving the church this broader view and in leading it into more and more fellowship and practical co-operation with Christians of other denominations.

It has been truly said that one of the greatest services rendered to China by Bishop Bashford was the interpretation of China to the Chinese themselves. Because the bishop so deeply appreciated their friendship and so consistently manifested his faith in the amazing potentialities of their country, many Chinese leaders willingly accepted his frank criticism of their national weaknesses, and took heart afresh to work unceasingly for the triumphs of real democracy.

Only a few of Bishop Bashford's closest friends had any realization of the tremendous influence he exerted in the relations between the United States government and the Republic of China. During the long controversy over the Twenty-one Demands made by Japan, this devoted friend of China labored indefatigably in behalf of the great people with whom he had identified himself. Yet never once did he act as a representative of the Chinese government, but simply as an ambassador of the Christian church. When, in the interest of China, he made a special trip from Peking to Washington he steadfastly refused to accept any money from the Chinese government, even to defray his traveling expenses.

More than a generation ahead of his time, this great bishop-statesman keenly realized the tremendous importance of friendly relations between China and the United States, as well as the bearing that such relations might have upon China's position in the family of nations. The following paragraphs written in 1916 by this far-seeing prophet are doubly significant in the light of recent events:

If the white races attempt to solve the race problem with selfish motives and through military power, we may witness a race-war in comparison with which the present European struggle will prove only a skirmish.

The influence of each race and each civilization will last so long as it deserves to last. If we read aright the principles of evolution or the unfolding moral and spiritual history of the race, or the teaching of the New Testament, Christ is set for the rise and fall of nations. If the Christian forces of the world respond to the divine summons, and Christianity takes deep root and spreads widely and rapidly around the Pacific, we may be sure that all will recognize that each race and nation has its providential work. In that event we shall approach the era

When each one shall find his own in every other's good,
And all men join in a common brotherhood.

Dan Brummit, then editor of the *Epworth Herald,* paid a worthy tribute to Bishop Bashford when he wrote:

James Whitford Bashford, statesman and saint, one of the master missionaries of the centuries, died last week at Pasadena, California. So our Methodism and the Chinese nation have lost a great and simple soul; to the one he was a leader of leaders; to the other a revered and trusted friend.

. . . .

The missionary work Bishop Bashford did in these years of his service in China was a genuine and consummate missionary service. He did the usual things but these were raised to unmeasured powers by a Christian statesman's influence on China's new life, troubled and bewildered.

. . . .

But Bishop Bashford was more than a great missionary. He was a discoverer and teacher of missionaries and men.

. . . .

The one thing which Bishop Bashford lacked was concern for himself, his own fortunes, his own needs, his own physical limitations. He would have shrunk from the suggestion, but in very truth he followed his Lord—he served others; himself he could not serve.

3. *China Elects Its Own Bishops*

On March 5, 1930, *Zion's Herald* commented on the launching of a new world-policy by Methodism:

What one of the most distinguished bishops of the Methodist Episcopal Church has characterized as "the most constructive piece of legislation since the separation of 1844," was put into practical operation on Thursday of last week by the General Conference of Eastern Asia, meeting in special session in Nanking, when, under the provisions of the new Central Conference amendments, recommended by the General Conference of 1928, and finally adopted by the concurrence during 1929 of the required majorities in all the Annual and Lay Electoral Conferences of the denominations, two bishops were elected for China.

Seven years before that, thirteen Chinese members had petitioned that the Eastern Asia Central Conference be granted "the power of nominating its own bishops for election by the General Conference, beginning from the year 1927-28." The year 1927 had brought Chinese administrators to Methodist institutions. Chinese superintendents had been administering conference districts since the organization of the Foochow Conference. Why not Chinese administrators for Chinese conferences? Could a Chinese be elected by a General Conference? Not without a policy of "bishops for races or languages," which the General Conference did not want, nor without electing him as a missionary bishop, which the Central Conference did not want. But the blueprints for the new Methodist Church were already on the boards, and the coming Jurisdictional Conferences had not been undreamed of; hence the leaders of the Methodist Episcopal Church felt that the Central Conferences abroad could be entrusted with this step towards autonomy without handicapping further negotiations for union.

Was China ready to elect Chinese bishops? Missionary members of the conferences were certainly exerting every effort to convince the church that it was. Three years had wrought great changes in some of their thinking! When, pursuant to the adoption of the amendment to the constitution of the church in 1929, a special session of the Eastern Asia Central Conference met in Nanking on February 24, 1930, the satisfaction that it had the power to elect two bishops was unanimous, but whether either or both of the two should be or must be Chinese was, at least, debatable and debated. The Committee on Episcopacy, meeting before the opening of the conference, passed a recommendation "to ask the conference to elect one Chinese and one missionary to the office of Bishop." But various parliamentary tactics met the presentation of that resolution on the floor of the conference, with the net result being passed by acclamation "that we cast our ballots for two bishops of whom two may be Chinese, but of whom one must be a Chinese."

On the seventh ballot John Gowdy was elected—the first bishop of the Methodist Episcopal Church to be elected by other than the General Conference. Gowdy had, since 1902, been a member of the Foochow Conference, and while most of his missionary career had been spent as president of the Anglo-Chinese College and the Fukien Christian University, he had made himself a much-loved leader of the conference, a man who had the respect of the church in the United States, an administrator of tact and vision, who had promptly made way for a Chinese administrator of the university, now to be made an administrator of the church by an overwhelming majority of the votes of his Chinese colleagues; for, as H. W. Worley, who was a member of that Central Conference explained, "certain of the missionaries, feeling that the time had come for Chinese leadership, refused to write the name of any missionary on their ballots." [12]

By action of the conference further ballots must be for Chinese, and on the fourteenth, on Thursday, February 27, 1930, Wang Chih-P'ing of the North China Conference became the first Chinese to be elected to this highest office in the Methodist Episcopal Church. No doubt the stars sang together as this spiritual descendent of Hu Bo-Mi and Sia Sek-Ong and their colleagues was escorted to the platform, signifying that China Methodism had come into its own as a co-ordinate and coequal portion of the Methodist Episcopal Church. Truly has Paul Wiant said: "Much the most significant event of the last twenty years is the election of Chinese bishops, starting with Bishop Wang in 1930."

Wang Chih-P'ing had for a quarter of a century been one of the leading pastors of the Methodist Episcopal Church in North China. He had come to this session of the Central Conference as both pastor of the Asbury Church in Peking and superintendent of the Peking District. Born in Peking, he had been educated in the Christian schools of that city, and had later studied in the United States, receiving the M.A., Ph.D., and D.D. degrees. He was a language teacher to missionaries when the Boxer siege called for his assistance in the defense of the British legation; in 1905 he was ordained a minister in the North China Conference and had been its representative in the General Conference of 1916, 1920, and 1928. From these years of preparation and service he was called to the position of chief pastor and leader of the church in China.

So significant was this session of the Central Conference that the Board of Bishops had delegated two of its number to share in it: Bishop John L. Nuelson, senior bishop of the Methodist Episcopal Church, and through most of his years of episcopal service resident in Europe, and Bishop F. T. Keeney, who through the 1920-24 quadrennium had shared with Bishop Birney in the administration of the China Conferences. Bishop Nuelson was presiding when the result of the seventh ballot was presented to him for announcement, and Bishop Keeney when that of the fourteenth ballot was presented, and here we quote the *Journal* of the conference:

Bishop Nuelson, in a short address, invited Bishop Birney to assume the chair as being eminently fitting on the occasion of the announcement of the first bishop to be elected by an indigenous Chinese church. Bishop Birney, in taking the chair, expressed his sincere appreciation of the honor done him and declared that he felt sure he represented both the bishop-elect and the members of the conference in expressing himself as bitterly disappointed that the first bishop elected by the Central Conference in China should happen to be a Westerner.

. . . .

Bishop Keeney invited Bishop Birney to take the chair and announce the result. Bishop Birney, after expressing his great appreciation of the continued courtesy of his colleagues, said that during the last five years of his residence in China, he had ardently hoped for this hour and now in his hands he at last held the evidence that a Chinese bishop had been elected. Were it not that the bishop-elect was confined to his room by illness he would be glad to clasp his hand, welcoming him to the highest office within the gift of the church. . . . [He] requested for himself the privilege of personally announcing the result of the ballot to the bishop-elect and asked Bishop Keeney and Wang Hou-Chai, a lay member of the bishop-elect's church in Peking, to go with him to the latter's room and if possible to escort him to the hall.

Maybe the church had taken this high step too soon. Yet other bishops of American and European birth, elected to office by the General Conference, had voluntarily or even under the advice of their colleagues or perhaps the Episcopacy Committee, asked to be relieved of the duties of their office. So it was not new in the history of the church that Bishop Wang, "finding it difficult to adjust himself to the responsibilities of the episcopal office," and sometimes "afraid to attack the proposition" which needed his pastoral leadership, "shortly after the Central Conference in 1934 ceased 'to travel throughout the connection.' " [13] To some this seemed the sunset for days—or years—to come of Chinese episcopal leadership; but the Central Conference in 1937 had no alternative than to adopt the resolution presented by the Committee on Episcopacy:

That we deeply appreciate the services of Bishop Wang Chih-P'ing to the church and very much regret his resignation from the office of bishop, but that under the circumstances we recommend the acceptance of his resignation by this Central Conference and that we approve of the action taken by the Ad Interim Committee of the Executive Committee in regard to the resignation of Bishop Wang and that further we instruct the secretaries of the conference to write a letter of greeting to Bishop and Mrs. Wang.

This left the administration of the Methodist Episcopal conferences in China on the shoulders of Bishops Gowdy and Herbert Welch (assigned by the General Conference of 1937 to the Shanghai Area), until the latter retired under the rules of the General Conference and W. E. Hammaker was elected in 1936 for assignment to the episcopal residence at Nanking. Bishop Wang's resignation made it incumbent upon the Central Conference of 1937 to elect a bishop for residential assignment in Szechuen, the re-election of Bishop Gowdy and his reassignment to the Fukien Area being "a foregone conclusion." On the ninth ballot Ralph A. Ward, though not a delegate to the conference and not present during the afternoon session, was elected. Ward had been a missionary in Foochow and Nanking, assistant secretary of the Board of Foreign Missions and executive secretary of the World Service Commission, promoter of the China Forward Movement of 1913, and of the Program Statement Conference of 1920—by experience, language ability, spiritual zeal, and favor with the brethren, eminently fitted for this fulfillment of a worthy calling and career. To many, especially missionaries, the election of another missionary was a matter of regret. H. W. Worley has grounds for his statement that "all the nationals for whom the Chinese were willing to vote were removed from consideration," because of unavailability at the time, but there must have been also some reluctance to repeat the experience of 1930-34, at least if "available" men could not command a high percentage of "desirability."

But in 1941 the church called to this leadership two of its master pastors. With the three churches now united, with Bishop Hammaker assigned to the Denver area, with Bishop Gowdy having reached the "three score and ten" that called for retirement at the close of this Central Conference session, and with the permission of the General Conference to provide four bishops for China's ten conferences, three bishops were to be elected. In the Committee on Episcopacy there had developed a rather general opposition to any rule to compel the election of two Chinese, but when the committee presented its report recommending the election of three bishops, and when a missionary member of the conference

moved an amendment that only such ballots be counted as carried the names of two Chinese, to the surprise of many his motion carried. But it wasn't necessary. It required seventy-four to elect, and Z. T. Kaung went in on the first ballot with eighty-four and W. Y. Chen had seventy-two.[14]

W. Y. Chen was elected on the second ballot with seventy-seven votes, and Carleton Lacy on the twenty-eighth ballot by eighty votes.

The church was now better equipped for intensive leadership than it had been since the days of R. S. Maclay and the two local churches in Foochow. The Rev. Z. T. Kaung, had been elected by a significant vote. With his training in the schools and churches of the Southern Methodist Church in China, his rare gifts as a preacher and spiritual leader, his masterful and spiritual direction of Moore Memorial Church since a few months before the war broke out, and a character that in itself preached Christ, there was no question that the church had chosen aright. Nor was there any doubt about the selection of W. Y. Chen, a product of Methodist Episcopal schools in Foochow, of Syracuse, Duke, and German universities. He was the capable pastor of Tieng-Ang-Dong, professor at the Fukien Christian University, executive secretary of the National Christian Council, and a fearless preacher of righteousness. Carleton Lacy was born in a missionary home in China, was a member of the Kiangsi Conference, was widely conversant with the church in China and its problems, had for twenty years been the China representative of the American Bible Society, and had for so long urged and prayed for Chinese leadership that he had written, at the suggestion that he would be elected at this conference: "The one thing that was perfectly clear to me was that I should not and could not serve unless there were two Chinese bishops elected." And continuing, of course, was Bishop Ward with four years of constructive episcopal leadership to his credit in Szechuen and extending to Kiangsi and Kalgan.

In full recognition of the worth of J. W. Bashford and Walter R. Lambuth, and the other great men whom the General Conferences had elected to administer the churches in China, it can in all fairness be said at this point that the church in China, in the six men that it had elected as its own administrators, had done as good a job as had the General Conferences. It remains for the Central Conference of 1949, perhaps, to give the church 100 per cent indigenous administration, and some believe this will be done, though "my own idea," thinks at least one missionary, "is that the fifty-fifty arrangement will very likely carry on for another generation." However that may be, the Chinese church came to its centennial, still a part of the world-wide Methodist Church, but competently led by men of its own choosing.

4. Other Problems of Indigenous Episcopacy

When the General Conference of the Methodist Episcopal Church had said to its central conferences in China, India, South America, and Europe, "Now you may elect your own bishops," it added, "and you may say how long they are to serve. In the past we have elected men to episcopal office for life; we intend to continue to do so, but you may elect them for terms of such length as you in your central conferences may determine; and whenever you wish to lengthen or shorten that term, you may do so."

In 1930 China was launching an experiment for the world-wide church: should it take over entirely the tried and tested plan of the general conference or should it move cautiously and democratically, at least until "it got the feel" of the new motor? The American Constitutional Convention had faced the same question in 1787, and as it had voted to elect a president for a four-year term, without any constitutional restrictions against re-election, so the Eastern Asia Central Conference voted in 1930,

recommending that the bishops be elected for a term of four years and that they be eligible for re-election, but that in view of the fact that we are now in the midst of a quadrennium, the bishops to be elected by the Eastern Asia Central Conference of 1930 be elected for a term of six years." [15]

Hence no election was called for in 1934, and the recommendation for the re-enactment of the four-year term precipitated one of those parliamentary "breadbasket" games that left everyone sometimes uncertain of the situation, and the four-year term emerged unchanged. The 1936 Central Conference session was not held until March, 1937, when Bishop Wang's resignation was accepted (by now that was more gracious than necessary) and Bishop Gowdy's term had expired. Before the balloting, in which he was re-elected and Ralph A. Ward was elected, the conference voted to change the term of the Central Conference bishops from one to two quadrenniums, and that they be eligible for re-election. Southern Asia was electing its bishops for a life tenure, but the China Central Conference of 1941 re-affirmed the eight-year term, which had also been adopted by the South American field. Perhaps the people of the United States should have amended their constitution to limit the term of the president to one of six years or two of four years each; perhaps the China Central Conference should do that, or perhaps it should withdraw the time limit and elect its bishops for life. Perhaps it will, but if so, that will be something for the future historian to record.

The location of episcopal residences was a matter determined by the conference which had elected the bishop to be assigned. Hence, prior to 1941, three conferences were each designating the official base of one or more of the China bishops. The Methodist Episcopal Church, South, because of its policy, at least in its later years, of electing a bishop and assigning him to all the foreign fields, had no residence in Shanghai. In 1930 the China Conference "asked for the *status quo,* begging that the bishop reside permanently in China." To this the secretary of the Foreign Department of the Board of Missions wrote this reply:

The Board will, I am sure, give careful attention to this request. Great skill will be needed in the management of our work in China during the next quadrennium. A Chinese General Superintendent might help in the solution of this difficult situation." [16]

But the *status quo* remained until the union, with Bishops Paul B. Kern and Arthur J. Moore giving a high quality of administration during those two quadrenniums.

We have already seen some of the moves made in this checker game in the Methodist Episcopal Church. In 1923 the church had general superintendents resident in Shanghai (an extraterritorial residence), Peking, and Foochow. In 1928 the Foochow Area was discontinued, pending the passage by the church of the proposed amendments relating to the election of bishops by Central Conferences.

The General Conference returning Bishop Birney to Shanghai and Bishop Grose to Peking, included the Fukien conferences in the Shanghai Area. The historical conference of 1930 assigned Bishops Gowdy and Wang to residence in Foochow and Chengtu respectively, and, Bishop Grose having left the field, the bishops included the North China and the Shantung Conferences in the Chengtu Area; and the General Conference of 1932 sent Bishop Welch to Shanghai. In 1936 the General Conference assigned Bishop Hammaker to residence at Nanking instead of Shanghai, and North China and Shantung were included with Kiangsi and Central China in the Nanking Area, and West China in the Foochow Area, until in the following year Foochow and Chengtu were both again designated as area headquarters. With the inclusion of the China Conference and the Kalgan Mission Conference under the administration of the united church, in 1941, the episcopal assignments and area designations were made as follows: East China Area, with residence at Shanghai, Bishop Ward—Central China, Kiangsi, and East China (formerly China) Conferences; North China Area, with residence at Peking, Bishop Kaung—Kalgan, North China, and Shantung Conferences; West China Area, with residence at Chengtu, Bishop Chen—West China Conference; South China Area, with residence at Foochow, Bishop Lacy—Yenping, Foochow and Hinghwa Conferences. With the declaration of war between the United States and Japan and the confinement of Bishop Ward in Japanese-occupied territory, the work in free southern Kiangsi and southern Anhwei was, by vote of the Central Conference Executive Board, placed in the South China Area until such times as normal political conditions could restore it to its Yangtze Valley affiliations.

The authority to elect its own bishops had confronted the church in China with several problems: The nationality of the episcopal personnel, terms of service, place of residence, and—charged with equally controversial tinder—salaries. Almost since the beginning of the Chinese ministry the question of pastoral salaries had provoked I. G. John to comment in the *Handbook of Methodist Missions*:

Few questions in mission fields require the exercise of more patience and wisdom than the salary of the native preachers. . . . While the missionaries realize that the co-operation of the native preachers is essential to the evangelization of China, they were conscious that the offer of salaries that were in excess of those paid in native business circles might present a temptation to men who were seeking the salaries and not the souls of their countrymen.

The action of Sia Sek-Ong in refusing to accept support from American funds had been an evidence that the whole problem was closely related to that of self-support. Should pastors, especially in rural churches be paid no more than their parishes could pay, and no more than their peers in those villages and hamlets? Could men competent to serve the cause of the church in town or city be adequately educated and induced to enter the ministry for such a stipend?

Unfortunately these and many related questions had not been settled when the Central Conference voted to elect two bishops, "one of whom must be Chinese." For now the question had almost as many facets as were possible on a 24-carat diamond. The delegates to the conference had been "given very definite assurance that a missionary, if elected, would draw his salary from other sources," declared Carleton Lacy's article "Buying a Bishop" in *Zion's Herald*, November 19, 1930.

The delegates to the meeting in Nanking knew full well that the Chinese churches they represented were financially unable to provide adequate financial support and allowances for the two bishops we were called together to elect. "Economic imperialism," "financial despotism," "buying a bishop," were phrases that occurred in the long debate. . . . To some degree the Chinese were prepared to accept this situation. They recognized the advantage to a Chinese bishop in being dependent upon the churches over which he presides for his financial support.

Perhaps this influenced the decision to elect one missionary. If the Book Committee was to provide the salary and expenses of a bishop elected by the China Central Conference from among the missionaries, should his remuneration equal that of the general superintendents assigned by the General Conference to reside in Nanking? Evidently not, for as Lacy pointed out, it soon happened that

the secretary of a bishop elected by the General Conference was left without appointment because of his absence from the field, while a bishop doing the full work of that office [on the appropriation] provided by Central Conference recommendation was unable to engage her services [because he had no funds to pay her salary].

But if these two bishops should receive the same remuneration, should the Chinese bishop be paid less than his brother bishop, chosen by the same electorate, bearing the same responsibilities, and himself equally entitled to all the rights and privileges of any bishop of the Methodist Episcopal Church? Chinese and foreign salaries were already on vastly different scales: no one considered putting missionaries and bishops elected from their number on Chinese salaries, and it was equally unreasonable to advance a man from the pastorate of a Chinese church to the salary paid a bishop resident in America.

Chinese delegates had left the General Conference of 1928 at Kansas City "distinctly disappointed," Lacy had written. "They had hoped," he continued in the *Zion's Herald* article,

that when the Chinese church declared in favor of remaining a part of the "world-wide Methodist Church" they would be treated not as a dependency but as one of the federated states. There is a distinct impression that the General Conference legislation and the subsequent discussion have misinterpreted the Chinese desire for independence and have in substance replied: "Take thou authority just as fast as you are ready to pay for it."

Thus we see something of the turmoil in which the waters swirled and eddied as the church faced its first major outlet to an autonomous part of a world-wide church.

Liu Fang of the North China Conference was the chairman of the all-Chinese Committee to recommend to the conference in 1930 the salary to be paid any Chinese who should become a bishop. On recommendation of that committee the salary was fixed at $3,000 (Mex.) annually. Bishop Birney described the steps which had led to this action in an article in *Zion's Herald* on August 6, 1930:

In a questionnaire submitted for daily discussion at the ten preceding annual conferences, one of the questions was, "What should be the salary of the Chinese bishop or bishops to be elected?" This was submitted in order that the Central Conference might have some idea of the view of the ministry and leading laity of the church on this question which was new to the Chinese church. On the last day of each annual conference these questions were answered in writing secretly, without names attached. The replies to this question averaged slightly less than $2,500 (Mex.) a year. In the Central Conference the question was submitted by the Committee on Episcopacy to an all-Chinese sub-committee for study and recommendation. This committee, after very careful work, recommended $2,400 to be the proper sum, keeping in mind a due relation to pastors' salaries and salary of other Chinese leaders, and the general attitude of the church toward it as they were asked to pay part of it at first and all of it ultimately. The Committee on Episcopacy changed this to $3,600 and so reported to the Conference. After considerable discussion it was submitted to another all-Chinese sub-committee for still further study. The committee reported $3,000, which was adopted. This is two and a half times the salary received by the Chinese bishops of any other church in China, and with rent allowances, etc., puts Bishop Wang on a financial equality with other Chinese leaders engaged wholly in Christian work. It represents the same percentage of increase over his salary when elected that was recommended to the Book Committee for Bishop Gowdy.

Before the annual conferences met the next fall, complaints were being heard that the assessments for the Episcopal Fund, even at six cents per member for the church in China, were bound to set back the efforts being made for pastoral support by the Chinese membership, and Carleton Lacy reported the Chinese felt that they had "bought a bishop as an expensive luxury."

All problems, especially those of changing situations, eventually are solved, as the rapid stream madly rushing among the rocks ultimately reaches a level stretch and flows quietly between grass-bordered banks—for a time, at least. And so this problem had reached a new stage.

The General Conference of 1936 approved the position of the Central Conference of Eastern Asia . . . that the Central Conference Areas need not be taxed at a higher percentage for the support of bishops "than the rate of apportionment fixed by the Book Committee from time to time for the church in the United States" and provided for grants-in-aid to the various central conferences . . . without causing too heavy a load to be thrown suddenly on the younger and undeveloped churches.[17]

The first General Conference of the united Methodist Church threw this problem into the lap of a committee of its designation, which met in July, 1940, and

decided that bishops elected by the General Conference or by Jurisdictional Conferences would receive U. S. $6,000, and that Missionary Bishops and bishops elected by a previous Central Conference would receive U. S. $5,000 until the next session of the Central Conference. This apparently leaves it for the next Central Conference through a representative committee to consult with the Committee of the General Conference to determine what salary shall be paid to the bishops which it elects. There is provision made also by these committees for certain allowances to cover rent, travel, and secretarial help.[18]

This still left several questions unsettled, and the conference in Shanghai in 1941 was again faced with the problem, with the following result: the salary of bishops was fixed at U. S. $3,000, with an additional expense allowance of $2,000 to the American bishops.

This conference also voted that an effective bishop, retiring under the age rule, although at the expiration of the term for which he had been elected, retired as a bishop, subject to all the rights and privileges of a bishop, and the General Conference and the administrators of the Episcopal Fund have recognized this action and the resulting status.

China Methodism had been given its coveted goal of determining its own leadership. Inside of a century of growth it had demonstrated its fitness for this permission and its good judgment in the selection of its leaders. Many factors had militated against its becoming a self-supporting church within the same period of time; if it could not adequately support its pastors, it could hardly be expected to support its chief pastors. Economic and social conditions might have to call for a different scale of remuneration for the American bishop resident in Chicago or Shanghai, the Chinese bishop in Chengtu, and the Indian bishop in Hyderabad; but the dominant desire for equality in status and treatment could be achieved by applying to all parts of the world the time-honored practice of the Methodist Episcopal Church, that of paying all its bishops from one treasury which was supplied by a membership apportionment of a stated percentage of the amount contributed by each church for pastoral support. As Worley has well said:

The Methodist Episcopal Church is a connectional church, with each part contributing to the extent of its ability and sharing according to its need. The Central Conference of Eastern Asia is a part of connectional Methodism and will contribute to all connectional activities but it expects to share in this connectionalism even if its part in the collection is small.[19]

The General Conference of 1944, being both broadminded and generously fair in spite of the relatively few delegates that war conditions permitted to come from outside the United States, recognized this principle, and gave the central conferences exactly that status when it adopted this paragraph for the *Discipline* of the church.

The amount of support and all other allowances, including office, house rent, travel, retirement allowances, and provision for health and education of children, for a bishop elected by a Central Conference shall be estimated by that Central Conference. It shall also determine the amount that it will be able to provide toward the General Episcopal Fund on the ratio of apportionment ordered by the General Conference. When the total estimated support shall have been determined, this amount in itemized form shall be submitted for approval to the General Commission on World Service and Finance. After approval the treasurer of the General Episcopal Fund shall pay the amount agreed upon to the bishop concerned, or as the Central Conference may determine.

Thus was given to China, and to other central conferences, the autonomy which they desire and deserve, and which at the same time keeps them on an equality with all sections of a world-wide Methodism.

VI

EARTHQUAKE SHOCKS THREATEN

For not like kingdoms of the world
Thy holy Church, O God!
Though earthquake shocks are threatening her,
And tempests are abroad;
Unshaken as eternal hills,
Immovable she stands,
A mountain that shall fill the earth,
A house not made with hands.

1. *The Tai-ping Rebellion and Antiforeignism*

THE WIDENING OF GEOGRAPHICAL BOUNDS, THE ONWARD AND UPWARD climb in ecclesiastical organization, the placing of the wheel in the hands of pilots who had grown up in and with the church, had not been accomplished on a calm, summer day. Political and military tempests had too often been abroad. Tnrough persecution and anti-Christian attacks the church had to climb the steep ascent of heaven. Before we look at the growth within the church, along its various paths and highways of activity, it will be well to look at the earthquake shocks which have formed so much of the stage setting.

To all the domestic and missionary troubles of the first decade was added the strain of rebellion throughout the land, destroying the Shanghai chapel, threatening the possibility of physical danger to the missionaries, and making their evacuation advisable. We pause at this difficulty only long enough to hear Maclay's comment in October, 1852:

In reference to the prospect before us as a mission, it grows more and more evident to my mind that a time of storm and conflict is at hand. The enemy is rallying his forces and the quiet and unostentatious course of our proceedings hitherto, may soon be exchanged for scenes of excitement and perhaps peril. But we will not fear, Christ will here triumph. Oh, that we had more faith, more zeal, more devotion to God's cause.[1]

Then in 1881 lightning struck in the form of the Chungking riots that caused a general withdrawal of Methodist missionaries from Szechuen. In 1884 France and China were at war, and the conflict disturbed all the China missions, although the sphere of action of this undeclared war was the southern coast of China. As a result, for the second time Methodist women and children evacuated Foochow, this time to Shanghai before the French ships entered the Min River and destroyed the arsenal, the ships at the Anchorage, and the forts guarding the river. In 1891 an antiforeign outbreak in the Yangtze Valley, as sudden as a tropical storm, forced the women and children to flee from Nanking, where their homes and schools were looted and burned almost before they were outside the city gates. War with Japan in 1894 was another source of anxiety and interruption to work, during which schools, especially in the north, had to be closed, and a riot attack on the mission premises in Chengtu in May, 1895, "wiped out at one stroke" the mission property there. To one writing since the Japanese invaded Manchuria in 1931 and attacked China in 1937, and remembering the American official attitude before 1941, a placard posted in Chengtu in May, 1895, is particularly interesting. "At a time,"—it reads—"when Japan has usurped Chinese territory, you English, French and Americans have looked on with your hands in your sleeves. If in the future you wish to preach your doctrine in China, you must drive the Japanese back to their own country." [2]

That same spring and summer antiforeign feeling, particularly active among the so-called "Vegetarians," resulted in the closing of schools in Kutien, Fukien. With the close of the Japanese War, and with seeming quiet among the hostile element, plans were made for the return of the women to Kutien, when, again without warning, lightning struck from an almost cloudless sky, and eleven of the Anglican Mission were massacred in a mountain village where they were spending the hot weeks of midsummer. Miss Mable C. Hartford of the Methodist Mission, also there, was one of the few foreigners to escape.

In spite of these hindrances, the church marched on to its golden jubilee in 1897, rejoicing that it was worthy to suffer these losses, and hardly dreaming that 1900, 1911, 1927, and 1937-45 would make the disturbances of the first half century but gusts which only made its roots take firmer hold in the earth.

2. Riots, Boxers, Revolution, Bandits, and Famine

But the clouds hang low and dark over the city on a winter morning, when the rose window seems almost opaque, and the blue coloring can scarcely be seen. So it was as the church entered its sixth decade, when the glorious sunrise soon faded and the heavy dark clouds of the Boxer movement overspread the sky.

The coup d'etat came in 1898, when the empress dowager relegated her nephew-emperor to the role of a near nonentity, and assumed drastic control of the empire. It was in this year that Mary Robinson wrote of the government school in Chinkiang that its "door had closed with a bang," as had many doors throughout the empire which had seemed to be open. It was in this year that Tang Hsi-I—whom Dr. J. H. McCartney described as "probably the first martyr given by the Methodist Episcopal Church for the redemption of China"—a promising medical student in Chungking, was murdered at midnight by a mob "because he had succeeded in renting a house against their wishes."

The riot in Chungking in 1886 and the Hwa Sang Massacre in 1895 were only two of the earlier manifestations of a feeling that was becoming more widespread. Rioting, rebellion, and persecution of Protestant and Catholic Christians were now particularly rampant in West China. Also, the North China Mission and the bishop felt they dared not send a missionary family to open the station which had been prepared at Tai-an, in Shantung, because of "the unsettled condition of the government." Miss Steere, who, with Dr. Mary Barrow, became the first Methodist missionaries to live in Tai-an, early in 1899, wrote that fall "that she had put all the deeds and other papers in a satchel and was ready to go at a moment's notice." The treaties under which—and probably well beyond the letter of which—the missionaries were living and working, had given to Chinese Christians, as well as missionaries, special protection of foreign powers. The fifth, and perhaps the sixth decade of Methodist growth probably witnessed the crest of the wave of appeals to the American consuls, and of presseure by them on local Chinese officials to protect the members of the church from persecution, some of which was real persecution but some only the manifestation of personal or clan hostilities. There was justification for feeling that such a foreign protectorate constituted a serious blow to the prestige and integrity of the Chinese state, and this feeling found its way into the imperial palace at Peking.

So "many have taken in hand to set forth in order" the causes and events of the Boxer movement of 1900 and the Revolution of 1911 that these need be mentioned here only insofar as they affected the deepening of Methodist penetration into the life of China. The feeling mentioned above had increased until "on June 20, 1900, an Imperial edict was issued in Peking which called for the slaughter of all foreigners in the Empire." [3] The very day that the North China Conference adjourned its 1900 session, and before most of its missionary and Chinese members had been able to leave for their homes, egress from Peking was terminated, and many were prisoners in the capital, first on the property of the Methodist Mission until that became untenable, and then for the long remaining weeks of the siege on the grounds of the British legation with all the others whose extermination was sought—Chinese Christian men, women, and children, and foreign missionaries, government officials, and businessmen and their families.

While Frank D. Gamewell, whose engineering training had qualified him for appointment in charge of defenses, and all the Chinese Christians, legation guards, and men and women who co-operated with him, were protecting the lives of these prisoners in Peking, elsewhere in China missionaries were evacuating their stations, and Christian people were being slaughtered. Missionaries from West, Central and South China, not yet in immediate danger, were evacuating their stations, reluctant to leave, knowing that their exodus would be interpreted as cowardice, that it would be a sign that the conflagration was becoming more widespread, that it would expose their fellow Chinese Christians to attack by those who were or could be considered Boxers, or their like, and that their going would be the signal for looters, like vultures, to swoop down on the property.

All this happened—not generally and very widespread, be it thankfully said. On the Peking District every foreign building was destroyed and every Chinese house used for church services was wrecked or damaged and all church records lost.

The son who years ago wheeled his mother three hundred miles to learn the story of "Jesus and His Love" was mortally wounded at the siege of Peking, and went to sleep praying, "Lord, receive my spirit." The old mother in Shantung, true to her faith, would not, when ordered to do so, take down the "Jesus sign" from over the door, but declared that she would stand or fall with it.[4]

Missionaries were killed, both Protestant and Catholic; and although no Methodist missionary lost his life, Chinese members of the church, especially throughout the North China Conference, suffered horribly. The following will serve to typify what might be written of scores of places:

One local preacher on the Shan-hai-kuan District was compelled to kneel over a bench, a basin was placed beneath to catch the blood, a sword was put to his throat, and he was told to recant or die. He recanted. But others were faithful unto death. . . . At Ch'ien-an the slaughter was terrible. Ninety-one were killed, chopped to pieces, and burned. Our helper at Ch'ien-an, Yang Nien-Tseng, was seized and the first time released. Then the Boxers came again and said he or his son must go with them. He replied, "I will go." They took him and killed him, but allowed his friends to take away his body. But when they brought it to his village the people there would not allow it to be taken into the village. Finally the Boxers came again, took the body, and burned it with the coffin.[5]

Many elsewhere also suffered much, many might have escaped the destruction of their property by bowing themselves before the idol temples, many might have assured themselves protection by denying their faith in Jesus Christ—but very few did.

But when the allied army had relieved Peking, when new treaties were dictated, when the fugitive empress dowager had returned to her palace—what was then the effect on the church? Had this "tragic set-back to Christianity" shattered the faith of the Chinese Methodists? As J. O. Curnow wrote of the work in Chengtu, so we might write of many places in the Yangtze Valley and the plains and mountains of Fukien: "True, it had made no aggression, but it had made no regression. It had held its own." Fletcher Brockman felt that the resentment which had been engendered against the foreigners among the non-Christians, especially the better educated, was more than a great wall of brick and stone: "As a boy," he has since written,

I had visited Stone Mountain in Georgia, a sheer precipice rising 700 feet from the plain. I now pictured myself at the foot of this great monolith drilling a hole with a pin and attempting to blast the mountain. My work for the literati seemed equally impossible.[6]

And although the historian of the Peking Mission records that "the year 1901 dawned upon a wreck," Dr. George A. Stuart, of Central China, was voicing the thought of many missionaries when he wrote: "We stand now at the beginning of a new era for China. . . . Our mind is burdened with the question of how the church is going to meet its new and increased responsibilities. How is it going to enter the opening doors?" [7] How was it? Uong Gang-Huo has said: "Here in China some of the strongest preachers came in direct response to the sacrificial deaths of their predecessors." And everywhere the readjustments necessary left the church "more compact, more independent, and more energetic than ever before."

The clouds of a dark winter morning break later in the day, and the sunshine again illumines the blue rose window. But politically the clouds were destined to gather again. In fact, as the historian looks back over the third quarter century of Methodism at work in China, the outstanding motif in the stage scenery seems to be the dark clouds of outrage, revolution, and war.

In 1902, Spencer Lewis, in his manuscript "Pioneering in West China," tells of reported "midnight gatherings in temples where seasoned Boxers, reported to have migrated from North China after the defeat in 1900, were practicing mysteries by which the initiated were rendered impervious to sword and bullet." In 1905 a riot in Nanchang forced the missionaries to take refuge in Kiukiang and temporarily arrested the work in Nanchang. In 1908 both the emperor and the empress dowager died within a few days of each other, and "hastened the inevitable." Kenneth Latourette, in his *History of Christian Missions in China*, does not agree that missionaries caused the revolution of 1911, which he says would certainly have resulted from "the commercial and political expansion of the West," but he adds, "What the missionary did do was to help give direction to the revolution." This he explains by continuing:

He prepared leaders and communities who were ready to assist in the re-shaping of China when the inevitable arrived. Because Christian groups and individuals existed and had become partly adjusted to Western ways before the general change began, the chaos and bewilderment were not as great as they otherwise would have been and the readjustment could be made more quickly. Moreover, by bringing to China moral, religious, and intellectual factors of Western culture, with which the Chinese could not have come into such intimate contact, the missionary helped determine the character of the new China.[8]

Again missionaries were being summoned by their consuls to leave their interior stations and seek safety in the port cities, not this time, as eleven years before, because the trouble was antiforeign and anti-Christian, for now both revolutionary and government officials felt it to their advantage to protect these groups, but because of the inability of officials in many places to do this very thing—Manchus fleeing from the revolutionary forces could hamper and discredit the latter by looting and plundering mission property. From Chengtu to Soochow, from Hinghwa to Peking, Methodist churches were affected, of course, by this struggle to overthrow the Manchu dynasty. But this was not the deepest aspect of this revolution. That, said Uong Gang-huo, a Chinese Methodist leader,

was the spirit of China trying to free itself from the bondage of custom and tradition and to awaken to national consciousness and achievement. The revolution turned the eyes of the world upon China, and it turned the eyes of the Chinese people upon their own country.[9]

Following the 1912 session of the Yenping District Conference, B. H. Paddock reported:

Last year there was not a man [in the conference] who had cut off his queue; this year there was not one with long hair. In the removal of the queue, as in other things, the church has taken the lead. Our preachers have preached the gospel of liberty and plied the shears until not a queue is to be seen in our churches. At this session of the district conference a few minutes were spent in instructing the people how to write their first ballots for the coming election of delegates to the provincial and national parliaments. The church is doing its share to prepare the people to take an intelligent part in the new government.[10]

Again the church in China and in the United States took heart and felt that a new day of opportunity was at hand—a day, that under the leadership of the National Christian Council now so soon to be organized, would mean a Christian church in a new China more truly supported and led by Chinese men and women than that which had yet developed.

In May, 1913, the missionaries were forced to leave Hinghwa. In June the bandits announced their purpose to destroy the Methodist Church, because it was destroying idol and ancestor worship. Houses and crops of church members were burned and plundered; preachers fled to the mountains or spent the nights with friends at safe distances from their chapels; men, women, and children who had connection with the church were kidnapped by the bandits. Yet none denied his faith! Bishop Bashford explained the "deep underlying cause" of this attack by the so-called "Sixteenth Emperor" as the "loyalty of our missionaries and of our Chinese Christians to the republic and to the opium reform" on the one hand, and, on the other, the inability of the government, because of the rebellion of 1913, "to re-establish order at an earlier date in that portion of the nation." [11]

But hardly had the National Christian Council been organized, the Christian school systems been better systematized, and the higher institutions been united for better training of Chinese leaders, when someone dropped a match on a keg of powder at Serajevo, and fighting took place on Chinese soil and missionary men and Chinese workers were called to the battlefields of western Europe. Had the Japanese authorities not felt that the circumstances made the time propitious to demand of the Chinese government certain rights and privileges that no self-respecting and sovereign nation could relinquish to another, the years of the war and its early aftermath would have caused little deterrence to the growth of the church in the Chinese Republic. But every fresh Japanese move which looked like—or was—a move of aggression, was for a number of years met by the students in the schools by insisting that "they could not study while such things were being allowed in their midst," and the question before many a school principal and his or her faculty was "To close or not to close?" From the college right down through the primary schools the story was the same. Thirty to fifty years earlier the aim of mission schools was "solely evangelistic," but with the elaborate educational system now built up to train Christian members and leaders, the influence of these political events could not but affect the work of the church.

And then came the famine of 1920, due to the soldiers, the locusts, and the drought. All through the North China Conference "the situation was really desperate. . . . The people were eating bark, leaves, weeds and chaff, and were in a most miserable condition. The strong were able to leave, but the young and the old had very little hope." [12] But the Methodists in the United States, in Sumatra and Singapore, in the Foochow and the Hinghwa

Conferences, helped generously. Methodist missionaries and Chinese pastors gave of their time and strength unstintedly, and much non-Christian help and support came to the church because of the aid it brought to these people in their need.

During and between these catastrophies in many parts of the country, bandits—sometimes called soldiers of contending war lords—harassed and plundered. Neither missionaries nor native pastors nor Christian laymen escaped the robbery, the demand for ransom, and the arson that terrorized especially the mountain provinces of Fukien, Kiangsi, and Szechuen.

From 1897 to 1922 had been a quarter century during which the political and economic background had done all a background could do to check the growth of the church. Riots, the Boxers, revolution, war, aggression, bandits, and famine had followed one another, almost "toe to heel"—an expression Bishop Lewis repeatedly used in one of his sermons, much to the perplexity of his interpreter—and with them came other domestic difficulties which can best be described in the words of the Episcopal Address to the Eastern Asia Central Conference in 1923:

> In China, governmental impotence, piteous inactivity, sectional strife, and local defiance of the Government's decrees; brigandage, bold and oppressive in many parts; merciless abuses of peaceful and helpless populations, and heartless taxation of the poor; vast moneys spent for military waste while education languishes; the poppy forced again into the fields and gardens as by military order, and smuggled in by connivance of foreign tradesmen and mendacious Chinese officials; whole villages in part of China fleeing to the mountains to sleep more safely under the stars than under their own home roofs; uncertainty and distrust that blocks the wheels of industry and throttles economic initiative; increasing skepticism in foreign capitals concerning political conditions and the power of China to set her own house in order; immeasurable and unblushing graft and petty squeeze deadening the moral perceptions of the people; gambling well-nigh a national characteristic; superstition, idolatry, plural marriage, footbinding, still the rule rather than the exception.

But with the faith and the farsightedness which characterized the bishops of these years, they also said: "We have chaos and disorder, but here, too, are signs of a new and greater day."

3. The Nationalist Campaign

But the new and greater day was to be ushered in with another storm. In the foreign-controlled city of Shanghai, in June, 1925, had occurred a clash between Chinese students and British police, which had had its echo in Canton a few weeks later. The trickling stream of anti-imperialism and anti-foreignism, whose babblings had been heard in 1900 and then lost in the woods, was emerging as the European war and the Japanese demands had been intensifying the feeling of nationalism. By 1927 the stream had risen so rapidly that the babbling had become a roar, and there seemed to be no stopping of the flood as the armies of the revolution made their way northward through Kiangsi and Fukien to the cities of the Yangtze Valley, and then on through Taian-fu to the north. The struggle was one for supremacy by southern forces, under the inspiration of the late Sun Yat-sen and the leadership of his former pupil Chiang-Kai-shek, against the northern regime, which was held to be too conservative and too subservient to foreign domination. Hence at places along the advance of the southern soldiers, looting and destruction of foreign property occurred, and at many other places it was feared.

All missionaries south of the Yangtze were ordered to the ports—for the first time the radio was used for the transmission of such orders. As had always been the case in the past, many missionaries preferred to disregard the advice of their bishops and the call of their consuls; those who for conscience' sake stayed sometimes found themselves, if not in actual danger, handicapped for supplies and help. Joseph Beech, of Chengtu, tells this story:

One of the daily duties of the president of the University was to make a "nightly" visit, avoiding spies while so-doing, to a quiet spot out in the country and bring home a bucket of milk for the Methodist families. He was accompanied by his young son. On the first night's escapade this youngster remarked: "Well, Daddy, if I live through this, I will have another subject for an essay." We did not fear being caught. We did fear lest the milkman be discovered, his cows taken from him, and he be otherwise punished. That state of affairs continued for fifteen days, then middlemen began to talk terms.

.   .   .   .

Agitation still continues and it is not unlikely that there will be an attempted recurrence of the strike in the near future ostensibly to secure better terms for the workers, but actually to again endeavor to carry out the program of opposition to foreigners, and the closing up of Christian work as one step in the program of the revolution of the radical party now in the saddle in a good part of China.[13]

Foochow was the first city where Methodists were molested, and Siong-Iu-Dong and the Woolston Memorial Hospital were thoroughly looted, Dr. Hu King-Eng being forced to flee to Singapore. Missionaries were hurriedly evacuated on a United States destroyer to the Philippines.

In Nanchang, stood that valiant soldier of Christ, Dr. Ida Kahn, as a mediator between missionaries and anti-Christian agitators, and her influence frequently made friends of bitter opponents. Through the reign of terror her hospital stood open, and 12,800 treatments were given in 1927. Refugees by the hundreds came.

Soldiers ravaged the beautiful garden, but injured women and wounded soldiers alike were healed and shown what the spirit of Christianity is.[14]

Truly it was said of her: "In her own person she is doctor, teacher, preacher, and many find Christ through her."

Nanking was looted, burned, and raped; missionaries there were assaulted, their property destroyed, and one killed before the American navy offered its barrage of fire. Taian-fu was evacuated, but the southern troops did not reach there until the spring of 1928, by which time the missionaries had returned. Then as reported by Perry O. Hanson, "fighting occurred all around our Taian compound, missionaries and Chinese friends crowded into basements and cellars for several days, and Mrs. Hobart . . . was killed by a bullet sent by a soldier on the city wall," which position commanded the mission compound in which every house was struck by bullets.

Missionaries had evacuated their stations, sometimes never to return. Some were transferred to other fields, some went on furlough and accepted permanent positions at home, some felt the time opportune to withdraw when there were Chinese to take their places and appropriations were being annually curtailed; a few, in spite of the fact that they were "strong and effective missionary workers, . . . well-loved by the immediate circles which they served," were voted from the field by their Chinese colleagues coming into power; some accepted retirement a few years earlier than the stipulated age. The greatest exodus of missionaries in Methodism's eighty years in China took place in 1927-28.

4. The Japanese Invasion

Ten years later the international storm which had been brewing for years broke in North China. The shot fired at the Marco Polo Bridge, like that fired at the bridge in Concord in 1775, was "heard round the world." It is unquestionably true, as Nathaniel Peffer said, "the summer of 1937 marked the end of one historical period in the Far East and the beginning of another." Violent, seismic, and far-reaching as were its effects on the Christian church in China, it may be questioned whether these effects were more significant and vital than those which had risen from the flames of 1927.

Manchuria, Ethiopia, and Austria had felt the unmolested grip of totalitarian covetousness, and the Japanese militarists were realizing that every day's delay in their thrust for the final control of China was another day in China's increasing ability to resist. Japan was already strong enough, they thought, to win what it wanted from China within a few short weeks. China was not yet strong enough, but was steadily approaching a strength which could at least provide delaying action—or so some Japanese minds seem to have reasoned. And so the steel and flint were struck. The conflagration which resulted is a story for other pages; the processes of reconversion and reconstruction have not yet progressed far enough to appraise the final effects on the Methodists in China, but a few of the immediate, temporary, and short-term reactions are, of course, already a matter of record.

Three or four years of this raging conflict had passed when in January, 1941, the editor of the *China Christian Advocate,* in describing the demand for the gospel, said:

In occupied China, churches are filled. . . . Moore Memorial Church is overflowing already. There is not standing room at the regular services; every worker has more than he can do as it is. They cannot take care of the ones who come to study and to seek. They dare not invite more to come. . . . In Free China the opportunity is intensified. Evangelists and ministers find multitudes ready to listen to the Gospel and to study the Way of Life, whenever opportunity is given. "Come and help build our church," says Bishop Ward of West China. Many are going, but even so, calls for more are heard.

Left to itself, perhaps, the church could have met this demand; but left to its former self, perhaps the church could not have convinced the nation that it could satisfy the longing need. In its ability to survive, in its power to adapt itself to the drastically new conditions, in the devoted spirit of its missionaries, pastors, and lay members, the church was able to prove a tower of strength and to go forward; the roots which, for ninety years, Methodism had been sending down into Chinese soil were able to hold the church firm and keep it alive. "One church in Shanghai," reported Richard T. Baker, "lost two-thirds of its members by emigration, but by 1945 had gained back all that loss and more with new converts."

It early became evident that schools could not survive Japanese invasion. China's students had long been known for their hostility to Japanese ambitions in China; they could and would, the invaders well knew, be the breeding places for influences which would thwart Japanese conquest. Therefore, "bag and baggage," primary schools, middle schools, colleges, and universities, moved into safer locations. Faculties and students, on foot, by boat, by any available means, took themselves, sometimes a thousand miles or more, to places where they could teach and study with little outside disturbance. Noted the *China Christian Advocate:* "A college president said, after his return from weeks of fleeing with a nucleus of faculty and students, 'There is no food so coarse that I cannot eat it; there is no bed so hard that I cannot sleep upon it.' " Libraries and laboratories were dismantled and packed in boxes and baskets and boats and set up in remote locations. Some, like William Nast College, had to leave everything behind, but, as one official said: "With us we have brought the legal status and spiritual tradition of the school—thus symbolizing our faith in man and in God." Bathrooms were used for classrooms, ancestral halls were loaned for college buildings, temporary structures were erected for dormitories, several colleges were crowded into a single campus. And so the Christian education of China's youth went on, sometimes in remote villages where Methodists had had no previous abiding place.

Since nearly every Methodist school in China sooner or later transplanted itself, it will obviously be impossible to list them all by name and new address. Schools in the neighborhood of Shanghai fled to the protection of the foreign concessions in that city, Soochow University and Susan B. Wilson School to Moore Memorial Church, and Laura Haygood Normal School and Virginia School to the campus of McTyeire, only to have to move again before the course of the war permitted the Japanese to appropriate McTyeire for a convalescent hospital for soldiers. But in partial and suggestive summary, the following may be quoted from the executive secretary of the Division of Foreign Missions reporting in 1942:

At the outbreak of the war most of the Union Christian universities moved into the hinterland. . . . The University of Nanking, Ginling College for Women, and the medical department of Cheeloo University went to Chengtu where they were given asylum on the spacious campus of West China Union University. . . . After December 8th of last year the Japanese closed Yenching University in Peiping and established in the buildings a School for Scientific Research for North China. The Americans on the faculty are confined to the American Embassy, and the president is confined in a private house in Peiping. Forty-six members of the faculty and 227 students made their way to West China and during the summer Yenching was re-established in Chengtu on the campus where the other four Christian universities are functioning. . . . Some of the faculty and students from Soochow University . . . which first moved to Shanghai and then, early this year, closed because of Japanese interference, made their way to Shaowu. Negotiations were in progress for the establishment of Soochow University on the Fukien Christian University campus, but the advance to within a day's march of a strong military drive from the coast led to a dropping of the effort for the time.[15]

Later, for a time, the Arts and Science division of Soochow University located at Kukong, adjacent to Ling-nan University, and "finally abandoned its work," but the Law School joined with Shanghai University College of Business in Chungking, "keeping the charter of the university in effect." Hwa Nan had early found a satisfactory resting place 130 miles away from home, in school buildings, missionary residences, and temporary structures on the Methodist hilltops in Yenping.

But schools were not alone in feeling the effects of the Japanese invasion. In every part of the country which was occupied, residences, institutions, and churches were looted or destroyed—or both. West China, especially Chungking, which was at one period termed "the most bombd capital in the world" (that was long before the raids on Berlin and Tokyo began), felt the ravages of aerial invasion. But for the most part Fukien, southern Kiangsi, and Szechuen were portions of "Free China"; in North China, the Yangtze Valley, the coastal sections of Kiangsu and Chekiang, and, for two different periods, Foochow and its coastal environs, the church suffered from being in "Occupied China." Within a year after hostilities commenced, in many of these areas church work had been "almost entirely disrupted"; the population migrated to freer territory, so that congregations evaporated; preachers devoted their energies to the needs in refugee camps, "finding opportunities for expressing Christian love among these masses largely non-Christian." Annual Conference sessions, at first held months after the regular dates and very poorly attended, had eventually to be abandoned altogether.

Leland W. Holland wrote: "In occupied territory the church adapted itself to the necessity of emphasizing the evangelistic work without having the chance to run schools, and hospitals." But "make-up classes" for children and youth were being held in churches which were not interfered with. In one church alone there were a thousand children being taught to read, write, and to know the Way of Life; so, without a regular curriculum, although no diplomas could be granted, the youth of the church was being fitted for life. And even missionaries could, in some places, call in the homes of school pupils. Miss Nagler, carrying on alone in Chinkiang, says she had many invitations, even from non-Christians: "Do come to see me," they would urge, adding, "we have a nice dugout."

Petty annoyances and restrictions were not infrequent in territory occupied by Japanese troops. Schools, hospitals, churches and homes were seized and used at pleasure, sometimes to be returned, but in filthy and dilapidated condition. Opposition and obstruction tactics which were used are illustrated by this picture at the Wuhu Hospital, where incidents were created to endanger

the safety of the nurses and physicians, such as forbidding the hospital chauffeur to drive the hospital car; objection to the least ray of light from the hospital windows at night when lights in their own military quarters and other places in the city show clearly; refusal in some cases to accept the hospital certificate of inoculation against cholera and typhoid (the Chinese government has always accepted the hospital certificates), demand and forcible attempt to search American property of the hospital to abduct the Chinese lady doctor which was prevented. However, in spite of danger and difficulties and the fact that they are virtual prisoners, no member of the staff has resigned.[16]

But after Japan had commenced war against the United States, restrictions on work in Occupied China were increased and intensified. The Methodist Church in China, like others, was not only a Chinese institution, but even more, they argued, an American organization. Missionaries from Changli to Shanghai and Kiukiang were promptly limited in their movements, very soon they were restricted to the confines of their own homes or institutions, and subsequently and all too soon placed in concentration camps or prisons. Bishop Ward, at first confined to the hospital in Wuhu with other workers there, was later released, allowed to return to Shanghai, still later imprisoned in the Haiphong Road Jail and sometimes tortured. The demand for his repatriation had to be withdrawn as a condition for the second trip of the *Gripsholm* to repatriate most of the remaining imprisoned Methodists and others; and shortly before the Japanese surrender he was transferred to a Japanese prison camp near Peking, to remain until released in August, 1945.

The Chinese leaders of the church were also hampered and restricted in their activities. At one time Bishop Abe, of the former Japan Methodist Church, who had been sent to China to serve as liaison between the Japanese military and the Chinese churches, traveled a thousand miles to see what relief could be had from the pressure being put upon Bishop Kaung.

In North China, and somewhat less enthusiastically under the puppet government of the lower Yangtze Valley, pressure was brought to consolidate all branches of the Christian church, and to eliminate all existing church organizations. Before his imprisonment, Bishop Ward had written:

Since all such contacts between Americans, British and Chinese promote mutual friendliness which is deemed inimical to Japan, such contacts must be disrupted in "Total War." A union of existing churches with their Anglo-American traditions and friendly attitudes must, therefore, be utterly destroyed. The principle of religious freedom plus the principle of Sino-Japanese co-operation thus requires the creation of an entirely new Protestant Christian Church which is definitely Sino-Japanese. Co-operation of existing churches is insufficient. Differences of faith and connection are belittled.[17]

This reorganization, with headquarters in Peking, was a union Protestant body, following in general the organization forced on the church in Japan, having Chinese church leaders, including Bishop Kaung, making up the governing bodies, with Japanese pastors as advisors, and with branch organizations in the main cities of North China. Missionaries were barred from participation, and all financial support from foreign countries was forbidden. This might have resulted in a Chinese Christian Church, which would make strides towards unity and self-support, but the stimulus was too forced and external to be lasting.

"We are no longer Szechuenese, but Chinese, and we glory in the chance to work with down-river national leaders of the church in China." Thus wrote Grace Manly of "A District Conference in Free China," expressing one of the results of the great migration caused by the coming of the Japanese. History has few (if any) parallels to the mass movement of population thrown into flight by enemy invasion in China. Miss Manly may have caught an attitude among the Szechuenese which Carleton Lacy, two years later, thought was too largely lacking among the immigrants:

To some extent the government has caught the imagination of its supporters and employees as a national institution which operates on a nation-wide basis. No such appreciation of the church has as yet been secured and those who work in and for the church still think of it in regional and denominational terms.

The disturbing element in this whole situation is not that church leaders from the east should desire to return home and leave the field to the developing leadership of the west, but that the attitude generally expressed showed so little appreciation of the national dimensions of the church, so little missionary spirit, so little response to the challenge of a big job difficult to be accomplished.[18]

Occupation by unscrupulous military forces could not but have had hurtful effects upon church life and property. But the uprooting of forty million people from Occupied China and their resettlement in Free China —since many, many of them were Christian people—could not but affect the church for better or for worse in both Free and Occupied China. One thing it had done, especially in Free China, was to throw a great burden for Christian care on a church as yet unequal to this task, and to show the inadequacy of vision and responsibility which had been developed in the church, particularly in the lower Yangtze Valley, which was, of course, the source of the major portion of the migration.

Probably no one realized after three years of war between China and Japan that the mid-point of that war still lay some time ahead. And as the war lengthened, as the entrance of other nations into the fight against Japan increased the difficulties in China, this intermingling of east and west in China seems to have been somewhat cemented, the temporariness of the relationships lessened, and the feeling of national unity which Grace Manly early sensed, increased. And hence, even applying it to the life of the church, William P. Fenn seems to have been right when he said: "Above all, an advance from a traditionally regional to a national viewpoint has already been achieved. This opening of the interior and the linking of the people is one of the greatest phenomena in all history." [19] And so Dr. Charles H. Fahs spoke appropriately when, speaking at the funeral of Spencer Lewis, he said: "When the history of Christianity in China is written, Dr. Lewis will be known as one of the great pioneers of what was once the Western fringe, but now the great center of China."

In view of what has been said in the foregoing paragraphs, and because it is a typical etching of these scenes in this "great center of China," the following sketch is reproduced:

Ting-chia-ngao is a one-street market-town on the Szechuen highway, half a day's motor ride northwest of Chungking. . . . In the more prosperous days of Methodist Church work in Szechuen two decades ago this village became the seat of a church and a boys' and girls' higher primary school. Land was purchased and buildings erected of an attractive architectural design. Those palmy days passed and left the school buildings empty, the church nearly deserted, the resident pastor and the Bible Woman continuing year after year to visit in the homes and the tea-shops and to hold some sort of service on Sunday without a community program.

Migration brought a boys' junior and senior middle school [Methodist] from Kiangsi which was granted the use of the buildings and the remnant of equipment. Petty discord early arose. . . . The immigrants succeeded, however, in making necessary improvements to the plant. . . . In the process of migration this boys' school had become co-educational. With the teachers and students had come also some of the faculty families and of students as well, and a number of Christian workers and other friends from the same down-river community with old connections or associations. Some of these were persons of sufficient means to provide themselves with comfortable residence accommodations close by the village. . . . Church services were conducted by the local pastor. The school community practically filled the church. Very few people from the village, apart from immigrants, attended. The pastor was a fairly well-educated man with potentialities, but with no apparent program, and the school administration felt that he had no message for the students. . . . He seemed to have lost any vision, sense of mission, or very high ethical standards that may have taken him into the ministry. The Bible Woman appeared to be capable of developing under proper leadership and was willing to work along with the immigrants. She was the only local person at the mid-week prayer meeting. The school community appeared to be quite satisfied with itself with no sense of responsibility for the larger community. . . . It was impossible to avoid raising the question as to the type of Christianity which might be developing within this rather exclusive, relatively self-contained, educated immigrant community.[20]

With the outbreak of war in 1937 there arose, of course, the question that missionaries had faced time and again in the past ninety years—during the Taiping Rebellion, the Boxer Uprising, the Revolution, the Nationalist Campaign: "To go or not to go? To evacuate under orders or as a precaution, or to stay with the property and the people and ignore the physical risk?" Of course the question was answered both ways. The attitude of the officials of the Methodist Episcopal Church at the beginning of the hostilities in 1937 was that mothers and children should leave, that others who "freely elect to remain" if needed should be guided by the exigencies of the situation and the maintenance of the church program, but that in every case "those who are evacuated and those who elect to stay are alike assured of our sympathy and of our moral and financial support." An official attitude, as expressed in China, is contained in the following incident related by Charles E. Winter in the *Michigan Christian Advocate* of January 13, 1938:

I never saw a more effective and affecting good-bye to a bishop than the one our Bishop Gowdy received today. A group of about a hundred preachers, Bible Women, and church members gathered at the gate and as he rode out they sang, "God will take care of you." . . . They know how, when a few months ago the consular officials would have sent all Americans home to America, he stood out against them. He said to our consul, who was himself acting under orders from his superiors, "If these are the orders of the Government of America, the Government has been misinformed. We cannot leave."

Evacuation in 1937, as reported by the *China Christian Advocate* of February, 1938, meant all it had meant in 1900 and 1927:

Often and again, the wife and mother has come to safety with the children while the man of the family has stayed to face whatever may come. . . . Two people and sometimes three are packed into a tiny room with double-decker beds. . . . Meals are in a common dining room with no possibility for having home life. . . . Week after week the missionaries are thus "living in public." Added to the strain of scanty news from their loved ones left behind who are in constant danger, is the knowledge that when they do go back their homes have been looted or burned. . . . Where furloughs have been due, missionaries have gone to America. Some who are nearing the age of retirement are pressed by relatives and by advisers to give up and return to a land where they can be free from the dangers inherent in this situation, whichever way the war turns. But all who have given their energies to spreading the Gospel in China are slow to give up.

But with the progress of the war, and particularly following the Japanese attack on Pearl Harbor, evacuation became more and more advisable, more and more necessary, more and more difficult, even from Free China. Bombings, shortages, inflation, put missionaries under physical strain which often made it physically imperative that they leave; restrictions on and internment of American citizens in Occupied China prevented their continued work and urged for repatriation when facilities were offered; fresh enemy advances provoked fresh evacuations to avoid the risks of arrest and imprisonment. Travel difficulties within China and government demands for transportation facilities between China and the United States prevented many who had gone to the United States from returning to China. In 1937 there were 254 Methodist missionaries in China; in 1940 there were 280; at the end of 1945 there were fewer than 20 there. Bishop Gowdy in 1944 expressed his realization of the changed conditions since his retirement in 1941 when he said: "Travel difficulties are infinitely worse than you or I ever knew them. I'm glad I got away when I did, because I couldn't have done the necessary travel, and nothing less would have been fair to the church."

Many experiences of missionaries getting out of Fukien in 1943-44 prove this and make the initial journeys of Moses White and Charles Taylor and their parties seem like de luxe travel. The Whites and Judson Collins were four months and twenty-seven days from Boston to Foochow; a party which landed in Boston on May 25, 1944, had been five months and two days from Foochow. And contrasted with sailing the boundless sea through these months, Edith Simester's story of overland travel is typical of war-time China:

> The trip across China was a nightmare. . . . In Kukong we were in despair for accommodations. Kweilin was an unpleasant experience. . . . We arrived in an air raid which delayed our getting in for three hours. . . . It never went below 100° day or night during my nine days there. . . . The next nine days were the most miserable I ever spent. The railroad was newly built and the road-bed was not in good condition. . . . Once we had to change trains in the middle of the night . . . and climb up a mountainside to the new train in the dark and rain. Three of the nights were spent in hotels. The rest were spent sitting up on the train in an overcrowded third-class car or sleeping on the station platform. We ate what we could get, . . . chiefly pears, steamed bread, and tea. . . . Flying was the most beautiful experience I have ever had. . . . It was strange to reach Calcutta and be penniless.[21]

However large it loomed in individual eyes, the attitude towards evacuation was a significantly minor problem. It was immediate and it was insistent. On the other hand, however, during the early months of Japanese occupation there seemed a hesitation to make long-distant plans for the future. Missionaries seemed to be "floundering," as one of them expressed it; whatever program they had was predicated on a hope-for early return to prewar conditions with little or no constructive program on which all could pull together. Carleton Lacy expressed it in a letter when he wrote: "Few have yet realized, at least within the administrative group, that a major cataclysm had taken place and that it is time to start in uninhibited or uncorrupted and unwarped by our traditional prejudices and ruts." The continuance of hostilities, the steady withdrawal of missionaries, the calls for the gospel and the Bible, and the demands for relief, resulted in a day-by-day development of policies and programs which, as had been the basis of too many missionary programs, would have eventually to be taken into consideration in any permanent policies that would later be shaped for the future.

Kalgan, North China, Shantung, Central China, and much of the territory of the Kiangsi Conference were occupied, as was all of the territory of the China Conference, and the question soon arose, as reported by the *China Christian Advocate* of July, 1938,

whether to stay by the property, where buildings and equipment are complete, but where the groundwork among the people must be begun again, or whether to release a number of missionaries who will go out among their educated leaders, and build again, with them in Free China a new social order that can be largely Christian, a new church that will be alert, forward-looking, courageous.

Only a few—perhaps too few—were transferred to Szechuen or moved into hitherto unworked territory in Southern Kiangsi, where foundations were laid on which new postwar structures may be built. When the United States entered the war all the missionaries who had elected to "stay by the property" in Occupied China were promptly interned; most of them had been evacuated to the United States, a few remained in India, and sooner or later some of the internees were exchanged and sent home on the Swedish ship *Gripsholm*. When the Japanese occupied Foochow the second time, in the fall of 1944, most of the Fukien missionaries had evacuated; the others who did not find safety behind the lines were interned. But the withdrawal of missionary personnel and the dispersal of church workers and members prevented the church from doing much more than maintain a holding program "for the duration," hoping, praying, and planning to make the church in all China, once more free, a new church, "alert, forward-looking, courageous," permeating with the Christian spirit the new social order that must and will be.

Not the least of the war results on church personnel staffs and programs was the disastrous financial inflation. The financial crippling commenced in 1937 when church members in all Methodist conferences (except West China) began moving out before the enemy should arrive. Usually those who could most easily afford to do so were the first to leave, throwing the burden of church and institutional support upon fewer and poorer members. Those who were left suffered loss because the migration of many threw many others out of work, the interruptions of markets and transportation deprived them of income, and the enemy robbed and plundered and bombed much of what they had. And the government levied for supplies and funds and pushed the sale of war bonds to prosecute the war. What was left? Hospitals that had been supported by patients' fees had no one to serve but wounded soldiers and impoverished peasants. Schools that had been largely dependent upon tuition found their pupils could not buy even enough rice. Bishop A. J. Moore, presiding over the Kiangsi Conference in 1940,

stated the case baldly but truly when he said that, save for the relief funds which were so generously contributed by American Methodists at the beginning of the war and are now rapidly being used up, the Kiangsi Conference faces financial bankruptcy. And that at a time when the Gospel message and the Christian ministry has never before been so needed and so genuinely appreciated.[22]

And Mary Mann wrote from Fukien in 1942, "Work goes on 'as usual.' 'Usual,' because of an inner assurance you good folks are back of us, and with even larger support than in 1941."

After the outbreak of war between America and Japan, our people realized that funds from America were cut off for the duration. Immediately we made a careful inventory of our funds. Bishop Kaung promised to raise $6,000 above the budget. By cutting our monthly budget from about $4,000 to $1,000 we found that we could keep the work intact until January first, 1943. Otherwise we would be bankrupt in a very few months.[23]

But war is relentless in its financial demands. The longer it progressed, the more persistent the call to meet military demands, the more difficult it became (almost to the 100 per cent mark) to secure goods from abroad or of marketing anything that could be spared. All this steadily increased the financial difficulties of the church, its institutions, and its personnel. Long before prices reached their peak, eggs sold at $3.50 to $4.00 apiece, the price of flour rose to $710 a bag, it took $1,100 to buy five gallons of kerosene, and rice brought $1,500 a load of 160 lbs. One pastor, for instance, as reported by Harry W. Worley, "with a salary of $520 per month could buy with it one third of a load of rice, but with six mouths to feed, he needed at least 180 lbs." In one week the cost of living in Chungking was reported to have advanced 22 per cent, missionaries were making single cash deposits of $1,000,000, and church budgets sounded like "New Deal" wartime expenditures.

Neither the horrors nor the suffering of war could destroy the church. Neither earthquake shocks nor devastating tempests could wipe it out. Methodism had been so fused into the mass that the fury of torrential rain could not wash it out, and no shattering by shrapnel could remove it from even the fragments that were scattered into the mountains of Szechuen,

Yunan, and southern Kiangsi. Immovable she stands! The church, stunned, scattered, impoverished, may not have been able to chart its future course with any measure of certainty, nor draw the blueprints for its postwar structure, but there is no doubt that its district superintendents and its bishops are farsighted enough and its membership—farmers, merchants, teachers, officials—devoted enough to make the Methodist Church of freed China one that will be alert, forward-looking, courageous, and Christ-centered.

VII
INFORM THE MIND

Thy word alone
True wisdom can impart;
Thou only canst inform the mind
And purify the heart.

1. *The Establishment of Educational Institutions*

"THE LONG DEBATE BETWEEN THE OPPOSITE POLICIES OF EXPANSION AND concentration is not yet ended," says Bishop Herbert Welch. That was perhaps the outstanding difference between the northern Methodists, starting in Fukien, and the southern Methodists, established in Kiangsu. Both churches during the second quarter century of their missionary work in China pursued both policies side by side, expanding their borders by evangelistic work, concentrating and deepening their foothold through more intensive contacts in schools. In individual instances the debate was often too heated to be called a debate; in some cases, there can be no doubt, the policy that won the argument was pursued to the detriment of the ultimate and highest good. But Bishop Welch, who has been first an evangelist, and secondly an educationalist, continues:

Missionary work never proceeded very far before it became evident that evangelism, in its simple and primary meaning, is not the whole of the missionary objective, and by itself is inadequate. It is not an end, but a beginning. Evangelism is a recruiting agency; it has accomplished its purpose at enlistment. But the whole process of arming and equipping, of drilling, and then of employing the trained forces in a campaign of conquest, is still to come. Evangelism must always be followed, or accompanied, by education.[1]

And those who have formed the policies of Methodism in China have agreed with this view.

Hence, as we have seen, Collins opened a school for boys in February, 1848, and Mrs. Maclay one for girls in December, 1850. The boys' school was started in a rented room on the island where White and Collins lived, the girls' school—which was "the first effort put forth by Christian missionaries for the instruction of the young girls" of Foochow—in a lath-and-plaster schoolhouse erected for the purpose in the yard of the Maclay residence at a cost of between $50-$60.

Collins' school for boys furnished, in its main outlines, the pattern for mission day schools for many decades to follow: A rented room, with a native teacher hired to teach the characters and classics, a half of each weekday devoted to the study of Christian books, the Sabbath devoted to religious exercises, all under the supervision of the missionary who conducted daily devotions and gave "such instruction as he deems profitable." This school started with an enrollment of eight boys, but soon had to be suspended because of sickness among the missionaries. As soon as possible, Collins restarted the school, but after he was compelled to leave Foochow it was moved across the river to Chong Seng Street near the residence of Maclay, who was to supervise it. Other similar schools for boys were being opened as rapidly as the growing missionary force was able to supervise them, until, by 1850, there were three, one with an average attendance of fifty, and one including both boys and girls. For several years following 1853, however, there was but one school for boys and one for girls. But it was not long until the missionaries were feeling the need of a seminary of higher grade, furnished, as the *Missionary Advocate* said, with "apparatus illustrating 'the laws of nature,' that by these also we may teach the heathen to 'look through nature up to nature's God.' "

In 1856—November 26, to be exact—the Boys' Boarding School, which for some time had been urged with assurance that some day it would be established, having now been authorized by the board, became a reality with four pupils. The oldest of the four was Iek Ing-Guang, whose admission because he impressed Mrs. Gibson, has already been mentioned. He was received into the church in 1859, and was the first pupil to finish the course in this school.

The following fall Gibson reported:

Twelve boys in all have been in the school. . . . There are now ten boys left in the school. Four of them are committed to us for a term of six years; three of them for five years; two who clothe themselves, and had previously been a long time in the Rev. Mr. Peet's school for four years; and one, lately received, for eight years.[2]

Before the first class had been graduated from the Boys' Boarding School it was decided to make this school specifically "a training school for candidates for the ministry," and in 1869 the mission decided that

hereafter we shall receive into the school only those who feel called by the Holy Ghost to preach the Gospel, and are duly recommended by the Quarterly Conference of the circuit where they live, and by the missionary having charge of the circuit.[3]

But on December 30 of the same year the Foochow Mission felt it incumbent, because no missionary was able to give the necessary time to the school, and because the young men seemed more needed for preaching than training, that the school should be suspended. This seems to have been an experiment between expansion and concentration, and one which evidently did not produce worthy results, for after a couple of years the mission, feeling "that there is an urgent demand for native preachers with more thorough Biblical and Disciplinary training," unanimously voted, "with the co-operation of the preachers," to reopen the Training School.

In Shanghai, as soon as possible after the mission had been established, two schools for boys were opened, but by 1851 lack of funds had compelled their merger, in one room, with one teacher, although there were twenty pupils making encouraging progress. That year Charles Taylor wrote the board expressing a desire to establish two boarding schools, one for boys and one for girls, with single ladies as teachers for both—"as the children would all be quite manageable by them"—though a male teacher for boys would be "so much the better." The appropriation for 1854 was "much larger than heretofore," and the $30,000 included "purchase of a press and the erection of a church and a building for school."

As at Foochow and Shanghai, one of the first moves at Kiukiang was to start school work. A day school was opened with an enrollment of seven which soon increased to fourteen. By the time that Kiukiang was made a separate mission in 1869 it had also a school which had for "its ultimate object the training of young men for helpers or assistant preachers," with four pupils, one of whom was self-supporting.

The baptism of Diong A-Hok and his family has been called "the chief event of this year's work" in the Foochow District for 1882. Diong had, in his early years, been employed in the home of a Christian woman in Amoy, whose influence had left its mark on him, and through him on thousands in the years to come. He had come to Foochow to live, had developed a prosperous mercantile business, and had become interested in the work of the church to which he gave liberally. But he refrained, until 1882, from accepting baptism and membership in the church until he could have influence enough with his business associates to close his store on the Lord's Day.

During these years he had known of the desire of the Methodist missionaries and preachers to develop a higher system of education for boys than any then in existence in Foochow. E. L. Ford says the delay in this development, each time the matter was discussed, was "partly because of the question of the study of English in a mission school." But when Diong came to his missionary friends in December, 1880, and offered a piece of property "to be used as an Anglo-Chinese College," and when, a few days later, Maclay, during a visit to Foochow, urged the acceptance of such an offer, the long-discussed project was launched. Diong finally changed his offer from a piece of property to $10,000 cash, with which, plus $4,000 raised locally, "the finest grounds and, with but one or two exceptions, the best building in Foochow," were purchased.

As soon as the institution was ready to open its doors, students were enrolled from the outlying districts of the Foochow Conference, as well as from Foochow itself, although during the first year Franklin Ohlinger, the president, had, in his annual report, vividly stated the need for such an institution (see Appendix A, item 11) and asked for financial assistance, saying:

Until we receive $5,000 from some source we must continue to refuse admission to those who do not live in the immediate vicinity, or who have no friend with whom they can board. . . . Many of these boys who had never been in a Christian chapel, listen with rapt attention to the persuasive discourses of Sia Sek-Ong and Hu Sing-Mi. Many of them are poor, but not one a pauper; all pay the stipulated rates. The example is stimulating the native church to renewed efforts in the line of self-support. . . . I commend the first Methodist college in Asia to the prayers of our beloved Zion.[4]

The following year George B. Smyth was appointed as head of this institution, and to him, more than to any other, belongs the credit for making this the outstanding Methodist educational institution in China not only of the eighties and nineties but also for a good many years to come. The argument for English as a medium of education had, in this instance, been settled by the terms of Diong's gift, but it persisted ever after, in varying degrees of intensity and manners; but perhaps nowhere were high accomplishment in Chinese and effective use of English combined with better results than under the inauguration and development of Smyth's leadership.

By January 10, 1890, when Ding Maing-Ing became the first graduate from the Anglo-Chinese College and commenced a lifelong career on its faculty, Smyth could write: "Let no one smile at our rejoicing over one [graduate in] our first commencement. . . . Some colleges which are famous now did not at first graduate many more." Bishop Fowler was saying: "Universities are needed in each of these three older Missions," and the appointments in the conference minutes included: "Foochow University, G.B. Smyth, President. Anglo-Chinese College, G. B. Smyth, Dean."

In 1844 a brave English woman, Miss Aldersey, had come at her own expense and commenced work for women in Ningpo. Not till six years later, however, did any mission board venture to send a single woman as a missionary to China; then the American Episcopal Church board, with faith and courage, sent Miss L. B. Fay to Shanghai, where she labored for nearly a quarter of a century. The year after her arrival in Shanghai, the missionaries in Foochow began appeals to the New York office for single women to be sent to open and conduct a school for girls. On February 19, 1859, the Misses Beulah and Sarah Woolston and Miss Phebe Potter had arrived in Foochow in response to these eight years of appeals, and on November 28 had opened the Waugh Female Seminary in the building which had formerly been occupied by the boys' school. It was such a novelty that at first none of the natives were willing to patronize it. At the end of ten months only eight of the fifteen girls who had been in the school remained. But these were being favorably impressed, and the school never was without pupils; in 1861 Miss Woolston wrote in the *Missionary Advocate* of two of them:

> We have lately taken in a scholar whose friends wish her to be taught "the doctrines" as the one she is to marry understands them.
> We have a new scholar; she is 68 years old and is gray headed. She wanted to come into school to be taught the Ten Commandments and the Christian doctrines, because she had no one at home to instruct her concerning them.

The need for suitable buildings for the school was met by the Female Missionary Society of Baltimore, and the "Baltimore Female Academy" was established, which, in turn, was succeeded by the Girls' Boarding School, in which, on March 9, 1862, Hu Sing-Eng was baptized and received into the church. Miss Potter, soon after her arrival, became Mrs. Wentworth, and the Misses Woolston, in 1871, became the first missionaries in China of the Woman's Foreign Missionary Society, which had been organized two years previously.

When Bishop Edward Thompson visited Foochow some five years after these women had come there, he wrote:

> Next day I visited Miss Woolston's school. The furniture is plain, rough, and cheap, but clean; the children are plainly but neatly dressed. There are benches for chairs, mattresses for beds, and bamboo frames for pillows. All this is that they may not be discontented on returning home. Misses Woolston are much encouraged by accessions recently received. There are now twenty-three girls under instruction.[5]

Although this school had been continuing to influence girls and fit them for Christian service, it was not till 1888 that there was a graduating class —six girls—and not till 1896 did it cease to be necessary to seek students and become possible to select students.

But in the meantime the influence of the Anglo-Chinese College and the desire of educated Christian ministers and laymen for educated wives created a vocal demand for higher education for girls, and the Annual Report of the Woman's Foreign Missionary Society reports the receipt of "one of the most remarkable documents received by our society: one from the native preachers, asking for the higher education of the females, and pleading for it with an eloquence and wealth of illustration thoroughly Oriental." [6] But it was too much for the Woolston sisters, and this same report includes this paragraph:

It is with regret that we receive this as probably the last report from the time-honored veterans of our work—the Misses Woolston, the pioneers of our distinctive woman's work for women in foreign lands. New educational methods, including the study of English, the Chinese classics, music and other accomplishments, are being introduced into China, which they do not approve, and, therefore, will not adopt; but, in retiring from this work, these sisters bring with them the highest appreciation and esteem of the oldest missionaries. [7]

Failing to find anyone to fill the places of the Misses Woolston after they left Foochow in December, 1883, the women's and girls' schools were merged in charge of the native presiding elder and a teacher employed by him, all under control of the Rev. G. B. Smyth, who wrote the American secretaries: "With an unendowed and penniless college on my hands, I could not give much time to another school." But by 1884 Miss Carrie I. Jewell had arrived and taken charge of the school, new property was occupied in 1893, and the school was creating Christian womanhood, while it was headed for that day, some quarter century distant, when it should be one of the feeders for a Methodist college for women in Fukien.

In the meantime the Foochow Seminary—started to fill a place in that port similar to that which McTyeire had created in Shanghai—had made possible advanced study, especially in English. But in 1904 a tentative organization, with Bishop Bashford as president, was effected by the Woman's Foreign Missionary Society for the development of a college for women in Foochow. Not until 1908, however, after a gift of $15,000 had been received for property, did Bishop Bashford appoint Miss Lydia Trimble as president with authority to enroll the first pupils in the preparatory department. Then began another of those matchless careers in the service of Chinese womanhood which can be only inadequately suggested in spoken or written words. After the class which had entered in 1908 had graduated from the preparatory department in 1913, in handsome buildings on a hill looking towards the Min River, regular college work was commenced; not until 1921, however, was Hwa Nan to graduate its first class of three girls with the degree of bachelor of arts.

Hwa Nan has continued a Methodist college. The tide of mergers into union universities did not sweep it along, nor did union with other denominational middle schools carry it into a union college for women. Hwa Nan was so far ahead of any other school for women in south China that, when union might have come, it could not be easy for any institution. Hwa Nan had too fine a piece of property to abandon to join with the union university six miles down river; and perhaps personalities had something to do with this reluctance—personalities have always had to be reckoned with in any decisions which have made this history, from the days that Moses White wrote his diary to—if we could only read them—the diaries that are being written today. And so Hwa Nan passed through the breakers that were coming in with the union tide, and remained, under the leadership and administration of Lydia Trimble, Ida Belle Lewis, Carol Chen, and Lucy Wang, a Methodist college, always a preeminent source of Christian inspiration and culture in the womanhood of south China.

In 1877 the boys' school which had been started in Soochow seven years earlier, and which had grown into the Buffington Institute, was commencing to do "good college work" which, during the next twenty-three years, provided training for most of the leaders of the church in that area. In 1881, the same year that property was secured for the Anglo-Chinese College in Foochow and its board of trustees organized, the Methodists in Shanghai were seeking to meet the demands of that commercial center by establishing an Anglo-Chinese college which should train Christian business men for that city. In 1895, as a step in co-ordinating educational work, Bishop Hendrix had made Buffington Institute a part of this college, with A. P. Parker as president. But a year later the demand for English in higher education was more than evident at Soochow (Buffington Institute had not become an Anglo-Chinese school), and D. L. Anderson was voicing the feeling that this institute "ought now to command an outside paying class of scholars, and I long to see the time when every boy will either pay his way or will be willing to work his way through school in an industrial department." To meet these two demands, the Kung Hong Anglo-Chinese School was commenced in Soochow in the early part of 1896, and within three years had an enrollment of 109 and had never cost the board a cent, except for Anderson's salary and for the temporary building which the school occupied.

Before this third institution of higher education had been started, however, Young J. Allen was calling for the unification of the higher educational work of the mission, and the immediate organization of a long-contemplated Southern Methodist University. "Our plans," he said, "are far in advance of any other mission here, and we have nearly all the elements or factors necessary for its successful inauguration." He wanted such a university to be chartered or incorporated in the United States and to be made in every way "a bona fide part of our great missionary enterprise in China." [8]

In the spring of 1899 the China Mission voted to move Buffington Institute from Soochow and merge it with the Anglo-Chinese College which, like others that might be mentioned, was a "college" in name only, to continue there the training of church workers and Christian children, and transfer to the Kung Hong School in Soochow the property and equipment of Buffington, thus greatly strengthening the school whose needs had been foreseen by Anderson some years before. In 1901 the New Orleans Missionary Conference pledged $50,000 for the building and equipment of Soochow University. Ten years later W. B. Nance reported the growth of Soochow University into "at least a respectable college." In 1911 the Anglo-Chinese College at Shanghai was moved to Soochow and merged with the university, the Shanghai property being retained for the use of a middle school and, later, the law school. During this ten years' growth, the medical training that had been given in connection with the hospitals at Soochow was made a department of the university, although in 1906 Anderson was not very encouraged about its prospects when he wrote:

In the medical department there are three enrolled: but owing to the confusion and uncertainty caused by the annual conference appointments this department is not so well organized as we desire. We trust that steps can be taken to put the organization of the medical school on a better basis, as it is a most important department of the university and there will be no lack of students.

And then he added: "The need for an organized theological department is becoming each year more pressing." [9] But with the organization of the medical department of Nanking University, and that of the Nanking Union Theological School, these two departments were transferred to Nanking.

On September 3, 1915, the university "had the honor of opening the first law school in China under foreign auspices." This school, known as the Comparative Law School of China, was located on the property of the former Anglo-Chinese College in Shanghai. Wrote Bishop Cannon in the *History of Southern Methodist Missions:*

The Soochow University system is one of the unique achievements of Southern Methodism in Chinese education. The seat of the system is in Soochow, where is located the college of liberal arts and one of the middle schools. Other units are in the remaining stations of the Mission. . . . Soochow was chosen as the center of the system because of its better climate, its standing as a center of Chinese education, the availability of sufficient land at a reasonable price, and the support of Chinese gentlemen at Soochow who subscribed $25,000 to aid in the scheme.

By 1920 the university embraced eight departments with a total enrollment of 1,603 divided as follows: At Soochow: preparatory, 67; middle school, 223; college, 138; at Shanghai: law department, 27; middle school No. 2,

127; at Huchow: middle school No. 3, 109; at Sungkiang: the Bible school, 27; and throughout the system, primary schools with a total enrollment of 885.

To D. L. Anderson, more than to any one other man, though largely and ably assisted by J. W. Cline and W. B. Nance, belongs the credit for this development of Soochow University during this score of years. Anderson was farsighted and a builder, he believed that "the missionary's best work is intensive, in the lives of those who have capacity for leadership among their own people," and as he knew how to "appeal to the highest motives in dealing with students . . . such a thing as a widespread or organized rebellion was unknown under his administration. His students looked up to him with reverence and affection." [10] The institution which he piloted through those early years has, under the later administration of W. B. Nance and Y. C. Yang, like Hwa Nan, surmounted the breakers of unionism and headed out to sea as a Methodist institution of unsurpassed influence and prestige.

The Clopton School for girls had been established by the Southern Methodists before 1876, at which time it could accommodate twenty-five girls through a course of study which "was largely a religious one." But in 1880, the failing health of missionary women made it necessary, as we have seen was the experience of the girls' school at Foochow some three years later, to leave the school in the care of native teachers with such help and oversight as Dr. Walter Lambuth could give until in February 1881 it was necessary for him too to return to the United States. Then Mrs. A. P. Parker was called from Soochow, for it was felt that the work in Clopton should not be allowed to fail nor decline, even if the new work in Soochow should be delayed for a time. But in 1882 the East Side School for girls was opened in Soochow with "two scholars and a woman from Clopton School as a native teacher. In the meantime Miss Dora Rankin arrived in October, 1879, to join her sister in educational work for girls, and in March, 1880, Pleasant College was opened in Nant-ziang.

In 1881 Young J. Allen had been appointed superintendent of the mission, and, under protests and offers of additional emoluments, resigned from his educational, editorial, and translation work for the government, which he had continued since the Civil War days of financial stringency, that he might give the remaining years of his life directly and undivided to the interests of the church in China. With his prestige as a senior missionary, a farsighted educationalist, a friend of the Woman's Board and its missionaries, and his passion for his church in China, Allen secured a generous response to appeals for funds for a high-grade school for the daughters of wealthy Chinese. Some one had raised the question: "Why multiply charity schools for beggars, when the souls of the rich and more intelligent might be brought to the light, thus multiplying indefinitely the power of the gospel through their efforts and influence?" A similar sentiment was expressed in Foochow when Miss Ruth Sites started the seminary there in 1893. In 1891 this Shanghai school was christened "McTyeire Home and School," in loving remembrance of Bishop McTyeire who, from its inception, had been cordially interested in all plans concerning it and had died before its completion. The school opened in March, 1892, with seven pupils, marking a new era in educational work in China—it was the first school which charged parents regular fees for the board and tuition of their daughters while in school.

By 1900, with the continued support and encouragement of Young J. Allen and under the master-builder that Laura Haygood was, McTyeire had become an institution worthy of the highest commendation. And so it has continued. No Methodist woman who came to China from the United States is more deserving of a place among that select number of missionaries whom all would agree had rendered conspicuous service of the highest quality to her church than Miss Laura Haygood. Her passing in 1900, as C. F. Reid said at the time, created "one of those great vacancies before which our missionaries must for a time stand helpless."

Never doing college work, there was no call for McTyeire to become a college or department of some university. Occupying a suburban area of nine acres (when it was secured in 1917) the school was in a position to receive the recognition and to touch the homes of the businessmen of the growing metropolis of Shanghai; and likewise it was able to influence and train girls who would be the makers of homes of business and official influence throughout China. If Methodism has colored the life of China at all, more of that dye has been poured into its womanhood through McTyeire than can be measured.

The development of day schools, boarding schools, and "colleges," with university dreams, that had characterized the work for boys and girls in both the Foochow and the Shanghai missions, was repeated in its essential characteristics in Central and North China, and eventually in West China. At the annual meeting of the Central China Mission in 1880, "it was seen fit to place Bro. Carter in charge of all our schools, with a view of increasing their number and efficiency and making them feeders to a higher school to be established for the training of advanced pupils," [11] and the next year—note the year 1881 again, as significant advances in Methodist educational work in all these missions is mentioned—"a high grade school was organized by Bro. Carter" in Kiukiang, which was "named 'Fowler University of China' as a mark of our high appreciation of Dr. Fowler, as a Secretary of the Missionary Society, as a gentleman, and as a friend." This institution opened with fifteen young men from the best families in Kiukiang in the English department, and an equal number in the Chinese. The students in the English department pay their tuition, and the amount received from this source has been used to defray the expense of the Chinese department.[12]

In 1888 Bishop Fowler appointed John C. Ferguson president of Nanking University, which had "neither land, buildings, nor even a school which might serve as a nucleus of an institution." The new president started the institution in his own home the next year with fifteen pupils, but within a couple of years the university had a large site, several buildings, and a constitution which provided for a local board of managers, a board of trustees in the United States, incorporation under a charter, and for the government of the departments. Ferguson described the first commencement, held in 1897, at which seven young men were graduated as

the goal to which eight years of constant labor had been devoted. It was made a memorable occasion by the presence of a large number of the members of our own mission and by the visits of many guests. Sermons were delivered to the graduates on Sunday by the president and by Rev. J. Jackson of Kiukiang. On Monday evening a lecture on "Educational Ideals" was delivered by the United States Consul-General, Hon. T. R. Jernigan, who came from Shanghai expressly to attend the exercises. On this day a reception was given to the local officials, at which all of the prominent mandarins of the city were present. On the following day the viceroy, Lin Kun-Yih, called at the University, and as a token of his interest in the work which had been done presented the graduates with $100 in prizes. Referring to this visit, the *North China Daily News* . . . said in an editorial notice: "This is undoubtedly the first time in the history of the new education in China when so high an official has taken an interest in the work of an institution under foreign control, and it is a most hopeful sign. It is gratifying that in this one instance, at least, the oldest viceroy in China, and now probably one of the most influential should have taken such an interest in an institution whose aim is progress." Of the seven young men, three were graduates of the College of Liberal Arts. Two of these have been retained as teachers in the college and one has become the head teacher in a newly opened government school at Tsing-Kiang. Two were graduates from the Theological School, and these are both leading pastors in our mission. Of the two graduates of the Medical School, one is our chief assistant in our Wuhu Hospital and the other is assistant surgeon to the new army corps at Woosung.[13]

The Chingkiang Institute had been opened in 1894, designed to be primarily a vocational school for the training of Christian mechanics, but E. L. Ford points out that this "did not become a permanent feature . . . doubtless due to the fundamental aim of furnishing intellectual leaders for the church, especially a well-equipped native ministry." But the experiment of omitting the Chinese classics from the curriculum, keeping the boys occupied "with studies of a more practical and edifying nature," may, missionary testimony at the time nevertheless to the contrary, have kept the school from attaining the popularity desired. Another unique feature of this school, which never became generally or permanently accepted, was the absence of a Chinese New Year vacation, replaced with Christmas, Easter, and summer vacations—transplanting American customs. Though his opinion has not yet, even after all these years, received much following, C. F. Kupfer said, "These changes must eventually come with the progressive triumph of Christianity, and to begin, we know no better time than now."

The urgent demand for native preachers, which had prompted the opening of the Theological Trainng School in Foochow in 1871, had been equally felt in the younger missions. In 1890 Nanking was building a "beautiful" theological school building with a "tower which will support a large four-faced tower clock and bell," but Peking was grieving that "not a single new candidate for the native ministry presented himself at the annual meeting." All agreed that for the successful evangelization of China, trained Chinese evangelists must be used, but in every mission the demands on the missionaries were so heavy that few, if any, were available to give their full time to such training. Hence in 1897, the fiftieth year of Methodist educational work in China, one of the missionaries was lamenting:

Much that was hoped from school work in Central China is being realized. One hope, is however, not being realized—it was hoped that they would produce a store of evangelists sufficient for the needs of our great field. Thus far they are not accomplishing it, and we need the preachers very badly. We need them to guide the very interest in the Gospel which the schools are assisting to awaken.[14]

The Female Boarding School in Kiukiang was opened January 1, 1873, by Gertrude Howe, "with seven pupils and a poor man of the literary class, as teacher." It was difficult to secure a matron who could read, but after some search, "a woman, with very small Chinese feet, and an unusually large head and lady-like manner" was secured, and she remained with the school several years without pay.

Some years later W. C. Longden expressed the opinion that "it is more satisfactory and easier to rear a Christian in China than to convert a heathen"; and some of Miss Howe's first pupils were foundlings, of whom she wrote, perhaps better than she then knew; "For the most thorough results, I look to the future of my babies." This policy was eminently justified in the case of Mary Stone and Ida Kahn, whose services to the women of China will forever keep their names among the sweetest flowers of the Methodist tree in that land. While not the first to practice western medicine among their Chinese sisters, Drs. Stone and Kahn were Miss Howe's greatest contribution to China, and when one recalls her own many years of devoted service, that is saying a great deal. Her own story of Ida Kahn is quoted by Eddy L. Ford:

> After some months one of us jokingly enquired of our language teacher whether he could not give us a girl. He replied, "My next door neighbor has a little girl two months old. This is the sixth girl. She has never had a son, and the five girls have been sent out to mothers-in-law. She says she cannot bear to send this one to a mother-in-law. I succeeded in getting her a betrothal in a good home, but when I took the cards to a fortune-teller he said that the stars clashed, the children were not born favorably, and the mother must not proceed." That day he saw the mother, who decided to risk us rather than the cruel treatment of a mother-in-law for her daughter. The family was a good one, named Kung, or, as it is pronounced in this dialect, "Kahn," direct descendants of Confucius.[15]

A girls' boarding school was opened at Chinkiang in 1883 and one in Wuhu in 1886, the accessibility of these port cities doubtless contributing to the extension of schools of this grade more rapidly in Central China than in other missions. The Chinkiang school very soon acquired a reputation that justified raising admission standards although "the parents or guardians were required to provide the girls with clothes, while the ladies claimed the right of arranging the betrothal," a practice which was not confined to this school only, and one which the times may have justified, but which, of course, has long since been universally abandoned.

The development of the educational system for boys in Peking began with resolutions of the Committee on Education at the annual meeting in 1885, which called for (1) a good school for boys in each station where a sufficient number of children from Christian homes can be assembled and a Christian teacher secured, these to become feeders to the Peking school; (2) the goal of the Peking school, which was to be named "Wiley Institute" —"in memory of our beloved Bishop I. W. Wiley"—to become a university as soon as possible; (3) to this end courses to be developed in classics, history, English, mathematics, natural science, medicine, and theology; and (4) the annexation to this school as soon as possible of "a boarding school for the children of missionaries and other foreigners residing in North China"— an aim that never materialized.

Six years later a board of trustees was formally organized in New York, with Bishop E. G. Andrews as president; S. L. Baldwin, secretary; and Chas. E. Taft, treasurer; and a resident board of managers provided—the pattern of all future university organizations. The Rev. Marcus L. Taft had raised $5,000 to purchase land, and the General Missionary Committee had appropriated $6,000 for the erection of dormitory buildings. L. W. Pilcher reported:

Large classes have been carried through a thorough elementary course in physics and chemistry; a number of the students have learned much of the science of telegraphy, and the junior class has completed a text-book in astronomy, and found much enjoyment, as well as instruction, in studying "the open face of the heavens." These studies have been taught in English; classes in the Old and New Testament Scriptures, elementary mathematics, geography, and the native classics, have been conducted in the vernacular.[16]

He also reported that feeder schools had been established at Tientsin, Tsun-hua, and Taian—"one of the most important advanced moves in our educational work during the year." Five young men were graduated in 1892, four of whom presented themselves to the Quarterly Conference asking for licenses to preach, and receiving appointments accordingly.

Mary Porter Gamewell wrote some time later:

One year from the time when Maria Brown and I sat at study by a wood fire in southern Foochow we sat in Peking before a stove in which burned a coal fire to keep out the cold of a northern winter. Then we were studying the language; now we were considering certain questions which ever since our arrival in Peking had been thrusting themselves more and more into view and could no longer be ignored.

One of the questions decided was, "Should or should not the feet of girls admitted to our schools be unbound? . . . Nowhere else in China were the feet of girls in mission schools being unbound. Some missionaries thought the movement to unbind the feet hurtful to the progress of the gospel. And we had been told that if we undertook to unbind the feet of pupils, we should never be able to establish a school for girls in China. . . . We decided to unbind the feet, and in so doing emphasize our teaching that the body is the temple of the true God and must not be profaned. Then we should leave the results with the God whom we tried to honor before a heathen people.

And then, she added, while the infant church grew, the girls' school, with its pupils with unbound feet, grew—"and it grew to be the largest girls' school in China." [17]

The sentiment against bound feet grew gratifyingly. That it had become the policy in Foochow was partly responsible for the desire for the seminary for high-class girls. Even in Kiukiang, where in the early days of the girls' school the tightening of the bandages was as much a part of the school routine as the morning teeth-brushing, and where Miss Howe never expected the girls to unbind, though she hoped their daughters would grow up with nonbound feet—even here the time came when one girl felt that she "could not be baptized with bound feet." Only after months of prayer and pleading with her parents was their consent gained. Other girls were "ashamed to go up on the platform with little feet" when preparations for Children's Day were being made. These girls won by prayer and effort the consent of their parents to free themselves from this terrible bondage.[18]

And even in remote Chungking by 1894 eight of the eleven girls in the school had natural-sized feet, and full support was required of those who did not. Mrs. Esther B. Lewis tells of one girl who had been in the school but a short time:

The father wished to sell her to some rich family as a slave, but the mother preferred her to be in school where she felt sure of her being "kindly treated." It was delightful to see her bright face when the bandages were removed and her feet were put into stockings and shoes like other girls.[19]

The Peking girls' school was opened in August, 1872, with two pupils:

The first one who came ran away again as fast as her bound feet could carry her just as soon as she saw us. She had never before seen foreigners, and the first sight she found very frightful. The child was captured and brought back, and put into the care of her aunt, who had been engaged as matron of the school to be. When the child had become reconciled to her new home her feet were unbound, she was bathed, and put into a new suit of clothes; and our school had its first pupil— Hui-Hsin, we called her—one of seven who remained.[20]

And years later one of the missionaries who frequently visited the churches outside of Peking, said: "If the Peking Boarding School never did more than to furnish wives for our native preachers, it would be abundantly worth all it ever cost."

A similar school for girls was opened in Tsun-hua in 1888, and others in the North China stations followed. The Girls' Boarding School in Chungking was opened in 1884 with twenty-eight pupils. It was closed in 1886, when the riot forced that step, and was reopened in 1894 by Mrs. Spencer Lewis with eleven boarders and nine day pupils.

While boarding schools for girls and for boys, and colleges and universities for men, were being started in every mission, the primary work was not being neglected. Probably the first Methodist kindergarten was that started in Peking by Miss Young and Mrs. George R. Davis (the former Maria Brown after the Sino-Japanese war conditions led to the "concerted wisdom of the conference" that the boarding school should be closed.

But of far more reaching effect in time and space was the development which resulted from an article published by Rev. George S. Miner of Foochow in 1892 or 1893. As a result, he reported in 1894:

I am receiving money whereby I am supporting and superintending sixteen day-schools with over 500 pupils. About forty persons have been brought into the church during the last nine months through the direct influence of these schools.[21]

And a year later,

The dear Lord is so blessing the "special gift" day schools work that instead of sixteen as last year, I now have about a hundred, with nearly 3,000 pupils. About two hundred persons are assisting me in the work. Seventy-four schools are in and near Foochow City. Where three years ago we had eight places in which to hold preaching services, we now have eighty-two. . . . At one place where we opened a school two and a half years ago, we have thirty-five members and thirty-seven probationers. If the Lord continues to bless, and the dear people to give, we will soon have this mighty city honey-combed with Christian day-schools, which will aid mightily in its salvation.[22]

Miner's dream was never realized fully, but for a quarter of a century "Special Gift Day Schools"—whatever the faults of the system that then resulted in its curtailment and practical elimination—were an important factor, not only in Foochow but in the spread and growth of the Methodist Church throughout China.

While gifts in response to this appeal were not the first "special gifts" for Methodist work in China, these appeals and the resulting schools gave the greatest stimulus to the practice which it probably ever received, a practice which, through the years to the present day, has been a necessary evil—necessary, because without such gifts much of the work would have been impossible, an evil because some of its projects should never have been undertaken; necessary because the church at home needed these personal contacts to stimulate its giving for the church work abroad, an evil because it sapped the strength and time of missionaries who could have been preaching the gospel and training with personal influence the youth in the schools; necessary because the church in China was growing faster than the local support was able to supplement the regular income of the board, an evil because too often a missionary's influence and prestige with his Chinese brethren depended upon his ability to secure funds for the work in which he or they were particularly interested.

By 1897, when the semicentennial of Methodism in China was celebrated statistics of educational work included the following: day schools 384; day-school pupils 7,381; high schools 24; colleges and institutes 6.

2. Developments in Schools

Systematization, co-ordination, and co-operation were the order throughout the Methodist educational field during the third quarter-century. In all the conferences schools had, during the earlier decades, just "growed," like Topsy. Miner's policy of establishing a day school in any village where a teacher could be employed and a group of boys enrolled, was an attempt to set a candle shining in heathen darkness, but the flickering flame never grew very bright, and was too often blown or snuffed out. E. L. Ford points out that "secondary schools were not usually established in a center until it was occupied by placing a missionary in residence," but he might have stated it conversely and said that secondary schools were usually established in every center in which missionaries, men or single women, were placed in residence. By the time the missions—I use that term instead of churches since, as Ford has pointed out, "the administrative control was still largely in the hands of the missionaries appointed as principals of the schools," although the annual conferences had "functioning committees on education" and "the better schools had organized faculties who assisted in administration"—by the time the missions had recovered from the Boxer devastation, nearly every mission station had its boys' and girls' schools which soon adopted the new government classification of higher primary, and each of these schools was being fed by from one to a score of day schools, except in the China Mission (Methodist Episcopal, South) which had then done almost nothing with primary education.

Hence the Committee on Education recommended to the Central Conference in 1903 "the appointment . . . of a Board of Education to represent Methodist schools and colleges in China." [23] But such board, if appointed, seems to have failed to function, for the same committee again eight years later repeated that recommendation, with the further proviso that "this Board shall have authority in all matters pertaining to the standardization and articulation of curricula and in the co-ordination of education with the other work of missions and in the general advancement of educational interests." [24]

Early in the 1916-20 quadrennium Frank D. Gamewell, who had already made unusually significant contributions to the growth of the church in North China and West China, was appointed general secretary for education, and during the next two quadrenniums rendered a major contribution to all China in the program of standardization of the Methodist educational work. Nevertheless, in the meantime the Central Conference in Peking, on February 14, 1920, was again calling for the organization of a national Methodist educational board to be composed of two members from each conference, elected by the conference Board of Education, and to be known as the China Educational Council of the Methodist Episcopal Church. This council would, it was hoped, seek to correlate the whole educational work of the Methodist Episcopal Church in China, in co-operation with the general secretary for education.

But locally, and in part, co-ordination and supervision were being advanced. The Foochow Conference, about 1913, set up district boards of primary education, which carried out, sometimes drastically, the belief which the West China Annual Meeting had expressed in 1896, namely, "that it is not wise to sustain day-schools unless they are carefully supervised," to which statement Manley added the comment, "and so one school was closed at the beginning and another during the year." By the use of centenary reinforcements, Yenping had a full-time conference superintendent of education, and a missionary had been added to the Foochow staff in the never-realized expectation that he would be assigned to a similar task. Like advances were being made in North and Central China, and everywhere Methodist educators were uniting with those of other denominations in Christian educational associations to systematize and coordinate all the work of Christian schools. West China carried this program to the highest degree of co-operation and efficiency attained anywhere, by the organization in 1912 of the West China Educational Union, charged with the control and supervision of all church schools from primary through collegiate, with a full-time salaried executive secretary.

Mergers were taking place in several localities because of a shortage of missionary personnel or to develop higher grade institutions. Two boarding schools, including the former "Fowler University," were merged into the William Nast College in Kiukiang in 1901. The school was incorporated on October 1, 1904, and $1,000 donated to its endowment by Mrs. Fanny Gamble of Cincinnati, but after the organization of Nanking University, college work at William Nast was discontinued in 1918.

We cannot devote the necessary space to tell of each of the Methodist schools which were making outstanding contributions to the advance of the church. Without attempting any invidious selections, a few contemporary snapshots selected at random from those schools which were active participants in the great program of Methodist education in China may give the reader an idea of what the church was doing through this means.

As illustrative of the absence of a long-sighted program, the Boys' Boarding School in Foochow became part of the Anglo-Chinese College in 1901 because of a demand for the study of English in the boarding school. It remained a part of the college until 1908, when it was reopened as a separate school. But after two or three years it disappeared by being combined with the Normal Training School.

Of the Chungking Institute, Joseph Beech wrote in 1902:

The introduction of English into the curriculum and the changed attitude of the Chinese towards Western studies have made the past year the most successful in the history of the Chungking Institute. . . . The amount of time given to Chris-

157

tian instruction is far more than would be considered proper in a school of similar grade at home. Including the regular church services every student receives at least twelve hours of religious instruction in a week.[25]

And when it comes to the teaching of English—still, as in 1883, a moot question—the Peking Girls' Boarding School in 1904-05 tried the experiment "of allowing any girl who had reached the high school grade to study English if she wished to do so and would furnish her own text-books. . . . The result is thirteen out of forty-seven in the high school are studying English and they are doing good work." [26]

No institution in China did more in the organization of a Student Volunteer Band for Christian service, or had a more successful band, than Peking University. In 1906 this band numbered 126, a larger percentage than could be found in any American colleges or theological seminaries. About half this number devoted their summer vacations to assisting pastors throughout the conference in their work.

The women came soon to realize that girls could, should, and would pay for their education. The Central Conference of 1907 adopted the report from the Committee on Women's Work which contained this paragraph:

Believing that the time has come for advance in respect to self-support in the schools of our Woman's Foreign Missionary Society, we recommend that it be made the rule that all entering our boarding schools, whether for women or girls, who are able to pay their board, be required to do so. That for those who cannot do this our goal be to require one-half the amount, or that each one pay something from the time of entrance into the school.

One of the teachers at the Lettie Mason Quine Day School in Taian in 1908 was a granddaughter of Mrs. Wang, of An-chia-chuang, thus adding another to the many contributions of that family to Methodism in Shantung.

"On receiving her appointment as Principal of the Girls' School," in Nanking in 1908, Miss Laura White "was instructed by Bishop Bashford to develop it as soon as possible into a Woman's College. Very wisely, we think, Miss White has obeyed his wish by emphasizing normal work." [27]

Mrs. Jewell wrote from Peking: "In the latter part of the spring term of 1909, a class of university boys came to Miss Baugh for Latin. It was arranged for mutual help that in the autumn an exchange of Latin from our schools should be made for mathematics from the university." [28]

Training schools for nurses were organized in 1910 in both Soochow and Foochow.

In 1912 President Bowen was appealing from Nanking University:

The famine relief work undertaken under the efficient leadership of Mr. Bailie has had a potent effect on the peace of the city. This, with the more recent developments of the colonization scheme, is bringing not a little credit upon the University. Is not this the strategic time for us to seek an agricultural department, where experiments may be carried on along all lines of modern methods and where new products suitable for the Yangtze Valley may be tested? Will it not be possible to get some of our state universities in America—for example, Wisconsin—to establish an experiment station here with us? [29]

His appeal met with enough response so that the university was able to develop a college-grade School of Agriculture, whose contributions to other schools, like Changli and the Foochow Normal, and to the betterment of rural conditions, has been strikingly conspicuous.

The first girl was graduated from the first Methodist high school— Chengtu—in 1915.

At Futsing, in 1915, a school for boys was established which, because of its co-operative basis, was unique. While initiated by the gentry of the city, and property worth $10,000 and cash amounting to $8,000 were donated by the people of the community, the property was deeded to the Methodist Episcopal Church, and all instruction in the institution was conducted under the supervision of the church. But, unfortunately, after 1927 the arrangements collapsed and the property was lost to the work of the church.

In 1916 the Laura Haygood School was converted into a normal school, thus meeting a long-felt need for the training of teachers for elementary schools and kindergartens.

The Peking Boys' Higher Primary School has the honor of being probably the first if not the only school in which the honor system was inaugurated —and it worked! Miss Felt, in 1920, "was surprised at the ready response of the pupils." "Through the charming personality of Miss Hopkins," Miss Felt continues, "and her assumption that the pupils could be entirely trusted, she accomplished much. At any time she could leave her boys in the class room with confidence that they would act as though she were present." [30]

From Guthrie High School, Hinghwa, in 1921, came a wail that is more or less typical: "For a biology class of 103 we have one microscope."

Much emphasis has been put on the educational institutions—too much, some critics have thought. But Methodism knew that it could never survive as a strong Christian church without strong Christian men and women to lead. And without schools giving the highest type of college and professional training, the Methodists—singly or in union with other churches— could never have produced such leaders. And when 1927 came, and the decades that followed, this faith and this program were justified.

3. *Unification of Higher Education*

At the diamond jubilee in Foochow, Uong Gang-Huo, a member of the Foochow Conference, and one of the most capable leaders that the Methodist Episcopal Church had produced in China, reviewed the third quarter century of that church in China. He began his paper with a phrase from the physiographers, comparing the period under review with "the period of advancement to maturity" in the life of a river, and then went on to say:

> Like a river system that begins its life as springs which soon become marshes, these in turn coming down in undeveloped tributaries—brooks, creeks, small rivers —then into a fully developed river sweeping on toward the sea, so the Methodist Church in China follows a şimilar life-history. . . . Now in the third period it has come to greatness as a wide-spreading river whose complete development is assured because effective work is well begun.
>
> This work is truly that of a river—erosion, transportation, deposit, and the bringing of life. Erosion in the wearing away of ignorance, superstition and sin. Transportation in carrying the Gospel and its application to the far places. Deposit in that it builds a better land through what it carries. And bringing of life because it spreads through the canals to vivify the land.[31]

To the historian who can think back through his own memory of those years, or who reads through the written records made by those who were the active participants, there is a very definite conviction that the major phase in this advance to maturity was that of systematization and consolidation of the educational system and the unification of higher education. No other phase of the process absorbed more constructive thought, required as many missionary years, or demanded as many American dollars as the educational work of the church. The church was showing its faith in what Bishop Lewis had once expressed:

> These facts make clear the duty and opportunity of the Methodist Episcopal Church to China, Asia, and the world's democracy. If the church can pour its life into the heart of the youth of the present day the next generation will witness a harvest time of such quality and regal proportions of democracy as to surpass the wildest dreams of the lovers of the race.[32]

Those two indomitable leaders of Northern Methodism who by their wisdom, sagacity, and spiritual life were molding the church, and both of whom had been prepared for their tasks in part by years of college administration, Bishops Bashford and Lewis, with the active help of John F. Goucher, and the recommendation of the Burton Commission, brought the colleges of the Methodist Episcopal Church into those union universities which are the fruit of the first two decades of the twentieth century.

We must recognize this development; we shall pass over most of the details. We might wish the Methodist Church could point with pride to a great Methodist college or university in each section of the country where the church is established; rather, we rejoice that Methodism can save and serve the youth of the nation through co-operation with other Christian forces in great universities with standards, staffs, and equipment second to none.

Nanking was the first center to start a thorough-going union in higher educational work and to make union and affiliation the normal development now in China. It was in 1910 that President A. J. Bowen reported the successful accomplishment of getting the union into actual operation—an organic union in which the title to all property, including that originally held by the missionary societies, is vested in the Board of Trustees. The initial agreement had been for each of the co-operating churches to provide $40,000 in endowment or lands or buildings, and the Methodist Episcopal Church transferred its valuable Nanking University property, joining with the Disciples of Christ and the Presbyterians and starting all departments of the institution. Within two or three years the Southern Methodists, and also the Baptists and Southern Presbyterians were sharing in the medical school, but this, as a part of the university, was discontinued within a few years in view of the union work at Tsinanfu and Shanghai. The department of agriculture was opened in the fall of 1914, by which time the property assets of the university amounted to $205,000 (Mex.?) including seventy-five acres of land, eleven buildings, and thirteen residences.

West China Union University may well dispute President Bowen's claim to priority. In 1906 land had been purchased and building operations were under way where Chengtu College was to be started. The first buildings were remodeled Chinese buildings. The first union work was started in 1909 in the Union Middle School opened in temporary buildings erected in the south suburb of Chengtu. In 1910 university teaching was begun in the two faculties of arts and sciences. The Methodists reported eleven students in the college in 1911. This university is

a union and a federation. Each mission represented in the union has some ten acres of land assigned upon which its missionaries and students live. This gives each mission perfect liberty with and control over its students at all times, except during hours of recitation. It also permits each denomination to direct in large measure the Christian life of its student body. In all other respects the university is a co-ordinate union, the university being under control of a Board of Governors, at the home base, appointed jointly by the several participating boards. On the field it is under the direction of the Senate, which is appointed by the several co-operating missions and by the Board of Governors.[33]

In 1914 the hospitals of the Canadian Methodist Mission, the Canadian Woman's Board, and the Methodist Episcopal Mission, located in Chengtu, became constituent parts of the West China Union University Medical School which was opened that year.

If Peking has any claim to priority in this matter of union universities, it is to the idea rather than to the fact. Discussions looking to such a union date from 1901 and 1902, but the several church organizations involved appear to have been unable to concede their own terms and accept those asked by the others. By 1917, however, Yenching University, partaking of the centralized federated type, had become the union institution so long hoped for in this national capital, located on the grounds of and adjacent to the Methodist Peking University, which had the previous year celebrated twenty-five years of service and development.

Fukien had no institutions doing full college work to become the basis for a union university. In the spring of 1915, however, an organic union, similar to that at Nanking, was launched, a president elected, a faculty organized, temporary property secured, and in February, 1916, the two upper classes of the Anglo-Chinese College in Foochow, and of similar institutions of other churches, became the student body of Fukien Union College. The following November plans were initiated to organize and incorporate the Fukien Christian University, which, it was hoped, would include the Fukien Union College, the union medical, normal, and theological schools already in operation in Foochow. But this hope was never fully nor permanently realized, and the college was the only one of these institutions which has continued in the present university.

Since this is a record of the Methodist Church in China, it is interesting to note at this point that the first president of each of these four union universities was a Methodist missionary.

In 1905 Bishop Bashford recorded in his diary: "We thought of union of the colleges for women with the colleges for men in these centers [Nanking, Foochow, Peking, Chengtu] as a possibility fifty years hence." But he lived to see the fulfillment of much of this dream long before the end of the fifty years he had anticipated. A Woman's Union College was already a going concern in Peking in 1905 when the Methodist preachers urged advanced education for women, and the Methodist women recognized that for them to join this union would be a very rational way of providing college opportunities. But a decade of remarkable and dramatic achievement passed before this union college for women became a part of the union university in 1920. In the meantime Mrs. J. W. Bashford's mother had given $3,000, of which $1,000 was to provide a perpetual scholarship for Methodist girls, though no Methodist pupils entered until 1915, and the

Woman's Foreign Missionary Society was not represented on the faculty until 1918.

Ginling College for women opened in September, 1915, with eleven girls enrolled, nine of whom were Methodists. Five mission boards, including the Woman's Foreign Missionary Society of the Methodist Episcopal Church, had united in establishing this college, which was organized under the trustees of the University of Nanking, but with a separate local board of control.

Union in medical, normal, and theological education had generally preceded that in college work, and almost without exception the Methodists co-operated in these unions; in a few cases, for a time at least, they were included as colleges of the universities, but this relationship never lasted long.

Peking University, before the union, had its medical school, which in 1906 was united with that of the North China Educational Union, and on the same evening that the union between the colleges was effected, it was proposed that the Women's Medical College—a new union venture— should be opened in connection with the Methodist Mission, to which the Educational Union at once consented, and a class was thereupon organized, and two girls graduated in February, 1914. The Anglican Mission in Foochow had opened a medical college in 1911 and the following year the Methodists began to co-operate in the work, and when the plans for the university were in the making it was hoped that this would become the medical department of the university. Nanking and Soochow were both providing medical education in connection with the hospitals at those places, both of which were transferred to the medical department of Nanking University when that was formed. But by 1923 the Committee on Medical Work was reporting to the Eastern Asia Central Conference:

The Methodists have discontinued the Medical Schools at Nanking and Foochow in view of the union work at Tsinanfu and Shanghai. We are, therefore, morally obligated to co-operate with Tsinanfu in order to secure our Christian Chinese doctors from this source. . . . We are definitely committed to the support of the Medical School of Chengtu University, to supply three physicians on their staff. This is the *only* Medical School in China in which we are now financially committed. . . . We are now giving only the *salary* of *two men* for medical education in *all China*. This is only one-third of what we gave before the Centenary. This is Union economy—because union does make for economy—but carried to meanness.[34]

In both Foochow and Nanking union in theological education for men was undertaken before the universities were launched, in those days when the movement toward union was in its vigorous infancy, and in both these institutions the Methodists joined at the first. Bishop Bashford's observation, recorded in his diary, that "seven foreigners teaching the Bible in Nanking is not a wise co-ordination of our forces" helped pave the way for the Union Bible Teacher's School for Women, which, in 1920, mentioned as the Nanking Union Theological Seminary for Women, was giving advanced work for those women who had completed the higher course in their respective conferences or the course in the local Women's Bible schools.

The Foochow Normal Training School "was opened," says G. S. Miner in 1903, "in my office with seven pupils," but it had grown so that with Methodists and Congregationalists uniting in 1913 it became the outstanding union normal school for men in the Methodist educational field. Of this school, Miao and Price, in their survey of Chinese middle schools, wrote:

The Union Normal School of Foochow is a courageous experiment in a new field. The sixty-seven students are drawn entirely from the farm. There are only two servants in the school, students doing most of the necessary work. Each student works at least six hours a week. There are three courses: general, normal, agricultural. Students work part of every day on the farm, in the garden and poultry yard, and in the carpenter shop.[35]

A union school for nurses started in Peking in 1905, which had but a short existence, the union kindergarten training school started in Foochow in 1910, and a union women's normal school in Chengtu, which received its first pupil in 1914, are three other examples of union in which Methodism generously undertook its share and shared to advantage in the results. For in such institutions as those listed in this section, Methodist missionaries and boards have realized that Methodism could have no monopoly; that such education, at least in the first half of the twentieth century, could never become a mass-production program for any one church nor therefore be operated efficiently except in union; and that in union of educational institutions there could come that strength which was necessary to compete with and to guide the non-Christian education being rapidly developed by the government through those decades. Church union might or might not be desirable; educational union did not depend upon it, and Methodism believed in educational union.

4. Educational Developments Since 1927

Education has always been the mark of Methodism wherever the church has gone. The starting of school work marked the first quarter century, its projection into middle and collegiate grades and its wide geographic extension characterized the second quarter century, union for greater efficiency and higher training marked the third quarter century. How shall we characterize the educational growth of the last twenty-five years?

Chinese control and government registration have been probably the most significant development. During the troublous days of 1927 a member of a college faculty received "a query from America about certain academic practices supposed to characterize the 'effective college.' This reply went back: 'In these days the effective college is the one that stays open.' " To stay open in 1927 and thereafter an educational institution had to register with the government and certain requirements had to be fulfilled to obtain registration. Among these requirements only a few need be mentioned here. One was that the principal or administrative head be a Chinese. Every Methodist institution complied. Leland W. Holland wrote: "Some of the Chinese principals of schools have done jobs which no missionary could possibly have achieved." Bishop John Gowdy, who had been a university president, is sure that the wisdom of the change has been fully demonstrated and that in the dealings with the government and the meeting of its requirements for reports and inspections no foreigner could have managed so successfully. And Bishop Birney wrote in *Zion's Herald* in 1929:

President Chen of Nanking University, President Lin of Fukien Christian University, President Ding of the Anglo-Chinese College, and many others in the lower schools in these six conferences are revealing the superb capacities for education and religious leadership that have been and are being developed by our Christian schools.

A certain amount of income was another registration requirement. This was not as happily met as that of administration. To reach this requirement it was often necessary to admit greater numbers of students who had not been previously "touched by Christian influences"; so it became often a question of no school at all or a school with a great preponderance of non-Christian students, and without required Christian teaching.

The removal of required Christian teaching and services was the "hardest pill to swallow" for the older and more conservative missionaries. If the introduction of English into the schools could force the withdrawl of missionary educators, it was certainly to be expected that the limitation of all religious work to "voluntary" and "extracurricular" status would do likewise. And coupled with this was the required Sun Yat-Sen memorial service on Monday mornings, which had all the aspects, if not the spirit and intent, of worship. But neither the Sanhedrin in Jerusalem, nor the anti-Christ dictators of modern Europe, nor other lawmakers in between—including the Chinese authorities of 1927-28—have been able to destroy Christian influence nor prohibit the working of the Christian spirit when men and women had known its power. It was found at William Nast, for instance, as in most Methodist schools, that religious education was not driven out of the school nor underground, that religious activities could still thrive, the goodwill of students and teachers be retained, and that all religious services and Bible classes were well attended.

And so they met the conditions of local and national authorities and kept their light shining. Nanking University completed its registration on September 20, 1928, being the first Christian educational institution recognized by the central government. It often took time to readjust curricula, replace administrators, replenish budgets and re-form paths for Christian teaching. Nanking University had done it in a year. In 1933 Ralph A. Ward, writing in *Zion's Herald* of a recent function, said: "Our hostess announced what some of us already knew: 'Lucy Wang has just accomplished the impossible. She has secured the registration of Hwa Nan College as a college for women under the Chinese Government' " adding parenthetically, "Most of the other colleges for women had sought or been forced to accept union with similar colleges for men." The next year Hwa Nan achieved another success when, on September 21, the Board of Regents of the State of New York granted an absolute charter to Hwa Nan College "the only woman's college in China to receive this independent recognition."

Few—only a very few—new schools were added to the roster after 1927. Some changed their status. Many—especially primary schools—were discontinued. Mergers of higher primary or junior middle schools were frequent. Coeducation commenced in all grades above the primary, and in the primary it had existed before. The increasing need for Bible schools for men and for women was stressed. The Christian character of the schools was upheld. Wrote one principal:

In our own middle schools, and in many others there has been a steady increase in Christian character since its lowest point in 1928. Probably now they are equal to 1926 and superior, in that they are more open to non-Christian influences and are Christian in character in spite of that fact.[36]

The women put their Bible training schools, "first in strategy," according to Mary Isham, who continues:

The necessity of separate schools for women was at once a burden and an opportunity to missionaries. . . . Until recent years a large proportion of the women taught were wives of the pastors, betrothed in childhood, bound-footed and illiterate, many of them still heathen when they entered the schools. . . . Some of the smaller schools gave way to central ones, better equipped and taught. The first, in Foochow, is now the Bible Seminary, and along with Knowles in Kiukiang and Hitt in Nanking (both established in 1893), Thompson in Changli, and DeWitt in Tzechow, offers six years in training and requires Middle or High School passes for entrance. . . . Taian and Peking Schools were opened mainly for the wives of pastors.[37]

The Great Wall Bible School was established by the Kalgan Mission, the only Bible School or Seminary in that area, to meet the need for evangelists—men and women—"the hope of the mission and the whole church in China."

Coeducation was frequently a result of financial needs, sometimes the result or the basis of mergers. On Bingtang Island, where "the cut in appropriation forced a coeducational plan, . . . the results are so good that the teachers plan to continue such classes even in the hoped-for day when Methodist missionary giving strikes the up-grade." [38] But, as was to be expected, coeducation was not universally approved, and probably never will be. One missionary—E. Pearce Hayes—described this situation:

It has worked well on the whole, although there is a China-wide questioning of the value of coeducation from the junior high up; there is a group making itself very vocal concerning the evils of coeducation; just how generally true are their charges, I do not know.

When, in 1924, women were admitted to West China Union University as coeds, Spencer Lewis noted that

it was thought advisable to chaperone the young women who attended the university, so for somewhat over a year the faculty wives arranged to sit in the classes where young women were registered. Soon it was apparent that both the men and women had accepted the new order of things with dignity, so this supervision was discontinued. [39]

The Yenching Women's College was combined with the men's university in 1926, and Fukien Christian University inaugurated coeducation in 1932. In 1928 the Women's Council co-operating, women students were admitted to Soochow University, and by 1935 fifteen women were enrolled in the law department located in Shanghai. In 1945 the theological seminary and the Bible Women's Training School in Foochow were merged for the training of both men and women for evangelistic work.

Mergers were sometimes the result of a shortage of funds, sometimes of government pressure, sometimes of evacuation and migration. The Foochow Conference, for instance, tried to federate its ten junior middle schools at Yuan-kang in 1944, but Bishop Lacy observed that the local boards of Kutien and Mintsing, which had not been "occupied," could not see why they should move, especially since schools of other denominations remained in those districts.

A change of status occurred, for example, when the Union Normal School at Foochow applied for registration with the government in 1928 and was required to change its name to the Union High School and later to drop its normal work which had been of exceptionally high quality. As a fine experiment in vocational training for rural life, the move made necessary by military invasion—which ultimately destroyed its buildings in Foochow—was perhaps not an unmixed blessing. Of this move, its principal, K. P. Lin wrote:

> On coming to our new destination new difficulties loomed large. At first we were not only unwelcome to the local authorities, but were flatly told to move out of their district. The local magistrate, looking upon us as a group of desperate refugee students, feared we might raise the level of consumption.
>
> .   .   .   .
>
> There are flowers and hedges everywhere. Hillocks have been leveled, rough lands cleared, dug up, and planted to vegetables and grains. Even the once inhospitable magistrate has marvelled at our rapid development, as he has observed it with admiration.
>
> .   .   .   .
>
> When we first came to Tsianglo there was not so much as a place to lay our heads, not one building, nothing but a rough wilderness of old graves and footprints of wild animals. Now we have thirteen buildings with bamboo or thatched roofs, folding slats for windows, wooden sockets for hinges, bamboo pegs for nails. Visitors are struck with the beauty of the location and campus, and impressed by the creative ability of the students. One person wished to compare our campus to the Peach Blossom Fountain of Tsing Dynasty, while another hailed us as "A colony of heaven!" [40]

The financial provisions for Nanking Theological Seminary must be briefly mentioned, since, as Ralph Diffendorfer has pointed out, they are "of special interest to Methodists because of the large bequest (the Wendel-Swope Fund) entrusted to the Division of Foreign Missions for administration on behalf of the Seminary." Property from this estate was bequeathed to the Board of Foreign Missions of the Methodist Episcopal Church as trustees for the Nanking Theological Seminary, and in 1937 the board of founders of the Nanking Theological Seminary was formally organized.

> The organization of the Board of Founders does not relieve the Board of Foreign Missions of its responsibility as the legal trustee of the Wendel-Swope Funds. . . . The Board of Founders, after studying the needs of the Seminary as presented by the Board of Managers in Nanking, makes request annually to the Board of Foreign Missions for grants from the Wendel-Swope Fund, for current expenditures and for property and permanent improvements. The recommendations will by legal necessity be reviewed by the Board of Foreign Missions serving as the Trustee.[41]

The Wuhu Hospital is one of the very few institutions to record a new school started during this period—a school of nursing for men opened in

1925. With Mr. Ren, a graduate of the Peking Union Medical College Training School, in charge, the national association was willing to register this as a nurses' training school, and said that "it will be the first school registered in China with a Chinese nurse in charge."

5. *Religious, Membership, and Rural Education*

In Occupied China the Methodist Church—as did others—confined its program largely to evangelism. This had become necessary because of inability to carry on its institutional work. Can we not rather say that this it was now able to do because it was freed from the absorbing effort to maintain its institutional agencies? Educational institutions of middle and higher grade had migrated to Free China, and hospitals, when they had not been bombed, were generally occupied by the Japanese. The reactions following the externally induced anti-Christian propaganda of 1927-28 had resulted in many parts of the country in a new hunger for the gospel message on the part of the common people as early as 1929. That hunger had persisted, and in 1937 the bishops were saying to the Central Conference that the church was then facing the greatest opportunity and challenge for preaching the gospel which it had had in this generation, but that "our evangelistic personnel, both national and foreign, has been decreased to a heart-breaking extent," a situation due in part to "the continued financial depression in the United States during the past quadrennium." [42] The outbreak of the war had not smothered this craving, for in their new needs the people longed for some new source of help. The effect of Japanese attacks on Hawaii, the Philippines, and Malaysia, were scarcely apparent when a missionary wrote of the evangelistic work in North China:

This work has no taint of nationalism, does not call for any investment in property or the organizing of schools. It comes the nearest, with one exception, to the *koinonia* of the New Testament times of anything I can think of. In it Japanese Christians are free to join, and they are listened to with respect. Christianity which is above national boundaries in its composition is the least shaken by present changes. . . . The church is carrying on under the changed conditions with adaptability and courage. Bishop Kaung calls this the "Golden Age" of opportunity for the Church, the hour for which she was called into being, to dispel misunderstandings about Christ and the Cross and Salvation and World Brotherhood, an unexampled opportunity for witnessing and fellowship and for demonstrating good will. [43]

But still, with all the effects of the global war, the preachers of Wesley's followers found a warming response in hearts throughout both Free and Occupied China.

And so religious education, which the church had been stressing for a decade, became a most important feature of the Methodist program. Mrs. Elizabeth F. Brewster called it "the great task of the church" in 1927, when she wrote of the program in the Hinghwa Conference, and in 1930 the bishops reported "that the Methodist Episcopal Church is in the lead of other bodies in religious education," and pertinently asked:

But what is meant by this intended praise? Is it that we are leading in organization, in methods, in curricula and theory? . . . Or does it mean that we, through all these, lead in the skill of bringing the youth of our churches and schools into a vital and redeeming relation to Jesus Christ which sets free their own capacities for fellowship with Him, high character through Him, practical service in the building of His Kingdom? [44]

Seven years later they answered this question in these words:

The Methodist Episcopal Church in China has been peculiarly fortunate in the number and quality of its trained leaders who have been determined to remove the stigma that rested upon the early efforts of Religious Education leaders, and to develop methods and curricula that would meet the needs of every day life and enable the people to realize the terrible sinfulness of sin, that they might turn from their evil ways and seek intelligently a new life in Christ. . . . Since 1928 the Methodist Episcopal Church in China has had an organization called the All-China Committee of Religious Education. This committee conceives of the church as the Central Teaching Agency in the field of religion and believes that in order to develop the highest type of intelligent, spiritually-minded Christians, it is necessary to conserve and apply educational method in all the phases of the life of the church.[45]

This development had been largely furthered in 1934 by the visit to China of the Revs. Jesse L. Corley and H. K. King. Corley, of the Southern California-Arizona Conference, a well-known specialist in religious education in the United States, had come to China under the auspices of the National Christian Council; and King, assistant secretary of the Board of Missions of the Methodist Episcopal Church, South, had been assigned to develop and carry out a definite plan of religious education for the Chinese church; and his mantle was taken up by the Rev. Z. S. Zia, trained and able to carry on with success. Methodists these men were, and the Methodist Church continues to feel the results of their work; but their influence in the whole field of religious education has extended far beyond the bounds of the Methodist Church.

Religious education embraced a threefold program: youth, adult, and rural education. Roxy Lefforge and S. S. Ding, of the Foochow Conference, had been appointed national secretaries for religious education in the church in 1934. Writing in the *China Christian Advocate* in August, 1937, on "Present Trends in Christian Work," Miss Lefforge drew this sketch which shows how the church was educating its youth:

Today many churches are sponsoring Children's Clubs. In a rural parish in the Mintsing District, we were invited by a group of 4H Club boys and girls to share in a worship program and then to contribute to their fund for buying low chairs and tables for their club room in the home of one of the church members. These children have complete charge of their activities with a very alert, sympathetic pastor as advisor, and they are a positive Christian influence in the community.

In other places, where primary day schools are being closed, either because of shortage of funds or to avoid competition with flourishing government day schools, a week-day program of religious education is caring for the Christian nurture of the children. Thus tension between the government and the church is eliminated and a specifically constructed church-centered program of religious education under competent leadership is being initiated. Although this is a comparatively new venture, already happy results are reported from a few centers in the Central China and Foochow Conferences. Closely connected with this week-day program are the Children's Centers, where not only the children are taught and given wholesome recreation, but the older sisters and mothers of these children receive instruction in home-making and parent education. South Gate Methodist Episcopal Church in Tientsin is doing very fine work in this line.

Such a program had been preceded, even as early as 1923, by an action of the Central Conference which appears to have been a dress rehearsal for the organization set up by Methodism when reuniting in Kansas City sixteen years later:

In order to secure the closest co-operation and co-ordination in the work of the youth of Methodism in China, the Epworth League and the Sunday School Committees recommended the organization of one advisory council to direct and promote the work of both. Conceding that the Epworth League meeting and the Sunday School class meet distinctive needs, it was nevertheless maintained that the two organizations might promote one program of expressional activities, such as general and personal evangelism, social service and recreation.[46]

Mountain and seashore have offered attractions for youth conferences for a good many years. The first in the China Conference was held on the island of Pootoo in August, 1933. The following summarization comes from the Rev. M. O. Williams, Jr.:

There were Bible study classes and discussions, vesper services, dramatics and stunts, beautiful morning watch periods by the ocean, and much fun and fellowship, especially when all went swimming in the surf—a new experience to most of the Chinese. . . . These conferences embraced *all* the youth of the church, college students, high-school students, young working people. Efforts were made to bring these groups together, demonstrating the real unity of the Christian church. Young people had a significant part in the planning and in the conducting of the conference, although the leadership was predominantly adult.

.   .   .   .

These conferences have fairly uniformly emphasized three phases of Christian living: personal religious living, social service and reconstruction, and the techniques of youth work and of service projects. . . . The conferences were centers of demonstration in Christian living and in methods for youth groups. They sought to present new experiences, for instance, having factory workers come and describe the conditions of their life and work, that would open new areas of thought and feeling to the young people. They have had experts in adult education, rural reconstruction and public health meet with them to plan what youth could do in these areas. Each conference has reached high points in private morning devotions, vesper services, small prayer groups. The climax of each conference has been a consecration service in which decisions are made and lives rededicated to the Master who had become more real through the days of fellowship in the conference.

In July, 1941, with tension mounting in the Far East, with missionaries called home from Japan, Korea, and Occupied China, with travel difficulties extreme, and surf-beaten Pootoo outside the Japanese patrol lines, 110 young people gathered at McTyeire School. At the close of this conference, under these conditions, the conference leaders felt, as reported by Williams, "that we came closer to having our message go home than we have ever done before."

The adult education program has been conducted largely through laymen's institutes. Some conferences sponsored "consistent and consecutive parent education classes for both present day and future parents and enlightening and enriching the Christian families of the church and actually serving as light to non-Christian neighbors." Thus has the spiritual life of the church been deepened; lay leadership has been the objective of the laymen's institutes, for thus can the Christianity of the church be intensified and extended, within the church and to those outside. "In the past in many instances," said Mary Sing-Gieu Carleton in a letter, "the members would have liked to have helped but they did not know how and there was then no provision made for teaching them."

These institutes brought together groups of men and women for periods of from four days to a month for Bible study, for instruction in methods, and for inspiration as pastor's helpers in every phase of church life, a program absolutely essential to help the church become a permanent part of Chinese society. From these schools came many local leaders and volunteers for Christian service. Bishop Lacy calls it "training by doing," and says:

The religious education approach to religion as distinct from the old type of evangelism is so much a matter of course now that it almost escapes notice. . . . There has begun to develop a variety of expressions of Christian activity within the church framework. We now have our young people's groups, choirs, gospel teams, community service groups, laymen's groups, women's missionary societies. This is an expression life in churches.

In 1936 Miss Lefforge sensed the waking of the church "to the fact that a great percentage of its membership lives in a distinctly rural environment." In the years following 1937 this percentage increased as factory employees from metropolitan Shanghai became co-operative workers in the valleys of Szechuen, as students from Foochow became residents in the center of the Lutu farm lands, as well-to-do-business men of Nanchang and Tientsin became refugees in their ancestral villages along the mountain roads of southern Kiangsi and western Shansi.

It was well, therefore, that rural education programs had been undertaken in several conferences and encouraged by the Central Conference before migrations and refugees came in to the current vocabulary. Facing the problem of a dearth of rural-minded Christian leaders, the Foochow Conference, in 1936, requested that all theological schools (men's and women's) rearrange their curricula to emphasize rural needs and the ways and means of meeting them. A rural improvement team was set up to work with the local pastor, district superintendent, and district missionaries (men and women) in the five rural experiment centers designated for the Foochow Conference.

North China attacked the situation in the rural churches with a program of educational evangelism, including requirements for a community-serving church, and training curricula for service in the local church by its whole constituency. Miss Lefforge described one program in the *China Christian Advocate* of November, 1936:

Kiangsi . . . decided upon five realizable aims as basic for their rural church program: (1) Winning the entire family to Christ and Christianizing each home; (2) Christianizing the entire village; (3) Developing a literate church membership with at least ability to read the Bible; (4) Developing a spiritually-minded, intelligent church membership; and (5) Planning for each church member to participate actively in the life of the church and community.

The Sunkiang District of the China Conference had inaugurated a short term Bible school, which included courses in Bible, storytelling, health, food, and gardening, and providing fellowship first and foremost with two music periods, one for devotional music in the morning and one for church services in the afternoon, and demonstrating daily the preparation of children's food as eleven babies and five little fellows under six were fed every morning at recess. (See Appendix A, item 12.) The other conferences were getting under the problem with more or less similar programs.

Results? Note a report by Frederick Bankhardt from the rural Church Center at Hsiashuenkeng in the Yenping Conference, which is typical of many:

> Church attendance in 1935 was 25, for 1939 the average was 105. In 1935 there was not a single voluntary worker in the church to assist the pastor, this year he reported ten. Again, in 1935 there were but three Christian families in the church, i.e., families in whom every member was a member of the church, this year there are 21 such families. Whereas in 1935 there were but 35 who were able to read there are now 115. Those who learn to read in turn teach others who cannot read. During the same time the membership has grown from 65 to 190. The work of supporting the church financially was not overlooked. In 1935 only $24 were given for the support of the pastor whereas this year $78 were given. The total giving for all causes in 1935 was $62, but this year it rose to $281.

Summarizing for the Methodist Episcopal conferences, the bishops said:

> The National Committee is also paying special attention to the necessary contribution of the rural church in bringing to the rural community the sort of abundant life of which Jesus spoke. . . . Several preachers resolved to return home and combine their spiritual ministry with one which recognizes that the whole of life is the concern of the church. . . . Thus, for the life of the whole church, is Religious Education coming down out of the realms of theory to the very practical business of functioning in the every day lives of the people for whom our church is responsible. Its leaders are deeply spiritual, clear-minded, undaunted men and women, many of them of the younger group, who believe with all their hearts that nothing short of a complete dedication of themselves to the task will bring permanent results.[47]

Rural institutes and "folk-schools," of course, had their place—so far, much the major place—in producing such results. But Ginling College, after it moved to Chengtu, saw an opportunity for a continuing service in this field, and the Jenshow rural service station was established with two objectives: "(1) To give the college girls experience in rural work and through research gather materials which will make possible curricular training based on the real needs of the people; (2) To provide in the future a two year short course in rural work for high school graduates."[48] Miss Irma Highbaugh, who had given much time and thought to the rural problem in North China, and who had been invited to join the staff of Ginling College to help in this work, commented: "One may say that our center is in the town of Jenshow. Actually the center of our work is in the rural homes."

Though perhaps wrongly included in this section on religious education, the experimental farm and horticultural station at Peitaiho, which has been called "a unique missionary service," is contemporaneous with this emphasis on religious education and is helping to solve these rural problems as it has improved plant varieties, recommended reforestation, and tried to salvage the soil and the life of the farmer. The work of C. R. Kellogg and his successors at Fukien Christian University, through their efforts to improve silkworm strains, better crop yields, and many other contributions to the agricultural betterment of the community, also deserves mention in Methodism's influence in rural China.

This rural problem, like the problem of self-support—on which it may have a bearing—will continue into Methodism's second century before either will have been satisfactorily solved. The two are closely, and to a large degree, connected, and China will still be an agricultural country when Methodism has been there two hundred years. Even though Shanghai and Tientsin and many smaller industrial and mercantile cities, Soochow, Chengtu, Peiping, and other student centers will require their degreed pastors to meet the problems of the city churches, "the great majority of men and women who undertake to spread the Gospel of Christ must have an understanding of rural life and an insight into the needs of the rural population." [49]

And so the church is becoming increasingly conscious of the need to strike a balance between adequate preparation for the ministry, particularly the rural ministry, and the ability of country congregations to become self-supporting. Institutes will help, but more and more the church is recognizing and must recognize that its schools for ministerial training and the women's Bible training schools must be preparing, as is Ginling College, to provide church workers such as China needs.

Returning to China for a visit after an absence of seven years, A. J. Bowen recognized in 1937 what the years since have continued to emphasize: "More and more the missionary and the Christian Church is being relieved of former tasks and set free for the main task of preaching the Gospel and nurturing men and women and boys and girls in the Christian Faith." [50]

A century of much preaching has produced in China the church in which that is, and in which it must continue to be, its main task; but it will never fulfill its destiny towards making China a Christian nation until it trains its leaders and teaches its youth the truths of science and culture and religion "whereby the nations live."

VIII
THEY HEAL

Empower the hands and hearts and wills
Of friends in lands afar,
Who battle with the body's ills,
And wage Thy holy war.

Where'er they heal the maimed and blind,
Let love of Christ attend:
Proclaim the good Physician's mind,
 And prove the Saviour friend.

1. *Medical Work During the First Fifty Years*

BOTH BRANCHES OF AMERICAN METHODISM HAD, WITH THE OPENING OF
their missions, provided for medical work—of a sort. Both White and
Taylor had a medical education, and both were ministering to the sick and
wounded long before they mastered the language (which has also been
true of every medical missionary who has come to China since). But a six-
months' supply of medicines, the burning passion to preach the gospel, and
the pressing demands of other duties, very largely limited any battling with
the body's ills during the early years of Methodist penetration. And so
the first quarter century of Methodist work had ended without formal and
organized medical work having been undertaken by either branch of the
church, and the growth of this field of service was distressingly slow during
the second quarter century.

To the women of the church belongs the credit for really beginning
medical work as a distinct and definite part of the development of the
church. Dr. Lucinda Combs was sent by the Woman's Foreign Missionary
Society to Peking in 1873, the first woman medical missionary to China
under any mission board. Within a very few years this work had attracted
enough attention that when Lady Li, wife of Viceroy Li Hung-Chang, was
taken ill, Dr. Leonora Howard (who had come in the meantime to join
Dr. Combs) was sent for. A steam launch was sent up river from Tientsin
to hasten her journey from Peking, and "every attention paid her." During
the month, more or less, that Dr. Howard remained with Lady Li, her
personality and her professional ability made so favorable an impression
that not only had she obtained entree to the homes of well-to-do and
official women in Tientsin, but Viceroy Li turned over for her use as a
woman's dispensary a temple which he had built in memory of his predeces-

sor. H. H. Lowry wrote from Peking to the secretaries of the Woman's Foreign Missionary Society that "Dr. Howard's attendance on the Viceroy's wife has made an opening such as has never occurred before in China, and, if lost, may never occur again. The homes of many of the best and most influential families of the city are open to the visits of your physician." [1] The women promptly made provision to take advantage of the opportunity. John F. Goucher, of Baltimore, whose first gift to China seems to have been $4,000 for a theological department of the Anglo-Chinese College in Foochow, and whose subsequent contributions were too numerous and too generous to chronicle, now donated $5,000 for the erection of the Isabella Fisher Hospital for women in Tientsin, which was formally opened October 15, 1881 after an official inspection by Bishop Bowman.

Another significant providence in Dr. Howard's work for Christ is narrated in the reports of the Woman's Foreign Missionary Society, in connection with a very favorable treaty which the United States secured with China through the new American minister at the court of Peking. James B. Angell, the minister, had come to Peking from the presidency of the University of Michigan, where Dr. Howard had graduated, and her diploma bore his signature. Hence when Lady Li asked Dr. Howard if Angell was "a good man," her answer can be readily imagined. Lady Li responded, "If you say he is good, he must be good." All of which disposed Viceroy Li "to listen with confidence and kindness to the words of President Angell, and so the Gospel of the Prince of Peace promotes peace." [2]

The year following Dr. Combs's arrival in Peking witnessed the arrival of Dr. Signoury Trask to open medical work for women in Foochow, and the Woman's Foreign Missionary Society report for 1880-81 contains the brief but significant sentence: "In Foochow, under the auspices of our Society, was erected the first medical hospital for women in China." The emphasis must here be on the word "erected" since Dr. Combs had, in November, 1875, *opened* in Peking the first hospital for women and children in all China, and the hospital in Foochow was not opened until April 18, 1877. In the report for 1882 appears this interesting and cryptic sentence: "The medical work in Foochow is our chief glory."

The next year "the most remarkable thing in all Chinese history"—to use the words of the Women's Foreign Missionary Society report—was an appeal from Foochow to provide medical training in the United States for Hu King-Eng, daughter of Hu Yong-Mi, and hence a third-generation Methodist, who had been for seven years the first medical student in China, studying under Dr. Trask. "Measures are on foot," the annual report stated, "by which, through private beneficence" she might be sent "to remain, if necessary, ten years that she may go back qualified to lift the womanhood of China to a higher plane, and then to superintend our medical work." On February 23, 1894, the Woolston Memorial Hospital in Foochow City, with Dr. Luella Masters in charge, had been dedicated as a "Hospital for the Sick and a Place of Worship for Almighty God." The following year Dr. Hu King-Eng returned from study at Ohio Wesleyan University and with a degree from Woman's Medical College in Philadelphia—the second Chinese woman to become a doctor of Occidental medicine, and the first of that noble quartette of Chinese Methodist women to make medical history in China, not only as outstanding Methodists but as outstanding doctors and outstanding women: Hu King-Eng, Mary Stone, Ida Kahn, and Li Bi-Cu. At Woolston Memorial, for thirty-two years, Dr. Hu brought physical and spiritual help and life to women and children until the building was wrecked during the anti-Christian activities of January, 1927, and the one who had saved the lives of so many was compelled to flee for her own life to Malaysia, where, a refugee, her earthly career ended in 1929.

Walter R. Lambuth, first of many second-generation missionaries who have helped to make this history, was born in Shanghai, the son of the Rev. and Mrs. J. W. Lambuth, and opened the formal medical work of the Southern Methodist Mission on December 8, 1877, making three short visits into the country districts, and treating eleven male and eleven female patients during that month. In 1882 this work was centralized in Soochow, patients being seen in the home of Dr. Lambuth. A dispensary was fitted up in the yard in January, 1883, and a hospital formally opened on November 8 of that year. Dr. Mildred Phillips reached China in November, 1884, but, owing to the difficulty of procuring land suitable for the erection of the buildings, the women's hospital was not opened until 1887, after which, adjacent to the men's hospital and "with two large doors on the street, one for men, one for women and children," the two hospitals were operated as one. By the time Dr. Phillips was on the ground, health conditions in Dr. Lambuth's family made it impossible for him to remain in Soochow, and he resigned, went north, took work with the Methodist Episcopal Mission in Peking and started the medical work of that church in that city. Here was a man who not only pioneered medical work for his own church in China but who served his sister church in like manner, who later helped to open work for Southern Methodists in Japan—as Dr. Maclay had done for his church—and still later, as missionary secretary and then as bishop, in a career that covered the world, was as great a statesman and inspiration as his church has given to China and as his church has produced in China for its world-wide field.

Following these early beginnings, hospitals had been started in each Methodist field. Dr. Edgerton Hart, another second-generation missionary, wrote of the work in Wuhu in 1896: "Suffice it to say that we have treated patients of all classes and conditions of men and women from the double-dragoned, red-buttoned, peacock-feathered Taotai, to the dirtiest, buggiest, tattered, opium-besotten beggar that walks the streets of Wuhu." [3] And similar statements could have been made of the hospital work in Peking, Chungking, Nanking, and Kutien in Fukien, and of the active dispensary work being conducted in Kiukiang and Tsungwha, all of which were commenced prior to 1897; and Dr. Ellen Terry, called on a four-day medical trip into Mongolia, was asking herself the question, "When shall the Methodist Episcopal Church raise the standard there?" Also, although there had been a medical school in connection with the Soochow Hospital since 1884 the call was being sent across the ocean from Central China: "We should have a medical school in Nanking. We cannot prepare physicians too soon. Young men are willing to pay their own way to get a medical education." [4]

2. *The Next Twenty-Five Years*

Read through the reports from missionaries written between 1897 and 1923, or read the minutes of Central, Annual, and Women's Conferences, and you will not find advances in medical work comparable to the great development that took place in the educational work in those years. As union in education was a motif of mission work, union in medical education, as already described, was inevitable.

Union, organic or co-operative, between hospitals conducted by the men and women doctors in the same station had occurred, such as that made in Soochow in 1887. But few of the Methodist hospitals were located in cities like Foochow or Tientsin or Chungking where there were hospitals built and operated by missionaries of other churches, and the move for union among such hospital authorities had hardly begun to glow. Where there was warmth to the idea, it may have been an afterthought of, and a need resulting in, the union medical schools, for how successful can a medical school be without the clinical facilities of a hospital? So Dr. J. E. Gossard was expressing it in 1919, seven years after the Foochow union Medical School had been organized: "The missions representing the three churches working in Foochow have before them a plan for establishing a Union General Hospital. One aim of this institution will be to furnish clinical facilities to the Medical College." [5] If union in hospital work could be effected, it ought to have been possible in Foochow under the conditions of which Dr. Ellen M. Lyon had written her society in 1909:

In the walled city of Foochow . . . are four hospitals, including our own, that take in women. The American Board is about to build a fine $15,000 hospital, well equipped, and in it will be a women's ward. The majority of the mission feel that our work should be concentrated, and only one hospital, and that in the city." [6]

But that was in 1909. A plan was before the Missions in 1919, but it took another decade to consummate it.

But if we turn back to 1915 we find the Southern Methodists joining their hospital at Huchow, which had been established in 1912, with that of the Northern Baptists. And with "a gift of $20,000 from the China Medical Board, and with additional funds to be supplied by the co-operating mission boards, a great medical plant at no distant day" was predicted. But while the couple lived together for more than a decade, financial conditions in the Baptist board made it necessary in the later twenties for it to withdraw from this union and most of its other work in Huchow.

A score of new hospitals and a half-dozen dispensaries were opened during the first part of the twentieth century, seven being started by the Women's Foreign Missionary Society, and one, that at Taian, being the only one specifically a men's hospital. Increase in staff and equipment hardly kept pace with increase in the number of institutions, even with the impetus of the centenary, for the ideal of at least two missionary doctors and a graduate nurse on the staff of every hospital was never realized. But let us not be misled by statistics, though there is a place for them. The outreach of the Lucie F. Harrison Hospital at Futsing, as an example of most of these institutions, and the service rendered there by Dr. Li Bi-Cu far exceed the pen-and-ink figures of bed capacity, patient days, and Caesarean operations. Here we pause to present Dr. Li, daughter of one of the pioneer preachers in the Hinghwa field, one of that quartette of Methodist women doctors already named, and goddess of mercy to hundreds of mothers and their babies.

The hospital at Peking, which in a new building had been dedicated in 1903 as the Hopkins Memorial Hospital in memory of Dr. N. S. Hopkins' brother John L., made a unique and significant contribution to the health services in China. Dr. Hopkins had made a beginning toward meeting the tremendous need for ophthalmological work for the Chinese, and in 1914 Dr. D. V. Smith was added to the hospital staff and gave fourteen years to this work. Through its manufacturing department it contributed to optical needs throughout the country, and its optical clinics brought patients from Korea, Manchuria, and many parts of China; but, as Dr. N. S. Hopkins said: "No less a contribution to Medical Service was made in the co-operative nature of the work, that enlisted the doctors and the employees in harmonious service to carry it on." [7] In 1916 Dr. W. B. Prentice was appointed to the hospital to conduct a dental school and dental clinics, and during the next ten years qualified men were trained who were able to carry the work on until the war interrupted, and who doubtless furnished the inspiration, if not the nucleus, for the school of dentistry started at Chengtu as a part of West China Union University.

In no aspect of the medical work was more advance made during the first part of the twentieth century than in that of competent nursing. Nearly every hospital had trained nurses, men or women, trained by the apprentice method reminiscent of Paul Revere's time. The establishment of certain schools of nursing has already been mentioned in a previous chapter. The organization of the Nurses' Association of China, which early secured Miss Cora Simpson, a Methodist nurse, as its executive secretary, did more than anything else to improve the quality of nursing education and set standards for nursing service in the hospitals. See what she thought of the situation in Methodist hospitals, as she reported her work to the Eastern Asia Central Conference in 1923:

The Methodist nurses have had a very important part in building up the nurses' work in China. I had the privilege of the early starting of the Association with Dr. Cousland and the school of which I was the Superintendent of Nurses, the Florence Nightingale School of Nursing and Midwifery of the Magaw Memorial Hospital . . . was the first one to reach the standard set by the Association and heads the list of registered schools in China. . . . Nine of the eleven Woman's Foreign Missionary Society hospitals have registered schools of nursing, and the Futsing School will be registered as soon as the new hospital is completed. Only three of the thirteen General Board hospitals have yet met the conditions necessary but two will be able to enter soon. The Woman's Foreign Missionary Schools are only for women nurses. One of the General Board is for men nurses only, and two are co-educational. The W. F. M. S. hospitals need some more foreign nurses but the General Board hospitals need them desperately. . . . The care of the sick in our hospitals is not yet a credit to our great Methodist Church, and in fact in some cases is almost a disgrace.[8]

A situation, significant in what it foreshadowed, was that in the hospitals in Taian in 1916. Because of political conditions the women's hospital was not opened after the New Year's season, and the men's hospital was closed in June. Nora M. Dillenbeck reported:

However, soon after closing the latter, the Chinese members of the church offered to take charge of the work and arrangements were made whereby with Dr. Chia as the physician, the work was carried on. The mission allowed them to use certain buildings and some apparatus while the Chinese pay for medicines and all running expenses.[9]

This story would hardly be complete without some reference to the medical work undertaken in China by the Rockefeller Foundation. Although not a Methodist institution and therefore, perhaps, outside the pale of these pages, its importance to the medical work of the Methodist and all churches is sufficient to allot a paragraph to it. The foundation undertook to co-operate with the China Medical Board "for the more intelligent conservation of the great 'what-is' as a basis for the 'greater-to-be,'" and the original plan called for the establishment of two adequately equipped modern medical schools, to be founded and financed by the Rockefeller Foundation, one to be located in Shanghai, where the work was to be done in English, and the other in Tsinanfu, where all work was to be done in Chinese, but the magnificent hospital and medical school erected in 1920 by this foundation was placed in Peking instead of either of the locations named. The effect of this project on Methodist and union medical schools has already been mentioned in connection with the schools in Foochow, Nanking, and Peking—rightly they yielded to the better preparation that a better equipped school and hospital could give the doctors whom they needed.

Has the peak of Methodist medical work in China been reached with the 38 hospitals and dispensaries, 98 doctors, 111 nurses, and 16,103 inpatients and 147,731 outpatients reported in 1923? Few of the hospitals were self-supporting and the amount of human suffering was scarcely being touched. The need of hospitals to secure entree for the church was about gone, though they will always be points through which men and women are brought into the church. Will the American church much longer finance these hospitals? Will the years that lie beyond 1923 see enough support from the local constituency and furnish enough qualified doctors and nurses to man these institutions as was done for a time at Taian-fu? But these are questions, not history. Perhaps the future will give the answer.

3. Two Hospitals Since 1923

The next twenty-five years saw few new hospitals and all too little increase of staffs and equipment. The failure to start new institutions did not indicate that the Methodist Church was failing to grow in China; rather was it an evidence of how well the church had laid its foundations in previous years. In 1937 the bishops summarized the medical work of the church in a few comprehensive sentences which noted an increase of hospital work and a steady growth in influence, due in part to a greater confidence on the part of the people, increased specialization on the part of the staffs, and some improvement in equipment. They might have added that most of their support was then coming from local sources. But then came the war, and every Methodist hospital in territory that was occupied was either bombed, occupied by the invaders, or used as a civilian imprisonment center. Bishop Ward, when first interned by the Japanese, was confined on the property of the Wuhu Hospital; American and British missionaries, including Miss Alice Wilcox of the Methodist Church, were interned in the Pierce Memorial Hospital when the Japanese occupied Foochow the second time, in 1944.

The Pierce Memorial Hospital in Foochow was the only new hospital built during this quarter century, although it had been projected in the early twenties. It was a long-looked-forward-to fulfillment of these dreams for a union institution, incorporating the Magaw Hospital and the American Board Hospital in Foochow City; a new building for this united enterprise had been erected on the American Board property, and the patients moved in and the use of facilities begun on a summer day in 1938 when Japanese airplanes were flying over the city.

The Syracuse University Hospital in Chungking deserves mention here. It was a restoration. The Methodist Hospital property had been unoccupied for seven years when the Syracuse unit arrived in 1921. It was thoroughly renovated, a new floor added, and patients came, the doctors were busy, and again the medical compound hummed with life. But within three years the entire Syracuse staff had been compelled for one reason or another to withdraw. Dr. Max Gentry, however, came to the helm in 1924 and remained with it for several years. Throughout his administration it was

his firm conviction that the hospital must be manned by trained Chinese. This conviction was aided by the development of a modern medical college in Chengtu, in connection with the West China Union University. Young people were able to receive proper training in Chengtu and after some years of practical experience, selected ones were sent to Peking Union Medical College for post-graduate work. At the present time [1927] there are nine well-qualified Chinese doctors working in the hospital. The Superintendent of Nurses and all technicians are Chinese.[10]

It was the policy to use Chinese materials and to adjust to Chinese customs wherever possible, consistent with a high standard of hospital service. How this institution had grown before the war is shown by these figures:

In 1925 there were 400 patients in the hospital; in 1934, 1,005 and in 1936, 2,136. The number of out-patients seen at the dispensary increased from 1,000 in 1925 to 58,381 in 1936. . . . The number of operations increased from 415 to 1,062 in 1936.[11]

With the coming of bombs to Chungking, it was more than ever necessary that this hospital should carry on, even though no missionary doctor was available to replace Dr. Gentry. C. B. Rappe wrote on July 7, 1942:

Administration is difficult due to the fact that hospital work is carried on in three widely separated places. The main work is done at Go Loh San, a mountain twenty miles west of Chungking, where we have accommodations for 150 patients in temporary buildings constructed largely of bamboo and plaster. Within the city limits in the old hospital compound, we do a large clinical work and have thirty beds where patients can be received and later sent to Go Loh San, in an ambulance donated by Madame Chiang Kai-Shek. Then in the western suburb of the city we have an emergency hospital, our surgical department, where we have cared for hundreds of air-raid victims. This wide separation of departments means an increased staff and more equipment, but since our hospital is the only institution of its kind in the city of Chungking, it seems wise to continue this arrangement for the duration of the war. During the past year we had a total of 2,559 in-patients; 54,355 out-patients, and 513 air-raid victims. To superintend is a full-time job in itself.[12]

Recovered from the war, schools, colleges, and hospitals will continue as church institutions to serve and build the church and the welfare of the Chinese people. Union, federation, and co-operation have marked and furthered these institutions, and though their number may decrease, their usefulness to and by the Christian church will increase. The glorious record of their past forbids anything else. •

IX
PUBLISH GLAD TIDINGS

Publish glad tidings;
Tidings of peace;
Tidings of Jesus,
Redemption and release.

1. *Presses and the Publishing House*

THE DISTRIBUTION OF CHRISTIAN LITERATURE HAD BEEN A PART OF THE
program laid down by the Board of Foreign Missions of the Methodist
Episcopal Church when commissioning Moses White and Judson Collins,
and White began handing out tracts on the streets of Foochow almost
before his wife had been able to unpack that delayed-in-transit trunk.
The next step would have been the production of Christian literature, and
the Methodist Episcopal Church, South, in making an appropriation of
$30,000 for the year 1854, included something for "the purchase of a
press." No money, however, so far as the records show, was ever used for
the purpose.

Although the establishment of a printing press had been proposed in the
earliest recommendations of the China Committee for the mission at Foochow, the initiative came from Moses White, then on the faculty of Yale
College, who, in 1859, wrote the Foochow Mission suggesting the possibility
of securing funds for the purpose from the American Bible Society. The
mission made the request, the board approved, and appropriated $5,000,
contingent on $3,000 of it being received from the American Bible Society
"for the publication and circulation of the Holy Scriptures in the Chinese
colloquial language of the province of which Foochow is the capital," and
in the belief that the "grant will be continued annually should the Bible
Society prosper and the publication and circulation of the scriptures be
satisfactory." [1] In the summer of 1861 Wentworth spent three months on a
trip to Hongkong and Canton, where he purchased "one of Hoe's Washington presses," and a font of double pica Chinese type, took practical
lessons in typesetting himself, and commenced negotiations to secure a
Cantonese foreman when the press was ready to open the following January. In the meantime a frame building was commenced in November,
thirty by sixty feet, erected within the compound on the Chong Seng Hill,
at a cost of $400. Before the end of 1862 Superintendent Maclay reported:

There have been printed in the office one thousand copies of a duodecimo tract of twenty-two pages, entitled, "Doctrines and Miracles"; five thousand copies of St. Matthew's Gospel, five hundred copies of St. John's Gospel, and five thousand copies of St. Mark's Gospel. We hope during the coming year to add to our font of Chinese type, so as to work the press with increased efficiency.[2]

The following year, the Rev. S. L. Baldwin urged the sending out of a "first-rate printer who, feeling no call to the preaching of the Word, will have no scruples about devoting his whole time to the printing department." While secular printing was at first prohibited, by 1867 net profits of nearly $800 were reported, and the China Committee of the board was authorized to apply these to the expenses of the press.

During the next fifty years the Foochow Mission Press contributed mightily to the spread of Christian intelligence throughout the Methodist areas (not yet Areas) and established a China-wide and interdenominational reputation for quantity and quality of work produced. L. N. Wheeler had been sent to Foochow in 1866 primarily for this work, but conditions had resulted in his pioneering, first in North China, then in West China, and this work continued through the years under the direction of S. L. Baldwin, N. J. Plumb, and W. H. Lacy.

In 1892 J. R. Hykes was reporting that the press in Kiukiang had "more work than it can do." In Foochow one of the presses and a font of Romanized type were transferred to Hinghwa, "for greater convenience in publishing literature in the Hinghwa dialect, as no one trained to read that proof could be found in Foochow," and the day of special delivery and airmail had not yet arrived. In 1895 H. H. Lowry was writing from Peking: "Progress has also been made in the printing press. . . . The work of the press is now entirely in the hands of our students." And the records of the Southern Methodist Mission carry not infrequent references to hopes or plans for the establishment of a press.

But everywhere the Chinese were commercially able before long to compete with and displace these small printing plants; the answer for the time being was the Methodist Publishing House for all of China Methodism.

But while hospitals had been united and disunited, schools had been merged and unmerged, mission stations had been opened, occupied, and closed, and, as we have seen, a whole conference was turned over to another church, the only institution that the Methodist churches in China organized, built up as a big business, and then liquidated, all within a period of twenty-five years, was the Methodist Publishing House.

The Mission Press at Foochow was, in 1895, still maintaining its successful and enviable reputation when C. F. Reid, writing from the China Mission, expressed at least his own convictions, and apparently that of his colleagues:

A Methodist Publishing House in Shanghai, even though built on a generous plan, would pay expenses from the day its doors were opened to business, and in a short time would doubtless become a fruitful source of income. . . . The question as to who will meet the demand is another thing. At first thought it would seem that such an enterprise would naturally fall to the Methodist Episcopal Church, South, and there is no doubt that our church is in a very favorable position for undertaking such a work. Some of us, however, prefer that the movement should be taken in hand jointly by the various Methodist bodies working in China. This preference arises from the profound conviction that Methodism will never fulfill her mission to this people in her present divided condition. Here we are, seven children of Wesley, without even so much as a common name to indicate we are kin to each other. These seven Methodisms bear names so unlike that no Chinaman would ever suspect that they are more to each other than they are to either Baptist or Presbyterian. Not one in fifty of our native members has any idea of the relationship. . . . It seems to this writer that the establishment of a Methodist Publishing House in Shanghai offers a working basis for united effort which may lead, in course of time, to such co-operation in additional departments of mission work as shall greatly add to their economy and efficiency.[3]

And with this preamble, Reid transmitted resolutions from the China Mission of the Methodist Episcopal Church, South, requesting the presiding bishop "to appoint a committee to confer with like committees, should any be appointed, of other Methodist bodies working in China, who shall have full power to act." Young J. Allen, C. F. Reid, and A. P. Parker were duly appointed as such committee, similar committees soon thereafter being appointed by the Central China Mission, North China Mission, and the Foochow Mission of the Methodist Episcopal Church, and by the Central China Mission of the Wesleyan Church. The following year the Southern Board of Missions added its blessing and referred the whole matter "to the Bishop in charge of the China Mission, and the Secretaries of this Board, with power to act."

The development of a union organization in China has always taken time—conferences within the missions, conferences between the missions, correspondence with the home boards, board actions, sometimes referral to the General Conference, again referred to the field organizations and the presiding bishop. And so it is not surprising to find in the minutes of the Central Conference of the Methodist Episcopal Church in 1899, a resolution petitioning "the General Conference to establish a Chinese Publishing House in Shanghai, whereby the uninterrupted progress of our publishing interests may be assured." [4] What is surprising in this resolution is that it makes no reference to the proposal or the negotiations looking towards a united Methodist undertaking, which, of course, were not unknown to the members of the conference.

Bishop David H. Moore had come to China for the quadrennial administration of 1900-1904, and within a year he was earnestly supporting the union project. By 1901, also, the Southern brethren were convinced that "the large amount of building now going on" in Shanghai, showed that the business men of that city had full confidence in the "safety of vested interests in the settlements"—a confidence that was not shattered for thirty years—and that, therefore, delay in the establishment of the publishing house was no longer necessary. A year later the mission asked the Book Committee to "take immediate action," and voted "that if the prosposed plan for union fails, we shall proceed at once to build our publishing house on the lot already selected on the Woosung Road."

By the spring of 1903, however, enough "of the machinery of the new Publishing House was in place" to commence work at 10 Woosung Road, Shanghai; and the official minutes of the Central Conference, held in November, 1903, bear the imprint of "Lacy and Wilson, Shanghai." At the close of the year, W. H. Lacy, northern Methodist representative in the management, reported:

The union of the Foochow Book Concern and the Methodist Publishing House at Shanghai went into effect June first, and from that date the business at Foochow has been conducted as a branch house of the Methodist Publishing House in China with headquarters at Shanghai. This completed the long-hoped-for union of the publishing interests of our own church with those of the M. E. Church, South. . . . We have taken fifteen of our workmen from Foochow to Shanghai, somewhat reducing our facilities [at Foochow] but we have left the Foochow plant almost intact and are quite prepared to meet the demands for local work.[5]

Then for twelve years, Hu Ung-Ming, son of Hu Bo-Mi, who had been trained in the business by W. H. Lacy, maintained—as manager in fact, though never given the title—a high efficiency in the continued work of the Foochow branch.

From the first month the Methodist Publishing House had all the printing and binding it could handle. Much of it—too much, the management felt—was commercial. The managers longed for more orders for church literature, but church literature was not appearing in sufficient volume, and commercial printing helped pay off the initial investment.

The influence which this arm of the church attained within a few years throughout the Methodist missions and conferences in China ("10 Woosung Road" was an address as well known among Methodists in China as "150 Fifth Avenue" was throughout the world) justifies the space we are devoting to it; nor was that influence confined to denominational or areal limits. By 1911 the Presbyterian Council had made overtures for union of the Presbyterian Mission Press (the only other comparably large Protestant printing plant in China) with the Methodist Publishing House, and the Methodists were giving favorable consideration to the proposal.

As a first step towards this larger union, the two plants merged their retail sales departments, forming the Mission Book Company in 1915, but continuing for the time their independent manufacturing plants. As a second step, we record the death knell of the Foochow Press, since the negotiations clearly showed that the union with the Presbyterians could not be accomplished with this branch included in the Methodist assets. Of this "radical change," W. H. Lacy wrote in 1915:

In view of the fact that the Mission Press at Foochow, which was established in 1862, had been doing most of the mission printing for over fifty years, the mission realized that the absence of a Mission Press would be a great inconvenience and a loss of some prestige to the Mission. It was first proposed that the Central Church in the city take over the press as one of its activities, but as this did not seem practicable, some who were greatly interested in maintaining a press for our church took steps to organize a stock company of Christian laymen. A special offer of the equipment was made to this company, and it agreed to allow a representative of the Mission on its Board of Directors, and to grant the Central Church one-seventh of its profits. Business was begun by the new firm Oct. 15. [6]

But the mission representative on the board of directors, and the one-seventh share of its profits to Siong-Iu-Dong, were terms of short duration —whether by mutual agreement or due to the default of forgetfulness, available records are silent.

Two steps had been taken on the field, and the Central Conference adopted the recommendation "that pending the consummation of union with the Presbyterian Mission Press our Publishing House in Shanghai be brought to a state of high efficiency." A third step was taken in the United States by the transfer of the Southern Methodist interests from their Publishing House to their Board of Missions. Representatives of the Presbyterian and the two Methodist boards met in New York in 1919, expressed their judgment for such union of the two institutions "unless conditions and sentiments on the field had changed," and authorized the managers of the two publishing houses to proceed with the making of inventories as the next step toward union. But the final step was never taken.

And so the bishops came to the jubilee conference of the Methodist Episcopal Church in 1923, and the story can best be closed in the words which they addressed to the church, and which appear in the minutes of that conference, printed by the Oriental Press:

For several years there has been a growing conviction in the minds of the committees in China and America immediately responsible for our Publishing House, that it would be the part of wisdom to discontinue the manufacturing and printing phases of this work in the interests of a larger publishing program. The conviction rested upon such grounds as the following:

The heavy debt which burdened the printing plant; the apparent impossibility of paying this from the profits of the business and the inability of the Boards to liquidate it; the fact that it now seemed possible to secure good printing in the city of Shanghai from other foreign or Chinese presses at a lower cost; that to maintain the press at all without rapidly increasing the debt required, in the judgment of all, the soliciting of commercial work bringing our plant into direct competition with the Chinese presses, which, from the standpoint of mission service is wrong both in principle and practice; the home boards found themselves unable to subsidize the press to make commercial work unnecessary; were the press to continue, a large amount of money would be required to repair and renew equipment, this the Boards were unable to furnish; the property occupied by the press has become very valuable to the Church, South, to which it belongs, and continuance therein would necessitate heavier expense than heretofore to provide for housing.

For these and other reasons the Advisory Committee thrice recommended to the Board of Managers in New York that the plant be liquidated on condition that ample provision could first be made for Methodist printing. The Board voted for liquidation to be effected if possible on or before Sept. 1, 1923. The business has been sold at a figure which will leave a considerable sum after the debt is paid. We suggest that the Central Conference make request to the Board of Managers in New York that the sum remaining after all debts are paid be made available for the publication of Christian literature in China.[7]

2. Literature Production

Some of the products of these presses and the Publishing House during these years, and some of the literary work of the missionaries, picked more or less at random, should here be placed on exhibit. In 1868 Young J. Allen began the *Chinese Globe* magazine, which, in seven years, had grown from ten to thirty-six pages and had increased from 30,000 to 96,000 copies annually. On November 11, 1874, the Foochow Press published the first Chinese issue of *Zion's Herald*, the name of which was changed later to the *Fukien Church Gazette*, later to the *Fukien Christian Advocate*, and eventually became the *Chinese Christian Advocate*, under which name it continued from 1898 until forced to suspend because of the Japanese invasion.

In 1866 a large-character colloquial New Testament was published, followed before long by a pocket edition. The *Alphabetic Dictionary of the Foochow Dialect*, a "portly volume" of nearly a thousand pages, and "truly monumental in the literary world," prepared by R. S. Maclay and C. C.

Baldwin of the American Board Mission followed soon after. The year 1891 saw the completion of the Foochow Colloquial Character Bible, with three thousand complete volumes printed and bound, twelve hundred volumes of the New Testament and Psalms, and three thousand New Testaments. Memoirs of Bishops Kingsley and Wiley appeared in 1885, on which the Rev. F. Ohlinger commented: "Our students ought to know more of early Methodism and the best means to convey this knowledge is Methodist biography." A few years later A. P. Parker was writing:

It is true that we do not come to this country to make Methodists or Presbyterians or Baptists, but Christians; hence we do not *care* to introduce our Arminian or Calvinistic controversies into the Christian Church in China. It is also true that the Christian books hitherto produced by the Presbyterians and other Calvinistic writers do not make their Calvinism specially prominent or offensive, and hence their books are in general use among the Methodists as well as among the Presbyterians and Baptists.

. . . .

And yet we know that the Church must be well established in sound doctrine. They must be taught the Truth as it is in Jesus. And the Methodists hold distinct views of Christian trust that it is very desirable that the Christian Church in China should know. It is the duty, therefore, of the Methodist Church to see to it that adequate statements of Christian doctrines as understood by the Methodists be put into the Chinese language, and thus be made available for the Church in China.[8]

Then followed a list of "the principal works by Methodist authors so far put into the Chinese language," which included, among others, a part of Ralston's *Elements of Divinity*, translated by J. W. Lambuth; McTyeire's *Catechism of Bible History*, translated by Mrs. J. W. Lambuth; *Jesus Is Coming*, by Vergil C. Hart; Binney's *Theological Compendium*, translated by Lambuth; *Peep of Day*, by Mrs. Lambuth; *Life of Tyndale*, by the Rev. F. Ohlinger; *Life of Wesley*, by Mrs. Nathan Sites; the *Discipline of the Methodist Episcopal Church*, translated by Nathan Sites; and the *Discipline of the Methodist Episcopal Church, South*, translated by A. P. Parker.

In the year 1897 nearly nineteen million pages were printed by the several mission presses, and that was before the Methodist Publishing House had been established. Yet in spite of this printing capacity and of the literature output just suggested, W. H. Lacy had observed in 1918 that "our missionaries are too busily engaged with other work to do much in the preparation of denominational literature." The bishops had more than once stressed the need for "Christian scholars engaged under our direction in putting the literature of our denomination within the reach of the Chinese church." In 1918 Clayton's *Index of Chinese Christian Literature* had been published, revealing that out of more than 2,600 titles "American Methodists, of both the Northern and Southern bodies, are represented by only sixty-six titles, including tracts, sheet music, and everything except a few contributions to Sunday School quarterlies," and also that of 624 translations of the Bible or Bible portions, American Methodists had shared in only fifty-three. Reviewing this book, Paul Hutchinson, general editor for the Methodist publications in China, observed:

> Save for the books with a distinctly denominational purpose few of the writings of Methodists have had a wide circulation. Exceptions should, however, be made in the case of H. L. Zia and Miss Laura White. Mr. Zia made the imprint of the Y.M.C.A. known throughout China, and it is largely due to him . . . that the publications of the Y.M.C.A. are today making a real impression on the thinking men of China—something that can be said of no other publications. Miss White seems to have caught the secret of the Chinese mind, and her stories, pageants, music, and other productions have found a large sale. She, too, has the help of enthusiastic Chinese, in her case young women who have graduated from the school of the W.F.M.S. of the Methodist Episcopal Church at Nanking. . . . It is true that there is little in this review of the past to make Methodism feel particularly proud. Facts are facts. To have the second largest number of church members of any denominational group in China, with by far the largest number of students in Sunday and day schools, and the largest native ministry, yet to walk almost at the rear of the procession in the matter of producing literature shows that we have left undone some things that we ought to have done.[9]

Several attempts have been made to provide periodical reading matter for the preachers and the members of the church who could read. The *Fukien Christian Advocate* and the *Central China Christian Advocate* had been united in 1898 into the *Chinese Christian Advocate,* and with this was combined in 1904 or 1905 the *Christian Advocate* which Young J. Allen had established in 1900. This *Chinese Christian Advocate,* under the successive editorships of F. Ohlinger, A. P. Parker, W. P. Chen, and R. Y. Lo, survived the vicissitudes of revolution, the liquidation of the Methodist Publishing House, and all those ills to which the normal weekly or monthly periodical is ever heir, but succumbed to the conditions resulting from Japanese invasion.

Likewise the *China Christian Advocate,* published in English. Replacing the *Fukien Witness,* the *Central China Record,* the *Forum,* and ultimately the *West China Messenger,* and started under the aegis of the Methodist Publishing House in 1913, the *China Christian Advocate* had, by 1915, been adopted as the official English language organ of the Methodist Missions in China.

But periodicals could never fill the need which could be supplied only by the translation and authoring of books on denominational, biblical, spiritual life, and religious education topics. In spite of the paucity of Methodist writers through most of these years, one branch or other of the church had the majority of one man's time devoted to this work, in addition to that of editing the *Chinese Christian Advocate!* Some of the publications from only some of these editors are named without any attempt at selection. Of A. P. Parker and George A. Stuart special mention must be made as men of scholarship and initiative and judgment, who, in spite of many hours a week devoted to the preparation of books for the Christian Literature Society, the China Educational Association, and other undenominational or inter-denominational organizations, were yet able to make a not inconsiderable contribution to the output of the Methodist press. There were, for instance, a *Handbook of Methodist Theology*, written by Sheldon, "at the request of Bishop Bashford, for special use in China," two Methodist catechisms, a *Life of John Wesley*, and a revision of "a volume of Wesley's sermons which had been translated into Mandarin by one of the Wesleyan missionaries at Hankow." There were also Parker's volumes on Nehemiah and Esther in the Bible commentary and his share, with that of some forty-odd other missionaries throughout China, in a translation of Hastings' *Dictionary of the Bible*. Sheldon's *System of Christian Doctrine*, his smaller book on the Second Coming, and a condensation of the *Discipline of the Methodist Episcopal Church*, 1916, were among the products of the 1916-1920 quadrennium reported by Paul Hutchinson, as book editor, who had come to China in 1916 to lend impetus to this phase of the church work, and he modestly added to his report: "I must confess that I have had nothing to do with even this modest achievement."

During these years two important editions of the Bible had been published. The first was in Roman letters in Hinghwa, with W. N. Brewster doing most of the preparation. The use of "Romanized" as a medium for church publications—although some felt for a good many years that the demand for it was sure to increase—never had any following outside of the Fukien dialects, and within those limits began to wane within a decade or two after the turning of the century. The other edition was a monumental work of revision, or rather, as Spencer Lewis said, the completely new translation of the Mandarin version of the Bible. Let us present Methodism's share in this work in the words of Lewis, who made this one of his several impressive and conspicuous contributions to the church:

The committee appointed later by the General Conference of Protestant Missions for the purpose of translation into the Mandarin and the Wenli were called revision committees, but as far as the Mandarin Committee was concerned, the outcome was a new translation. . . . Not until 1904 did I, after years of persistent efforts on the part of Dr. Mateer, yield to his persuasion that I become a member of the committee. . . . As soon as I consented to act on the committee, the bishop sent me to superintend the work in Central China so that I could combine that work with the translation and be nearer the other members. . . . After some years when we each did work in our own fields and came together for the revision on the passages under consideration only during the summers, it became evident that we must devote our entire time to the work, so we began work in Peking on the fourteenth of April, 1913. . . . We left Peking hurriedly in January [1914] when the bubonic plague, which had been spreading rapidly all over Manchuria reached Peking and Tientsin. The individual members of the Translation Committee agreed to go on with their work in their own stations, translating during part of the time. I went back to our old home in Chungking and acted as Superintendent of the district, spending a share of my time in translation. It was not till the fall of 1918, when Mrs. Lewis and I returned from furlough, that I had the satisfaction of reading the proof of the final version in our quarters in Shanghai.[10]

In 1923, R. Y. Lo, who had succeeded Paul Hutchinson as general editor in 1920, reported to the Central Conference, that "with the help of writers and translators we have been able to turn out" twenty volumes which are all named in the reports of that Central Conference, of which only the following five are here mentioned as typical: *The Institutional Church, Religious Education in the Family, The Need of Intercession,* Fosdick's *Christianity and Progress,* and *Biographies of Prominent Methodists.* It seemed in 1923 as though the Methodists were about started on a program for which many had long prayed, in which they might be handicapped by the liquidation of the Methodist Pubilshing House or might be helped by the funds thus made available—or perhaps both. But in 1934 the bishops were still lamenting the insufficiency of Methodist production and distribution of literature in these words:

Quite apart from the national efforts that are being made in China to create a literary people, it has been fully demonstrated in our own church that these efforts, wisely directed, furnish us with the most effective means we know of for "adding to the church daily those that are being saved."

. . . .

Most of us think we are too busy to attempt any creative work along this line, and doubtless this is true, but that should be no barrier to our distribution of what other people produce. Investigation in the American Bible Society reveals the fact that many of our missionaries and preachers do very little even in the dissemination of Scripture portions. . . . The whole history of the church in China, as elsewhere, proves that the spread of Christian literature is one of the most effective agencies for leading men and women to know Jesus Christ as their Saviour. This being so, it is much more than a mistake to neglect it, it is sin.[11]

Within another quadrennium war had come with its migrations and evacuations, with many new tasks and responsibilities for a much smaller staff of missionaries and Chinese workers, with facilities destroyed, and inflation prohibiting many endeavors. The *China Christian Advocate* and the *Chinese Christian Advocate* became war casualties, though the latter was succeeded by the *Wei Li Tung Hsin* with two editions, published in Chungking and Foochow; and the Division of Foreign Missions helped support the *Christian Farmer*, which had been published with the sponsorship and close co-operation of the National Christian Council in Shantung, but which, when invasion threatened its existence, had been moved to Szechuen.

But the writing and translating of Methodist literature has not ceased, in spite of war conditions. *The Meaning of Church Membership* needed two large editions to meet the demand in 1943; the Foochow Conference has continued to publish colloquial books of family devotions; Bishop Lacy's *Book of Revelation—Message of the Prophets* came from the press in 1944; and Methodists have shared in a great series produced by Nanking University and the National Christian Council, entitled *Early Church Fathers*. Of the new hymnal 300,000 copies had been issued for all denominations up to 1941, and the Bible Society had a staggering demand for Bibles and Scripture portions throughout the war years. As long as their printing facilities could be maintained in Shanghai, the Bible societies had only to face the gigantic problem of transportation in order to get their publications to churches, camps, and other distribution points in Free China. But with the Japanese control of Shanghai, publication and distribution facilities had to be shifted to West China—but were maintained.

Through all the decades the American Bible Society, a recognized agency of Methodism, has been of immeasurable help to the growth of the church in China. It was in 1875 that the China agency of the society was opened in Shanghai; from then on, and through the leadership of the Methodist men who later became its executives—L. N. Wheeler, 1890-95, J. R. Hykes, 1895-1921, and Carleton Lacy, 1921-1941—the society did much to further the Methodist Church through providing Scriptures in any quantity and any dialect, style, or script that would assist the church; and likewise, by its Publishing House and its several presses from time to time, Methodist facilities have contributed largely to the splendid work of the American and other Bible societies and their successor the China Bible House.

3. *Music and Hymnals*

The "Hallelujah Chorus" was sung in Tieng-ang-dong by student choirs from the schools of the three denominations in Foochow: such had been one of the triumphs of the sixth decade of church work. In the early days of ministerial training in Foochow, the Rev. F. Ohlinger had started the training in hymn singing that the local churches might join in vocal praise as well as reverent attention to the Word, heartfelt prayer, and silent worship. By the time the faculties of the several educational institutions included missionaries who were trained and accomplished musicians these schools were able to prepare boys and girls for church choral work, culminating in an annual Easter Monday concert during a number of years, with the climax of praise in Handel's "Hallelujah Chorus."

McTyeire School early began and soon developed outstanding training in Western music—vocal and instrumental—and everywhere throughout China Methodism, the youth from the day schools up and ministers-in-training, were learning to sing the "songs of Zion" and play on those four-or-five-octave baby organs the hymns which the churches in the United States and Great Britain were singing.

In 1860 the Rev. W. C. Burns had prepared for the churches in Foochow a hymnbook "in Foochow Colloquial, a translation of hymns written by Mr. Young and himself, which had previously appeared in the Amoy dialect. He added others, making up a book of more than thirty hymns. These were deemed so excellent that they were adopted by all three missions in Foochow and superceded others previously used, which were in Wenli." [12] This was, in 1869, succeeded by a Foochow hymnbook having 86 hymns and a doxology—words only, large type. The preface says that to Burns' original thirty, some hymns have been added: 13 translated by Maclay, 6 by Hartwell, and 29 from a Hong Kong hymnal. In this 1869 Foochow hymnal, the term *Siong-da* (for God) was restored, indicating the use of *Sing* in the earlier edition had been unpopular. Probably this book had been the basis of the 1878 Methodist hymnal—*A Hymn and Tune Book* prepared by the Rev. and Mrs. F. Ohlinger—the first "Methodist hymnal" in Chinese, though in the same year the Central China Mission had brought out a hymnbook which seemed to fill its niche. In 1883 a *Union Hymn Book*, largely, if not entirely, the work of J. W. Lambuth, was in use throughout the Southern Methodist field where later, in many places, the Kiangnan hymnal was used. Throughout the Mandarin-speaking conferences—i.e., in North, Central, and West China, and the Yenping Conference—the Blodget and Goodrich hymnal was in universal use in both Methodist and other churches. The *Union Hymn and Tune Book* which had succeeded the Methodist hymnal in Foochow in 1889 was in turn succeeded in 1915 by the *Foochow Union Hymnal*, prepared by representatives of the three churches, a great advance on either previous publication, although criticized at the time by some as "too classical," and by others as "too colloquial." The Hinghwa Conference, with its own limited dialect, had translated into the Hinghwa Romanized the *Foochow Union Hymnal* of 1889. F. P. Jones wrote in the *China Christian Advocate* that in its Romanized and character editions [it] continued to hold the field without question until the coming of the Union hymnal. . . . The *Foochow Union Hymnal* was known and respected among choir leaders and school music teachers in the Hinghwa regions, but never succeeded in displacing the older book for church use.

By 1930 all parts of China, and many denominations, were feeling the need for something better than the Blodget and Goodrich, the Kiangnan, and the Foochow union hymnals—better in style, more appropriate to the modern views of the church, and more truly Chinese. As the Yenping Conference expressed it in a Memorial: "There is great need in our churches of Methodism for . . . a change in the words and tunes of Christian songs; and there ought to be a general Methodist Hymnal for all China."

Hymns of Universal Praise, published in March, 1936, was the well-received answer to this need. This book differed from previous hymnals in that, in addition to 450 hymns whose music had been appropriated and whose words had been translated from Western hymnody, it contained fifty or more original hymns from Chinese writers set to Chinese musical compositions, thus making a real Chinese contribution to Protestant churches. The Rev. J. W. Dyson, of the East China Conference, who modestly omits his own important share in this work, says:

This event, largely unheralded in the West, will no doubt come to be recognized as one of the significant achievements of the Protestant church in China; for it was the joint effort of six bodies, comprising three quarters of the entire Protestant membership of the country who had combined their talents and resources in a single task, and who felt in its consummation the new uniting bonds of a common fellowship of love and praise.

The history of any one of these six bodies during the recent decade of church life in modern China would be incomplete without some mention of its part in this great addition to the hymnody of the Church Universal. Both the Northern and Southern branches of Methodism shared in the total enterprise. [See Appendix A, item 13.]

Other Methodists who made significant contributions to this book were Francis P. Jones, through his music criticisms, Edward James, with his practical gifts, and Bliss Wiant, who carried the music editorship.

The Central Conference of 1934, in anticipation of this hymnal, requested "the Hymnal Committee to prepare a special Methodist edition, including ritual, responsive readings, etc., and to make arrangements, if possible, for a union in this material with the Methodist Episcopal Church, South, and with the English Methodist Church." [13] To secure such a union ritual was found to be impossible at the time, however, as both of these churches found themselves unable to adapt their ritual to any united form. The union of the three branches of Methodism five years later removed the first difficulty, of course, and closer co-operation and affiliation, if not organic union, with the English Methodist Church, will probably remove the second in the near future.

The Rev. N. J. Plumb had discovered "efforts made to adapt some of our Methodist hymns to purely Chinese music" in Hinghwa in 1885, but the formal introduction of Chinese musical compositions into this hymnal was another distinct advance in making the church at home in China. But James Burke mentions the conservatism with which his father viewed this trend, a conservatism that has been detected again and again as missionaries have seen the church become less American and more Chinese. In spite of this bit of conservatism on the part of W. B. Burke, he stands as one of the best beloved and most loyal to the Chinese people of all the missionaries whom the Methodist Episcopal Church, South, had sent to China. After he had retired and been asked by the Chinese to return to Sung-kiang, he was interned by the Japanese, and repatriated on the *Gripsholm*. And whether in their tunes or those he loved, the Methodists of Kiangsu will ever sing their hymns of thanksgiving for the life that W. B. Burke lived among them. Said his son:

Expressions of nationalism met Burke's all-out sympathy until they touched on church singing. It was becoming increasingly popular to put hymns to Chinese music. Translating the words into Chinese had never brought a murmur from Burke, but the idea of changing the tunes in his Methodist Hymnal was a little too much.[14]

But in this case, as in many others, this trend has become a healthy growth, the hymnal is popular, the Chinese tunes are liked. The war popularized music and singing in the army and in society, and this new hymnal is making the church more of a singing church than ever before.

In connection with this development of Chinese Christian music and this hymnal, this story by Everett Stowe in the *China Christian Advocate* of April, 1936, is worth repeating:

In the early dusk of Saturday evening, January 25, 1936, three Chinese students were approaching the great doorway of International House, New York City. Suddenly one stopped. He looked up with incredulity at the tower of Riverside Church which raises itself over twenty stories above Riverside Drive. It was the hour of the usual Saturday evening carillon concert, but the tunes from those bells had to this student a strangely familiar sound.

Excitedly he grasped the arms of his companions and said, "Isn't that tune 'Man Chiang Hung—All Red the River?' " It was. And the one following was

"Chi Lo Yin." For almost an hour the concert of the bells sent out over Broadway and over the Hudson these age-old tunes of China.

There is a little story back of this. . . . Earlier that week I had sent to Mr. Kamiel Lefevere, carilloneur of Riverside Church, three of the hymns harmonized by Prof. Bliss Wiant for the new Union Hymnal. In the note accompanying them it was suggested that since Chinese New Year came at the end of the week, the many Chinese students resident on Morningside Heights might be heartened to hear in the carillon concert some of these ancient Chinese tunes. Mr. Lefevere became so much interested that he sent back for more of these folk-tunes, from Mr. Wiant's and from other collections, and made up nearly the entire program of them, even though it required him to sit up until eleven o'clock at night to complete transcribing them.

From the days of John and Charles Wesley, Methodism has been nothing if not scriptural and musical. While much remains to be done to "publish the glad tidings" by Methodist men and women in China, the foundations have been well laid for the church to "search the scriptures" in which are the words of eternal life, and to sing praise unto Jehovah in the congregation, which is both pleasant and comely.

X

WE GIVE THEE

We give Thee but Thine own,
Whate'er the gift may be:
All that we have is Thine alone,
A trust, O Lord, from Thee.

1. *A Start in Self-Support*

"AMONG ALL THE QUESTIONS RELATING TO MISSION WORK IN CHINA," THE belief was once expressed that self-support was "signally the most difficult one." Whether "signally" and "most" have always been true of it, there is no doubt that from the appointment of the first Chinese pastor to the consecration of Chinese bishops and on through the war years, with their terrific inflation, this question has been a major problem and an essential aspect of the growth of the church. J. H. Worley in 1885 voiced the sentiment of missionary leaders at that time in words to which missionary and Chinese leaders will both subscribe at the present time: "Self-supporting, self-governing, and self-propagating, is the proper motto. Without the first the second is dangerous and the third is impossible."

The story began in 1861, when the members at Goi-hung, in Fukien, contributed both money and labor toward the building of their church. The twelve men who were members of the class gave an average of a month's work each, thus contributing about one eighth of the whole cost, a share which encouraged the missionaries to feel that the work was taking sufficient root so that the future independence and self-sustenance of Christianity in China was assured.

This is one of the three phases of self-support within the area of a young and growing church: (1) Provision of land and buildings for the local church; (2) Payment for services received in institutions—schools and hospitals; and (3) Support of the ministry and the current expenses of the local churches and the church as a whole. In the earlier days the providing of property may have been the easiest form of self-support to secure in China. From many a mountain village and highway town people interested in the church would appeal to the missionary: "We will provide the church if you will send us a preacher." And the churches provided in this way in South, East, North, Central, and West China during the first decades following 1861 have been far too numerous to name.

Institutional self-support did not begin as early, chiefly because there were no institutions to support except day schools and boarding schools, and at the beginning, as we have seen, girls had to be induced to enter the schools, while of the first twelve boys admitted to the Boys' Boarding School in Foochow, two "clothed themselves." But as the value of education for both boys and girls became more manifest, financial response was more willingly provided, although "where mission boarding schools have, as in Foochow, so long existed in which all expenses of the students have been gratuitously met by the mission, it is not strange that the native church hesitates" over the plan that was projected in the Hinghwa District in 1878, namely, "that the buildings, apparatus, and teachers be provided for by the benevolence of the church, and that the scholars board and clothe themselves." [1] But by 1892 all the pupils in the Hinghwa Boys' Boarding School were self-supporting except eight preachers' sons who were given an allowance of fifty cents a month. "The self-supporting feature," wrote R. L. McNabb, "although new in China, is a grand success." And even in the newer field of Szechuen, W. E. Manly was reporting, as early as 1895, that the aim with regard to all new pupils was one of self-support, partial if not entire. The families of all but one of the boys were providing their clothing and the expenses for their board, for the most part, were met from sources other than the missionary appropriation. These are not isolated but typical illustrations of what was being done as well in Soochow and Peking, Chinkiang and Kiukiang, and equally applicable to practically all the day schools, even the "Special Gift Day Schools," during the second quarter century.

As rapidly as schools for higher education were developed, and especially when the commercial asset of English was added, the cost of operating the schools was borne more and more largely by student fees. Even buildings were provided by local philanthropy, as in the case of Diong A-Hok's gift to the Anglo-Chinese College in Foochow, and the erection of the second dormitory for that institution.

Likewise with the medical work. The Isabella Fisher Hospital in Tientsin was started with donations from the family of Viceroy Li Hung-Chang, and under Dr. Lambuth's administration the hospital at Peking showed a steady "swelling" of receipts from the fees of Chinese ladies, merchants, and officials, and "generous subscriptions" from local sources which Dr. Lambuth said "should be jealously husbanded and deposited in the bank upon interest, looking to the day when the hospital shall no longer be dependent upon the Home Church."

At Soochow, where no unfavorable precedent of gratuitous treatment had been set, from the days that the doors of the hospital were opened the experiment which had been inaugurated was a success, and the hospital was self-sustaining. But it was not always easy, as witness this story told by W. W. Pinson in his biography of *Walter Russell Lambuth:*

This reminds me of a family of soreheads who lived outside the water-gate of Soochow. Materfamilias came in one day, leading two children. . . . "I'll reward you, Mister Doctor, indeed I will. We are poor, but there is one thing we have got and we will bring you plenty of them." . . . True to her word, she brought the doctor's pay in the shape of a sack of water-chestnuts. In spite of all remonstrance, those water-chestnuts must be left, and they were. Next week she appeared with six children and water chestnuts. . . . Another week and cousins began to appear, accompanied by the inevitable chestnuts. . . . We ate water chestnuts raw, we had them fried into cakes, we made water-chestnut pudding: they were in the kitchen, we found them in the store room, a bag full in the back entry, another under the filter. We gave them to the servants, we gave them to our medical students, we fed hungry patients, and yet we had more and to spare.[2]

And so the story might be repeated, with variations, of course, but without destroying the theme, in the several cities where Methodist hospitals had been opened.

But the crux of the difficult problem was and is in ministerial support. In 1868 an effort was made to raise the pastor's salary at Cing Sing Dong, $72, and during the first half of the year, while the contributions were not quite at that rate even with the help of Wheeler and Baldwin, real advance was being made and there was hope that this would soon be a self-supporting church.

The following year at the annual meeting it was decided that each charge should raise a certain amount towards its pastor's salary, mission funds being appropriated only to make up the difference. At the next annual meeting Sia Sek-Ong, who had had difficulties in his work because of a suspicion among his neighbors that he had been "hired by foreign rice" to preach the gospel, renounced all claim on mission funds. After a year without financial help from the mission, being asked if he regretted the step, Sia replied: "I have not the thousandth part of a regret. I am glad I did it, and I expect to continue in this way as long as I live." When asked: "What will you do if supplies fail and your family suffers?" he answered, "They won't fail; but if they do—if I come to where there is no open door—I will just look up to my Saviour, and say, 'Lord, whither wilt thou lead me?' "[3]

The movement which had begun was attracting favorable attention outside of Foochow and outside the church. The *North China Herald*, in its issue of January 11, 1871, contained the following:

We are glad to see that a movement in the right direction has been lately made in regard to missionary work at Foochow. Some of the native preachers have advocated the propriety of native Christians supporting their own pastors, and if the principles be carried out it will be at once a proof of sincerity in the converts, and a step towards allaying the distrust with which the new religion is now viewed. . . . The strongest test of sincerity that can be applied is that suggested from Foochow.[4]

The theory stated by J. H. Worley was generally accepted as sound, but opinions varied as to its operation. Some held that no native minister should be employed until his support could be provided locally; others held that qualified men should be employed by the mission regardless of the ultimate ability of the native membership to maintain them on the same salary. The Foochow Mission took an intermediate position on this question, namely,

to employ men who give evidence of "gifts, grace, and usefulness," and pay them very moderately, insisting that the native congregations, as they grow up, shall contribute according to their ability, and aiming to put the whole burden of the preacher's support upon them as speedily as possible.[5]

The Mission felt that this could be done through the proper education of the Chinese church, by care not to give too much help lest indolence or indifference should be encouraged, and at the same time, by care not to discourage the brethren by "putting them on their own" too suddenly. It also felt that the system of classes and stewards gave the Methodist Church such an advantage over churches organized otherwise that they had "faith to believe that we will be the first mission in China to establish a self-supporting and self-propagating native church." That the Methodist system was adapted to a program of ministerial support warranted its application in many instances, not the least noticeable of which was that in Asbury Church in Peking in 1885. Said Marcus L. Taft in 1886:

Last year for the first time in the history of our North China Mission, the responsibility for collecting the native preacher's salary was placed upon the stewards, where, according to the *Discipline*, it properly belongs. Shortly after the last annual meeting, a meeting was held in Asbury Chapel and a certain amount to be paid monthly was pledged by the natives and foreigners. Formerly the missionary with his own hand paid the salary to the native preacher. Now this is all changed. The native stewards collect the amount each month from both foreigners and natives, and they pay the native preacher. On this station the contributions of the native members alone equalled about one-third of the preacher's salary.[6]

The reports from the several missions make it difficult to determine how rapidly self-support was progressing. Its progress through the years must have been like one of those charts showing votes cast for the candidates of any one political party through a series of elections, now up, now down, but with a definite upward trend as the population of the country increased. In 1874 three preachers in the Hinghwa District received their entire support from the native church, and the Presiding Elder "Sia Sek-Ong received, for salary and travelling expenses, 124,000 cash (salary, 100,000, traveling expenses, 24,000), about $108, which is regarded as liberal support." [7] The following year the presiding elder of the Foochow District was also entirely supported by the native church, and 60 per cent of the salary of the presiding elder at Futsing and part or all of that of several pastors came from the same source. In 1877 a missionary collection was taken at the Tartar City Church in Peking, "at which the greatest enthusiasm prevailed, and which, with amounts since added, will realize $24.13."

In several sections of the country—Central China, Foochow, and North China in particular—missionaries were expressing themselves in the early eighties that neither preachers nor members showed any enthusiasm for increasing local support of the churches. This lack of interest was attributed to the extreme poverty of the church membership—at least to making that the excuse, while "they do not seem able to understand or appreciate the spiritual blessings promised to the cheerful giver."

The church at Soochow determined as from December 1, 1886, to pay its pastor's salary and all the incidental expenses of the church, the pastor having "declared that he would gladly suffer for what he knew to be the good of the church, rather than have the members lean on the foreigners." Contributions immediately increased and interest in the services of the church grew steadily. In 1889 the Kiukiang District raised, for the first time, more than its apportionment for the Missionary Society, $9.24, without the other benevolences suffering, and with $637 raised "for self-support." In 1890, Chungking "collected for self-support $20; contributed for other local purposes, $10." And Dr. Lowry in Peking noted a change over ten years earlier when he said:

Self-support has made commendable progress. . . . Three preachers are supported entirely by the contributions of the local churches and several others are supported in part, . . . but the special interest during the past year has been in the line of church extension. The collections for this purpose on several charges have indicated a spirit of liberality that is not often surpassed by congregations of like ability anywhere.[8]

In 1893 the advance made in self-support in the Chien-Li-Huei was clearly shown, the Shanghai church now also being self-supporting, paying its pastor in full $20 per month in addition to liberal contributions to the poor and the meeting of church expenses in full. In 1895 the territory of the Hinghwa Mission Conference raised $1,283.74 for pastoral support, in 1896 the conference treasurer reported $2,432.12; in 1895 it gave nearly $300 for "home missions," in 1896, $1,431.78. In 1897 the Chinese members of Tieng-Ang-Dong in Foochow said they would undertake the entire support of that church without the help of the missionaries who were members of that church, and supported not only their pastor but "three assistants who worked in neglected districts some distance away. Besides they have contributed liberally towards the new church" building.

These are but a handful of straws which show the direction of the wind. Four specific cases picked from the reports of missionaries at the time will serve to illustrate the attitude of ministers and church members. Pang Ting-Hie, speaking at the twelfth annual meeting of the Foochow Mission in November 1876, said:

I think this self-support business ought to be accomplished. . . . We must learn from Paul and be ready to go to all places, and make up by labor what the people don't make up. Because of foreign money some preachers are not yet converted, and many members are not yet true and faithful. The Saviour said to the disciples, "Go," and they went and were supported. We must not wait to know first that we will certainly be supported, but go out, and trust the Saviour.[9]

Deacon Ding Mi-Ai of the Ka-sioh circuit, Futsing District, on full native support in 1874, testified:

I used to be paid in round foreign dollars which were very nice to have; but they were an obstacle to the contributions of the people, who thought we had plenty of money. This year I have been paid in *potato money*. But I have found potato money as good as any other kind. I can get rice or wood, or anything else I need with it, and I have better heart to preach the Gospel than ever before.[10]

The reference to "potato money" was to round slices of sweet potatoes, which are dried and extensively used by the people of this region, many of whom cannot afford to eat rice.

An instance of sacrificial giving came from Tsung-hua, in North China, in 1882:

Among the members is an old blind man who lives about three miles from the city. He barely supports himself by peddling small cakes on the street. At most he can only earn a very few cents during the day, but on Sabbath he voluntarily gives up his business and feels his way to the city and back so as to attend the services in the chapel. When the missionary collection was taken no one thought of asking him for a contribution, but greatly to the astonishment of all, he gave three hundred cash (about four cents) which he had carefully saved up for the purpose one cash at a time.[11]

And another from the Futsing District, Foochow Conference, in 1890:

This is the second year of drought and famine, and yet the contributions do not decrease. One of the pastors recently [told of a member who] expressed a fear that his cow, which lived in the only room in the house, would eat his bed-covering, "for," said he, "we felt we ought to pay our subscription, and to do so we were compelled to sell our bedding, and have filled a cotton cover with straw as our only covering!" [12]

There was much sacrificial giving to and for the church, it is true. But perhaps too much emphasis was being put on the need for the Chinese church to support itself and not enough emphasis on the spiritual value of tithing. It would not be strange if this were the case, for certainly fifty years later the Methodist Church in the United States was still a long way from knowing this value; perhaps the difficulty lay too largely in the abject poverty of Chinese farmers and peddlers, yet there was a feeling in some parts of the church

that the missionaries can and ought to change Chinese methods of commerce and labor by the introduction of Western machinery. Such fabulous profits are believed to be possible that many people see great fortunes amassing with very small capital. The members of the church, of course, will be chiefly benefited under this new order of things. In some quarters it is believed that native ministers should not depend upon the missionary society for support, but form companies, borrow money, and purchase machinery or mills, from the earnings of which they could support themselves and families and be independent.[13]

Naturally most of these examples come from the older sections of the church. One of the missionaries in Soochow hoped, in 1897, to attend the jubilee conference in Foochow, "to study carefully," he said, "the question of self-support," because "they have the best work in the empire in that province." But even there, as has been seen, the goal was far from attainment. These specific cases of giving cited above suggest some of the reasons for the failure of the church to move constantly and steadily forward; perhaps also a reliance, conscious or unconscious, on "special gifts" was beginning to have a deterrent effect on this upward trend. At any rate, nearly a half century had passed since the first Chinese had been baptized in a Methodist church, but Methodism in China was much farther from being self-supporting than it was from being self-governing or self-propagating.

2. Self-Support Still in Its Infancy

Said his Chinese secretary to one of the missionaries one summer morning: "Nine out of every ten letters you get these days tell about trouble. Either it's brigands or soldiers that are causing trouble." Frederick Bankhardt, who himself personally knew what it was to be captured by brigands and held for ransom, tells the story in these words:

Letters were coming in from every part of the field. One day comes the news of a Christian being taken captive. The Christian is poor, and the brigands are demanding an outrageous ransom. I am asked to help, but am powerless. The next day comes a letter telling how soldiers have taken a member prisoner claiming that he was a brigand. The preacher testifies to the faithfulness of the member. Again what could I do? Then one of our preachers is badly beaten by the northern soldiers. False charges were brought against him by some who were opposed to the church in the village where he was preaching. We hardly get over the effect of this report when a messenger brings us the news that the town in which one of our most flourishing chapels is stationed has been burned by the brigands. With my own eyes I have seen villages that were still smouldering. I have seen the dead lying around. I have seen the dead bodies of women, who with their little feet tried to escape from these terrible robbers by running into the river, still lying in the river, though more than twenty-four hours had passed since it all happened. . . . Our district superintendents and our preachers have showed great courage on many occasions in the brigand infested regions. They have stood loyally by their people, interceded with the brigands for members of their church who were captured and held for ransom. They themselves have been taken captive and their lives threatened; they have been beaten, their homes and churches have been burned, but they have stayed on, helping the suffering and encouraging the people. In many places farmers dared not work their fields through fear of being captured and being held for ransom, and the poor people have been robbed by bandits and soldiers alike. . . . One district reported an increase of 80 per cent over last year in contributions for the support of the native ministry on the district.[14]

That, in a nutshell, is the story of self-support during the turbulent years that followed 1900. From the Great Wall to the mountains of Yung-chun, and from the upper and lower parts of the Yangtze Valley, following the Boxer devastation, the unsettled conditions that were the aftermath of the revolution, the civil "wars" that seemed to be raging interminably in some part of the country—all were making life hard for the people. The local military forces had their own policies and methods of collecting taxes, often for years in advance. Fields which farmers refused to plant in opium were taxed, and the poppies which other fields produced were taxed because they were grown, and capture for ransom was often a fruitful means of producing revenue.

Hence it is not surprising that the advance towards self-support was not more rapid during this third quarter century of the church. What is surprising is that Bankhardt could report one district making an advance of 80 per cent! By and large the self-support problems of 1872-97 were pretty much the problems of 1897-1922, plus the conditions of the above paragraphs. Brigandage, however, was not the whole trouble. New aspects of the problem were being recognized. J. L. Hendry, of the China Conference, voiced not alone his own feeling when he complained of the church's failure to find the right system for making itself financially self-dependent: "On the one hand," he said, the pastors

are supposed to look after the interest of their churches, while on the other they are to take care of the interests of the Board of Missions. Should they recommend a liberal advance on self-support, strong objection may be raised by some of the stewards; if a small advance is advised, or perhaps no advance at all, the presiding elder may not be pleased.[15]

And the Committee on the State of the Church of the 1903 Central Conference faced "the dangers connected with self-support and how to avoid them" in these suggestions:

(a) That, insofar as those connected with us are able to avail themselves of the privileges of extra-territoriality, there will always be the danger that unconverted persons, having no interest in the Gospel, will be attracted to the church and give liberally to its support because of legal and political advantages that may accrue to them.

(b) It may sometimes transpire that pastors supported by native congregations will be subjected to undue pressure to secure their co-operation in matters at variance with the teaching of Christ and His Apostles. In the Hinghwa Conference the Home Missionary Society has sought to meet this difficulty by setting aside a percentage of its receipts to be used in making up to pastors any loss in salary that may be incurred by a refusal to be coerced into wrong-doing. A consecrated ministry and a soundly converted membership, intent upon the achievement of spiritual results, will be the surest safeguard.[16]

Beginning in 1874 it had been the Hinghwa Conference territory that was making the greatest gains in this major step towards the reality of a Chinese Methodism. It was always one of the objectives of that sincere, enthusiastic, capable, and much-loved missionary, W. N. Brewster, who almost singlehanded molded the Hinghwa Conference out of the clay which had been the Hinghwa District when he came to it in 1889. His enthusiasm for a self-supporting church, his ability to see and solve the problems, the loyal following which the membership gave his leadership, made it possible for him to report nearly $16,000 "contributed to the support of their pastors this semi-famine year" of 1902; to tell of contributions towards self-support increasing more than 400 per cent in 1911 while the membership increased not quite 250 per cent; and to rejoice in a 35 per cent increase in 1914 when the membership increased 40 per cent in a year which had "been one of destructive floods, severe drought and high prices, especially the latter half of the year, when most of the money is paid in." As early as 1904 the Hinghwa territory was furnishing 84 per cent of the funds necessary for pastoral support with about half the "foreign money" received being applied to the salaries and expenses of the presiding elders, while "fourteen years ago this ratio was reversed," Brewster said. And even faraway Yungchun Circuit had "advanced to the point of entire self-support" by 1906, and in another ten years the Yungchun-Tehwa District was "entirely self-supporting including the salary of the Chinese district superintendent."

Foochow Conference was developing tithers, and conference reports indicated from time to time so many in this and so many in that district; but in every such case it could always be assumed that the pastors and the day-school teachers were included 100 per cent, although too often they felt it, not a tithe unto the Lord, but a tax by the church—meaning, not the local church, but some church authority: the presiding elder, the annual conference, or generally the missionary. Ling Mi-Ing, presiding elder of the Haitang District in 1907, reported that in the first year of a self-support program on that district, it could be counted as "a settled fact on this district." This was not only because they had "been able to meet in full the expenses of the work without decreasing the number of men appointed or changing the scale of salaries," but because there had also been a corresponding deepening of the spiritual life.

And in the year before their separation into the Yenping Conference, the Yenping District recorded a 47 per cent increase, the Chang-hu-ban District increased 57 per cent, and the Yuchi District gained something over 60 per cent and "assumed complete self-support as the program for the future."

But in that same quadrennium the figures from the Chinkiang and Wuhu Districts, even "after making allowances for the fact that many of our members are poor," were, as in several sections thirty and forty years earlier, felt to be unsatisfactory, as tho there were not "an earnest effort in this direction by the Chinese ministry and churches," who formally "requested, that without lowering the amount now paid to any preacher, a maximum" double the salary of the previous year be allowed, and "this without any provision for the Chinese Church to assume a fair share of the increase." Ten years later, F. C. Gale felt that "the giving of our people of Central China compares very favorable with that of any other people; our weakness is in numbers," although he was still in the early stages of local giving when he concluded "that finances for property or equipment will be easier than for pastoral support and current expenses," and although, by 1920, the Hwangmei District (Kiangsi Conference), exclusive of centenary giving, had increased over 29 per cent over the giving of the previous year. Here again Christian stewardship and tithing were being emphasized.

The records of advances in North, West, and East China are not as numerous nor as specific as those which we find from Central and South China.

But progress was generally steady, if often slow, and Bishop Lewis was observing:

The Chinese are, at the present moment, only in their infancy on the subject of self-support. Indeed, very little had been done in any of the conferences before 1904. I deem this the most important problem affecting the evangelism of the nation that we, now, as a church, have to consider.[17]

Te Jui, district superintendent of the Shanhaikwan District, tells of one method that may not have been tried often enough:

At the first quarterly conference the stewards of the church reported that they did not have enough money to pay the pastor this year, and asked me to help them pay him. I answered them that it would be better to pray to God to help them pay the money. Then we knelt down and prayed about it. Finally one of the stewards named Lei Ju-Chu stood up and said, "I will give one thousand tiao." . . . He had given four thousand tiao before. . . . "Now," said he, "use the interest to pay the pastor." Others added to their contributions. So at once they obtained enough to pay the pastor.[18]

Self-support of schools and hospitals is, as has been suggested, quite a different aspect of the subject. While William Nast and some other schools followed a policy based on the premise "that at this stage there are in this land higher claims upon us than rigid self-support which closes its doors with a bang against all who cannot meet the fixed regulations," many schools found that the demand for education and the fall in the rate of exchange were so far outrunning the support available from the United States that increased fees and contributions from the local constituency were found to be not only necessary but possible. School after school throughout the Methodist field was meeting all its expenses, except that of missionary salaries, from local sources; and as these schools were sending their alumi into the customs, the postal service, the salt gabelle (government salt control and tax bureau), and private business, where salaries were high and income was more that a mere living, the laymen of the church were getting under the burden of school and hospital and church.

In 1910, for instance, the authorities of the Peking Hospital felt that the time was fully ripe for the Chinese Christians to provide in full for the current expenses of Christian work through that institution. But already in the same year, Dr. McCartney of the Chungking Hospital was claiming credit for that institution's being "the first medical work of our church in Asia to become self-supporting," since for seventeen years it had received no financial support from Missionary Society appropriations. And Dr. Park was campaigning for $100,000 from local Chinese sources for a new hospital in Soochow, and although it seemed that every time he started a new effort of the campaign, a new war started, he was finally successful.

C. F. Kupfer, notable gift to China by the German Methodists of the United States, wise builder of William Nast College, and consecrated missionary, said in 1904; "Self-support is a thing to be greatly desired where it is the intelligent, spontaneous fruit of Christianity." Perhaps, even after seventy-five years, that was the trouble—the fruit was not ripe enough. "It is educational evangelism which manifests its results in self-supporting churches," the secretaries of the Southern Church were declaring, and Kupfer was continuing; "But self-support can be no blessing to the cause of the Christian Church among a heathen people when it is secured by high-pressure methods." Was the church at home, and were the missionaries on the field, forcing a hothouse variety of flower or fruit? In 1914 Bishop Lewis wrote Frank Mason North, corresponding secretary of the Board of Foreign Missions: "Everywhere I hear them say, 'You praise us for our liberality, but if we should pay the entire cost of the church we would not be paying as much as idol worship cost us before the Gospel found its way to our hearts." [19]

3. New Motives and Methods

The years 1897-1923 had brought gains—very definite gains, often disappointingly inadequate gains. Some of the fruit, too much, no doubt, had been prematurely forced; much of it was genuinely ripe and firm. But the problem of a self-supporting church was not solved, and at the end of a century it is questioned whether it is much nearer a final solution than it had been twenty-five, fifty, or seventy-five years ago. Missionaries have continued to ask, "Who will show us the way forward?" In 1870 Sia Sek-Ong had renounced all claim to pastoral support from missionary appropriations, but seventy-five years have passed and the church is nearer than ever to being in the dangerous situation to which J. H. Worley referred of being self-governing without being self-supporting, of moving toward the impossible position of being self-propagating without being self-supporting. In fact during the fifteen years following 1923—up to the devastation wrought by military invasion—the Methodist Episcopal Church not only decreased 30 per cent in the number of full members with a consequent decrease in total contributions, but the per capita giving by the church declined with the same persistence; total church contributions reported were averaging $3.05 in 1923 and in 1936 only $2.53.

Hothouse forcing had been repeatedly used. The program adopted in the China Conference had been used with variations in plan and results in most conferences; Wesley Smith reported (after it had become the East China Conference) that no one could record the history of that conference for the preceding twenty-five years without noting both the desire for and the progress made in this matter of self-support, which, starting sporadically, had, by the time the Japanese aggression halted the program in its sixth year, become a successful, united, determined effort. Then he called it another hothouse variety when he said:

Every charge in the area covered by the conference was to become self-supporting in ten years by paying one tenth more each year. The weaker charges—those paying less than 50 per cent of their pastor's salary—were to be helped by money from other churches. The balance was to be used to open new work.[20]

Pump priming had also been tried. When appropriations for "evangelistic work" were decreased year after year, and when the board ceased to "underwrite" the "special" or "designated" gifts, to the Conferences abroad, the missionary could often secure gifts, direct or extra-appropriation, for the support of pastors and evangelistic workers in the crisis.

Neither of these methods produced widespread or long-range results. Let us look at a few specific snapshots. Of the centenary period, W. B. Cole wrote from Hinghwa: "The gain in giving for the support of the ministry . . . is only 8 per cent. We have slipped back in the self-support of the ministry. This 8 per cent is more than overbalanced by the increase in salaries." [21] The same year Lan-shien District in North China had shown great advance in self-support,

in some places the increase amounting to 100 per cent and more. At the opening of the year there was not a single self-supported church on the district, but at the close there were five churches which paid their pastors' salaries in full, and in addition three of these churches carried their school budgets as well. The most notable advance was that of Yenkechuang church, formerly the deadest church on the district, which not only reached self-support, but increased the pastor's salary;[22]

but within two years "many of the business houses went bankrupt and the people were reduced to poverty. The pastors accepted a one-third reduction in salary, and the people had difficulty in raising that." In 1924, J. W. Hawley reported from South Fukien: "The entire conference gave for all church purposes and exclusive of school tuition fees, more than the conference received from the Board of Foreign Missions in appropriations for all forms of work." [23] But the next year he had to say this:

Last year word was received of the cut in appropriations just at conference time. After due consideration of the matter, it was decided to try to carry on the work for the coming year with but slight diminution, all of the Chinese leaders feeling that with special effort the cut could be made up from increased local receipts as far as the preachers' salaries were concerned. Their hopes were vain. Economic conditions over all the area have grown so much worse that any increase in giving was found impossible. . . . The outlook for self-support of the ministry is discouraging.[24]

Frank Cartwright, writing from Foochow, said that, after a "slashing cut in appropriations from America," harassed members of the conference "have been tempted to give up in bitterness," but that "the District Superintendent of the South Mintsing District in a five-year survey shows a 47 per cent increase in membership and a gain of 145 per cent in support of the ministry." In Shantung "one of the preachers gave a whole year's work without salary, and many others gave up one or two month's salary because of the shortage in appropriations." The giving by one district superintendent on a salary of $480 per year

indicates the spirit in which some of the Chinese workers are giving to the work of their own church. Others could probably equal this record, if not exceed it. These figures were given without any expectation of their being used for any public purpose, and are known to be authentic.

To Junior Middle School budget	$ 54.00
To local church where family holds membership	20.00
To general district budget	13.00
To individual churches on the district	12.00
To church benevolences	9.00
To outside benevolences	5.00
To miscellaneous collections	8.00
	$121.00

or 25.2 per cent of his cash salary.[25]

However, still thinking of external stimuli, the bishops felt in 1934 that it "is not all to the bad" if the church realized "that it is absolutely true that America can no longer be depended upon to furnish the funds we have relied upon for support. . . . In one annual conference alone in 1932 twenty circuits declared themselves ready to assume entire self-support."[26] In Kiangsi, as in other places where pastors have had to supplement their salaries by other means of support, one district superintendent reported: "Some live on the interest drawn from their inherited properties, some have almost exhausted their capital, some let their wives work as servants, and some simply get along on loans."[27] Hence it ultimately became inevitable that sometimes pastors who could find other support were officially advised to sever their conference relations, although the ministerial ranks were thereby reduced to the point of too few men to fill the existing pulpits.

Having followed this problem for seventy-five years, one can easily be led to agree with a missionary who felt that effective leadership was lacking because missionary leaders had not been able to clarify their own thinking on this subject. In 1932

a leading official of the International Missionary Council, a man who for many years had formerly been a missionary in China, and understood Chinese life and conditions, made a tour of investigation in China, and came to the conclusion that churches which have been receiving a subsidy for forty or fifty years and were no nearer self-support than at the beginning should be cut off from all such help.[28]

But, as we have seen, stimulation by starvation has been no more the solution than hothouse forcing or pump priming. A deepening of spiritual life within the church seems to be the only solution. No one can express this better than the bishops did in both 1930 and 1934:

It is here in this high fellowship which shares the cross with God, that this troublesome, homely, embarrassing, threadbare theme of self-support is caught up from its lowly, superficial, materialistic meaning and is revealed in its true character to be an effort to share with God His transcendent task of redemption. And without that fellowship of sacrifice there is no full and final redemption, nor can there be in any final sense a Church of Jesus Christ.

. . . .

And we urge it never as a final goal, but as a long step forward in the development of a church of Christ, whose inner passion always is, not to save itself, but to save the world.[29]

How much more direct and immediately effective it would be to give Jesus Christ the central controlling place in the life to make subsidiary to Him all we are, all we have. Then such a passion for others will take possession of us all that we shall not stop to count the cost either in effort or in money. This is the position to which we all must come if we are true followers of Jesus Christ. This we conceive to be the most reliable solution of our self-support problem.[30]

To this end the new emphases on religious education and rural evangelism will probably afford the major impetus for the next few years. In the meantime stewardship needed to be stressed, as it had been in Foochow and elsewhere at various times, and thank-offering programs could furnish a part of the desired motive. Of stewardship in the China Conference, Mary Culler White drew this sketch in the *China Christian Advocate* in 1935:

For the last two years our emphasis has been on Stewardship. Text-books have been written, a primer has been prepared, and original songs on this subject have been set to Chinese tunes. In every short-term school all who enrolled have been required to take one of the graded courses on this subject, and much enthusiasm has been generated. As some one has said, "The women chartered a steamer called Stewardship and started across the Sea of Depression to the Port of Self Support; but the men hailed the boat and said, Come back, and let us get on. So now we are travelling together and singing Stewardship hymns, while we all stoke the fire." God grant that the port may be reached! [31]

And of the new psychological appeal of 1943 Pearce Hayes has written:

In place of the old phrase "the pastor's tax" . . . we have shifted completely to a thank-offering basis. The old tax was collected as a tax on each member and paid with other bills before China New Year. The thank-offerings are held four times a year, the attempt being made to place them to coincide with harvest or ingathering times. Another factor is that giving this year is held over for use next year, thus making appointments easier on the basis of actual available cash, not mere promises. Furthermore it has greatly saved the face and self-respect of the pastor. In the past he had to urge payment on his own salary; now he urges collections for the pastor next year and under Methodist policy, appointments are merely one year appointments. Now no member is asked to pay one cent to the church; he is given the opportunity four times a year to express his gratitude to God as he desires.

Self-support, as considered in these last few pages, has been confined to ministerial support. We have seen before that the problem of institutional expense has been a steadily diminishing one, as it continued to be until all institutional work was disrupted by invading armies. Perhaps the emphasis on the support of the ministry was wrong, as Olin Stockwell had thought just before the war, when he wrote in the *China Christian Advocate* in February, 1936:

No one else in the church circles is expected to become self-supporting, with all of the meagerness and uncertainty of income that that usually entails. Even the salary of the Bible-woman on the charge comes in regularly from the hands of a foreign missionary, a missionary who sometimes complains because the Chinese pastors are not entirely self-supporting. The teachers in the church schools, the doctors and nurses in the church hospital—all of these receive their salaries with a fair degree of regularity and there is no word concerning them becoming "self-supporting." Moreover, the missionary always seems to have enough to meet his own needs, in spite of frequent "cuts," and in the view of the Chinese pastor is making no great financial sacrifice. With all other church workers having assured incomes, why should he be expected to make a special sacrifice?

It should be noted that by 1943 "the Bible-woman on the charge" was expected to get at least a part of her support from the local church, "thus introducing new complications and resentments." But Stockwell also makes the well-taken point of another stubborn fact:

A ministry, set aside for the directing of the spiritual life of a church group and spreading the good news of the Kingdom, is new in China. To expect the small groups of Christians which compose our churches to give sacrificially to the support of the ministry may not be expecting too much, but it is certainly expecting "something new under the sun" as far as China is concerned.

Even after seventy-five years! And perhaps the support of the Buddhist priesthood was provided without sacrificial giving!

Many a Chinese church building had been erected, in part or in whole, by the voluntary labor of its members and their sympathetic neighbors. Labor had also been donated to support churches, as, for example, that at Wufenshi, in West China, which, Earl Cranston related in 1922, "has a unique congregation who meet in a temple and support the church by cotton spinning." The Manchu dynasty had for years collected taxes "in kind" and many a rural pastor in Ohio and Alabama has had his cash salary supplemented by food donations from his parishoners. Hence there was nothing new in the fact, after the war broke out, that "advances were made in self-support" at various places throughout the country. Note these illustrations:

The Fifteenth Township in Mintsing District reported 150 chickens given on one Sunday for pastoral support. Gang-cia, near Foochow, reported 60 birds of the same species donated for the expenses of the church.[32]

October 20, 1940, was an eventful Sunday at the Ankechuang Methodist Church, one of the experimental parishes under the Joint Council on Extension Service to Rural Churches in Hopei, North China. For two weeks preceding Pastor Ts'ao and Mrs. Chang, the Bible Woman, had made trips by bicycle to the church members' homes in all of the surrounding villages informing them of the plans for this Harvest Festival Sunday.

When the great day came one-hundred-and-twenty men, women, boys and girls, filled the church by 10 o'clock. The two-hour service united them in worship, thanksgiving and testimony.

The church was decorated by the offerings they themselves had brought. The pulpit was encircled by the sacrificial offerings of 48 sacks of beans, corn, millet and rice; a little pink paper pennant at the top of a little bamboo stick in each sack bore the name of the giver, written in black characters. Strings of peanuts, red radishes, white turnips, and yellow ears of corn hung from wires above the pulpit. Along the wall back of the pulpit were baskets of sweet potatoes and peanuts, and large green cabbages and russet squashes. Little pink paper envelopes hanging from the wire above the pulpit contained gifts of money from the town people who had no grain nor vegetables to contribute.[33]

There are many churches that are not able to give actual cash for the support of their pastors, but they bring what they have: rice, potatoes, peanuts, oil, and livestock. Sometimes these products are sold and the proceeds used for the church expenses or the pastor may use the products in the place of cash.[34]

And Pearce Hayes, writing from Futsing in 1943, said:

Giving is increasing on the basis of kind, not money. In fact these four districts are making it almost unanimous. My discovery is that where members give in rice, oysters, wood, whatever they have on hand, they actually give at least three times the amount they give in actual cash. The reason is evident: few have actual cash, all have some kind of goods, thus giving is easier. Minutes of the future may read: "Hai-kau, 20 loads unhulled rice, 20 loads sweet potato money." This is partly a war-measure, due to inflation, but its effectiveness was actually proved before the war and it will probably remain.

"Here is a road," as W. S. Bissonnette called it, which may—in part—provide that "something new under the sun" which Olin Stockwell was seeing.

The progress towards the self-support of the pastoral and evangelistic work of the church would doubtless have continued a normal—albeit slow—advance toward that consummation devoutly wished by all, had it not been interrupted by the shocks and quakes of the war. Giving in kind was only a partial remedy, and probably spottedly localized. It could help little in those areas where the enemy took all the produce the populace could not conceal, nor in those into which millions of refugees migrated. The team which surveyed the problems of the church—all denominations—in this area in 1940, had this to say: "With a fettering tradition, a very small membership, outrageously high prices, and an uncertainty as to what to expect or count on, the financial outlook for the churches in this field was not bright." [35]

Reviewing what has been written in this section, one outstanding conclusion must be reached: however real and however many the reasons, adequate local support of the Methodist ministry in China has not yet been realized. As Bissonnette said: "Until this obligation is more fully recognized by the average member there can be no true planting of an indigenous Christianity with a rooting in the native soil." The one sure, universal, and permanent solution of the problem has not yet been made sufficiently effective—"to give Jesus Christ the central controlling place in the life, to make subsidiary to him all we are, all we have." But, "in spite of war, famine, flood and drought, the church has moved forward in self-support," and since the Japanese cut off all the inflow of funds into the areas which they controlled, and froze the funds in the hands of the mission treasurers, cutting off the possibility of thus caring for the current needs of our large staff of Chinese Christian workers hitherto depending upon such funds in those areas, the church members have come wonderfully to the fore in giving for the work of the church. Even in Free China, where inflation has been a greater handicap than any of the many handicaps of former years, one Chinese worker—Mary Sing-gieu Carleton—testified. "Giving in the church has increased during these years. . . . Formerly if anyone gave a substantial gift for the church they wanted their names attached. Now people give to the Lord and do not care whether their name is known or not." That's what counts, that's what spells progress: "Now people give to the Lord."

XI
BOUNTIES RECEIVE

May we Thy bounties thus
As stewards true receive

THE FLOW OF FINANCIAL NOURISHMENT FROM THE UNITED STATES WAS being cut by 1910, and, as we have seen, local increase in self-support had not kept pace with this decline in the face of ever-increasing and expanding needs. West China's missionary salary budget exceeded its total appropriations from the Board of Foreign Missions; Hinghwa would have been "in the red" except for a generous response to a special gift appeal. In fact, Homer C. Stuntz reported in November that the cut had come "more nearly bringing disaster to our work in China than to any other portion of the field with which the assistant corresponding secretary conducts the correspondence." [1] To that meeting of the Board were presented requests for a total increase in appropriations to China alone of $137,769.

The demand for Western education that followed the Boxer episode and continued intensified after the revolution was requiring more, better, and bigger schools and universities; institutions that had been struggling houses of mercy found a need which only hospitals of enlarged capacity and the best of equipment could fill; the open doors of opportunity were calling for more mission stations, adequately staffed for both men's and women's work—all of these, as the branches of this Methodist tree grew in length and diameter, meant that the local supply of financial nourishment could not keep pace with the demand. The increasing financial need was putting additional burdens on the missionaries to secure help through special gifts, and thus creating calls for more missionaries to do the work that these men and women could otherwise be doing.

Under this urge and under the leadership of Bishop Lewis, there was launched at the Foochow Annual Conference of 1913 the China Forward Movement, for the spiritual development of the church, and "a financial forward movement involving the principle of self-support." The bishops, at the close of the quadrennium, expressed their gratification that the first objective had been obtained to an "exceedingly fruitful" degree as systematic Bible study throughout the local churches had resulted in "deepening the religious consciousness of the church and awakening interest in the cause of Christianity throughout the entire conference."

The financial effort was none the less successful. Twenty thousand dollars had been subscribed by members of the Foochow Conference before it adjourned; Ralph A. Ward was sent to the United States and within a year had added $55,000 gold from the Methodist Episcopal people; local contributions and subscriptions brought the Chinese giving to $49,-000 by the time of the next Central Conference.

But that was merely as if it were "a shot in the arm." Necessary advances had been made, but, like so many military campaigns, the advance slowed down. India, Japan, and Korea were likewise needing large help from their American brothers and sisters; the cessation of the war in Europe meant a need for hundreds of thousands of dollars for reconstruction in Methodist work there; and the opportunity for advance in Latin America, long desired, seemed to have arrived. The centenary was the answer. The church in the United States, both North and South—its membership, at least—had prospered during the years of the war; missionary needs at home and abroad had increased. The church would furnish millions of dollars during the next five years to give the missions the staffs they needed, to repair or erect the buildings where conditions had been too long unsatisfactory or overcrowded —in other words, to equip the foreign work and let the churches in those lands devote their energy to maintaining and advancing the life of the church.

At the end of the first centenary year, the corresponding secretaries of the Board of Foregin Missions reported that the board had done six things for the Methodist Episcopal Conferences in China, and the Methodist Episcopal Church, South, had done fully as well for its China Conference. Those six things were:

1. Restored operations to their pre-war basis.
2. Made our missionaries more efficient by an increased operating budget.
3. Enlarged the missionary staff.
4. Repaid advances made during the Centenary campaign when ordinary special gift solicitation for increase of funds was suspended.
5. Given a margin for some minor building projects.
6. Aroused an expectancy in the Chinese Church and an increasing enthusiasm for self-help.[2]

Two or three of these results call for further comment. An increasing operating budget had done two things: additional missionaries could relieve some of the older men and women of some of their responsibilities, thus affording them more time and strength for more intensive attention to others, while at the same time removing from them much of the need for the taxing and time-consuming job of securing "special gifts"—thus their efficiency had been increased. Several new missionaries had been added to the staff in each conference, thus, as just said, relieving the existing, overburdened staff, and making possible long-hoped-for undertakings; this gave what Bishop Ward has since described as "a bulge in missionaries," for the increased staff began before long to taper off, and long before the end of the century most of those who had come to China under the impulse of the centenary had, for one reason or another, withdrawn from the field. The repayment of advances during the campaign had been a temporary help which had, of course, been a capital expense from the Centenary Fund, which simply meant a return to special gift solicitation when that fund was exhausted. To say that the centenary roused "an expectancy" in the church in China is to suggest by the very use of the word a subsequent disappointment, which, we shall see, it did.

Meanwhile the church in China had risen to the occasion. Carleton Lacy had asked concerning the Kiangsi Conference goal of $50,000 in addition to the increase in regular missionary contributions, pastoral support and local support of the medical and educational institutions: "Can it be done? Well, it is a bigger task than raising $8,000,000 from the entire church. But we intend to do it." And while a year later F. C. Gale said the pastors in that conference had accepted their quotas "with an absence of optimism," but with "an earnestness of purpose to fulfil their promise made to the bishop," he also said that one district had, within a year, subscribed $7,881 out of a quota of $12,000, and added the experience at Mei-chuan which, he said,

leads the rural circuits of the conference—likely in all China—in the amount of its *bona fide* pledges to the Centenary. Mei-chuan is but a country village whose people have already subscribed $1,620 and are confident that within the four years they will exceed $2,000. There is no suspicion attached to the subscription lists. There is no misuse of the name of the church for personal advantage. No official there is called upon to decide any case in favor of a Christian. The folk there know that the church with its loyal pastor and its two flourishing schools is an asset to the community.[3]

And at the same time Mark Brown was writing from North China:

Many things have combined to hinder the work, but due to the inspiration of the Centenary program and the indefatigable labors of District Superintendent Wu and the district force . . . every church has committed itself to the task of doubling its membership. Convinced that a larger measure of self-support and less dependence on foreign help is the most crying need of many of our older churches today, the emphasis of the financial appeal was laid on trebling within five years the amount paid for pastoral support; and every church has pledged itself to reach this goal. . . . No more conclusive evidence can be afforded for the providential character of the Centenary movement than its ability to so stir and invigorate our Chinese churches. Our people have received a new vision of duty; they still need a new vision of Christ.[4]

Came 1921, and the secretary of the Foochow Conference was writing: "We have actually tried to hold back the giving of Chinese money to Centenary projects, owing to the unlikelihood of receiving from America the necessary Centenary assistance." And Ralph Ward, then secretary for China in the New York office, was reporting to the annual meeting of the Board of Foreign Missions:

All through the year there have been cases of keen disappointment on the part of missionaries and Chinese over the necessity of delaying urgent enterprises. Tens of thousands of dollars of Centenary pledges have been paid in by the Chinese with the understanding that American money would be ready to help. In instance after instance building materials were actually purchased; foundations were laid; walls were raised, in confidence that the promised pledges would soon arrive. "We are standing with our toes on the line ready for the crack of the Centenary pistol to start for the coveted goal," writes one of our missionaries whose hospital building has been held up by Centenary shortage.

. . . .

Missionaries are still trying to explain to the Chinese that American pledges will, eventually, be redeemed. But the Chinese know that the Centenary campaign ended successfully. They are accustomed to take Americans at their word, and it is hard for them to understand why American promises remain so long unfulfilled.[5]

They were "long unfulfilled"—many of the pledges were never paid. Receipts by the Methodist Episcopal Church in the United States fell from $6,071,107 in 1920 to $3,101,359 in 1925, while those by the Methodist Episcopal Church, South, in 1924, showed a decline of 28 per cent as against 1923, and of 57 per cent compared with 1920. Well did the bishops, in the Episcopal Address to the Central Conference in Foochow in 1923, say:

We shall never forget the inspired words of the pastor of this church [Tieng-Ang-Dong] when, in an all-China council at one of the darkest hours of the quadrennium, he lifted our faith to high levels by proclaiming that God might even make the Centenary disappointment a blessing, by calling forth the hidden resources of service and sacrifice from the Chinese church, which too great benevolence from abroad could easily weaken and discourage. The wisdom of a truly Christian insight is in these words.[6]

With the nonfinancial aspects of the Forward Movement of 1913 and the centenary of 1918, must be mentioned the Program Statement Conference in Peking in 1920. Five months of study of conditions in, and plans of advance by, the seven conferences representing Northern Methodism had been made. Most of those who composed this conference had had the privilege of personally seeing the work being done by several of the annual conferences.

So 146 Chinese and American leaders of the church from all the Methodist Episcopal conferences, men and women, met in Peking in January, 1920, for two weeks of intensive group and committee study. The purposes of this conference, the months of study and the miles of travel which had preceded it, were to provide the church leaders, Chinese and American, with a sense of the current movements in China and the several conferences an identification of the goals and policies that should be immediately ahead of the church, and "to support them by consensus of judgment rather than by a mere majority vote."

When the report of this conference had been submitted to the 1920 session of the Eastern Asia Central Conference, that conference accepted its recommendations and requested Bishop Lewis to immediately appoint a directing committee of at least three from each conference who should have power to co-opt others in order to devise the "means necessary for moving forward with all possible strength and speed in carrying out the all-China program of advance for the next five-years." A committee of twenty-one was accordingly appointed, which elected an executive secretary for the quadrennium— the Rev. J. M. Yard of West China—and opened a central office in Shanghai.

Serving somewhat the same need as the financial purposes of the Forward Movement and the Centenary, was the Stewart Fund, which was made available for Methodist work in these years. On November 2, 1916, Bishop Bashford wrote in his diary, that J. H. Blackstone, a member of the Central China Mission, "tells me of the strange providence by which Mr. Milton Stewart of Los Angeles has put $3,000,000 into the hands of W. E. Blackstone." Ten days later he had a long interview with J. H. Blackstone, a part of which is recorded in the bishop's diary:

I told him I understood the aim of the trust to be the speedy evangelization of the world. He told me that the aim of the trust is "to fill up what is lacking on the evangelistic side of mission work." I told him that I understood Jesus' program to be threefold: Miracles—to reveal the Father, Teaching—to train Apostles, Preaching—to evangelize the multitudes. Mr. Blackstone consents to supply (1) chaplain evangelists for schools and hospitals, (2) chaplain evangelists for colleges —at least four [?] colleges. (3) To support entirely four Bible Schools in connection with the four universities (Peking, Nanking, Foochow, Chengtu). (4) To build Primary Stations and use or rather support graduates of the Bible Schools and others to teach in Day Schools throughout the week and preach in the Primary Stations on Sundays. (5) He has not yet agreed to give $25,000 for Bible School buildings and grounds at Peking or to support a Bible School at Hinghwa or at Yenping. (6) He favors Bible Conferences of four to six weeks within the conferences and will finance them and wants us to aid him in a large and successful Bible Conference of four weeks at Nanking. He would pick out men as candidates for the Bible Schools from these conferences. This certainly is a providential answer to prayer for our evangelistic and Day School work.

A year later Bishop Bashford was perplexed as he wrote in his diary on August 29:

> Wrote J. H. Blackstone . . . in regard to $30,000 and $40,000 special gifts sent direct to Presbyterians of China and over $100,000 sent direct to Methodist for India. My perplexity at not hearing from him or from any of the conferences of any sum being spent by him through our Methodist preachers or for our Methodist work. Surely with Methodist administration using funds given chiefly for China and with the Methodist Church in China having a better record in evangelistic work than the Presbyterians, India should not receive $100,000 and China Presbyterians $40,000, and China Methodists nothing.

But over the next year or two the missionaries on the field were able to report of the Stewart Fund that "it has gotten under the entire budget of the district"; "it has helped send out evangelistic bands on every district of the conference"; "at many points special relief has come to overstrained budgets through this co-operation"; "the establishment of the Yenping Bible School with the assistance of the Stewart Fund"; the fund made possible "the new work in Southern Anhwei, a large and promising field"; "gospel teams were organized to travel from church to church . . . and many were converted"; "the new church at Chu-fu has been made possible."

But Bishop Lambuth's biographer tells us that he was worried by some of the situations accompanying the use of this fund—a worry that others felt—and quotes Bishop Lambuth:

> Some of the beneficiaries of the fund, if not the administrators themselves, are actually promoting the pre-millenial theory of the second coming of Christ. This activity centers in Kuling, a considerable sum having been expended the last year in meeting the expenses of missionaries and Chinese to these Kuling meetings. I have not called Brother —————'s doctrinal view in question on this subject or any other. . . . I did not question his right to his own views, but I did object to his attempting to line up our missionaries, thus dividing them into separate groups. . . . As my predecessors know, there was a time when the China Mission was not a unit. It is more nearly so now, in spirit and cooperative effort, than ever in its history. It would be nothing short of a tragedy to have it divided again.[7]

Looking back, the dangers that were feared, however well-founded they may have been, were less than the benefits, for much that the current appropriations could not do, that the Forward Movement failed to do, and that the Centenary was not yet ready to do, was done for the Methodist churches in China through the income from the Milton Stewart Fund.

Much of the advance of the church in the third quarter century was unquestionably stimulated by these financial bounties. No previous period had seen such intensive development of the church, but no previous period had seen so much money poured into it. Perhaps it was now stronger and better prepared to weather the storms that another quarter century would bring.

XII
WOMEN ACT LIKE THAT

Gentlemen, how can women not be mighty,
when they act like that?
—I Esdras 4:32 (Goodspeed)

TWO OF THE FIRST THREE PERSONS IN CHINA TO JOIN THE METHODIST
Episcopal Church, South, were women; three of those among the first to be
baptized in the Methodist Episcopal Church were women; four of these five
were closely related to men who were received at the same time. From every
part of the Methodist work in China, almost from the first day, there had
been a persistent call for special work by women for women. Mrs. Maclay
and Mrs. Lambuth were doing what they could through schools for girls,
but such measures were entirely too feeble to count much or soon toward
the winning of women to the church. However largely the men may then or
now control the activities of the Methodist Church—and others too—the
church could never have an assured and permanent place in the life of any
nation without a feminine touch and without its being a real factor in the
homelife.

Hence the Woolston sisters had been sent to Foochow in 1858; hence
the Woman's Foreign Missionary Society had been organized in 1869, and
these sisters were made its first representatives in China. Hence also that
society had sent Maria Brown and Mary Porter to Peking in 1871, who had
started the movement against foot-binding in schools, and who, as Miss
Porter's diary tells it, raised the question: "What should be the limit of our
intercourse with our brethren among the missionaries?" Her diary continues:

The presence of single women in China missions was an offense against all
Chinese ideas of propriety. . . . There were missionaries on the field in those pioneer
days who believed the introduction of single women workers into China missions
to be a mistake. In conference that night Miss Brown and I agreed that we should
be misunderstood no matter what course we might choose. . . . We decided, therefore, that we should conduct ourselves in all our relationships according to the
conventions of our own Christian land.

There is evidence of divine guidance in the fact that we were brought to these
decisions about the time that our infant Methodist Church of North China was
born. . . . The new church grew into new ideas concerning the dignity of womanhood, and the possible partnership of womanhood with manhood for the benefit
of both.[1]

226

This section of her diary was written too soon to record both her own and Miss Brown's marriage to members of that North China Mission!

The Woman's Foreign Missionary Society had also sent Gertrude Howe and Lucy Hoag to Kiukiang in 1873, causing some one to say they "would be no addition to our general work, but rather a hindrance," but V. C. Hart, superintendent of the mission, commented: "I am happy in stating to our Society that no more valuable reinforcement has reached this mission." Likewise the sending of Dr. Combs to Peking in 1873, Dr. Trask to Foochow, and Dr. Lettie Mason to Kiukiang in 1874, and Dr. Mildred Phillips to Soochow in 1884, had a definite objective, and became a decided asset to the work of those missions.

None the less valuable, though somewhat delayed, was the result which followed the organization of the Woman's Missionary Society of the Methodist Episcopal Church, South, in 1878. Funds had already been raised, and Miss Lochie Rankin had been accepted and appointed to the China Mission. The new Woman's Missionary Society immediately adopted her, and she became the first of thirty-three to represent that society and labor in China during the next twenty-three years for the winning of Chinese womanhood for Christ. To Miss Rankin and her sister Dora, who soon joined her, belong the credit of being the first Methodist women to undertake that doubtful, albeit usually successful and fruitful, policy of opening and "manning" a mission station not occupied by any missionary family— Nantziang, some sixteen miles from Shanghai, was the site selected for the first girls' school and women's work outside of Shanghai. Work for women, under the Woman's Missionary Society, was not undertaken in Soochow, "noted for the learning of its men and the beauty of its women," until 1881.

By the time the West China Mission was commenced, as we have seen, the work for women, supported by the women's missionary societies, was so fully an established policy that Miss Frances Wheeler accompanied the first missionaries of the missionary society—the first second-generation missionary appointed to China by the Woman's Foreign Missionary Society. But after the riot had temporarily closed the work at Chungking, the women were hesitant to re-enter. When, however, there was noted "a growing need of a class of helpers to do general work—a 'whatsoever' staff," the idea of sending deaconesses to meet the need was accepted, women's work was again commenced, and Miss Clara Collier, one of those deaconesses and for many years a devoted worker in Szechuen, accepted work under the authorities of the church and immediately commenced the study of the language and the teaching of English in the university.

Many stories could be related of the results of this work—of women who themselves became evangels, as Bible women working in the homes, of access secured to well-to-do families through the calls to women doctors, of devoted Chinese women living their Christianity in the face of family opposition, of girls winning their parents to Christ and contributing their "cash" to the cause of the church. We pause, however, for only one brief but inspiring incident. A Christian woman in North China, recognizing that her earthly life was close to its end, gave a string of "cash" which she had accumulated to the society through whose workers she had found Christ— "probably the first legacy left in the Chinese empire to the cause of Christ."

With the missionaries of the women's missionary societies increasing in number—often ultimately faster than the men missionaries—and with the growing importance of schools and hospitals for girls and women, and with Bible women working side by side with the native pastors, it is not surprising that questions of the legal relationship between the representatives of the two societies should crop up. Harmony generally prevailed but there were times when masculine authority was resented—even to the point of resignation from the mission. But the General Conferences which had approved the organization of these women's societies seem to have failed to stipulate adequate policies or regulations for their relationship to the parent societies or that of the missionaries on the field. Hence, before 1883 these field relationship problems were solved, or left unsolved, by mutual conference, or by the bishop who came, saw, expressed his solution, and left the field until an episcopal colleague should visit it some year or years later. Bishop Merrill, in 1883, while visiting China, expressed the hope that the next General Conference would remedy the situation, but, pending such action, decided

(1) that the ladies of the W.F.M.S. are not members of the Annual Meeting; (2) that he has no jurisdiction over their work; (3) that he cannot appoint them to the respective departments of their work; and (4) that the Annual Meeting cannot receive their reports.[2]

To avoid the entire abandonment of the practice which had prevailed "from the founding of the mission," the North China Mission appointed a committee which should receive the reports of the women and present them to the annual meeting. But the General Conference of 1884 enacted that

all missionaries sent out by this Society shall labor under the direction of the particular conferences or missions of the Church in which they may be severally employed. They shall be annually appointed by the president of the Conference or Mission, and shall be subject to the same rules of removal that govern the other missionaries.[3]

"Subsequently," as A. H. Tuttle tells the story in his biography *Mary Porter Gamewell,* one of our presiding bishops at Peking declared that under this law he could not appoint women to work who were not regular missionaries of the Woman's Society. Mrs. Gamewell contested the point with the bishop, and directed his attention to the rule of the Woman's Society which states, "Lady missionaries in charge of work and all missionaries of the Woman's Foreign Missionary Society are appointed by the president of the Conference at the same time and in the same manner that the appointments of the Conference are made." The bishop gracefully acknowledged the strength of her contention, and calling her the constitutional lawyer of the mission, rendered his decision accordingly.[4]

The oversight of all work by one board in Nashville had avoided any such problem in the territory of the Methodist Episcopal Church, South. But not until the union of the three branches of Methodism at Kansas City in 1939 was there the attempt at unification in administration which should have been effected in all Methodist Episcopal Conferences many years earlier. Although the relationship between the general and the woman's societies and their workers had been clarified in the eighties, it was without any organic co-ordination, much less amalgamation, and sometimes seemed to lack even co-operation. This had led, in 1934, at the Central Conference meeting in Nanking, to action that in each annual conference a joint advisory policy committee should be appointed, an equal number of "men by the Annual Conference and women by the Woman's Conference," whose duty it should be "to formulate policies concerning the work and make recommendations to the authorized committees of both boards." The organization of the field committees, which resulted from the union of the churches and the formation of the one Board of Missions and Church Extension, has been the long-delayed culmination of the question raised in Peking in 1883 (if not earlier and elsewhere also) and one which is "going on towards perfection" in making all the Methodist work a unity.

Co-operation, it has been said elsewhere, between the men and the women sometimes seemed lacking—but only sometimes. Many examples of the closest co-operation could be cited, and in these later years that in education, especially in co-education in primary and higher primary schools throughout the country, has been an outstanding success. An interesting and not altogether insignificant illustration of co-operative work at Changli has been called by Dr. Clay "a practical union between W. F. M. S. work and that of the Board of Foreign Missions along lines of health, education, and preventative medicine," which he describes as follows:

We have this term had a noble experiment in training the senior girls of our W.F.M.S. school. These girls all go out next year to teach in village schools. We have been taking them into our hospital dispensary and teaching them to do dressings, vaccinations, bandaging, first aid, etc. Each girl gets a month of this training coming to dispensary five days a week for one-and-a-half hours each day.[5]

But we must turn back to 1886, when, during the Foochow Conference one of the members of the conference, praying for the Woman's Conference then in session, called it "one of the most wonderful events, stranger to the Chinese than the electric telegraph," adding, "that seemed so wonderful, we thought we would never see it here in China, but last year the telegraph came, and now the Woman's Conference." This first Woman's Conference was a meeting of women gathered together from the several sections of the conference for examination and instruction as Bible women and teachers, for feminine discussion and consideration of the methods, views and sentiments of women's work, and "also for a deepening of Christian experience. Although this was literally a "conference," without legal sanction or legislative powers, one of the missionaries of the Church Missionary Society in Foochow said "his heart was so full and burning, that he must speak and express his pleasure, that the Methodist women had taken this step."

So successful was this experiment that it became an annual conference (no capitals) in Foochow and similar organizations were formed in the other conferences and missions. By 1891 the Foochow Woman's Conference met on November 18 as a delegated body, conferences of women on the several districts having elected their representatives. This ten-day "intellectual and spiritual feast" is reported to have been well-attended, "fifteen of the teachers at one gathering bringing their babies with them."

China was in the midst of war when, in 1941, a national Woman's Society of Christian Service was organized during the Central Conference. Some of them through routes of danger and some of them on foot, these women had come with that interest in missionary work for China, India, and Africa which is described more fully in chapter sixteen. Thus these several groups were united in a national organization that preserved their local and regional interests and activities and added a national project of an Easter offering for the children of Belgium. Conference organizations were thus encouraged and strengthened, and local societies were promoted as the national and conference organizations developed local leadership and emphasized imperishable and permanent values. Just as a sample of the results, this is quoted from many encouraging reports: "In this rural area, so often disturbed by the enemy, the work of the Woman's Society of Christian Service was just like a lily planted in the thorns."

The ordination of women, following authorization by the General Conference of the Methodist Episcopal Church, benefited the church in China, but did not become any more general than in other parts of the church. Janet Ho was licensed as a local preacher in the Foochow Conference in

1923, the first Chinese woman so honored. Three followed—the Misses Chen Pei-Yin, Chiang Feng-Chen, and Chu Sheo-Chen—in the Kiangsi Conference in 1924, and Miss Cheng Mei-Yin the following year, and a long line into the future years had commenced.

And so the women continued to work like that, ever increasing their share in the spread of the Kingdom, starting and maintaining women's missionary societies, receiving ordination as local preachers in 1923, becoming college presidents in 1927, and sitting as delegates from the annual conferences as early as 1912 when Dr. Li Bi-Cu represented the Foochow Conference. Women had come to China to win women to Christ and make them vital in the church; the relationship between the general and the woman's societies and their workers had been clarified; and Chinese women were already taking over from their American sisters a major share in this privilege of making Christian Chinese women. Perhaps no testimony illustrating how wonderfully the Chinese women were acting for the Christianization of their country is more fitting with which to close this chapter, than this paragraph from Fletcher S. Brockman of the Y.M.C.A., referring to Dr. Ida Kahn and her medical work in Nanchang:

I was walking through the city with a Chinese friend who had been educated in America. We were pressing past the crowd—such a crowd! Coolies carrying bales of paper and tea, wheelbarrows crowded with passengers, jinrickshas jolting over the uneven flagstones, sedan chairs, for which way must be made because an important person within lent authority to the insolent bearers, members of the literati walking leisurely in the midst of the common rush, modern students from the near-by government colleges with books and pens, beggars repellant with filth and disease, cooks hastening on with chickens and vegetables under their arms—what a medley of high and low, an impression of infinite numbers! "There is not one of this crowd," said my friend as the conversation reverted to Dr. Kahn, "who does not know her name." [6]

XIII
NEW OCCASIONS TEACH NEW DUTIES

New occasions teach new duties,
Time makes ancient good uncouth.

1. *Sabbath Observance*

ROBERT HERRICK, IN "CEREMONIES FOR CANDLEMAS EVE," PRESENTS A thought which, in terms of its life, is true of the Methodist Church in China.

Thus times do shift,—each thing his turn does hold;
New things succeed, as former things grow old.

The essence, the very life of this church and its adaptability to the social conditions by which it is influenced and to which it in turn imparts its influence, is grounded in its ability to leave by "life's unresting sea," its "outgrown shells," and to "build more stately mansions" of methods, ritual, and institutions, that "each new temple" may be "nobler than the last."

Judson Collins had early tried to make a difference between the Sabbath and the other days of the week, that foreign division of time called "the seven days of the worship period." His Sabbath school in Foochow in 1848 had been but the first of hundreds which, by 1897, were scattered over the country. That at Asbury Church, Peking, had attracted nation-wide attention because of its high degree of organization and efficiency in producing desired results, and in many parts of the country the missionaries looked to it as a model for them to follow. But "heathen Sunday schools" (mark the terminology!) were doing their part—tens of thousands of picture cards, the gifts of hundreds of American Sunday schools, sorted by the missionary children, with Bible texts on red paper pasted on their backs, given as a reward for attendance, were attracting children from heathen homes and carrying the Christian message to their families as the children carried them home. These Sunday schools were having a real influence in making the "worship day" different from the others.

But the Sunday schools were not enough to create a real attitude of Sabbath observance. Missionaries who had come to China from cities and towns in Iowa and Carolina, Massachusetts and Mississippi, during the last half of the nineteenth century could not quite appreciate the difficulty which the Chinese Christians faced in observing the Sabbath—the idolatrous or materialistic environment was so different from that of the church-going, Sabbath-observing communities of their home towns of that period.

However difficult it might be to secure the proper observance of the Lord's Day, and in spite of the lack of such observance by Roman Catholics and some Protestants, Nathan Sites was by no means the only Methodist who felt that "the Methodist Church must have a Christian Sabbath, or there can be no Methodism in China," for, he added, "a pure, high-toned, spiritual church alone can become the light of China." But it was a difficult problem. The Christians constituted so small a proportion of the population that there were many competitors ready to take business away from their Christian rivals during their day of rest, making it hard, for example, for Diong A-Hok to secure the consent of his associates to close their business. The result was, in other cases, that church members would work in the morning before service, come to preaching, and then continue their work afterwards. In one case at least, a young man who was in the employ of a heathen made arrangements with this employer to have the Sabbath for himself by furnishing a substitute on that day. But business competition was not alone to blame; the Chinese regarded all days alike, and they had a considerable following among the foreign residents.

But as Sabbath observance in the United States was steadily passing from the strict rigidity, and perhaps frigidity, of Puritan days to that of the automobile-golf-baseball days, in the Methodist membership in China the advance from previous years was steadily, though slowly, moving to meet it at a common denominator. Many Methodist men in cities and villages closed their shop doors on "Worship Day" and hung out the sign: "Today is worship day: tomorrow business will be resumed as usual." In some cases this Sabbath sign was placed on the counter, but shoes were being mended and lacquer-ware was being decorated behind the counter or in the back room.

The attempt was made to require Sabbath-observance as a condition of church membership. It is doubtful if that was, or could be, as effective as the results to the faithful observers. Take these results as reported by J. Fred Hayner from North China as early as 1900:

The consciences of the members are at work. Two members of the same church had resolved to keep the Sabbath, but harvest time was too big a temptation. They stayed away from church to reap millet. Both were wounded with a sickle, laying them up for several days. They took it as a direct judgment from heaven, and since they have faithfully observed the day. The Lord is prospering several members who have kept the Sabbath. Their gains in six days exceed those formerly made in seven days. One farmer not only stops all work from Saturday to Monday, but also requires his hired men to attend church and learn to read. Several illiterate men who work for him can now read the New Testament. Since beginning to keep the Sabbath he has nearly doubled the size of his farm, now owning over a hundred acres without a mortgage. . . . One of the helpers was nominated a steward, but the Quarterly Conference failed to confirm the nomination. The objection raised was that this member, although otherwise acceptable, did not regularly keep the Sabbath.[1]

Could that have happened in Ohio, Oklahoma, or Oregon? Or elsewhere in China?

2. *The Epworth League*

The Epworth League, which by 1897 was becoming a mighty force among young Methodists in the United States, had found its way—can we say its place?—among Chinese Methodists. A "Young Men's Epworth League" was probably not known in the United States, but it was to be a good many years before the social aspect of the American leagues could be a factor in the Chinese societies, and the Young Men's League of Asbury Church, Peking, was more active in evangelistic work than most of its contemporaries between Los Angeles and Boston.

Fukien province not only boasted the oldest Epworth League chapter in China—that at Hinghwa—but by far the largest number of chapters in the country. Almost wherever the Methodist Episcopal Church established a station in South China, there also was started an Epworth League. Their greatest weakness lay in their numbers. Churches had Epworth Leagues before they had young people. In 1899 it was feared that the league would crowd out other departments of church work, and their elimination from all but educational centers was recommended. By this time also the China Mission reported 10 leagues with 386 members.

But where educational work was strong, attendance at Epworth League meetings was, as in Hinghwa, often compulsory for students in theological schools, women's Bible training schools, high schools, and primary schools for boys and girls. Hinghwa Epworth League considered that it had a membership of a thousand. Seventy-three charges throughout the country reported Epworth Leagues with an uncertain membership of 7,464, and three charges reported junior leagues with a membership of 228. Most of the Epworth Leagues, in the south at least, were such in name only. The same older people who attended church services dominated the Epworth League meetings. Trained leadership was lacking. The few junior leagues had been organized where some missionary was prepared to undertake this specialized work for children, and as far as they went, the junior leagues were much more like the real thing.

Sarah Bosworth, conference secretary in Foochow, was right in noting that "good work has been done and we hope gradually to educate the people to an appreciation of the meaning of Epworth League work." And the

Rev. W. B. Burke had observed that the league at Nantziang was as "wide awake" as any in the United States, and that "its exercises were so interesting that outsiders came from quite a distance to attend them."

The Committee on Epworth Leagues recommended, and the Central Conference of 1911 voted:

That a Union National Secretary for the Epworth Leagues be secured as soon as possible. To this end we urgently request our Epworth League Board of Control to assume the partial support of such a secretary, and to negotiate with the Epworth League authorities of the Methodist Episcopal Church, South, and the Canadian Methodist Church concerning the joint support of such a secretary.[2]

But it was not till the fall of 1919, after Paul Hutchinson had presented the need for such a worker at the centenary in Columbus, that the central office of the Epworth League in Chicago sent Miss Geraldine Townsend to China as associate secretary of the Epworth League, almost from the beginning to become full-time secretary in name as well as in responsibility.

When her work started it was viewed with some suspicion. The Epworth League had been in so many mission stations an empty form with no program throughout the field as a whole that both missionaries and pastors were dubious about further "promotion." But with the assistance of an advisory council, Miss Townsend began a reorganization of the loosely defined chapters, a modest program of genuine service was suggested, lesson "Topics and Comments" in Chinese were prepared, and "Christian Social Service" and other useful helps were written for translation.

The first quadrennial report of the secretary, in 1923, told of the decrease in the number of Epworth League chapters reported, but an increase of 25 per cent in the number conforming to the constitution. Membership in junior and senior chapters conforming to required standards was placed at 5,289. To an encouraging extent also, devotional meetings were changing from a preaching service to one of general participation in prayer, testimony, and discussion. The annual yearbook on the league topics prepared in Shanghai was now used in China, Malaysia, and the Netherlands East Indies. The social service work outlined for third department activity was the thing most needed in Chinese communities, and fortunately the thing which most appealed to Chinese young people, and included suggestions for making a social survey of a Chinese community, especially suggestions for health work in the community, suggestions for work against such enemies of China as opium, vice, foot-binding, a complete outline of activities and program of daily vacation Bible schools, and encouragement for starting free day schools, night schools, reading rooms and libraries.

The social life which had helped so largely to build up the Epworth

League in the United States could not be transplanted to China in these early years, and until changes in the social life of the young people of China could come—and they were not very fully developed in 1923—the program started in the previous quadrennium seemed best suited to the conditions. The board of Young People's Work, authorized by the Central Conference of 1923 along lines later adopted by the General Conference of the united Methodist Church, was set up to plan, co-ordinate, and promote both Sunday school and Epworth League work throughout all the conferences of the Methodist Episcopal Church; it might change the character of any Epworth League that continued to survive as such, but it was a logical step in the inevitable forward movement that the church would take for its youth.

3. Conference Obligations and Procedures

With the growing strength of the church and its Chinese leadership, as well as because of the shocks of warfare, the last quarter of a century has been marked by many changes, some making the church more truly at home in China, some foreshadowing changes which the union of Methodism and the subsequent general conferences would adopt, some being temporary emergency expedients and no more, and others proving themselves permanently fit. Some of these changes may have seemed at the time to have been almost heresy. All of them were made with a view to making the blue dye of Methodism a more real influence in the life of China's people.

As early as March, 1890, a writer in the *Missionary Reporter* had felt that the authorities in the United States were failing to appreciate the needs of the growing church in China, complaining, not without some justification, that the General Conference had refused—or so it seemed—any special legislation for the work in foreign lands, and that to continue the use of the *Discipline* in China, certain changes were necessary; that while the *Discipline* might be well adapted to meet the needs of the church in the United States, it was not therefore equally well adapted to meet the wants of infant churches overseas. Hence, he concluded, that unless changes were permitted, its use would only hinder the foreign mission work and put an unnecessary burden upon "these little children." Eventually this plea bore fruit.

By 1934 the Central Conference was able to adopt a recommendation "that the baptism of infants be replaced by a consecration service when the parents dedicate the child to Christ. The child may then be baptized when reaching years of understanding," and added to this action the statement that "it is understood that such a child may accompany his parents to the Communion Table." The legality of this action was, of course, contained in several general conference authorizations to central conferences to provide their own courses of study and to revise the ritual to fit native conditions. At the same time the Central Conference authorized a revision of the *Discipline* to exclude "all matters of no immediate need or importance to the Church in China," and to include "(1) all commonly used parts of the *Discipline;* (2) all General Conference legislation pertaining to Central Conferences; (3) all Eastern Asia Central Conference actions and legislation." [3]

The admission of laymen to the annual conferences of the Methodist Episcopal Church, authorized by the General Conference, was approved by the Central Conference of 1934, which took its own action to ensure "that the lay members in Annual Conferences will not be in excess of the ministerial members"; but other than calling for a plan for effecting this, the only action taken was to stipulate minimum educational standards for lay members without requiring middle school graduation. "The best thing that has happened to the church in China in many a long day," said the bishops, "is the active participation of the laymen in the annual conferences."

The 1927 session of the West China Conference met with two American and fourteen Chinese members present. Bishop Grose had been unable to arrive, and, while he had telegraphed the time and place for the session, he had not appointed a presiding officer, as Bishop David H. Moore had done in Foochow in 1900, and as had been done on other occasions. After the opening devotions, the conference balloted for a chairman. The result was a tie between Spencer Lewis and the Rev. Lincoln Chang (Dsang Lin-Gao). An American conference would have ordered another ballot to break the tie; this Chinese conference, not hampered by precedent or Robert's *Rules of Order,* insisted that both serve as chairman. Two years later the Chengtu West China Conference went its predecessor one better: Bishop Birney had held the Chungking West China Conference, but was too ill to take the ten-day overland trip to Chengtu, and, as reported by the *China Christian Advocate,*

the conference, to the amusement of some, elected three chairmen, Dsang Lin-Gao, Joseph Beech, and Spencer Lewis, each receiving the same number of votes. . . . The Conference opened for business at 9:00 A.M. Monday, the three chairmen presiding on different days.

Thus it was demonstrated to the Central Conference of 1930, which was to elect the first Chinese bishop, that the church in China had produced at least one man who could take a bishop's place as a presiding officer, and one who had the confidence of his confreres that he could do so.

This same West China Conference of 1927 took another step to cut the apron strings that were tying the China conferences perhaps too closely to the General Conference. In every conference most of the business was transacted in Chinese, an interpreter for the bishop being necessary until the election of Bishops Wang and Ward and those elected later. But because General Conference regulations had precluded other action, each conference each year had taken a formal vote making the English minutes the official minutes of the session. Disregarding any possible disciplinary action or failure of approval by the General Conference of 1928, the West China Conference voted for a Chinese secretary only, the minutes to be translated into English afterwards. Perhaps this had been an exigency action in view of the fact that only two Americans were present, and one of those was a presiding officer. But it established a precedent, and the Central Conference of 1930 adopted the following (which, however, seems a bit ambiguous):

> We request that the Chinese Minutes in the national language be made official for the ten conferences in China. Your committee recommends that the English and Chinese Minutes be carefully compared and made to correspond, and that the English Minutes be made official for English requirements and the Chinese Minutes for Chinese requirements.[4]

West China accordingly made its Chinese minutes "official," stating that the English minutes are the "official translation." Shantung, ten years later, hoping that it would not "incur criticism from the examiners at Central Conference," adopted a new plan for printing the minutes, of which Perry Hanson wrote in the *China Christian Advocate* in October 1940:

> The Chinese and English records will be in the same book with the Statistical Report in the middle of the book. Hereafter the Chinese Minutes will be of greater importance than formerly because the English record will no longer travel to General Conference but the Chinese record must go to Central Conference.

In 1941 Kalgan went all the way and set the pattern which all the conferences very soon would copy; in the terse words of Horace S. Williams, attending the conference for the last time before repatriation was necessary: "There were no English Minutes of the Conference."

The reverence for ancestors may have made the Chinese of all peoples the most conservative. Perhaps it is because of that very conservatism that, while they eagerly accept the church for the spiritual values it has brought them, yet they want to dress it in costumes and adorn it with the jewelry of their own choosing. Hence these changes in ritual, *Discipline*, conference procedures, and so forth.

4. *Administration, Promotion, and Construction*

Meanwhile in financial and business matters the church had found it necessary to add new organizations. North China, pioneering along a line of activity too often not considered "missionary," secured a missionary who was "a specialist who could give his whole time to the financial and business work of the Mission." The time came, therefore, when the officials of the board in New York, after many conferences with China missionaries, and helped, no doubt, by the advisory action of the Mott Conferences, proposed to the Methodist Episcopal Missions in China the establishment of a central treasurer's office, which could relieve some missionary in each conference of much business detail and so promote efficiency and economy by consolidation. The plan was underwritten financially for a three-year experiment, and Edgar K. Morrow was sent to China to organize and carry through the experiment. Morrow's first report, that for 1915, mentions these early results:

The Kiangsi, Central China, Foochow, and Hinghwa Missions, in order, after thorough discussion, adopted the proposition without a dissenting vote. . . . The West China Mission is too far distant to adopt the central plan in its entirety. A local treasurer is absolutely necessary. They can get the full advantage of better exchange rates and the business agency, however, and there are other factors that will prove helpful to West China. . . . All of the work of the Kiangsi, Central China, Foochow, and Hinghwa treasurers was taken over January 1.[5]

And in November, 1915, the bishops in their address to the Central Conference referred to the undertaking as "one of the events of this quadrennium which promises much for the weal of the church in China," and which had already saved "several thousands of dollars . . . in exchange and financial adjustments to the missions." Within three years the treasurer reported that "the expense of maintaining our central treasurer's office in Shanghai, aside from the Treasurer's salary, is entirely covered by the profits accrued" from such exchange transactions and financial adjustments.

Morrow's first report also contained a dream which had in it much of merit, but which seems to have lacked the personnel to make it real, or was too far in advance of the real condition in the churches and missions:

If a policy for developing indigenous resources can be worked out along practical and comprehensive lines that will in part relate the giving in China to the gifts of the home church, a central financial office may offer a valuable co-operative agency, for it is not premature to predict that more and more the special giving of the home constituency will become more and more *supplemental.*[6]

When the Centenary Movement came into being, promotion of the work in China was necessary, both in China and by China in the United States. Hence in response to the Program Statement Conference (as has been mentioned) the centenary office was established in Shanghai, which, with its executive secretary and its publicity, photographic, lantern slide, and other bureaus, did a fine piece of work along lines which were developed; but this office was never anything but promotional, and, like all promotional enterprises, was transitory.

Then 1923 saw the creation of two groups for better nation-wide co-ordination of the work of the Methodist Episcopal conferences. First, the Board of Foreign Missions authorized the creation of an All-China Finance Committee in the fall of 1923, which functioned for a few years in co-ordinating estimates and appropriations to the several conferences and the centralized work in Shanghai. In time, however, it ceased to function as, second, the executive board became an effective co-ordinating body, acting meanwhile for the Central Conference. This board had been organized when the Central Conference, on November 24, 1923, adopted the report of its Committee on Temporal Economy, recommending "that there be an Executive Board of the Methodist Episcopal Church in Eastern Asia," a board whose existence, albeit in skeleton form, was able to function through the war period when the Central Conference could not meet in regular quadrennial years.

The release of professional missionaries from activities for which they had not been prepared, as in the case of the North China and the central treasurers' offices, was furthered by the establishment of the Fukien Construction Bureau. Ever since Moses White, during his first year in Foochow, had become "heartily tired of fixing and repairing," other missionaries, who in every field, had to devote much of their time to the building of homes, churches, schools, and hospitals, felt much the same way. As the Rev. W. C. Longden expressed it: "I am hoping this will be the end of my building experience in connection with mission work." Then he went on to say: "Apart from money considerations, we cannot afford to do much building in China. Not only does it consume the missionary's time, but by distracting his mind in business relations with the people, is, of necessity, attended with loss of spiritual power." [7] This expression found a hearty echo from many a man who wanted to preach the gospel, heal the sick, or train the youth.

Not only were building operations distracting and trying to one's patience, but what of the results? On many a country hilltop or busy city street churches were built that furnished a place where people could meet and listen to the pastor expound the Scriptures, but little more. The Rev. F. Ohlinger once said that he believed the Pocheng District, in the Hinghwa

Conference, had "the unenviable distinction of having within its bounds both the smallest and probably the poorest chapel in all Methodism." By 1910 there had been some improvement, for H. R. Caldwell, a tiger-hunting and church-building missionary, writing from the "coast districts" of the Foochow Conference, said: "Methodism here has outgrown the age of the mud hovel and has entered the age of brick and stone. The handsome church buildings now ready for dedication mark a new era in this work." But still, in 1920, the Central Conference Committee on the State of the Church was able to complain:

In some conferences we are glad to report that the majority of the churches are substantial brick buildings, clean and well ventilated; alas, in many places in China we are still using old shops that have been done over and they are dark and damp and not well adapted to the purpose to which they are being put.[8]

But, even these, to one who has sat Sunday after Sunday facing beautiful stained glass windows, or who has stood in reverent silence before handsomely carved pillars supporting gracefully curved roofs over the gods made by men's hands—even these handsome and well-ventilated brick church buildings lacked the lines and the color that would lead one's thought to God.

When it came to the building of schools and hospitals it was easy to plan a building with four plain walls, some windows, and a simple roof; and residences could be built to keep out the rain and the heat, in both summer and winter; but they were sometimes, as James Burke said, "odd architectural assortments, . . . the only known species of their kind, . . . unique, but not indescribable." And what of the quality of construction? Perhaps no better houses have been built in Methodist "compounds" than those—considering only the quality of construction—that were built before 1890. But there came a day when bricks were laid in mud with all too little sand and lime, and when the ends of floor beams could be spared their termite-repellant bath and duly covered. And so Joseph Beach, builder and maker of West China Union University, and missionary par excellence in that great western empire, said after the university campus was well under way:

Six permanent brick buildings have been erected on the campus. . . . Our own mission has one of the six buildings, which has cost about as much in patience as in money. One thing is clear from the experience: we should have a builder to give his entire time to the workmen and see that the material goes into the building and not into the workmen's homes.[9]

To meet these problems a beginning was made in 1916 in Fukien, a beginning which proved its value but was not made a permanent and essential part of the Methodist staff and program elsewhere until called for on a China-wide basis for the postwar reconstruction and rehabilitation. After the Anglo-Chinese College had been forced to close its engineering department because of insufficient paying demand, E. F. Black, who had engineered that department, was recalled from the United States to undertake the organization of the Fukien Construction Bureau. Under his initiation and the consecrated energy of Paul P. Wiant, who has devoted many years to this work, and of the others who came as colleagues and successors to Black, this bureau has been able to meet the building problems of which missionaries had complained. Devoting itself to planning, designing, and supervising the construction of churches, schools, hospitals, and homes that are suitable and well-built, this bureau has been erecting buildings that will stand for years to come to the credit of Methodism, art, and God.

Increased efficiency for evangelist and doctor was not being produced alone by architectural and financial experts, nor through centralized offices only. Not the least of the advances in this direction were extramural as far as offices and mission compounds were concerned, and of these the improvement in means of travel has been a mighty factor coming from new conditions arising from the impacts with the West. The excellent postal service which the Chinese government developed during the first quarter of the twentieth century was a boon to the missionary living far inland and to the district superintendent in communicating with the pastors on his district. Maclay and Sites, Brewster and Owen, had covered many thousands of miles of Fukien rivers and cobblestone roads on foot and in arduously-poled "rat-boats"; Lambuth and Allen had taken their families to Soochow by slow-moving canalboats; Dr. Terry and Dr. Hopkins had answered calls for medical aid by bumpy cart or perched on the side of a wheelbarrow; and the wind to propel their houseboats, or trackers to tow them laboriously through the Yangtze rapids, had provided Hart and Lewis, Nichols and Longden, with travel facilities in the river provinces. Those days had not gone in 1906 when Bishop Bashford was the first episcopal visitor to the Methodists of Shantung, when mules, buckboard, cook, driver, food, and bedding were sent to meet the bishop and Dr. Hobart at Suchien-Hsien; nor had the shrill squeak of wheelbarrow axles disappeared when members of the Program Statement Conference visited Taian in 1920. But those delegates had arrived at Taian by railroad—a travel luxury many of them had not enjoyed west of the Pacific. Many of those who had visited the Fukien conferences had been taken up river by steam launch covering the forty-five miles to Mintsing in less than a day, and the steamer which an English merchant had succeeded in taking through the Yangtze gorges to Chungking in 1898, while not saving Bishop Bashford and Bishop Lewis from that slow trip by boat, was, nevertheless, a step forward toward the day when Bishop Gowdy would fly from Chungking to Chengtu in a couple of hours instead of the ten days by sedan chair—one of the reasons for the division of the West China Conference.

What could be done in Kiangsi could and would soon be done throughout China. Listen to the enthusiasm of an evangelistic missionary at Kiukiang in 1920:

The "Baby Scout" has helped the itinerant this year. . . . It has been possible to make former four and five day trips in one day, and those who know the difficulties of waiting on a sulky wheelbarrow man, or deferring to the grizzly and hard chair-bearer, will appreciate what this has meant. Recently it was possible to go to a distant outstation, hold a quarterly conference, and return to Kiukiang the same day, attending a wedding feast in the evening. This is the first time in Methodist history that one has done a thing like that in Kiangsi. The time of slow travel in this conference has passed—we now have three motorcycles, and the next agitation will be for good roads.[10]

New temples, architecturally and structurally, have been built for church, institutions, and homes, by men trained to do that. The outgrown shell of the "heathen" Sunday school and the "Epworth League" that was just another preaching service have been succeeded by co-ordinated and planned young peoples' programs. New occasions have demonstrated the value of a central treasurer's office and a Central Conference Executive Board. Even Christians who formerly knew few holidays other than New Year's will, in spite of the competitive society, in time find the good in the Christian Sabbath. More stately mansions, in that they are better adapted to Chinese life and culture, have replaced certain sections of the ritual and *Discipline* developed by the General Conferences in the United States; conference procedures of the American pattern have grown old and been succeeded by those better adapted to the Chinese mind and habit. Good roads have come for the Good News, and mailboxes, station wagons and airplanes, are helping the forward march. And so, while many new things may succeed "as former things grow old," the Methodist Church in China will have its hue enriched and will ennoble its place as a part of Wesley's world-wide parish.

XIV

ALL ONE BODY

We are not divided,
All one body we,
One in hope and doctrine,
One in charity.

1. *Early Suggestions for Methodist Union*

WE HAVE FOLLOWED THE DEVELOPMENT OF THE METHODIST EPISCOPAL Church in Fukien, the Yangtze Valley, and North China; we have witnessed the growth of the Methodist Episcopal Church, South, in the populous delta of the Yangtze River; and we have seen the establishment of the Methodist Protestant Church in the mountains and valleys around Kalgan. We have also noted the entrance of the Canadian Methodist Church into Chengtu and its neighborhood, but very scant reference has been made in these pages to the Wesleyan Church, and none to the United Methodist Church, or the Free Methodist Church of North America. Methodism was divided, and the Chinese who could see little or no difference in creed or theology, polity or administration, could not appreciate the background of the separation which had produced these seven varieties of Methodism. Sooner or later some or all of these churches must—it was inevitable—consider union, or at least federation, in China.

The union of the Methodist Episcopal Church and the Methodist Episcopal Church, South, was naturally the first church union in China considered by either of these bodies. If any earlier proposals looking to such a union have been recorded, they must be in diaries or personal letters to which I have not had access. Those letters, reports, and minutes which have been available disclose, as might be expected, only vague and hesitant suggestions of the subject until we find the following notes by Bishop Bashford in his diary under date of February 2, 1906:

> Had a long talk with Dr. A. P. Parker of Shanghai over union of the two missions. In favor of union: Workers of both missions and especially of the mission of the M.E.C.S. would lose their sense of isolation and become more hopeful and aggressive. . . . On our side we should gain an entrance into the metropolis of China and strengthen our work.

The motives were not, it seems, all for union as such!

Following the Centenary Missionary Conference in Shanghai in 1907, at which there was considerable talk of church union, Bishop Bashford "met a second time with the representatives of the various Methodist churches in China," and made, he records, "some progress towards union." His diary goes on to say, under date of May 4, 1907:

I do not think we have yet reached the point where any branch is ready to yield much for the sake of union, especially to surrender its peculiarities. I am also inclined to think we are talking too much about separation from the home churches before we have made any progress towards union here. It also seems unfair to ask or expect the Chinese Christians to do what we have never been able to do at home and we are not seriously proposing to do. With all of our talk of union in the Centenary Conference I have not yet found any church proposing to surrender any principle or so-called principle.

A few days later, the Central Conference, in session in Shanghai, adopted a memorial to the General Conference of 1908 asking for the creation of "a commission with power to originate, receive, consider and consummate proposals looking toward the union of the Methodist Episcopal Church in China with any other Methodist body or bodies in China." [1]

But James W. Bashford was not one to sit by and wait for the General Conference to act—or reject. By the time he had held the North China, Central China, Foochow, and Hinghwa Conferences in the summer and fall of 1907, they had unanimously adopted resolutions authorizing the Central Conference to receive delegates from the other Methodist bodies in China who should have been elected by their respective missions, synods, or conferences, on the same basis as that on which members of the Methodist Episcopal Conferences were elected, so that all delegates would have equal and co-ordinate authority on all matters of mutual interest. Commenting on this action, we find Bishop Bashford writing in his diary on October 25, 1907:

If the other Methodist bodies accept this action and select delegates we shall have certain sessions of the Central Conference for China in which we shall consider and act upon matters which are common to all the Methodist bodies in the empire, such as publishing interests, creation of an Arminian theology for China, establishment of common newspapers to represent us all, common educational institutions, hospitals, etc. The plan contemplates holding the Central Conferences for the various Methodist bodies at the same time and place and then having one or more united sessions for consideration and action upon subjects of mutual interest.

What action the other bodies may have taken is not available for record here. At any rate the plan, with all its advantages, was never consummated. The next Central Conference session was that held in Foochow in 1911, which did not receive delegates from the other Methodist bodies in China, but seems to have been more concerned with the possibility of expanding itself to become the Central Conference of Eastern Asia. But it renewed the 1907 memorial to the General Conference requesting also that the commission be instructed "to submit a plan to the Central Conference of 1915 and to the General Conference of 1916," which commission the General Conference approved, but stipulated "that such plans shall not involve a severance of organic connection with the various home churches."

By 1915, however, the proposals for union of the Methodist Episcopal Church and the Methodist Episcopal Church, South, had progressed far enough in the United States that the Eastern Asia Central Conference only endorsed that progress and did not call for any report from a commission that had apparently never been appointed. The union had, however, not been completed in 1923, and was not for another sixteen years, but faith if not fact foretold its ultimate ratification, and the Central Conference in session in Foochow, went on record as favoring the plan of union that had been submitted to the church for its action in 1924, and further resolved:

That we urge that immediate provision be made for unified episcopal administration of all the conferences of the united church in Eastern Asia. *Resolved*, That the Eastern Asia Central Conference record its willingness to accept the term "Wei Li Tsung" as the official name for Methodism in China, contingent upon similar action by other branches of Methodism in China. That we refer our action to the bishops requesting that they ascertain the decisions of other Methodist bodies in China on this subject. When, in the judgment of the Bishops, an adequate majority of the other Methodist bodies shall have signified their acceptance of this name it shall become the official name of our church, with "Mei I Mei Hwei" written in small characters or in parenthesis where distinction is necessary, and that we request the other churches of Methodism in China to observe the same practice.[2]

Methodist union in China was practical. For twenty years it had worked in its publishing interests, and the liquidation of the Methodist Publishing House had not occurred because of any relations or lack of harmony in action between the high contracting parties. Union in a monthly church magazine had also been successful, and there was no thought of terminating that.

And of course Methodist union was more fundamental than union with other churches which claimed no blood relationship, lacked a common background, and functioned through widely different systems of polity. The slavery issue on which episcopal Methodism had split in 1844 was dead; the racial issue which was handicapping reunion in 1922 was of no more than academic interest to Chinese Methodists. In their tenets of systematic theology (with which very few Chinese concerned themselves), in their forms of worship, in their church administration and organization, it would have required an ecclesiastical microscope or a sectarian chemical analysis to reveal the differences between the Mi-I-Mi-Huei and the Chien-Li-Huei. Only in name did they differ; and in this case, certainly, "What's in a name?" Any bishop assigned to administer the China Conference could have gone on up the Yangtze River holding Methodist conferences at Nanking, Kiukiang, and Chungking a good many years before 1939, and have been wholly acceptable; while the members of the China Conference would have recognized only those differences which are true of all personalities had the bishop resident in Foochow administered their conference for a quadrennium.

It is possible that only the flood tide of union, clearly evident in 1923, prevented that union in China which had been slowly gathering strength since 1907, and which otherwise might have made a Chinese Methodist Church after the pattern of the Japanese Methodist Church.

2. The Methodist Churches United

Then came 1939. For over a century the church that Coke and Asbury had been commissioned to nurture in the United States had been divided. During that time its several divisions had made themselves world-wide churches. Like banyan trees rooted in the United States, they had dropped into foreign soil new rootlets, which had themselves become essential parts of trees that were covering the earth. All of these churches had taken root and were making noticeable growth in Europe, Asia, Africa, and Latin America.

Three of these had roots in China, which was furnishing beauty and strength to the trees that were spreading themselves over the world. And each of these churches had been making its particular contribution to the Methodist spirit which was being fused into the life of China during a century when that life was so fluid that the dyes which it received would affect its permanent hue.

The episcopacy could be much more democratic under a world-wide church than it probably was under the influence of an Asbury and a McKendree; and furthermore it was much less vital than the strength of union which could be made possible by its acceptance. The churches which had permitted withdrawals because the laity had been excluded from their legislative councils had long since admitted laymen and even women to the general conference and more recently to the annual conferences. The slavery issue had been officially dead for seven decades, but its aftermath —race discrimination in the United States—was still a factor to be reckoned with in a church that could sing with its lips but not believe sufficiently to shape its action,

> For what are sundering strains of blood?
> . . . .
> One claim unites all men in God.

But that was a factor that could be resolved by compromise. "The spirit in which Methodism has made its real advances . . . has been in its readiness to adventure in unaccustomed ways." [3] And out of the prayerful agonizing of Bishops W. F. McDowell and John M. Moore and all those men and women of the church who worked and prayed with them for the day when Methodism should be one church again, there appeared such an adventure in compromise: the Jurisdictional Conferences, a compromise which recognized the racial feelings. This was a compromise also which, in many ways, placed the central conferences of China, India, South America, and Europe, and others to follow, on a par with the jurisdictions in the United States and which may yet pave the way in the General Conference for greater equality of all parts of the world church in its several jurisdictions and central conference areas.

By 1939, when the representatives of the three churches assembled at Kansas City could declare the Methodists one body, these three branches of Methodism in China had already taken steps to consummate their union as a part of this round-the-world Methodist Church. In 1935 a Joint Commission on Unity of the Methodist Episcopal Church and the Methodist Episcopal Church, South, in China, had met in Shanghai in April. This joint commission had been composed of Dr. Z. T. Kaung, Dr. J. C. Hawk, the Rev. S. R. Anderson, President Y. C. Yang (absent) of the Methodist Episcopal Church, South, Bishop Herbert Welch, Dr. Handel Lee, Dr. R. Y. Lo, and the Rev. Carleton Lacy of the Methodist Episcopal Church, and by invitation as visitors, Bishop John Gowdy, Dr. Frank T. Cartwright, the Rev. Liu Fang, Dr. C. P. Wang, and the Rev. Paul G. Hayes. Cognizant of the negotiations that the churches were carrying on, and confident of an early fulfillment of that union, this commission pledged that the two churches which they represented would work together as intimately as possible, would do together those parts of the work which could be easily united and carried forward more efficiently in union than independently, at the same time proposing that the commission explore the possibilities and the means for concrete united activities and complete church union. Among concrete measures adopted toward the realization of this program were the following: (1) The joint consultation of the two committees on literature, with a view to possible co-operation in the publication of literature; (2)

The transfer of their membership to the church where they reside, wherever members of either church move into the territory of the other church, and that the pastors of both churches concerned encourage and facilitate such transfer of membership; (3) The appointment by the bishops "in special cases, and on request of the church concerned," of ministers to work in the sister Methodist Church, even though their conference relations be not transferred. (Had this been done thirty years sooner, probably the Foochow-speaking church in Shanghai would have escaped notice in this chronicle.) Two additional recommendations of this commission were: (1) Co-operation in leadership training; (2) A consideration of participation in the Central Conference of the Methodist Episcopal Church on the part of the China Conference of the Methodist Episcopal Church, South.

These recommendations had not all been made effective by the time the General Conference of the Methodist Episcopal Church, South, in 1938, had approved the Plan of Union by a large majority. "No sooner had this good news reached Shanghai," however, said the editor of the *China Christian Advocate* in 1938, than the two Methodist groups there began to plan for closer union and co-operation, without waiting for the formalities of a uniting conference in the United States. An Aldersgate commemoration service was held in the Moore Memorial Church, which brought new life and inspiration to the many who attended the several days program. It was also arranged for the Southern Methodists to have a larger participation in the *China Christian Advocate* at once, and the Rev. Z. S. Zia was appointed as their special correspondent to the *Advocate*. This same editorial concluded with this prediction: "By the time the official unifying actions have taken place in America, we shall expect the union here in China to be in full swing."

The Methodists in China knew and rejoiced that the results of the Kansas City conference in April 1939 would mean the complete union of the three churches in China, and eagerly awaited the fulfillment. The first word of the actions of that conference which was to reach Shanghai came on May 12 in a cablegram which read: "Moore appointed China Conference. Also Central and Kiangsi. Hammaker to Denver. One Board plan adopted."

The Methodists were one people. More than that, the "one board plan" meant that henceforth the men and women in China, the work for boys and girls, the evangelism by men and women, were united and would function under one board with offices at 150 Fifth Avenue, New York. To some extent this work was still amenable to a board office in the United States, but "the bulwark of the new unity" was to be the new Field Work Committee which is to be the only official body (of the Board of Missions) on the field and that it alone is supposed to write to the Division of Foreign Missions and the Division of Woman's Work as an official body, aside from Annual Conferences which of course always have the right to address directly the Board.[4]

But still more, union had been made concrete. With the transfer of Bishop Hammaker from Nanking to Denver, and the assignment of Bishop Arthur J. Moore to the Shanghai Area, the Central China and the Kiangsi conferences of the Methodist Episcopal Church were united in one area with the former China Conference of the Methodist Episcopal Church, South, under the administration of one bishop. In the fall of 1939, moreover, the Kalgan Mission Conference met under the presidency of a bishop for the first time, when Bishop Ward held the three conferences in North China. At the same conference Bishop Ward appointed three district superintendents. "This is one new thing," wrote Mrs. Soderbom six months later, "but even in this short time, we can see the advantage this is to the work."

Thus immediately and administratively were the former branches of Methodism united as a single church in China. With the adoption of Wei Li Kung Huei as the Chinese name of the united church, the major steps in consummating this union had been taken. But the Chinese were rightly feeling that these steps were not the whole; as Z. S. Zia well said,

A new name for the Church in China will not necessarily make the Methodist Church a new and united church unless the new *Discipline* should be rigidly followed. Otherwise, the practice of having one *Discipline* for the entire Church may lose its significance. . . . The building or re-building of the Methodist Church in China will depend much upon the enthusiastic application of the new legislation as embodied in the 1940 *Discipline*. . . . No local church may be permitted to ignore an express provision in the *Discipline* regarding the organization and program of a local church.[5]

However, that is a process which requires time; all over the world this process is still taking place. And in China, as elsewhere, patience will triumph over conservatism, until, as Bishop Ward said, "oneness simply is, with fine meanings and strength."

An old name is hard to eradicate. Many still think of Leningrad, formerly Petrograd, by its still older name of St. Petersburg, and Peking has not yet been perfectly supplanted by Peiping, even after nearly two decades. And so those in the villages and mountain valleys of China will for many years to come think and talk of the Mei-I-Mei-Huei, the Chien-Li-Huei, and the Mei-Pao-Huei. And for many years to come the shopkeepers and the wharf coolies in many a Chinese city will continue to give and receive directions in these timehonored names. But "What's in a name?" asks Perry O. Hanson, answering his own question as a member of the Mei-I-Mei-Huei in these words:

Well not very much in the name which our branch of Methodism has been bearing all the years. Of course there has developed a loyalty to the name, "Beautiful, Yea, Beautiful Society," but it is difficult to explain what connection the name has to the work of building the Kingdom of God in China.

The use of the same word as that used for America brings inevitable misunderstandings as to possible connection between our church and our country.[6]

In the adoption of the formal and official name Chung Hwa Chi Tuh Chiao Wei Li Kung Huei the church has become united under a name which to the historian has significance and to the Chinese scholar has a wealth of meaning: "China's Christian Church Bearing the Name of Wesley."

In June, 1942, with the war clouds over Asia at perhaps their darkest and blackest, Bishop Ward wrote:

When clouds were very threatening in April, 1941, the Methodist Church in China held its China Central Conference, implementing the last major part of the new organization. Very timely did it increase a China-wide Methodist consciousness and a sense of stimulating unity for widely separated regions which presently would be more sternly separated by political and military conditions. That oneness does not need to be advertised. It simply is, with fine meanings and strength. Other organizations which may be temporarily super-imposed are but super-imposed. The church continues, whether some of its organizational acts may be formally suspended or not. One annual conference is under one political regime. Most of the territories of two are under another. Two conferences and one half of another are under a third regime. Five conferences are under still another regime. Five are under general Japanese control, though with varying local regimes. Five are under control of the Chinese Nationalist Government. Yet the Church is one—and decidedly one in spirit.[7]

Now, at last, as Methodists in China,

> We are not divided,
> All one body we,
> One in hope and doctrine,
> One in charity,

one in organization, one in name, one in spirit.

The preceding sentence is, of course, not strictly true in that Methodists coming into China from England are not a part of this "one body." Outside of Tientsin and its neighborhood the British Methodist Church is working in sections of China where The Methodist Church had been doing no work until Zau and Mau went to work with the British Methodists in Kungming during the war. Union of its China organizations with its relatives in China would be welcomed, some have said, by members and officials of that church. Paul F. Wiant believes "that they were not particularly interested in the Church of Christ in China; they would be much happier in the world-wide Methodist communion." It would be welcomed by many in the Methodist Church in China; wrote one missionary—Pearce Hayes—in 1943:

The last year or so there have been efforts on the part of the Methodist Church from America and the Methodist Church from England to join hands in a larger China Methodist Church. Such a union would geographically spread the Methodist Church over China in such a way as to make administration and influence more effective than under their present division.

Perhaps some working union can be effected. Both churches might well use the same Chinese hymns. Both churches had in 1947 combined in a book of worship and united in a monthly magazine. Complete, organic union such as the other churches have attained may have to await that day when American and English connotations shall have been removed, and all shall be parts of one global Methodist Church.

3. Co-operation Preferred to Union

But meanwhile another question had been before the church from time to time: Could Methodism stay Methodist? The question is not based on the defections to the Roman Catholic Church, which had worried the missionaries in North China, for that was temporary and local. Famine in that area made the offer of four dollars per person too much of a temptation "to weak Christians of but a few months, or, at most, a few years, who do not appreciate till it is too late the difference between these two branches of the Christian church in China." [8]

The extreme poverty of the people, owing to the crop failure, made the temptation to eat Catholic food and a consequent acceptance of Catholic baptism, seem a necessary step during the first part of the winter. . . . For days there seemed to be no choice but to accept the Catholic food or starve.[9]

The question was raised, however, because of the union of other churches in national Chinese churches, and the invitations and sometimes urgings that the Methodists should join one of these as a further step towards the consummation of that day when there should be one national Christian church of China. Wisely did the bishops, in the Episcopal Address to the Central Conference of 1920, point out "that complete organic union of the Christian denominations of any of these lands is a thing scarcely to be anticipated

... and a partial union, perhaps a minority church, cannot assume to be *the* Church of Christ in any exclusive sense."

But during the next quadrennium the question continued: Should the Methodist churches sever their connection with the mother churches in the United States and become a part of a national Christian church in China? The question was far from settled by any clear-cut pronouncement or vote of the church when China Methodism was seventy-five years old. H. W. Worley says: "When Bishop Bashford made his quadrennial report at the General Conference of 1912 ... the other bishops and leaders of the church sat enthralled, and it may be said that from that hour the Methodist Episcopal Church was committed to the idea of a world church." [10] But the church membership in China was not so committed. A year later J. H. Pyke reported from North China that at one point in the conference an independent church, evidently desiring a purely Chinese church with full power of self-government, had been organized. This church, he said, had called and was supporting its own pastor and managing its own affairs. It had no connectional bonds with other similar movements, but was fast increasing in membership. In West China there had been a union movement which had led "to the adoption by the great majority of the foreign and native workers [implying the inclusion of those of the Methodist Episcopal Church] of the slogan 'One Protestant Church for West China.' " Whatever undercurrent or minority sentiment there may have been, officially the Methodist Episcopal Church in China was making or considering no overtures towards becoming a part of a national Chinese church when in 1923 its Central Conference invited the General Conference to hold its 1928 session in Peking, thus keeping in the foreground the world conception which Bishop Bashford had always upheld, and which the bishops expressed in their address to the church at this conference (1923):

That there is in the Methodist Episcopal Church in China and Korea practically no agitation toward and much opposition to an independent church is due largely to the independence that is already enjoyed. Witness the personnel of this important conference: 73 per cent native, chosen in annual conferences that are already predominantly Chinese or Korean. If any of our foreign brethren have the privilege of being members of the General Conference, the supreme body of their own church, it is by the grace of the native membership.

We believe in a world church: certain that if this, the greatest Protestant Church in the world, can remain essentially a unit, organically as well as in spirit, it will be a far more effective instrument of power to our common Christian hope of a universal brotherhood of man of every race and tongue, than it can ever be if broken into a sectionalism that may easily tend to emphasize racial prejudices. Organic and spiritual unity are more deeply related than we dream.

· · · · · · · · · · · · · · · · · · ·

But the only world Methodism in which we can believe—the only church that can really conserve and deepen either inter-racial or ecclesiastical unity, is a church which provides for that degree of local freedom and autonomy which is the essential condition of all normal indigenous development, not less morally and spiritually than in matters of self-support and the creation of a native leadership.[11]

This conference had urged haste in union with Southern Methodists, or at least in joint administration in China, but it also pressed for federation with the other branches of Methodism in China, especially because of the fear "that at least one large Methodist Mission is so committed to union . . . that it will speedily be absorbed into non-Methodist churches" though preferring "federation or union with other Methodist bodies";[12] but there was not a word recorded in the conference journal or in any preserved committee report favoring—or opposing—union into the growing national Christian church.

But if not in union with other Protestant churches, the Methodists did believe in co-operation. We have seen it in the universities and other institutions, we have seen it in the translation of the Holy Scriptures, we have seen it in the preparation and adoption of a common hymnal, and it became most evident and most powerful by sharing in 1922 in the organization of the National Christian Council. Yet in 1946 F. T. Cartwright sensed the same sentiment when he wrote after his study of postwar conditions and attitudes, "While church union is not a particularly live subject in China, unity of work is an extremely living one." [13]

Episcopal Methodism wanted to co-operate with its sister denominations but had no yearning to withdraw from a world-wide Methodist Church, of which it was in spirit already a part, alive and at home in China. When its representatives gathered in Foochow in 1923 to take stock of what had been wrought since Judson Collins and Moses White had commenced preaching on the streets of Dong-ciu Island, it numbered 73,000 full members, 265 Epworth Leagues, 600 preachers in ten conference organizations, and 500 Bible Women—a church that was better equipped to face the baffling problems of the two or three decades ahead than its bishops, its ministers, and its laymen could realize.

4. *China Methodists Favor a World-wide Church*

At the General Conference of 1944 Abbott Lee Fletcher, attorney and lay delegate from the Northern Minnesota Conference, said on the floor of the conference: "I have been greatly impressed at other General Conferences by the presence of delegates from India, China, Malaya, Africa, and the ends of the earth. Their brilliant costumes have been a constant reminder to me that Methodism is a world-wide enterprise." Their absence then, as Fletcher pointed out, was due to war conditions around the world which would not permit the nationals of other lands to attend, and not because the church was no longer a world-wide enterprise. The intense nationalism which swept China in 1927 might very easily have carried the three branches of Methodism into a Methodist Church of China, similar to that which had resulted in Japan in 1907 and in Mexico in 1930. Perhaps, as has been intimated, the measure of local autonomy which these churches had in China had kept Methodists from being swept by such a desire; perhaps the church had enough of the spirit of Bishop Bashford, when he had said at Canton on one occasion: "The New Testament puts the Cross above the flag, and not the flag above the Cross."

No better summary of the Methodist feeling on this question following the nationalist advances of 1927 can be made than to quote from Bishop Birney, who wrote in *Zion's Herald* of April 25, 1928:

For months before the annual conferences, the writer said repeatedly to our individual Chinese leaders that if they felt the time had come to merge Methodism into the National Church, he would help them in every possible way, and he assured them that financial support would still come from America; at the annual conferences they were asked daily to discuss this and other problems, which they did with great frankness; at the closing session of each conference, they were asked to vote secretly (without names) on this and other questions, it being distinctly stated in the printed question that financial help would still continue if they wished to join the National Church; at the All-Chinese Conference, composed of ninety Chinese Methodist leaders of both sexes, ministerial and lay, from all China (no foreigner present) they voted again on this matter; following this was the Eastern Asia Central Conference, at which they again voted on the same question. To the last named conference, the writer asked that Dr. Cheng Ching-Yi, the Moderator of the National Church, be invited to attend and set forth the claims of that church, which he did at length, and with power, making a direct appeal to the delegates present to merge Methodism with the National Church. The vote in all these conferences was overwhelmingly to remain with World Methodism. Bishops Grose and Brown not only were sympathetic with but aggressively co-operated in securing what we believe to be an honest expression of Chinese conviction and desire. . . . To question its sincerity on the part of the Chinese is only to betray ignorance of the kind of men and women who did the voting, and of the refreshing frankness with which they now speak their minds.

Retaining their organic relation to world-wide Methodism, at least for the present, is not . . . to use the Chinese equivalent, a "rice" conviction with our Chinese. The following are some of the arguments used repeatedly at the annual conference discussions, in which no foreigner was supposed to participate: "We already have more real autonomy in Methodism than we should have in the National Church." "We believe an international church is more Christian than a national church." "In this great Nationalist Movement, China is cutting many international ties; the church ought to be the last institution to do that." "Methodism has made and is making a distinctive contribution to China, a contribution that was never more needed than now, and which could not be made as effectively by losing its identity in a national church." "Other churches that have joined the National Church could do so with little or no change in their organization and foreign connections, while it would completely destroy the Methodist organization."

Three years later the bishops, addressing the Central Conference, pled that if there had been any change in the sentiment of the church since the last conference, if there were reasons not foreseen three years earlier, the greatest frankness be expressed in their discussion preliminary to whatever action the Chinese members of the conference deemed desirable. Then they added this challenge:

But we cannot pass from this grave matter without seeking to make clear the responsibility which the Methodist Church in China assumes should she choose to remain a part of our church's world organization rather than sever that organic bond to become an independent church. There is but one reason that will ever justify that choice, the profound conviction that in her present form and relation she can be a more vitally effective means in the power of God to develop the spirit and likeness of Christ within the church, and to carry the redemption to the multitudes beyond the church. Whoever does not share that conviction should with prophetic courage make his voice heard for any change that will achieve that which is the only valid excuse for the existence of any church. But upon all who do share that conviction, God lays the high and unescapable obligation to see to it that Methodism is increasingly that kind of church, or that she surrendered her ecclesiastical life to nourish her life in the Spirit.[14]

But the conference took no action to alter its former position.

In 1934, moreover, in spite of a recommendation by a commission which had been appointed to bring in preliminary suggestions to the Central Conference, that, because the Methodist Episcopal Church had shown the right spirit through the years in entering many union enterprises, it should now affiliate with the Church of Christ in China, the report of the commission was not adopted by the conference.

On the eve of the consummation of Methodist union, the editor of the *China Christian Advocate* wrote in February, 1939:

The only anxiety that China has in this matter is whether or not she will be cut off from the home churches even more than in the past. Those who knew the warm enthusiasm for missions of two decades ago cannot but feel that a close fellowship between the churches in America and those in China, is a spirit to be strengthened rather than weakened. . . . Therefore we view with anxiety any plan that would prevent a close unity between the churches of America and other lands. . . . Let us not forget that "The world is our parish," and until we have brought the saving grace of Jesus to each needy one, our task is not done.

And in 1940 H. W. Worley was sizing up the Chinese attitude, as he saw it, in these words:

In other words, the Chinese leaders in the Methodist Episcopal Church have passed through a period of growing national consciousness and have merged as a part not of a distinctly Chinese church but of an organization which encircles the globe. Through the Central Conference, it has been possible for them not only to realize national aspirations but also to find that wider fellowship which comes from stepping over the boundaries and limits of nations to join the world federation about which Bishop Bashford so often preached—an international and inter-racial church.[15]

Interviewed in America in 1944, and asked "if there was any movement among Chinese Christians toward setting up a 'Methodist Church of China' as an expression of the new Chinese nationalism," Bishop Chen replied: "The Methodists of China would rather belong to a church that is world-wide in its scope. There is no place for nationalism in our Christian faith." [16]

On the other hand, one must recognize that the Methodists in China—missionaries and Chinese—do not unanimously favor a global Methodist Church in preference to one Chinese church; also, that the sentiment for a Chinese church may be growing in strength. But sentiment of a nationalist tone has until recently been somewhat sporadic and individual: one conference in 1930 thought that "all churches in China ought to unite in one big church, but Methodist branches should first unite." [17] Mrs. H. C. Jett, a missionary, felt:

The National Church appeals to the Chinese people, and at once makes an appeal to their sense of independence and their willingness to sacrifice in order to make it self-supporting. Such an urge is lacking in a church that is very conscious of the Mother church and her maternal care.[18]

But this is to forget that perhaps the church is growing so closely into that of a united family, all members of which are so mature that maternal care has given place to a mutual sharing by all of privileges and obligations. F. O. Stockwell, working in West China, where the Southern Methodists were not represented but where other denominations were active, had said in 1937:

I do not see that a union with the Methodist Church, South, will affect our situation here, and I fear that it will only strengthen the feeling of self-sufficiency of the Methodist body as a whole to the place where any hope of uniting with other than non-Methodist forces will be pushed into a distant future.[19]

This same missionary expressed himself similarly in 1944 when he wrote that the Chinese Christian leaders were expressing the hope that the post-war church may be one; he continued:

The cry for church unity is coming from many quarters, and most of all from our Chinese friends. This is not a denial of the values of the past. We came to China nearly a hundred years ago, each denomination bringing the flower of its Christian faith in the particular denominational flower-pot that it loved best. But through these hundred years that little flower of faith has been watered by Chinese rains and warmed by a Chinese sun and its roots have grown strong and deep, so much so that many think that it has outgrown its original pot. Many feel that it is time to take these flowers out of their original containers and plant them together in a Chinese garden. Each flower will still retain its beauty and its particular grace, but they will be growing in Chinese soil, unhampered by foreign "pots." The objection to denominations is not only that they divide the church, but that the divisions have been imported, having no reality in Chinese life and experience.[20]

It is true that the war developed with new force the need for unity. The union forced on the church by the Japanese was external and only temporary, but in working together there and in free China where migrations erased many denominational lines, there was very definitely a feeling developed that the postwar task will be too tremendous unless the churches face it together. Yet Frank Cartwright, from his contacts as associate secretary for China in the Division of Foreign Missions felt, in 1943, that among the recent events and trends which stand out significantly in the development of the church, is "a marked growth of interest in organic church union." In a letter he wrote:

I would not want this interpreted as meaning that Chinese Methodists are now a unit in believing in one Protestant church for China. But there has been a significant development along that line. You and I can well remember when there was practically unanimous judgment against uniting with the Church of Christ in China. There has come the union of our American Methodism which followed shortly upon the union of British Methodism. There is now a Central Conference Commission which is negotiating with the representatives of the British Methodist group looking towards the union of our Methodism in China. I have had letters and have had conferences with Chinese men and missionaries who desire that this shall be only a step toward a union of evangelical Protestantism.

But after his tour of China in 1946, Cartwright said that, outside of the membership of the Church of Christ in China, he found "almost no suggestion of interest in 'one Protestant church.' "

Perhaps one must distinguish between a union of Protestant denominations into a national Chinese church, organically separated from the church in other parts of the world, on the one hand, and, on the other, the union of the Protestant churches throughout the world, with the separate churches in China becoming one part of one global church. Perhaps that distinction must be remembered when Henry Van Dusen, reporting as a non-Methodist in his *Methodism's World Mission,* says: "Workers for Christian unity have reported their sadness to find one of the most influential leaders of World Methodism casting his influence against long-desired and promising unions in two far-distant sectors of the World Church." [21] He does not name the leader who may have been using his influence against national unions only until such time as the union of world churches was possible.

In another place Van Dusen says:

The youthful Christian churches born of the missionary enterprise are so far out in advance of their parent churches of the West in the matter of co-operation and union as to have achieved almost a New Age in the history of Christendom. . . . This is one of the most vivid impressions from a world survey of Christian Missions.[22]

There is, then, a third alternative: the union of Protestant churches in each nation, and then a world federation of these national churches.

But these are problems for the statesmen of the church, not the historian. The historian may merely record the growth of the church in China from the time when it was an infant, looking across the seas to its mother, until, having attained its "of-age-ness," it must decide whether to leave its mother and with its fellow workers in China set up its own establishment. The historian may show that what the bishops of India said in issuing a *Discipline* of the Methodist Episcopal Church in Southern Asia in 1937 has been equally true in China: "After eighty years of continuous testing the polity of the Methodist Episcopal Church has been proved beyond a doubt to be adapted in a peculiar way to the needs of church organization on this mission field." The historian may even—as I have tried to do —point out the trend of thinking by this hundred-year-old church as to its relations and co-operation with its relatives and its neighbors. And yet it was an historian who said: "In these days when such a struggle is in process to set up means of tying in the world together in interests which transcend national boundaries, such an organization as the Methodist Episcopal Churches have might seem to be a providential one." [23]

Thus far that has been the major thought of China Methodism. Local autonomy and complete parity within a world-wide church have never yet been fully effected. This story of a century of Methodism in China points to the belief that The Methodist Church become such a church.

XV

THE NOBLE HOST

He who, in fealty to the truth,
And counting all the cost,
Doth consecrate his generous youth—
He joins the noble host.

BEFORE WE TAKE A LOOK AT THE TRANSFERS OF AUTHORITY AND THE undertaking of responsibilities which demonstrated that the church was definitely rooted in China and ready to reach out in its own right and vigor, we ought to pause to meet some of the individuals who were the fruit of the church through the years, who typify the membership which is making the church today, and who are laying the foundations of Methodism in China for centuries to come.

The Rev. Nieh Chen was right when, after a year as presiding elder in the North China Conference, he said he would "chiefly report the work of proclaiming the Gospel." He must have read a good many of the reports that have not been quoted in previous chapters, and perhaps some that have, for he was criticizing their pattern when he said: "Although I received the appointment of presiding elder, yet I need not report particularly the work of schools and hospitals, of furloughs and returns to China, as foreign missionaries do, but will chiefly report the work of proclaiming the Gospel."[1] So we too must pause here, not for statistics of the growth of the church but for evidences that the followers of John Wesley in China were also genuine disciples of Jesus Christ, for evidences that the blue dye of Methodism is in reality being fused into the life of China, and that the long-nailed scholar and the paddy-field worker, the bound-footed housewife and the skillful maker of lacquer, have all found it the form of religion for them and made it their own. As one of many illustrations that might be used, witness

a barber, named Chou, who united with the church and, getting into foreign employ, disposed of his barber's kit. He soon, however, lost his place and was persuaded to return to his former occupation. With a little help he bought a new outfit, and now makes his living as a barber, and at the same time is doing the work of a self-supporting evangelist. He carries in his shaving-stool a good supply of Christian tracts which he distributes, at the same time bearing faithful witness to all who engage him.[2]

Just before the Boxer outbreak a graduate of Peking University, a layman, had written, with more evangelistic fervor than English rhetoric: "I had gone out every day with Chia or Wang to preach in different villages by foot. Sometimes we come into rain we walked on our bare feet three or four miles long." [3]

Mother Wang, when past eighty years of age, still continued to preach the gospel at Taian and longed "to be permitted to make a journey to Peking to give the Gospel message in person to the Empress Dowager." But there were times and places when a dim-out of spiritual glow, a genuine backsliding, was a source of anxiety—even at An-chia-chuang, where there had once been a church attendance of one hundred and fifty, there were "only a few gathered for Sunday services," and in 1903 it was all too apparent to Dr. Pyke, who was one of that sextette of missionary master-architects who had built the North China Conference and gone with it through the fires of rebellion and persecution—Lowry, Davis, Pyke, Gamewell, Hobart, and Hopkins—it was all too apparent

that the churches had sustained other and even greater loss than that of property and life. The mind and spirit of Christ were wanting. . . . The collection and distribution of indemnity for losses sustained had awakened a spirit of covetousness that was all the more subtle because associated with losses which pecuniary compensation could not restore. . . . A spirit of forgiveness, charity and patience [was lacking and needed, and] must be obtained and exercised by the Christians toward their enemies, that would overlook and ignore if not forget all injuries.[4]

But how gloriously it had been acquired forty years later!

But lulls and dim-outs, pruning of church "members" and defections from church attendance were, thank God, local and temporary. Harvests were ripening on every hand, and, if the labors of other years were to be conserved, the board secretaries were saying, "Our work there should be steadily pressed to victory."

The Bible women in all conferences were doing a marvelous evangelization job, doing their share in pressing on to a Christian victory. To some of them Bishop Bashford paid this tribute in his diary on November 5, 1908:

On returning home tonight at 10 P.M. thoroughly tired, . . . I found twelve Chinese Bible Women who had come to me this noon and again at the close of meeting with a petition for Miss Wells' appointment as evangelist. Still waiting to see me. They were not stubborn nor persistent. They said, "We realize tonight since altar service that you do not make the appointments but Holy Spirit working through you. Hence we do not dare ask unconditionally for Miss Wells, but if it be God's will we wish her." It was heartening to meet them. They were in better state spiritually than the original twelve. May the Lord use them to take China for Christ.

Station classes, street meetings, house-to-house visiting, and special help to pastors in the regular service of the church were bringing "harvests in proportion to the seed sown."

During a series of revival meetings led by Miss Dora Yu not long before 1920 a non-Christian girl was heard to remark concerning the confessions and restitution which were frequent occurrences: "Why, the Chinese people must be tortured to make them confess; but here are girls confessing, with no visible pressure brought to bear upon them. Surely there is an unseen power at work, and I no longer question that there is a God, for I have seen His work." [5]

The church was now coming into that stage of its growth when it could count on its laymen. As men had gone out from the Anglo-Chinese schools, and as they were beginning to graduate from the union universities, they were going into business and official positions which paid good salaries, and they could, and gladly did, help to support the church and its institutions. But the time had come when they were beginning to take responsibility for leadership as well as give financial support. F. T. Cartwright illustrated this by the case of one official board which, for instance,

felt that too many outside calls were being made upon the popular pastor of that church, and they asked the officials concerned to do one of two things: appoint a pastor who would stick to the immediate job or else appoint a strong assistant pastor to help them through the frequent interruptions. [6]

"This church," he added, "is self-supporting, having raised a budget of $2,200 last year, and the men feel that they have a right to some control of their work." How happy Maclay and Hart and Allen would have been to have known the church they longed for was growing up like that!

From that day to this an increasing number of laymen have been witnessing and laboring to make Methodism a vital force in China. W. S. Bissonnette describes the influence of that "example of energy and sacrifice" who "flashed upon the vision of the people of Kutien" in 1920-21, and in eight months had done his lifework so well that "God called him away."

Dr. Ciu Do-Gieng, just back from the United States, was appointed to head this [Kutien Social evangelism] work. . . . His work had just begun to take root when his death by a bandit's bullet late in August brought it to a stop, but not an end. What he began is being carefully conserved and the precious legacy of the memory of his Christian spirit is already a living influence. Those who saw him in his many and ceaseless activities, especially the younger Christian workers, are taking up his burdens. Some are preaching on the streets and in shops; others have opened night schools; one is gathering the street boys on Sunday afternoons; and the spirit of seeking for opportunities and thanking God for the privilege of labor for humanity is gaining upon us all.[7]

On the main street of Foochow city, there had been started in 1915 an institutional church, similar in program and direct objectives to those of Kiang-tang-kai and Moore Memorial, which a few years later had far outstripped it in China-wide eminence. Ralph A. Ward, who promoted and founded this church, is authority for the statement that Siong-iu-dong or Central Church, after six months, had a larger indigenous congregation in regular Sunday attendance than any other church of which he knew had after several decades, a congregation which had raised during the first year over half its current expense budget, which was expressed in four figures. At this church, on September 5, 1915, a young man was baptized (whose name Ward did not give us) who typified many whom these "institutional" and the other churches were winning in all Methodist-occupied territory:

He was a member of one of the proudest families in Fukien Province. His father-in-law held the highest position under the Manchu dynasty of any man from his province in the present generation. His own father held the highest literary degree obtainable in China. More than that, for a period of five years, after competitive examination, he held first place among all men of this highest degree throughout the empire.

For years the mission had endeavored to open a preaching place in this man's village. Now he, only an earnest layman, preaches to his aristocratic relatives every Sunday. Following conversion he began the habit of asking a blessing before eating his rice. Members of the same clan laughed at his new religion, but in a few weeks became interested learners. An employee of the government on good salary, he feels it no compromise to proclaim everywhere his relationship to the church. Practically all his spare time is given to the church work.[8]

Though the ardor of General Feng Yu-Hsiang's Christian life and activity did not remain at the high level which it reached in the decade around 1920, yet as an outstanding lay member in the North China Conference, elected a lay delegate to the General Conference of 1924, perhaps the nearest counterpart which China Methodism has produced to Captain Webb with his sword laid across the pulpit, this chronicle would hardly be complete were his name omitted. Many stories have been written of the life and work of this general of military influence and power in the war lord days of China's recent history. Here are a couple of paragraphs. The first is from the Rev. Liu Fang, pastor of Asbury Church, Peking, who baptized Feng Yu-Hsiang, and who continued his intimate and loyal friend:

Three of those added to the church this year were majors in the army. Of these Major Feng has since become a general. He has led most of his officers to become Christians, and on Sunday morning he may be seen regularly sitting in the church with these men. Very soon after accepting Christ he sent once a week a minor officer who understood Chinese music to learn the church hymns in order to teach the soldiers to sing, and in about two weeks all the soldiers in his company were singing Christian hymns instead of heathen songs while they were drilling. There is a preaching service every Sunday for those who have joined the church and all interested since they were moved to San Chia Tien, a place ten miles west of Peking. Three hundred Bibles have been sold to the men, and Bible classes have been organized. So that the regiment now seems to me like a small church set down in the midst of the Chinese army, and my heart overflows with gratitude to God for these soldiers of the Cross.[9]

The other comes from George Davis, who was closely associated with General Feng, and tells of the Christian work in his army in 1923:

The men stood and sang at the word of command, and while no Carusos have been discovered among his soldiers they certainly enjoyed making a joyful noise unto the Lord. . . . It was a wonderful eye opener to the Christian workers to live in the army for four or five days and see what the men are really like. Their earnestness was surprising. The first meeting of the day was called at seven in the morning, and it was always dark when the service opened, [and the men stood] for an hour or more three times a day in the open in February to hear a Gospel sermon. . . . The last day of the sojourn 3,719 men were baptized and taken into the church.[10]

With the Christian spirit thus permeating the highest strata of literary and military influence as well as the humble farmer, barber, and soldier, and with non-Christian officials and reformers aware that "true reform is stimulated by the atmosphere created by the church," it was to be expected that the church could sometimes secure the support of the government, after the Manchu dynasty had been exiled. Hence "few more profoundly impressive events have taken place in all these days of transformation," wrote Frederick Brown of New Year's Day, 1913, than an evangelistic campaign in "The Temple of Heaven." Here is his account:

The covered altar did duty as a platform, and for ten days preaching was carried on in this sacred building—the Chinese holy of holies. The emperors of China had supplicated here for five hundred years, but on January 1, 1913, the Gospel of our Saviour Jesus Christ was proclaimed by an earnest band of preachers, and thousands heard for the first time the message of salvation.[11]

Again in 1947, this time on the Altar of Heaven itself, a Christian service of worship was held when the Methodist Youth Institute of the North China Conference was held in August.

Early in 1913 "came a request unparalleled" in the history of the Chinese government, namely a request that the church of God in China would unite in prayer that wisdom might be given to the new republic for the drafting of her constitution and the selection of a president. The first meeting in response to this request was held on April 13, 1913, in Asbury Church, Peking, a union meeting of all the Protestant churches in the city, to which President Yuan Shih-Kai and the minister of foreign affairs sent their representatives. It was attended by many prominent officials from other boards, and C. T. Wang, the vice-president of the senate, C. C. Wang, and others, offered earnest prayer. A second such prayer meeting, also requested by the government, was held in the same church some days later when C. T. Wang gave an inspiring address followed by earnest prayers on the part of the people. And on May 17, 1917, another great meeting was held. The use of Asbury Church was a part of Methodism's share in the celebration by delegates from all over the country of the victory for religious liberty in China. Confucian forces had tried to have Confucianism made the state religion of China; but the Religious Liberty Society was organized and defeated the Confucian Society, and Chinese leaders in the Methodist Church spent a great deal of time and contributed not a little to the victory.

From the plains of Manchuria to the mountains of Szechuen, and to the island of Haitang, the Methodist Church had been established. But it was not geographical extent nor the number of occupied cities and counties that made the church strong. Schools, colleges, and hospitals dotted the map, and were (many of them) well staffed and equipped—though not too well. But it was not its institutions that made the church strong. Ten conferences under leadership of their own choosing have been year by year fusing Methodism into the life of the Chinese people. But it was not its organization and leadership that made the church strong. Its strength lay in all these, it is true, but much more in the spirit which all of these had combined to produce. Elijah found his strength neither in the earthquake nor the thunderstorm, but in the still, small voice. So the strength of the church lay in the spirit which after nearly a hundred years had been breathed into the life of its members, giving their widow's mites, carrying the gospel to remote sections, enduring hardship as good soldiers of the Christ, training themselves to serve the church better. Humble villagers and high government officials, school administrators and army officers, doctors, lawyers, merchants—some master writer should rewrite the eleventh chapter of Hebrews in terms of Methodist men and women in

China. Though to name only a few is to do an injustice to the many who are not named, the strength of the Methodist Church in China cannot be appreciated without seeing a few more of these vignettes thrown on the screen from an immense volume portraying persons in all walks of life.

The Rev. Hwa Hsing-Tung had done much work among the military men who were living in his compound. . . . Though his church was often occupied by soldiers, he never suspended a single Sunday morning service. Sometimes the soldiers moved out on Sunday morning and moved in again in the afternoon. One Sunday Pastor Hwa held his meeting over at the Girls' School. Mr. Kung, one of his church members, said that one day one of his friends met him on the way and said to him, "Your church is abolished." He answered him, "No, how could that be?" Then his friends said again, "Look here! Your church has been occupied by so many soldiers." Mr. Kung answered, "See, I am still here! Unless they struck me down they could never abolish our church!" [12]

Bah-sua, on Haitang Island, is an almost inaccessible village, which can be reached only by so hazardous a trip that the conference finally abandoned it as a regular appointment. Why, under the circumstances, a district missionary or a district superintendent would ask a Bible woman to go to Bah-sua, is a question perhaps not to be asked here; but we will let the missionary tell the results:

Two years ago we asked Mrs. Siek Hua-Saeng, a Bible Woman, to go to Bah-sua as pastor. She went. She made no complaint. And she is still there in service. When Mrs. Siek went to Bah-sua there were but nineteen families of Christians left in the group of villages making up the circuit, and the spiritual life of the church was just about nil. Last year we held one of our sixteen-day series of evangelistic services, followed later by a ten-day training conference. New life, and an entirely different kind of life, has been imparted to the church. I found more than one hundred families of earnest worshippers. . . . It was said of Mrs. Siek by a leading layman of the church of Haitang, "She casts out more devils of those demon possessed, destroys more gods in home and wayside shrine, visits in more homes administering to the spiritual and bodily needs of the people, and preaches the Gospel with greater fervor than any six men preachers on the district." [13]

These stories will illustrate the type of strength which can be found in China's villages. But as General Feng Yu-Hsiang sought to win his men to Christ, and as Paul won the officers of his guard, so Chinese staff officers were convincing their superiors of the truth. This story, in the *China Christian Advocate* of December, 1938, comes from Nanchang before the Japanese took the city:

Perhaps the most significant event of the month for us Methodists was the baptism and reception into membership of the Teh-shan Church of Marshal Shang

Cheng, the Commander of the 32nd Group Army and the Garrison Commander here. In a service ... with twenty-five invited missionaries and Chinese Christian leaders present, the Marshal was baptised and received. Then all participated in the Sacrament of the Lord's Supper.

The Marshal had become known to us only within the last few weeks. He was a schoolmate of Chiang Kai-Shek at the Paoting Military Academy and later in Japan, and was active in the north in the early days of the Revolution. He has since been governor of Shansi and held numerous other prominent civil and military posts. He says that Dr. Sun Yat-Sen back in the days before the Revolution of 1911 used to read the Bible to them, but it seems that it made little impression upon him at the time. More recently he had contact with numerous Christians, and recently has studied English with various missionaries in places where his military campaigns have taken him. Some months ago he was located at Kaifeng during the campaign along the Lunghai R. R.; and before leaving there announced his decision to be a Christian. Perhaps the Christian influence and example of a member of his staff, General T. C. Liu, has been as strong an influence as any in helping to shape the Marshal's decision. Certain it is that on arrival here General Liu made immediate contact with the Christians and brought about the introductions and cordial relationships that preceded the service this week.

Janet Ho was the first Chinese woman ordained a local preacher. But she was much more than just a local preacher. Raised in a Christian home—and the coloring is now so infused that there are many Christian homes making third and even fourth generation Methodists—educated in the schools of the church, graduated from an American College, Miss Ho took a graduate course at Boston University School of Theology. Listen as Miss Lydia Trimble tells the rest of the story in the *China Christian Advocate* of June, 1937:

I know of no one of our girls who is making a finer contribution to the kingdom. Deeply spiritual, always on the job, keenly alive and up-to-date; gentle, quiet, poised, with good judgment, she has decided initiative, and is resourceful. The number of people who come to her for consultation and help is large—preachers, teachers, Bible Women, students, and those in distress. Outside the church, people in the government, not excepting the magistrate, look to her for leadership in many ways. Being principal of the only girls' junior high school in the county gives her an outstanding position of influence, and right royally is she measuring up. She is always true to the church, and to the highest ideals.

Methodist schools in China have produced no more beautiful flower, Methodist homes in future China will have had no richer influence in their making, and the Methodist Church will have had no more devoted Christian than Lucy Wang, who has measured fully to the responsibility from which she shrank. The *China Christian Advocate* published her own story of "My Call":

Having been born and having lived among the echoes of "Lack of ability among the fair sex is considered a virtue," and "Boys first," in everything, on all occasions, the question came to me, "What can a woman do?" "What does a woman amount to?" Throughout my childhood days, I realized that a Chinese woman found it impossible to live happily. As a child, I often rebelled against the fact that I was not born a boy. When I grew older I did at a great cost many things which a girl would not have done at that time. More than once my heart was "heavy-laden." Inequality of treatment of boys and girls made life even bitter for me at times.

Hwa Nan College was the open door for me. I owe to Hwa Nan what I have and am. It was during my student days at Hwa Nan that I heard Christ call, "Come unto me all ye that are heavy-laden and I will give you rest." "I am the Way, the Truth, and the Life." It was within these halls of learning and within these walls of love that I found the way of life which is Jesus Christ. Since then life has become brighter and full of promise and adventure instead of despair and darkness. I began to realize that it was my responsibility as well as my opportunity to help the mass of Chinese women to seek for a more abundant life.

When the call came to me to become President of Hwa Nan College, on the one hand, this seemed to open an avenue of service for the womanhood of China of which I had dreamed when I first received my Christian education and, on the other hand, I shrank from accepting this great responsibility.

Then there is Hsu Wen-Liang, familiarly known as "Bill" Hsu, graduate of Methodist schools and Yenching University, with an A.M. degree from the University of Michigan. While in the United States, Hsu worked on farms, in nurseries, and a year in the Ford Motor Company plant, and Henry Ford wanted him to return to China to represent the company. But "Bill" went to teach in the Methodist Boys' School at Changli at a much less salary than many that had been offered him. He became its principal, went as a lay delegate to the General Conference of 1928, and then "prowled over farms" in the United States, Holland, Denmark, and Sweden. When the Japanese invaded the neighborhood Hsu went to Szechuen. "He saw Chinese soldiers crawling in their own filth, louse-infected, underfed, dying by the roadside," and he organized the Friends of the Wounded society, whose workers were nurses who "prepared food, washed bloody clothes, deloused garments, treated skin diseases, mended clothing," in every way serving "the lowly, forgotten, suffering, starving, freezing soldiers of China." Four million people contributed to the support of this work, and the organization grew to two hundred units on the several military fronts. Then Hsu Wen-Liang went back to Changli to rebuild the school and to build his life into the young men there as he had into the lives of wounded soldiers.[14]

Then there was "Yui Hsieu-Lien, daughter of a Methodist pastor, [who] bravely faced the Japanese when they came to take over Moore Memorial Church in Shanghai, gaining time for the escape of some of the leaders and cleverly effecting the removal of important papers." [15]

What shall I more say? Time would fail me to tell of men whom the church has developed, who rank high as thinkers and writers, who are making the church strong by their lives, men like T. C. Chao of Yenching University, recognized as a leading thinker of religious themes; James Ding, president of the Anglo-Chinese College in Foochow, with whom the provincial authorities are in constant consultation; Mrs. Herman Liu, a Methodist by birth but a Baptist by marriage, writer of a prize novel and a national leader in the movement for women's rights and position in national life; Y. C. Yang, president of Soochow university, worthy and capable representative of Chinese Methodism to American Methodism for several years during the war disturbances; and member of China's delegation to the United Nations Assembly; R. Y. Lo, a Ph. D. from the United States, a former member of the Kiangsi Conference, and then an active layman serving in the legislative yuan of the national government, writing frequently on various subjects, and editing Methodist publications and journals.

To be able to include Generalissimo Chiang Kai-shek in this chapter is possible because of the faithful Christian work and prayer of both American and Chinese Methodists, and the sincerity of the man himself. Wendell Willkie called the generalissimo "one of the truly great men of the age," and much of that greatness lies in his sincerity and his loyalty to his people and his faith. After his leadership in the Nationalist campaign of 1927-28, he had wooed and wed Mayling Soong, daughter of Charles Soong, whose place in the Southern Methodist impact on China has already been mentioned. This had not been accomplished without difficulties. "No non-Christian should marry into the family if Madame Soong could prevent it." When she finally pressed the question whether he would become a Christian, he replied,

that his understanding was that a real Christian is one who has a personal experience of God, and so he would not profess conversion as part of a matrimonial bargain; but he would study Christianity, read the Bible with an open mind, and pray sincerely for divine guidance to a right decision. No answer could have pleased Madame Soong more, since it bespoke the honesty of the man, and she believed that any person who would read the Bible and pray would certainly be led by the Holy Spirit into an experience of Christian faith.[16]

The Generalissimo fulfilled this promise, and with the Christian influence and prayers of his mother-in-law, and the devoted spiritual encouragement and guidance of his wife, who was ever near him, even in his military campaigns, he advanced in his understanding and his faith.

Dr. Z. T. Kaung, who had prayed with the couple before the marriage service tells the result:

It appears that in a local war between the Central Government and recalcitrant elements the Generalissimo was trapped and surrounded near Kaifeng, and capture and death appeared imminent. There was a little country church near his headquarters, and Chiang entered it to pray. There he made a vow to become a follower of Christ if he survived. Said Dr. Kaung,

"His prayers were answered; a heavy snowstorm broke and held up his enemies' advance, and reinforcements arrived two days later. Thus his life was not only saved but an apparent defeat had been turned into victory. Then it was that he made his mind to accept Christ. When I returned from America I was asked to baptize the leader of China into the membership of the Christian Church." [17]

Some cynical critics of Chiang's conversion—taking note of the eight million odd Methodists in America and Chiang's need for American support in the inevitable clash with Japan—said, "There's Methodism in his madness." But there were many, Christians and non-Christians, who would vouch for the Generalissimo's sincerity.[18]

That sincerity breathes through the words which the generalissimo addressed to the Central Conference, meeting in his capital on the eve of the terrific struggle with the Japanese:

I have now been a Christian for nearly ten years and during that time I have been a constant reader of the Bible. Never before has this sacred book been so interesting to me as during my two week's captivity in Sian. This unfortunate affair took place all of a sudden and I found myself placed under detention without having a single earthly belonging. From my captors I asked but one thing, a copy of the Bible. In my solitude I had ample opportunity for reading and meditation. The greatness and love of Christ burst upon me with new inspiration, increasing my strength to struggle against evil, to overcome temptation, and to uphold righteousness.

The life of Christ reveals a long record of affliction and constant persecution. His spirit of forbearance, His love and His benevolence shine through it all. No more valuable lesson has yet come to me out of my Christian experiences. . . . Today, I find that I have taken a further step and have become a follower of Jesus Christ. This makes me realize more fully that the success of the revolution depends upon men of faith and that men of character, because of their faith, cannot sacrifice their principles for personal safety under circumstances of difficulty and crisis. In other words, a man's life may be sacrificed, his person held in bondage, but his faith and spirit can never be restrained.[19]

It is even more vividly attested in the following story of a Canadian visitor to the home of Generalissimo and Madame Chiang while at war with Japan, a story which is not a unique incident, but a typical daily experience in their family life:

The Canadian had come to the moment when he felt he should excuse himself and return to his hotel. As he prepared to go, General Chiang said, "Must you go immediately? We would be happy if you would stay and join us in our evening's devotions."

Such an invitation comes to very few, and the Canadian quickly acquiesced, seating himself again. With that a Bible was produced and the General began by reading some Scripture. Then the three joined in prayer, the General leading.

Says the Canadian: "I never expect to hear such a prayer again in all my life. The General began with a simple expression of thanks for their personal safety. Then he added thanks for the courage of the nation under fire. Then he prayed for strength for the men in the field and along the firing lines; he prayed for strength for himself, and added a most earnest plea for guidance and wisdom, that he should not fail the people.

"But the most amazing thing in his prayer was a plea that God would help him, and help China not to hate the Japanese people. He prayed for the Japanese Christians, and all the suffering multitudes of Japan whose impoverishment was making the war on China possible. He prayed for the people who were bombed, and for forgiveness for those who dropped the bombs.

"In the simplest and humblest terms he laid himself at the service of Almighty God, and begged that he might know the Divine will and do it on the morrow."

When the thirty minutes of Scripture and prayer was concluded, the Generalissimo and Madame Chiang arose, extended their hands in friendly good-nights, and escorted their guest to the door. As he went out into the night and started on his way to the hotel, he was saying to himself, "At last I have found two Christians." [20]

Their motives were often questioned and impugned, their judgement often criticized, their political and military decisions often under fire; but for eight long years of self-defense, and through the many months of struggle which followed the Japanese surrender, these two Christians held their nation to its task, trying through their New Life Movement and their own Christian living to infuse their non-Christian nation with the only Spirit that would lift its people to a higher level of spiritual and economic life.

It was because the church was made up of many such men and women, dedicated to the task of making it stronger, who could, also be depended upon to advance the program, that the Central Conference Executive Board in 1943 adopted a Five-Year Program of Church Advance with which to close the century. This program was to emphasize a membership rally for service in the first year, then a year of improvement in worship and prayer, a third year devoted to stewardship, missionary service to neighbors and friends through the fourth year, and in the fifth year personal evangelism and "forward in service to other groups." It was immediately adopted by the several annual conferences where war conditions permitted, and by the others when conditions made such adoption possible; it is being empasized in institutes and training conferences and made a matter of private and group prayer continuously. As perhaps the strongest program of such church advance inaugurated in this century of Methodism, it follows somewhat the Crusade for Christ in the United States.

"Just as in other lands, churches with a history behind them contain some members who are merely blind followers, some who know something about Christ, and a small vital group that really knows Christ as Lord and Savior." [21] In this latter group lies the hope of the future: Christian men and women on fishing boats and in college halls, praying for their enemies while planning military campaigns for defense, preaching to church congregatons, serving wounded soldiers, or sitting in legislative chambers, for "whom to live is Christ"—these are both the fruit and the seed of a Methodist Church which has been, which is, and which is to be.

XVI

WE ARE ABLE

"Are ye able?" Still the Master
Whispers down eternity,
And heroic spirits answer,
Now as then in Galilee,
"Lord, we are able." [1]

1. *Chinese Ability to Take Leadership*

ONE OF THE OUTSTANDINGLY SIGNIFICANT YEARS IN THE HISTORY OF the church in China was 1927. It was eighty years since the "good ship *Heber*" had sailed from Boston harbor with the first messengers of Methodism. For eight decades the flow of Methodist coloring had been giving its hue to the religious life of the Chinese. That had begun in 1847. It was 1867 which marked the beginning of expansion into other parts of China. In 1881 the present educational system received probably its greatest impetus with the founding of the Anglo-Chinese colleges in Foochow and Shanghai, the initiation of McTyeire, and what later became William Nast, and the opening of work which was eventually to make possible the great union school system of West China. The year 1897 marked the consciousness of a China-wide Methodist Episcopal Church, with the coming of bishops who could stay long enough to administer and inspire all the conferences, and with the organization of the Central Conference to co-ordinate and further the church which was never again to be made up of isolated conferences. And 1927 was the year when the Chinese leaders really began to increase, while the missionaries really began to decrease.

Pearl Buck, writing of the missionary career of her father, says:

I have not seen anywhere the like of Andrew and his generation. . . . Ah! well, they are all gone now! . . . It was the policy of the missionaries to stand together at all cost against the "natives." If any individual missionary had a clash with a convert or a Chinese preacher, all the missionaries upheld the white man, regardless of right or wrong. . . . . "It wouldn't do," it was often said, " to allow the natives to undermine the authority of the missionary." For then what would become of the authority of the church? [2]

Yes, thank God, those days were gone. The missionaries were far from being fully aware of it, however. Bishop John Gowdy, a college president at the time declared:

I can say in all honesty that until the law made the change obligatory it had never occurred to me to think that our Chinese could head our schools, nor do I recall any missionary ever suggesting such a thing. As I look back I am amazed at my own stupidity! It was not because I was so anxious to be the head of a college as was demonstrated by my immediate resignation as soon as the law was announced. It is simply that the idea never previously entered my head.

And yet, in 1923, Uong Gang-Huo had challenged the church in these words:

But today it is the consensus of opinion that Chinese leadership must be depended upon *right now*. It is time for the responsible leadership and the hard work to be taken upon our own shoulders, so that before long may be realized the high ideal of a self-governing, self-propagating, self-supporting Methodist Church in China.[3]

The missionaries had early felt that the burden of purely evangelistic work must be borne by the Chinese. "The foreigner," they thought, "must direct the battle, but for standing face to face with the foe and winning an early victory, the native has the advantage." And in all sections of the church men and women had been coming to the church, and coming with the church and its blessings to their own people. Yet one of the Methodist missionaries had said in 1892 what others felt, but feared to express, even thirty-five years later:

While as a rule the natives cannot stand alone, and are not gifted with the power to plan and intiate, they nevertheless are most valuable workers under proper guidance and are most patient in attention to many details which somewhat tax the patience of a foreigner in this country.[4]

Never before in the eighty years of its history would the church have been able to survive such an exodus of missionaries as we have seen took place in 1927; never before had the missionaries realized that Chinese leadership was ready to accept Uong Gang-Huo's challenge.

Yet the whole policy of the Methodist Church during these decades had been preparatory to this demand. Class meetings, quarterly and district conferences, so acceptable to the democratic system of Chinese life, and so effective in giving the church member an interest and share in the work of his church, had developed lay leadership in churches; pastors had received their salaries from their own stewards; district superintendents had reported on the work and character of preachers and missionaries, and had advised bishops in cabinet sessions; the itinerant systems, even though it meant moving pastors every few years, had developed an able ministry. Institutional boards of managers had been increasingly composed of Chinese members; and the Tai-an hospital, for one, had been operated by Chinese, and Dr. Chia at Changli was doing "most of the operating" there "in accordance with the new idea of putting responsibility on the Chinese workers and making our mission seem less like a foreign institution." District finance committees had been taking the annual appropriation and "sitting down to the task of making the work fit into it," while since 1916 in Central China, and later in other conferences, finance committees, the legal representative of the Board of Foreign Missions on the field, had had Chinese ministers and laymen as members. Now the evacuating missionaries could turn administrative duties over to their Chinese fellow workers, and, often to the surprise of the missionaries, find that they had done a better job of preparing these men and women than they had known, for they made good, carrying on the work in spite of the near-by presence of soldiers and the anti-Christian activity.

Two years later the Methodist Episcopal Church, South, carried further this transfer of authority and responsibility by an organizational step that was in advance of anything its northern sister had done, even of that of placing Chinese in more than token membership on its finance committees. The first meeting of the China Central Council thus organized by this conference, was held in September, 1929. It was designed that this council "should in a large measure take over the work hitherto done by the Mission" and be the medium of connection with the Board of Missions. "The trustees of schools, of hospitals, laymen's movements, and all other departments of the work are to elect members of this Council," so that it was composed of about eighty "Chinese and missionaries—preachers and laymen, men and women, without discrimination, representing the thought of the Chinese church and missionary policies to the Board of Missions and administering affairs on the field."

The anti-Christian seeds that found soil in many hearts and minds—most of it was the shallow soil on stony ground—could not but check the growth of the church. Spencer Lewis saw in many of the churches "a weather-beaten aspect," and writing of 1928 said, "Christianity is unpopular, and who wishes to belong to an organization which is the object of defamation and ridicule?" But W. B. Cole was finding in the Hingwa Conference a year later, that church school enrollment was increasing again after the withdrawals to government and private schools, due to the propaganda of 1927. He added: "There seems to be something in the mission school that they want and do not find elsewhere."

If anyone had thought in 1927 that the day of the missionary was past, or that the church was ready to cast off the hawsers that moored it to a home dock, he was mistaken. The day of Andrew and his generation and his type of missionary had been rapidly passing; now it was certainly gone forever. But Methodism in China may still have needed financial help from the United States; more than that, it still wanted spiritual support, as witness the following from three of its leaders:

Y. C. Yang, president of Soochow University, felt:

The Chinese Christian and the American missionaries are working in closer and more cordial co-operation than ever before, and the "home church" and "mission field" are knitted together by warmer sentiments and closer fellowship than ever before.[5]

James Ding, president of the Angle-Chinese College in Foochow, wrote two or three years later:

The new Anglo-Chinese College is characterized by a new spirit—the spirit of co-operation between West and East, between the Board and the officers of administration, between the faculty and the students. There is a genuine family spirit; the Chinese people know well what that means.[6]

And it was Carol Chen, who had taken the helm of Hwa Nan College in 1927, who had said:

We Christian nationals are facing a big task. We are trying to establish an indigenous Christian church and nation that will be a true incarnation of the living Christ. We are calling to God and to our friends. Can you not tarry and watch with us? If there is any time we need you, it is now. You are welcome as a missionary movement. If the missionary movement was worthy to be started, it is worthy to be continued forever! . . . Accept our welcome; accept our invitation to come to the field, to walk with us the trail of Jesus Christ, the Man who saved others, but would not save himself. Be assured that even a warmer welcome is awaiting you over there.[7]

The year 1927 had brought to Chinese Christians a big task. Missionaries, many of them reluctantly, and church workers, many of them hesitantly, now knew that if Methodism was to become indigenous it must be through Chinese leadership. Missionaries who could cease "directing the battle" and walk with the Chinese in a co-operative family spirit were still wanted, but henceforth the Chinese must lead the church ever forward. And the church quickly realized that they could and would do it.

2. Chinese Ability to Hold Property, Promote Church Work

The transfer of administrative responsibility to the Chinese, into which the missions had been jolted in 1927, was one of the major steps toward making the church indigenous. What about church property? No church can be completely indigenous as long as the title to its property is held abroad.

In its awareness of this truism, the Southern church seems again to have been ahead of its Northern sister. At the 1886 session of the China Mission Conference, Young J. Allen, C. F. Reid, and A. P. Parker were appointed a committee to secure from the United States consul general a legal opinion as to the holding of their church property in China, particularly in respect to the following questions: (1) Can a board of trustees elected by the China Mission Conference legally hold property in China? (2) If so, what steps are necessary before it can take over such property from (a) the Board of Missions of the Methodist Episcopal Church, South, and (b) property held in interior cities in the name of individual members of the church, whether absolutely and in fee simple, or in trust for the church.

To this Consul General Kennedy replied that the General Conference of the Methodist Episcopal Church, South, had that year, by an "express mandate" provided that "The China Conference should hold and control all church property here," but he advised that the transfer of all properties, by whomever held, be by deed to such board of trustees.

The committee therefore recommended to the Conference (1) that it elect a board of trustees to hold all such property in trust for the Methodist Episcopal Church, South; and (2) that it instruct the attorney for the Board of Missions and all persons holding deeds to interior station property to deed such properties to this board of trustees. A year later the trustees reported that all the church property in Shanghai had been regularly transferred and duly registered but added:

The instructions in reference to church property in the interior have not been carried out, for the following reasons: (1) The titles to property now held in the interior are, in our opinion, valid and secure. (2) To attempt any further change in reference to them would certainly involve us in a considerable expense, and should any difficulty arise with the Chinese officials, might endanger the tenure of some of our property. We therefore deem it inexpedient to take any further action in the matter.[8] [See Appendix A, item 18.]

Although those actions had been taken in 1886-87, this board of trustees was not functioning as fully as designed when the union of Methodism occurred, and when later the invaders of Shanghai had all this property at their mercy. Property outside of Shanghai, purchased by the Chinese, had not come into title of this board, except in the case of "large" transactions. The board continued to be composed entirely of missionaries and was responsible to the Board of Missions at Nashville. But for a quarter century it had not taken any actions which had not been thoroughly considered by church organizations, such as, for example, the China Council, in which Chinese participated fully. Unification had not reached action altering this arrangement when invasion froze it, except such parcels as the board could turn over to the governing executive body of the East China Conference, pending the organization of the holding body authorized by the Central Conference of 1941.

Through all the years the Northern Board of Missions had been in no hurry to act in this matter though it had "long acknowledged . . . that the so-called mission properties in China have been given by American Christians . . . with the expectation that ultimately they would be under Chinese management and control." [9] But in 1927 this board was quick to act. On September 22 of that year its executive committee on China recognized "that any well-grounded and throughly-founded church in China cannot progress in initiative, responsibility and self-direction unless it owns and controls its properties," and then definitely stated:

We feel that the time has now come when we should say to the church in China that it is our expectation that proper legal steps will be taken by those having the power to transfer the local church properties to Chinese control as soon as some satisfactory plan can be agreed upon.[10]

The committee then urged that the bishops and field finance committees in China recommend as soon as possible the best way for church property to be held safely and permanently in China. Having taken that step and having declared its intention to its Chinese brethren, further haste appears to have been not incumbent, either on the field or in New York. Nearly seven years elapsed before we find the Central Conference in April, 1934, voting to "appoint a commission to prepare a plan for taking over all properties of the Methodist Episcopal Church in China, including those of the Board of Foreign Missions and the Woman's Foreign Missionary Society, except missionary residence property." [11] Three years later a board of trustees, consisting of thirteen members, was created, by action of the Eastern Asia Central Conference on March 29, 1937, to "have in trust the property of the Methodist Episcopal Church in China." (See Appendix A, item 19.) *Zion's Herald* called this "the first serious proposal of its kind in the history of Christian missions," not remembering the action of the China Conference in 1886.

The China Committee in 1927 had considered all the property of the Board of Foreign Missions in China under three classes: First, the local churches together with the local parsonages and primary schools which are sometimes built on the same lot; second, the educational, hospital, and other institutional properties; third, the compounds and the residences for missionaries. Its action for holding property pertained only to the local church, parsonage, and primary school group; it believed that further study should be made of the legal questions in view of developing national requirements, before the institutional property should be transferred, and that probably the transfer of each institution would have to be considered on its own merits. The Central Conference in its proposals in 1934 was preparing to take over the institutional property as well; in 1937 it organized a board of trustees "which shall have in trust the property of the Methodist Episcopal Church in China," thus providing the machinery against that day when it could "take title to all Methodist Church properties in China." Thus Paul Wiant, in reporting that conference, "hoped," it would seem, that "all" would be taken to include "missionary compounds and residences," although the September, 1927, statement of the China Committee had considered them "definitely a part of the provision and equipment for missionaries which should therefore be considered the permanent property of the Board of Foreign Missions." [12]

Perhaps the China Committee had been right in 1927 in believing that the holding of institutional property "must be studied," and that the "transfer of each institution must be considered on its own merits." Probably the Central Conference was right in 1934 in preparing to take over "all properties of the Methodist Episcopal Church in China . . . except mission residence property." American contributions had made possible such varied institutions as Moore Memorial Church in Shanghai and the chapel at Geng-giang on the Lungtien District, which had been erected only after years of opposition and litigation; the boys' boarding school at Tientsin and the buildings of Hwa Nan College; the Danforth Memorial Hospital at Kiukiang and the great Syracuse University Hospital at Chungking. Churches had their local official boards, institutions had their boards of managers, which were predominantly Chinese, and schools and hospitals were definitely coming under the administration of Chinese men and women. If a connectional board in the United States could hold the property of a local institution, why could not the board of trustees established for the church in China hold the property of institutions as well as that of churches? The only answer, of course, is, "Give it time, and it will." The chaos due to the Sino-Japanese War prevented for some time anything further along this line. By 1941 the churches had been united, but only the conferences in Free China could come under any provisions for holding property under the Nationalist government. Hence the executive board of the Central Conference, following the conference session

voted to appoint a committee to study the whole matter of registration with the government and the formation of a Property Holding Corporation. This Committee will act for the conferences in Free China in relation with the National Government in property matters. The Committee: William Hsu, convenor, Dr. D. Y. Li, C. B. Rappe, R. Y. Lo, Russell Hsiung, Miss Dorothy Jones, and the bishops.[13]

Then the General Conference of 1944 gave its blessing, voting that:

A Central Conference, through a duly-incorporated property-holding body or bodies, shall have authority to purchase, hold, or transfer property for and on behalf of the Methodist Church, and of all the unincorporated organizations of the Methodist Church within the territory of that Central Conference; or on behalf of other organizations of the Methodist Church, which have entrusted their property to that Central Conference,

subject, of course, "to the laws of the country or countries concerned." [14]

This has raised another question—that of the source of funds for repair and upkeep when the property is held by the board of trustees registered with the Chinese government. "In earlier days major repairs were in a large measure financed by funds from America. Today," wrote E. Pearce Hayes in 1943, "such aid seems almost impossible, or at least difficult. It is now evident that we have built on too large and expensive a scale for the indigenous church to be able to carry on repairs." That looks like another problem of the whole self-support question!

Some valuable church properties were ready for the new board of trustees to take over—valuable in the services they were rendering rather than in the number of dollar figures shown on the balance sheet of some of them. These, to name only a few outstanding churches among the many that might be named, include the following: Cing-sing-dong, still standing, valuable because of the people it could reach and as a sentimental shrine— the first Methodist Episcopal Church erected in Asia; Tieng-ang-dong, almost as old (though the first building was replaced in 1896), ministering to a large student group and as fine a church membership, both in quantity and quality, as almost any city church anywhere; Siong-iu-dong, the first complete city institutional church in the Mi-I-Mi Huei; Wesley Church, in Nanking, brought, as was Siong-iu-dong, to the fullness of wonderful usefulness in the large city (at the time, China's capital) by Ralph A. Ward, who knew how to promote church work in China's cities; the great Lewis Memorial Church in Chungking, which had been reaching the multitudes and all classes of that city before enemy bombs blasted it to pieces; Asbury Church, in Peking, a church of modified renaissance architecture that had housed the best Sunday school in China, made worship a joy to students and officials, and served as a house of prayer at the request of the non-Christian government; and Moore Memorial, Shanghai.

Moore Memorial Church, with a $325,000 (Mex.) edifice which would not have been out of place in Atlanta or Tacoma, and from which the church bell, which had been secured by Young J. Allen, rings out its worship call to the hurrying throngs and the heavy-laden multitudes of Shanghai's International Settlement, and with the only pipe organ which Methodism owns in China to lead its vested choir in praise to Almighty God—this is one aspect of Moore Memorial which is otherwise "a veritable bee-hive of activity" and which has also been called "a Christian laboratory; an evangelistic center; a religious education base; and a temple of worship."

It would be interesting to list its ten educational features, its eleven evangelistic features, and its fourteen health, social, and literary features, including the Bootblack's Co-operative in which forty unemployed young men support themselves by polishing shoes on a co-operative basis, and give part time to service projects, such as selling rice, and keeping the neon cross lighted one week of the month. There is time however, for a few of the "Highlights of the Past Year" as reported to the Central Conference of 1941:

Better Baby Contest in which 405 children took part—the best fifteen were given prizes, the fifteen poorest were given medicines and vitamin foods. Joint Baccalaureate Service of six refugee Christian Universities and colleges with their affiliated Middle Schools, . . . Five hundred graduates and faculty members marching in impressive academic procession. Weddings are solemnized on an average of one a week—fifty-seven was the total for last year. . . . Rice Line. On account of the rising cost of living the selling of cooked rice which had been a feature of the earlier months of the fighting in Shanghai was resumed. Last year 350,000 catties of rice were sold at a cost of $80,000. Of this amount $16,000 represented a loss sustained by the church, which was met by unsolicited contributions for relief. A mat shed was built to permit the five hundred people who buy rice daily to eat it hot with the free vegetables supplied. Many take home a supply for the family; the average amount bought by a person is three catties daily. Communion Service was changed to 8:00 A.M. after long years of experimentation to find a satisfactory time at which a quiet communion could be observed. . . . Christmas candle-light choral service in which 150 gowned choristers of the six choir groups of the church took part, with over a thousand of our church people lighting candles in the Service of Light. . . . Christmas Baptismal Service for babies at which fifty-eight children were baptized. . . . More than two thousand people entering the church doors daily.[15]

As far as church legislation was concerned, China Methodists could own their own property: it was to be theirs to use to further the Kingdom of Christ, as soon as legal steps for its transfer could be provided by governmen action. As "Dr. Taylor's little chapel" had paved the way for the city church that could minister to two thousand people daily, so the place of the church would be increasingly useful as such assets become increasingly indigenous. The time would doubtless come when, instead of towers (even though of pagoda-like architecture), glass windows, and Berean pictures on the walls, Methodist churches would be built on Methodist property in China, possibly adapting the architecture of the Chinese temple with its courts and halls to the needs of choir, congregation, social rooms, and church school; worshiping, perhaps, in services no longer following the conventional Western pattern; its curved roof and carved pillars affording sacred beauty; the rich-toned chimes and organ of the Christian temple replacing the gong and drum, and the bronze incense burner supplanted by the communion altar and its Christian cross.

3. *Chinese Ability to Carry On Missionary Work*

Chinese Methodists were administering the church and its institutions, and provision was being made for them to hold its property. Those were two major steps in making the Methodist Church indigenous. When the church took the responsibility for sending the gospel to places and peoples outside of its own boundaries, it was exhibiting another major responsibility of a self-governing church—that of being self-propagating. Though not yet self-supporting, it was supporting work beyond its borders. Here was an opportunity for those who would criticize: but the giving church is a living church; it is likely to be a singing church, for the congregation which has shared its "crust" has usually had more for its own nourishment.

> The Holy Supper is kept, indeed,
> In whatso we share with another's need.

The West China Mission, as we have seen, had sent two missionaries to Tibet in 1907.

The sending of Ethel Li to Yung-an was the beginning of this missionary work by the women. "Come unto me," was the call which Isabelle White had wanted to give to the women of China, and the call which Maria Brown, Lochie Rankin, Gertrude Howe, Mable Hartford, Esther Lewis, and hundreds of other American women have heard accepted by Chinese women. But those Methodist women of China have also heard the other call, "Go ye," and have responded magnificently. As early as 1899 or 1900, the women of the Futsing District had made a thank offering for what the Woman's Foreign Missionary Society had done for them and sent $36.45 to support an orphan in India. This was repeated in subsequent years, one old woman once walking ten miles to bring $3.00 as her dues for three years which no one had in the meantime called to collect. The Woman's Missionary Society of China was organized in Foochow on October 10, 1913, by Elizabeth Strow and May Hu, daughter of Hu Sing-Mi, and rapidly became a missionary society "by and of the women of China," which has grown and spread as it has devoted itself to the carrying of the gospel to the women of China and the world. The work was still being carried on and the interest was unflagging in 1940, when, with

prices soaring and living conditions growing more pitiful they gave more than they did the previous year. The star auxiliary is Lungtien, situated on the sea coast. Most of the members are poor under ordinary conditions and now during the blockade their main source of livelihood, fishing, has been made unsafe. In spite of poor crops of both their sweet potatoes and peanuts these poor women handed in $761., almost $200. *more* that they gave last year. At their mite-box opening, all two hundred members were present in spite of an air-raid in Futsing not far distant.[16]

It was evidenced by many reports, such as one from Edith Able written in 1943, when eggs were selling for $1.20 each:

Our women's societies are growing in number and in giving. Last year the women on our four districts gave nearly $10,000 with Lungtien heading the list with $4,000. This fall we expect to celebrate in Foochow the thirtieth anniversary of the founding of our society and great plans are being made for that.

At least two of the churches are paying the full salary of their Bible Women, and all the others are helping in part. Our Women's Societies of Christian Service are not only helping their local churches but are also continuing to support their home mission school at Yung-an.

Nor were they afraid of hurting their "home mission" project, when, in the thirtieth year of their existence they sent their Easter Thank Offering to India, for Christian work in some village, and hoped some day to send "one of their own Chinese women as a missionary to that country."

A woman's missionary society was also organized in the China Mission Conference in 1917. Composed of several auxiliaries and the women "so lately come out of heathendom," living, many of them, "in abject poverty," they gave generously to send the gospel to their fellow countrywomen in the interior of their own country and in Africa. This society had, moreover, opened and maintained a mission at Chitong, almost within its own conference territory, north of the Yangtze, where it enters the Yellow Sea, and where it maintained two women workers, and a home for Bible Women, "the first building ever put up on any field by the China Conference Women's Missionary Society." Meanwhile it also supported a Chinese woman missionary in the prewar frontier of Yunnan and joined in the larger conference project in Manchuria, and yet "not once during the twenty-two years has the Conference Treasurer failed to send the full amount of money to Africa." [17]

In 1935 a woman's missionary society was organized in the West China Conference that they might send the gospel to the aboriginal Miaos, near the border of Tibet. Volunteers from among the leading women in places of responsibility in churches and schools offered to go to carry out the motto, "We received to give."

A glimpse of how it was being done in the Yenping Conference is shown in the followng account from the river town where the Anglo-Chinese College had sought safety from the bombs, as told informally by one of the faculty women interested in the women of their new environment as well as in the boys of the institution:

This afternoon we are having a meeting of our women's missionary society. Once a month we bring our thank-offering and most of the women bring it in rice. I wish you could be there to see the two bushel baskets filled. The women take a little from the rice supply for each day. The family never misses it, but by the end of the month it counts up. We have averaged about $130 in our monthly offerings. And the spirit has grown amazingly since we began this method. Our first three years up here we had only faculty wives and refugee women. Now more than half are local women. I get quite a thrill out of our mixed crowd and the fine friendly spirit. Once we all had supper together and it was great fun. There was no feast, just rice and soup and four bowls. Last month Mrs. Ding Guang-Deu reported on Women's Work in Singapore. This week Emily is going to give the history of the Yungan work. Next month I am going to tell about India. The following month Isabel Hwang is going to talk on Child Care and Christian Training. The next month will be the Christmas program, and then Muriel is going to talk about the United States. The intervening weeks, Emily, Mrs. Ding, and Mrs. Kiu give talks from their personal experience and get the women to give brief testimonies. The church is quite flourishing.[18]

Evidently an interest in others was a factor in keeping "the Holy Supper" at home!

In 1922 the China Conference made a "momentous decision" which Dr. A. P. Parker of Shanghai said marked "an epoch in the history of our work in China." It has been previously noted that the Southern Methodists in Korea had heard a Macedonian call from Manchuria, and had sent men to plant the Christian seed. But Manchuria was a large field, and Korean Methodists could not, for many years to come, expect to meet the need of the native Manchus, the settlers of Korean origin, the Russian immigrants, and the large Chinese population. The China Conference was therefore by no means trespassing when it "decided to open a mission to Chinese in Manchuria, to be manned and financed by the Chinese themselves," and to be "administered as the Chinese section of the Siberian Mission of the Methodist Episcopal Church, South." Twelve thousand dollars was subscribed and paid towards the enterprise. Of the opening of the work, J. C. Hawk, who moved his family from the China Mission to Harbin in July, 1924, wrote in a letter:

On April 10 [1924] Rev. Tsoh Kwe-Sung, Mr. Mei Dzei-Si, and I started for Harbin. . . . Work had already been started by the Chinese brethren but . . . formal opening . . . on August 10 was followed by an evangelistic campaign for two weeks which resulted in more than seventy-five probationers. Since then that number has been increased to more than one hundred. . . . In order to meet the great need of a worker with the women we have secured the half time service of a young lady who is a native of Mukden, a normal graduate, and a graduate of our own Bible School in Nanking. Her salary is being provided for locally. Part of it is given by the Woman's Missionary Society of our Russian Church, and the remainder from our own local church.

Rented property was secured for evangelistic and educational work in a section of the city selected in agreement with the other churches already in the city. A year later, with funds available with which to build a church, Hawk was regretting that "we have not been able to secure a building site, as the Chinese and Russian authorities have not settled the question of control and ownership of land," but he was encouraged enough about the work to add: "We wish to recommend opening work to the west of Harbin centering around the town of Mankow."

Thereafter the reports of the China Conference are strangely silent about the Manchurian Mission. The conference appointments each year to and including 1932 included, on most of the districts, a "Secretary for Manchurian work." In 1933 and 1934 the appointments list one or two men appointed to the "Manchurian Mission," the appointment appearing under Changchow District. Then from 1935 through 1940, the appointment appears under Soochow District, the single appointee for the last several years having been Tsang Hai-Iung. For a number of years the Women's Missionary Society of the China Conference had a representative in this work. The local church financed the advance program, i.e., the opening of out-stations and the salaries of local workers; but the China Conference continued to carry the support of all workers sent from within its bounds.

These and the earlier missionary activities of the church can hardly be considered as major phases of the church's growth during the century, but they are fundamental and significant enough to justify the recognition that has been given them. Nor has the war decade written a finis to any of them.

But when "the tumult and the shouting dies," we shall probably find "our farflung battle line" extended beyond any recognized conference boundaries of 1937. Evacuation and migration had seen Methodist schools relocated in villages and towns not previously listed in any roster of conference appointments, and pastors and Bible women were scattered with their members everywhere through Kiangsi, Hunan, Kweichow, Yunan, Shansi, and other provinces. Just as Captain Ding had carried the gospel back to his native island of Haitang in 1870, and as Wang Jui-Fu had opened An-chia-chuang to the Christian message, so Hsiang Shui-Kong had established "a little place of worship for the villagers in his own home" at that "farthest north" point beyond the Great Wall, laying the groundwork for the church in "the busy market-town of Ta-ching-tzu" in 1923. So the sending in 1938 of the Rev. Zau Tsong-Foh, experienced district superintendent, student pastor, and religious education secretary, and the Rev. Mau Nyung-Zo, district superintendent, editor, and intellectual leader, with a team of Bible women and teachers, may have been the opening move, if not for a future Methodist conference centering at Kunming, perhaps for ultimate union with the Wesleyan Methodist Church. These cannot be called strictly missionary undertakings by the local churches; this Kunming appointment had been a war-emergency provided from the budget of the conference relief committee "as a relief project for one year" for work "in co-operation with the Christian organizations at work there," especially the Wesleyan Methodists with whom Zau, Mau, and their companions were appointed to serve. Many wartime assignments were voluntary or supported by mission, relief, or local funds; many new churches had sprung up beyond previous borders because of the reality of the Christ newly found by a humble villager.

But whether by the force of war or the spirit-filled service of "new-born" men, or the sacrificial giving of humble women, the Methodists of China were making Christ known in "regions beyond," and demonstrating that a living church, firmly rooted in the soil, and though it have but two mites, will inevitably be a giving church, and that a church that gives will be a church that lives.

XVII
THE CHURCH WILL REMAIN

Crowns and thrones may perish,
Kingdoms rise and wane,
But the church of Jesus
Constant will remain.

FOR A HUNDRED YEARS AMERICAN METHODISM HAS BEEN POURING INTO changing China the rich blue of its life; the molten flux which the century has produced has had the spirit of the Wesleys fused into it. As a part of this process there has taken root a church with the richness, beauty, and strength of Methodism now destined to remain a force in the Christian China that is to be. Yes, Methodism is very thoroughly and very permanently a part of the Christian life of China. But how fully is the yearning of the Chinese being realized of being able to interpret it in their own way to their own people? Asks Hu Shih:

How can we Chinese best assimilate civilization in such a manner as to make it congenial and congruous and continuous with the civilization of our making? This larger problem presents itself in every phase of the great conflict between the old civilization and the new. In art, in literature, in politics, and in social life in general, the underlying problem is fundamentally the same.[1]

In church life too the problem is fundamental. Are the Chinese people assimilating the spirit of Methodism so as to make is congenial, congruous, and continuous with the background into which it is being poured, and at the same time maintain its purity and its virility and be a vital and integral part of that church which can be "one o'er all the earth"?

Henry P. Van Dusen has coined a new word when he says that sound and desirable "indigenization" is not yet completed. And while we cannot but agree with that statement, the story which has been told in the foregoing pages clearly shows that the Methodist people in China have, in a hundred years, gone a long way along this road of "indigenization."

Bishop Ralph A. Ward says, "The Church was their Church." In his last official report before the Japanese confined him to three years of imprisonment, he had written:

Over a year before December 8, 1941, definitely began the process of preparing district superintendents, pastors, regular and special committees, other church

287

officers and local congregations to assume their official responsibilities as necessary if, and when, foreign missionary personnel and co-operation might be further or entirely removed. In plan and attitudes and practice they began getting ready. Essentially December 8th did not take them by surprise. The Church was their Church. It was in their hands—and in the hands of God.[2]

This special process may have been going on for a year, but the whole process of preparation had commenced on October 9, 1858, when the first quarterly conference was held in Cing-Sing-Dong, and when, "wishing to train our converts," the missionaries asked the brethren to "provide the symbols of brotherly love for the feast," and they chose tea and seedcakes instead of the conventional and alien bread and water. Thus from the very beginning, Maclay and Gibson and their successors tried to free the church from that ecclesiastical baggage which Kenneth S. Latourette mentioned when he wrote in *A History of Christian Mission in China*:

> Missionaries have been too often controlled by ecclesiastical authorities outside China who conscientiously insist upon the maintenance of the traditional system. This inflexibility . . . insists upon more of a dislocation of the older culture than is essential to an entrance into the Christian experience. It burdens Christianity with an enormous amount of baggage . . . of which it must some time rid itself if it is ever to be at home in China.[3]

It took another step when Hu Bo-Mi was made a member of the Wyoming Conference, thus recognizing the right of every Chinese who should prove worthy to become a part of the basic governing organization of his church. And when in 1869 Bishop Kingsley ordained three deacons and four elders, when in 1877 the Foochow Conference was organized and to every district a Chinese appointed as Presiding Elder, when S. L. Baldwin's character and effectiveness had to be recommended and approved by Hu Bo-Mi as his superior officer—then the "indigenization" of the Methodist organization was well under way. Repeatedly through those early decades the missionaries testified that in their judgment the organization of the Methodist Episcopal churches was marvelously adapted to take root in Chinese soil and bear fruit with a Chinese flavor.

With the spread of the church organization of the Methodist Episcopal Church from Fukien to the Yangtze Valley, North China, and Szechuen, the organization of the Central Conference in 1897 is now seen to have been a necessity in this process of "indigenization." In twenty-six years this conference had grown from a body of eleven American missionaries and two Chinese ministers to one whose composition was 66 per cent Chinese, and had demonstrated to the general conference that, not only was it becoming more and more Chinese in its composition, but also more and more competent to make the Methodist Episcopal Church more Chinese in its interpretation. Hence the General Conference of 1920 had

recognized the necessity of allowing differences in ritual, forms, of worship, "special advices," and even membership and ministry, in order to make the church fit in more closely with local conditions and customs. Instead of fearing what "the heathen members of Conference" would do to time-honored Methodist customs, there seems to be a hope that the missions in foreign lands would eventuate in indigenous developments.[4]

The church authorities and membership in the United States wanted this hope to be realized. At the General Conference of 1924, Bishop Berry, speaking for the bishops, expressed their belief that the conference would be wise in providing for an increasing amount of self-determination and self-government in all overseas sections of the church. And after another four years, the General Conference was seeking to make possible what was perhaps the largest step in decentralization of authority and increase in local autonomy which it had ever taken or would ever take—the election of bishops by Central (and subsequently, as a corollary, by Jurisdictional) Conferences. Hence on February 27, 1930, the Eastern Asia Central Conference had elected to the episcopacy of the Methodist Episcopal Church and to the administration of the Chinese portion of that Church, a Chinese. By 1941, with seventy-eight Chinese members (seventy-four per cent) of the Central Conference and twenty-seven Americans, two of the three bishops elected were Chinese. Only because this conference, predominantly Chinese, wanted two of their episcopal leaders to be Americans, and not because of any inhibitions or instructions from elsewhere, has the church not placed its administration entirely in Chinese hands. Organizationally little remains to be done in the "indigenization" of The Methodist Church in China—even *Official Minutes* are now published in Chinese.

Bishops Wang, Kaung, and Chen all came to this high office after experience in the churches of Methodism, preceded by training in Methodist schools. The significance of this is seen perhaps by contrast with the results in the Nestorian Church. While we may be able to agree that the failure of that church, with its "otherwise bright missionary progress," was due in large part to the preaching of a "Christ who is less than Divine," we must also note the comment of a recent writer on Nestorianism in China who says:

I should like to point out one other cause to which the overthrow of the work may be traced—I mean the neglect of school work and the training of Chinese pastors and teachers. . . . No effort seems to have been made to use and develop the Chinese Christians as teachers, speakers, doctors, or pastors, and in China any mission which neglects this branch of the work is foredoomed to failure.[5]

Granting the soundness of this view, we must not fail to see a warning in what one missionary—Paul S. Wiant—has said, if he is right when he said:

It is most heartening to every forward-looking missionary to see our Chinese brethren and sisters take upon themselves the responsibility of planning and doing the work of the church. Some phases of it which the missionary community have been very keen about in the past are not so fully supported by the Chinese; particularly the educational work beyond Junior Middle School. The missionaries have to continue their support for the few Senior Middle Schools until the average educational level of the pastorate is raised.

But if more can be done than has been done to "indigenize" the Methodist educational work from kindergarten through college and professional training, it will be done. Long since, the controlling boards of these institutions have been predominantly Chinese. The meetings of boards of education in the Foochow Conference behind the lines of Japanese occupation after most of the missionaries had been evacuated, their careful study of the postwar problems of these institutions, and their decisions to make reorganizations and mergers, all attest that the Chinese educators in The Methodist church are wisely making these institutions conform to the needs of Chinese Methodist youth and leadership.

With men and women of outstanding spiritual lives, intellectual ability, breadth of vision, and depth of understanding of both Chinese and Western educational conceptions, called to the lead of Methodist and union high schools, colleges, training schools and seminaries; with such men and women as Lucy Wang, and Janet Ho, James Ding and C. J. Lin, Y. C. Yang and Dsang Ling-Gau, and a host of others, there can be little doubt that Chinese Methodists are competently training the leaders for China Methodism.

The need for hospitals to secure entree for the church has about gone, and although the healing of bodies has always been a ministry of the church, and hospitals will always be points through which men and women are brought into the church, it is altogether possible that the "indigenization" of policy determination and financial support during the decades of postwar reconstruction may restrict or prevent further development of any hospital program by the church.

The "indigenization" of financial support for The Methodist Church in China is still far from accomplished. Through eight decades mission boards and finance committees, missionaries and Chinese, have wrestled with the problem without as yet having found the satisfactory formula. The x is still unsolved. In 1870 Sia Sek-Ong renounced all claim to financial support from mission funds lest he be accused of being "hired by foreign rice." In 1885 the church stewards at Asbury Church, Peking, were collecting the pastor's salary from the church membership. In 1914 church members were confessing to Bishop Lewis that they were not paying to the church as much as idol worship had cost them, or else the entire expense of the church work would be more than met. Giving rice, oysters, wood, or water chestnuts has been hailed as a means of local support, though it is doubtful if it will ever be found the adequate underwriting.

Nor has the organization of conference finance or field committees, composed of a majority of Chinese members, met the problem. To put the appropriation in the hands of the district superintendent may have "been a great relief and delightful fun" to the missionary who could then say: "Why, I don't have the money; please go and see the D. S."—but it has still been an "appropriation" from New York. The organization of an All-China Finance Committee was hailed "as the most encouraging development in years, with its work only just begun." Composed of "Chinese and missionary members from each of the seven annual conferences, together with certain of the general officers of the church," it viewed the financial problems of the China conferences as a whole, but was usually concerned with securing and distributing funds from the United States.

When the expense of carrying the total program of Methodist work in China can be reduced to meet the rising financial resources of the Chinese membership; when people "give to the Lord" in proportion to what they spent for idol worship, then, and not till then, will the "indigenization" of church finances be attained.

As long as the Division of Foreign Missions appropriates funds for capital and operating expenses in China, so long will it retain a measure of control over the church administration in China. But when the China Conference organized its China Council, predominantly Chinese, a long step was taken toward the transfer of this administrative authority to the China church, which was further advanced after union by the formation of the field work committees which, though largely Chinese, are the sole source of communication in China with the Board of Missions, other than the annual conferences and the bishops whom they have elected—then the "indigenization" of administration has moved a long way toward completion.

In *China's International Relations and Other Essays,* Harley Farnsworth MacNair has well observed:

In the minds of too many who contribute financially for Christian work in China there is the idea that Christianity and foreign clothes, architecture and customs are synonymous. Consider, for instance, the surpassing foreign-ness of much of the Christian church and mission architecture in China at present.[6]

The union universities and the Fukien Construction Bureau have stimulated the "indigenization" of this movement to express "Christianity in stone" in China. John E. Williams of Nanking University urged

that a Chinese type of architecture be followed, and pointed out the beauties of this ancient and indigenous art in China and states strongly his opinion that the university would become more truly national and indigenous if this course were followed. . . . The University of Nanking was the first of the larger Christian universities to adopt this type of architecture. . . . At the dedication of Swasey Hall, a visiting trustee remarked that it was "Christianity in Stone." It is not too much to say that the Christian colleges have had a profound influence upon the architecture not only of educational institutions, but of government buildings in China, and such action and influence help to refute the accusation . . . that their influence is too alien and non-Chinese.[7]

The church at Nguong-die—to pick at random one example of many—was architecturally neither Chinese nor American. The "handsome church buildings" which H. R. Caldwell had built from American contributions, and which were ready for dedication in 1910, could hardly have been described as Gothic or Oriental. Asbury Church in Peking had been copied from many an American church of modified Renaissance architecture. But the postwar reconstruction should see many a Methodist church in Kiangsu, Kiangsi, Fukien, Hopei, and elsewhere through China, built with carved pillars and upward-curving roofs, with stained glass screens enclosing "heaven's wells," and graceful pagoda-like towers, all of which will give to the best of ecclesiastical architecture a style that will refute the accusation of its being too alien and non-Chinese.

Recognizing that no church can be completely indigenous as long as the title to its property is held abroad, the Methodists have made progress in transferring property titles from the American corporations to Chinese holders. Methodist missionaries had been in China only forty years when the China Mission Conference organized a board of trustees which took title to the church property in Shanghai. Forty years later the Board of Foreign Missions of the Northern church took a first step in the same direction. Seventeen years then passed before the General Conference of The Methodist Church voted that "A Central Conference, through a duly incorporated property-holding body or bodies, shall have authority to purchase, hold, or transfer property for and on behalf of The Methodist Church." [8] China was then at war, much of the country was occupied by enemy forces, title to much property was for the time being not worth the paper on which it was written, many deeds held in mission safes and missionaries' desks may have gone up in smoke. Hence the groundwork has been laid and the early years of Methodism's second century will almost certainly see the "indigenization" of property holding as a major secular step towards the complete "indigeniization" of the church.

It has been hard for many a Chinese to accept the Western ways of doing things, though many things have been accepted because Western ways were wanted. But the time is past when the church in China wants to do something because it is the Western way. At the same time it has been very hard for many missionaries to transfer their authority to their Chinese brothers and sisters, or even to hear them sing the old familiar hymns to Chinese tunes, but the inclusion of fifty original hymns "set to Chinese musical compositions" in the new hymnal of 450 hymns from the West, "transplanted and acclimatized in the East," has been another large step in the making of the church at home in China. This intermingling of the praise and melody of both East and West will be one of the valuable assets of the church, when, "one o'er all the earth," all people will sing hymns whose words and music will be the contributions of the German and the English, the Americans and the Brazilians, the Indians and the Chinese.

Churches may revert to the lay leadership of primitive Methodism, dedication of infants may supplant infant baptism, new orders of worship may be evolved, Western parliamentary rules may give way to others more efficient in Chinese deliberations, the English language is about to disappear from conference sessions and minutes, and entirely new methods of financing the rural churches may spread over the hundreds of thousands of China's villages and hamlets. All these only show that the Chinese are at least beginning to have realized their yearning to interpret in their own way the spirit and purpose of The Methodist Church, and to refute the idea that Chinese churchmen are not gifted with the power to plan or initiate. "So," suggests Paul Wiant "will the Chinese church Christianize the festivals and feasts of the Orient, and the Church become truly indigenous." As R. C. Spooner said: "With the recognition of the value of Christian life and character, all sense of Christianity being a foreign importation into China and of alien culture, has vanished." [9] This is the real evidence that Christianity, and The Methodist Church in particular, are now an integral part of Chinese national life. Just a few names recalled from earlier pages of this story will demonstrate that: Ling Ching-Ting and Ciu Do-Gieng, whose flaming passion showed their fellow countrymen that Christianity was more to them than a Westernism that they had put on like a raincoat; Ida Kahn, whose name was known to everyone on the crowded streets of Nanchang, where she had become a living exemplar of the genuineness of Christ in Chinese life; Ethel Li, Chinese missionary, sent by the Methodist women of Fukien, to live

Christ for and among the Chinese women of the mountains of western Fukien; Mother Wang, whose name will be ever remembered and blessed in Shantung; that unnamed but not forgotten degreed scholar who, though an employee of the government on good salary, felt it no compromise to proclaim everywhere his relationship to the church; Diong A-Hok, who devoted his business to the observance of the Sabbath and the establishment of the Anglo-Chinese College in Foochow; Liew Tsoh-Sung, accepting Christ when he had no Christian companions, preaching in season and out of season, and going to open the new station at Soochow; R. Y. Lo, minister, editor, and legislator, and Feng Yu-Hsiang, whose political and military careers made Christianity felt outside the circles in which missionaries were in control; Chiang Kai-shek and Madame Chiang, who, while praying daily for their enemies, brought China through its years of "blood, sweat, and tears." Scattered through the century, pictured on the pages of its history, known and unknown, Methodism in China has produced scores and hundreds and thousands of men and women like those named above, who show better than words, institutions, or church buildings, that the Methodism that came from the United States a hundred years ago has become a part of Chinese life and culture, as it has been fused for the enrichment of the nation for ever.

If we are to test the "indigenization" of the Methodist Church in China after a century's work, we must define the word "indigenous" before we leave it. Said Latourette in *A History of Christian Missions in China*:

The word "indigenous" . . . was usually taken to mean a church led and supported by Chinese, and in doctrine, forms of worship and organization conforming as far as possible to Chinese rather than Occidental traditions. The immediate emphasis was upon transferring leadership from foreigners to Chinese.[10]

Wrote Roderick Scott not long ago: "The old roles have been reversed, which shows how far the missionary business has gone in China: formerly *they* said it couldn't be done and *we* did it; now *we* say it can't be done and *they* do it! and how well!"

That is the glory of it! That is why the church will remain! The gospel that Collins and Taylor wanted to bring to China a hundred years ago is making Methodism indigenous from Foochow and Shanghai to Chengtu and Kalgan. These from the Land of Sinim are making it genuinely and permanently a living part of that organism which is Wesley's world-wide parish. And how well!

APPENDIX A

SIGNIFICANT DOCUMENTS, STATEMENTS, AND RECORDS

1

Preamble and resolution adopted May 20, 1835, by the Missionary Society of the Methodist Episcopal Church

WHEREAS, There were collected and pledged at the late anniversary of this Society in Greene Street Church upwards of $1,400 for the support of a mission in China, therefore,

"*Resolved,* The Bishops be and they are hereby recommended and especially requested to select some person or persons, as soon as practicable, for the purpose of opening a mission under the patronage of this Society in the Empire of China.

"*Resolved,* That the clerk of this Board be requested to communicate the above resolutions to Bishops Hedding and Emory.

2

Letter from S. P. Williams of the Vermont Conference to the editor of the Missionary Advocate, January 5, 1846

DEAR BRO. STEVENS,

I was just in the act of taking up my pen to inform you that the North District in the Vermont Conference had resolved upon a mission to China, when the last *Missionary Advocate* came to hand. And it brought along with it the cheering intelligence that our Board at New York are seriously meditating this matter. Thank the Lord for this most *cheering* omen. . . . The Board may depend upon $300 from this district for that object.

3

Letter from H. C. Wood to Zion's Herald and Missionary Journal, July 29, 1846

A Mission to China. . . . When I consider the moral condition of that vast empire, the millions, aye, more, the hundreds of millions that are perishing for the lack of knowledge, the means of access to them, and the ability of the M. E. Church, my feelings are indescribable. . . . Whence the necessity of so much delay and such feeble efforts? Do we doubt that Christianity is adapted to that single people? or do we distrust the wisdom of our policy as Methodists? . . . The little Vermont Conference, by paying 10 cents a member, can raise about $1,000 yearly. . . . If each of the New England Conferences would send one, we should have five; and if New England would do this, we have no reason to doubt that our brethren South and West would do as well, and we should have a glorious little army that would pull down the strongholds of Satan and plant the blood-dyed banner of Prince Emmanuel on that soil, where superstition has had her seat from time immemorial.

4

Report submitted to the General Conference of the Methodist Episcopal Church, South, Petersburg, Virginia, 1846

The Committee on Missions respectfully report that they have duly considered the subject of the expedience and importance of instituting a mission to China, and are unanimously of the opinion that such a mission ought to be set on foot without delay.

Your committee have formed this opinion, not only because half of the pagan world belongs to the Celestial Empire, and the Emperor has recently, in the providence of God, opened a great and effectual door to missionary operations, and other churches, Papal and Protestant, are entering into it; but also because many respectable portions of our own church have been for some time past calling earnestly for a mission to China, considerable sums of money have actually been contributed for this express purpose, and the Board of Managers of our Missionary Society have recommended the same.

Moreover, your committee have been informed, from sources to be relied on, that two excellent men of rare qualifications for the work can be immediately obtained for this service. And they therefore recommend that you adopt the following resolution:

Resolved, That under a full persuasion of our being providentially called thereunto, we, the General Conference of the Methodist Episcopal Church, South, do solicit our bishops to take measures, in connection with our Board of Managers, for the appointment of two missionaries to China at the earliest day in their convenience.

Respectfully submitted,
W. CAPERS
Chairman, Missionary Committee

5

China Committee recommendation to the Board of Managers of the Board of Missions, New York, March 26, 1847

Our advisers agree in saying [that the number of missionaries may with greatest advantage be employed at our mission] should be three at least, with their wives, if married; but that the more of the right stamp the better. Those most thoroughly acquainted with Chinese missions assure us that fifty missionaries will be desirable at Fuhchau.

6

Letter from Bishop Hamline to the Rev. H. Hickok, August 31, 1847

DEAR BROTHER:

. . . And now, my Dear Bro., go in the strength of the Lord God and penetrate the darkness of that Empire of Heathenism. Go, and with the thunder of the Divine word shake the Idols' Temples, and with the fires of the Holy Spirit consume their altars from off the earth. Israel's GOD shall go with thee and with thine. He shall give thee a rod to carry in thine hand mightier than Aaron's and plagues more potent than fell upon Egypt shall follow thy footsteps as thou goest out against the enemies of thy crucified Lord; and potent, too, not to destroy, but to *save.* Live by the Cross and by the Cross expire. If you do this life and death shall be equally welcome. Should you live and labor long may the chariots of GOD surrounding you be your defense and above all may the *everlasting arms* be beneath. If called to martyrdom may the grace of GOD be in thee to sweeten its cup and make its cruel tortures as a bed of roses. He shall be with *you* who said—Be thou faithful unto death and I will give thee a crown of life.

Affectnly yrs.
L. L. HAMLINE

7

Letter from the Rev. B. Jenkins from Shanghai in 1851 to the secretary of the Missionary Society of the Methodist Episcopal Church, South

It is an encouraging thought, that from this mighty mass, dead in trespasses and sins, even a *single* soul is found willing to come out on the side of the true God and the religion of Christ. The man who has served me during the past year as a mandarin teacher, Mr. Liew, ... a native of Nanking, applied to me about six months ago for Christian baptism, but at that time I had little hope of him and opened up to him very fully the way of salvation by Jesus Christ. Since then he has conducted himself with such uninterrupted propriety and advanced so much in Christian knowledge and experience that I told him two months ago that I had admitted him on trial in the Methodist Episcopal Church, South. Prior to thus admitting him on trial, he had frequently spoken of his own experience of the utter folly and absurdity of Buddhism, in which he had been brought up, and of the value of Christ and his religion, and this so openly and fearlessly and with so good a grace, before his countrymen, to the number sometimes of 400 or 500, that I had in reality permitted him to preach Christianity before he had even been admitted on trial; but this I hope you will pardon, as China is so opposite to America in everything that we have even no such thing as a washerwoman, but a washerman, here. Mr. Liew now preaches a sermon or two every Sabbath, which is Sunday with most of us in China, and sometimes on week-days, when the weather will permit preaching out of doors, in the large enclosure in the city which contains the temple dedicated to the tutelary guardian of the city.

Letter from the Rev. B. Jenkins dated January 13, 1852

Although he has been on trial for a whole year, it was not until Sunday, the fourth of this month, that I gave him baptism. On that day, at two in the after noon. . . . Mr. Liew and his wife took their seats in brother Taylor's little chapel, for the purpose of publicly renouncing idolatry and receiving Christian baptism. The house was soon filled with Chinese: Messrs. Milne and Edkins and Dr. Lockhart of the London Mission, Mr. Yates of the Southern Baptist Mission, and Mr. Wright of the Presbyterian Board, were also present to witness the scene. Brother Taylor gave us an appropriate discourse in the local dialect of Shanghai; your correspondent then put all those pointed questions which he supposed the nature of the case demanded; all of which were intelligently responded to by both the candidates—the man being a native of the ancient Chinese capital, Nanking; and his wife of the Foo city of Chang-chau, in the province of Kiang-nan. Having received baptism, Liew Sing-sang mounted the pulpit and gave the people a capital talk in the Mandarin or general language of the Chinese empire. This was his first discourse from a pulpit, although he has been my constant companion in out-door preaching during the year. He declares the Gospel message very pointedly to his fellow countrymen; and who cannot but hope that he may be eminently useful? He is in the prime of life, about twenty-eight, his wife a year or two younger. They have no children.

From the Review of Missions, *May, 1898*

As a man [Liew] was frank, generous, and gentlemanly; in manner dignified and courteous; as a Christian, he was simple, sincere and brave—qualities not always found in his countrymen. He was not ashamed or afraid to declare himself a Christian anywhere, even in the presence of enemies who threatened his life. More than once he was assailed by angry mobs while preaching, but his courage and presence of mind never for a moment forsook him.

For a native to become a Christian is, in all heathen countries, a very serious matter. It means the loss of all things; to be disowned by kindred, hated and persecuted by neighbors, and despised as an outcast. Liew suffered this for Christ's sake. He never faltered.

As a preacher Liew was a marvel. He seemed to grasp the great themes of the Gospel as by intuition, and to expound them with great clearness and vigor. He assailed the popular vices and superstitions of his countrymen with unsparing severity. He was a "son of thunder" rather than a "son of consolation"; "a voice crying in the wilderness."

. . . .

Always animated as a speaker, he was sometimes impetuous—almost boisterous. This was playfully attributed by other missionaries to the "Methodism" that was in him. He was a Methodist. He loved class-meetings and love-feasts; he was lively and earnest in manner when relating his experience or exhorting sinners to repent and believe on the Lord Jesus. He was an itinerant, always ready and anxious to press into the "regions beyond," and was, at the time of his death, laboring on an advanced out-post near the city of Soochow. . . . He was instrumental in bringing into the church many of the members of the society of Shanghai, and his usefulness seemed to be increasing when he was smitten by disease and brought down to the grave. He died in great peace on the twenty-first of August, 1865.

8

Membership of the Methodist Episcopal Church, South, in Shanghai, October 3, 1859

(1) Liew Tsoh-Sung, a native of Nanking, a dealer in precious stones, baptized on the first Sabbath in January, 1851. (2) . . . Mrs. Liew, baptized with her husband. (3) Kwe Tsang-zz, a widow, baptised October 7, 1855. A native of Shanghai. (4) Yung Kuing-San, a carpenter from the vicinity of Soochow, baptised July 1856. (5) Li Tsz-Yen, a native of Nanking, a button-maker by trade, baptised April 1857. (6) Wong Sing-Loh, a native of Ka-shung, also a button-maker,

baptised April 1857. (7) Tsung Sa-Sung, a native of Ka-shung, a button-maker, baptised Dec. 27, 1857. (8) Shu Sia-Yun, a native of Nanking, a teacher, baptised September 6, 1858. (9) ... Wife of Shu Sia-Yun, baptised with her husband. (10) Kwe U-Bong, a native of Nanking, a hatter, baptised January 2, 1859. (11) Hu Ngun-Ti, a native of Teen-sing, a scholar, baptised January 6, 1859.

9

Letter of R. S. Maclay describing some of the first hundred members of the Methodist Episcopal Church in Foochow

Brief notices of some of our converts may, perhaps, be interesting to the friends of the China Mission. I note them in the order of baptism.

1. Hu Bo-Mi, aged 31. He has a good common education, is a soldier by profession, has taken the lowest military degree, and is entitled to hold office in the army. Baptised January 17, 1858, he has given us much satisfaction by his humility, zeal, courage, and desire for a thorough knowledge of the Bible. He is a fluent speaker, and has rendered us efficient aid in the public preaching of the Gospel. His wife, also, has been baptised and received into the church.

2. Ngu Teng-Hai, aged 37. He is a scribe by profession, and has been connected with missionaries three or four years. His education is respectable, and he possesses some ability as a public speaker. He was baptised March 21st, 1858, and renders us important help in public preaching. His mother, aged 69 years, has also been baptised and received into the church.

3. Wong Cheng-Kuong, aged 50. He is a common day-laborer, but has sufficient knowledge of the written character to enable him, with a little study, to read our books. He was baptised March 21st, 1858, and exhibits good evidence of the genuineness of his conversion.

4. Ding Seng-Mi, aged 20. He is quite illiterate, is by trade a basket-maker; and, so far as we know, has the honor of being the first of our converts in Foochow who has suffered open and violent persecution for embracing Christianity. He was converted while serving his apprenticeship, and after making arrangements with his master for a proper observance of the Sabbath, he was admitted to baptism March 21st, 1858. His friends soon began to persecute him. They commanded him to get back from the missionaries his ancestral tablets, and coming to the shop where he was at work, they applied to him the most insulting and abusive language. They charged him with various crimes, and under the pretense that he had been bribed into a profession of Christianity, they sought to extort money from him. Seng-Mi meekly bore their abuse, denied that he had received money from the missionaries, and firmly refused to ask for the return of his ancestral tablets. From words, the enraged friends proceeded to harsher measures, and laying hold of Seng-Mi they beat him severely. Even blows failed to shake the resolution of the young convert; he remained firm, and persistently refused to yield to the demands of his friends, declaring, in the true martyr spirit, that he would die rather than renounce Christianity. At first the tradesman under whom Seng-Mi was serving took no part in the affair, but becoming alarmed by the continued threats of the persecutors, he determined to dismiss him from his service, thus

throwing him at once out of home and employment. Hearing of these facts, Brother Gibson went to see the young man, and offered him a home in his school until he succeeded in finding another place. Seng-Mi gratefully accepted the offer, saying that now he desired above all things else, the ability to read the sacred Scriptures. He is now in the school and applies himself closely to his books.

5. Hu Ngieng-Seu, aged 57. He is the father of Hu Bo-Mi, is a man of more than ordinary talent, has a common education, and has filled some inferior offices in the government service. He has attended our preaching for nine years, and has treated us with uniform courtesy. During the past four years he became more frequent and regular in his attendance on our preaching. It was evident the Holy Spirit was striving with him, and many prayers were offered for him. About a year ago his eldest son became interested in Christianity, and the father encouraged him, saying, "Go forward, and I will follow." May 9th, 1858, he together with his wife and two younger sons, was admitted to baptism.

6. Wong Tai-Hung, aged 35. He belongs to the literary class, and is our first convert from this influential body. He has been connected with the missionaries nearly eleven years as a teacher, first of the Rev. J. D. Collins of our mission, then, for a much longer time, of the Rev. J. Doolittle of the American Board Mission in Foochow. During all these years he had the respect and confidence of all who knew him, though he remained a proud and persistent idolator. It seemed as though nothing could subdue the pride of his heart. Even after his mind opened to receive, one by one, the cardinal truths of Christianity, his pride still seemed to present an insuperable barrier to his conversion. But grace triumphed at last, his proud heart yielded, and after counting the cost, he applied for baptism. He was admitted to the ordinance September 19, 1858. The brethren in America who formerly lived in Foochow will rejoice with us in the conversion of Wong Tai-Hung.

10

"Plan of the Work" in the Foochow Mission, year commencing October 1, 1863

    I. North Fuhchau Circuit, comprising East Street Chapel, Teng-iong and Lo-nguong City.

    II. South Fuhchau Circuit, comprising Cing-sing-Dong, Lien-kong, and Ming-au cities.

    III. Nantai Circuit, comprising Tieng-ang Dong, Tiong-loh, and Yenping cities.

    IV. South Nantai Circuit, comprising Guang-ing-cang, Sieu-liang (A-do) and Futsing City.

    V. Western Circuit, comprising Ngu-kang, Goi-hung, Gang-cia, Sieu-meh-ka, Yeh-iong, and Mih-ka.

    VI. Work to be organized during the year: Mintsing, Kutien, Bing-nang, and Ing-hok cities.

11

Letter from R. S. Maclay to Dr. Harris, secretary of the Board of Missions, Methodist Episcopal Church, December 16, 1870

Have you plans for the establishment of a mission in Japan? That country now seems to be open to the Gospel, and it is high time Protestant Christianity were entering the field in earnest. In this glorious enterprise American Methodism must not refuse to act a worthy part. It seems to me you might safely take advance action in the matter. "Speak unto the children of Israel that they go forward." Japan, it seems, is moving rapidly towards modern ideas and civilization: she appears, in fact, enthusiastic on the subject. Not a moment is to be lost, if we would save the nation from Atheism or Romanism. She is now drifting inevitably in this direction, and nothing but the Gospel which is "the power of God unto salvation" can rescue the nation from social anarchy and ruin.. . . . You cannot begin the mission in Japan too soon. That country exerts a powerful influence on China, and missionary operations there will most efficiently aid us here. Japan is just entering the portals of modern civilization. Shall not American Methodism extend to her a cordial recognition and a strong helping hand?

12

Carleton Lacy, on the great migration and the church in West China

The conclusion forced itself home that, whatever the explanation, the actual church-going population of the western provinces without the migration influx was surprisingly low, and that there was an investment in church buildings and property out of proportion to the number of people now prepared to avail themselves of this generous investment.

. . . .

The result is a good deal of dissatisfaction among immigrant Christians with the type of church they have found in the west. Empty churches with poor preachers and no program is their three-phrase characterization of the church they have found. These they might have found much closer to home had their flight not brought them so far.

. . . .

Our observations left no doubt of the deficiency in leadership training here in the past, of the resultant weakness of the church, and of the very real service rendered to this weak or infant church by the immigrant leaders who seem to have come providentially for this critical period. It is generally agreed that this immigrant leadership is for the most part temporary, that most of these trained pastors at least will return whence they came at the earliest opportunity, and that the church in the west and southwest during the years to come must depend upon locally provided leadership.

. . . .

More than once the view was expressed that the leaders in the Christian movement in China were unprepared for and incapable of presenting the Christian apologetic in a convincing manner in the face of the present situation.

. . . .

The only point of these paragraphs is to emphasize the failure of the church to produce in its well-trained down-river leaders this sense of mission or responsibility for the great section of the country in which the church is as yet undeveloped and where the need for the gospel in its best expression is distressingly urgent.

13

The attitude of the Methodist Episcopal Board of Foreign Missions toward evacuation of missionaries in 1937

That the Christian movement must go forward even under war conditions in the Far East is the conviction of the Board of Foreign Missions and the Woman's Foreign Missionary Society of the Methodist Episcopal Church. . . . These agencies and, it is believed, the church they represent, are confident that the struggle between Japan and China does not nullify the Christian obligation but strengthens it, and that the missionary contribution ought to be made even more vigorously than before. . . . We shall endeavor in co-operation with others to maintain all possible activities which make for reconciliation in both China and Japan, which minister to the relief of human suffering and which exalt the Person and Way of Jesus Christ. We are convinced that all activities in China of hospital and nursing service, schools, and churches which can be continued deserve and should have the utmost support of the Board and the Society. . . . We advise the evacuation of mothers with children, and authorize the continued service of only such missionaries as freely elect to remain, and whose remaining is approved by their field groups and the resident bishop. Those who are evacuated and those who elect to stay are alike assured of our sympathy and of our moral and financial support.

14

First report of the Rev. F. Ohlinger as president of the Anglo-Chinese College, Foochow

Many from all parts of the province not connected with the church are enquiring eagerly: Have you rooms to rent, and teachers to teach us? We are willing to pay room-rent, board, matriculation, tuition and incidentals in advance; we will submit to the Christian rules and government of the college—only admit us.

I. What will become of these young men if the college is properly sustained by the church? 1. A few will become first-class vagabonds. 2. A larger number will become trusty servants in European families in the East. 3. The next larger number will become officers and diplomatists. 4. A still larger number will become intelligent prosperous merchants. 5. An equally large class will become preachers of the Gospel and teachers. 6. The largest class will, probably like true angels of mercy, bring to the hovels of this suffering people the boon of intelligent medical aid and advice.

II. What would become of these young men without the college? 1. Many of them would become first-class vagabonds. 2. A larger number of them would become opium-smoking chair-coolies and burden-bearers. 3. One or two might become petty officers. 4. Quite a large per cent would become merchants—selling peanuts, chopsticks, and idol paper. 5. A pretty large class would become Christian preachers —barely able to read the Bible in their own classic style, trembling when confronted by the pupils of infidel and Roman Catholic Europeans, everywhere denounced as propagators of ignorance, unable to converse with the Bishop who ordains them, to say nothing of participating in the great council of the church that sends them forth. 6. The majority would become ordinary Chinese literary men—of all men most proud and bigoted. This is a calm view of the case, sustained by such men as Sia Sek-Ong and Hu Yong-Mi and by our whole church.

15

Description of a short-term Bible school on the Sungkiang District of the China Conference by Miss Nina M. Stallings

The delegates were eager for everything offered in the course, Bible, Character Study, Story telling, the discussion group on Children's Work, Health, Food, and Gardening, but they were seeking fellowship first and foremost. They had seen so few congenial people in this two and a half years and they wanted to do things together, so we had two music periods, one for devotional music in the morning and one for church services in the afternoon. Of course they still sang incorrectly when we closed but they did have such a good time.

. . . .

The most whole-hearted response from every delegate was in the discussion hour on Health, Food and Gardening, but before we had finished we had included every need of a small community. Children's Diseases and How to Care for Them was very well treated, also household remedies and first aid. The preparation of children's food was a daily demonstration for we fed our eleven babies and five little fellows under six every morning at recess. We had hoped to carry on our regular clean milk service while the institute was in session but our equipment and space was too limited, so it had to be suspended. An agricultural worker discussed "Intensive gardening, fresh vegetables all the year," and raising chickens and pigs.

. . . .

They are poor and have lost so much but had not lost the habit of giving; we hope this is only the beginning of the deepening of the spiritual life, more generous and better living and better service to their church and community.

16

The Rev. J. W. Dyson, of the East China Conference, a member of the commission which prepared Hymns of Universal Praise, *discusses the importance, the difficulties, and the results of this work*

This event, largely unheralded in the West, will no doubt come to be recognized as one of the significant achievements of the Protestant church in China, for it was the joint effort of six bodies, comprising three quarters of the entire Protestant membership of the country who had combined their talents and resources in a single task, and who felt in its consummation the new uniting bonds of a common fellowship of love and praise.

The history of any one of these six bodies during the recent decade of church life in modern China would be incomplete without some mention of its part in this great addition to the hymnody of the Church Universal. Both the Northern and Southern branches of Methodism shared in the total enterprise.

. . . .

Its 450 translated hymns were still essentially the hymnody of the West transplanted and acclimatized in the East. Its unique merit, however, derived from the fifty or more original hymns which were included and thus became a contribution from the Chinese church to the whole movement of congregational singing. These fifty hymns of these Chinese writers are set to Chinese musical compositions, which include some in the modern manner, and some of the traditional chants and ancient lute and verse tunes adapted and harmonized and thus appropriated to the service of the church. Mr. Bliss Wiant, as music editor, . . . searched out and mobilized a great body of Chinese musical talent, who collaborated in the production of these Chinese hymn tunes. . . . Certain of these tunes will in time become a part of the heritage of the universal church and will be incorporated in the books of America and Europe. The future will thus witness the enrichment in the life of the church coming from East to West.

.　　.　　.　　.　　.　　.　　.　　.　　.　　.　　.

The average churchman may not fully appreciate what is represented in a good hymn, as he is likely to be unmindful of the literary and theological criteria by which a sacred poem is judged as a vehicle for spiritual truth, and the vocal fitness of it must show in phrasing and accent for the chosen tune, which too must previously have met its own standards in the musical arts. These difficulties are further compounded when a translation is attempted from one language to another. The exacting requirements of Chinese poetry, for example, with its differing and sometimes conflicting systems, imperial, traditional, or modern scientific, as to accent, the poetic foot, the couplet, the interlacing rhyme, the weak and strong syllables, or other elements in style which must be employed in a hymn—all these make the task so formidable as to be almost impossible.

It will appear at once that such a task must await the appearance of Christian poets and musicians within the framework of the Chinese church: men and women with literary and musical gifts, and with a depth of spiritual experience that enables them to combine and sublimate the three in the final creation of a worthy hymn. The church today is notably richer in such spirits than it was a generation ago.

.　　.　　.　　.　　.　　.　　.　　.　　.　　.　　.

Mr. Ernest Y. L. Yang (of the Anglican-Episcopal Church), musician and poet in one, in fulfilling his tasks had reread the entire Bible three times during the three years, that he might better be imbued with its language, its message, and its elevated mood. . . . Their musical and literary assets were greatly augmented by contributions such as the music criticism of Dr. F. P. Jones, the poetical gifts of Dr. Edward James. . . . Mr. Bliss Wiant of Yenching University . . . assumed the music editorship.

.　　.　　.　　.　　.　　.　　.　　.　　.　　.　　.

The new union hymnal of the Chinese church, in its humble way, is thus a symbol and signpost: a symbol of the goals already achieved by the unifying processes of the Spirit; and a signpost to that still higher order of life that awaits a synthesis of East and West. And as such it deserves acclaim and pointed recognition in the annals of the church.

17

Effects of the Centenary in the Methodist Episcopal Church in China as summarized by the corresponding secretaries of the Board of Foreign Missions

The first effect of the Centenary in China has been to strengthen existing work.

A. Exchange. The war made serious curtailments. . . . Exchange has been heavily against China since the middle of the war period. The war increased prices. Living costs and the cost of building jumped an average of 25 per cent for all China. . . . Transportation costs increased 100 per cent. . . .

B. Offsetting losses during the Centenary Campaign. . . . In compliance with the wishes of the Centenary Administration China folk ceased their normal campaigning for special gift increases.

C. Increased operating budget. . . . For many years funds were insufficient to equip our men on the fields. Several resigned simply because they were given no working budget. . . .

D. New missionaries. . . . Some of these were replacements. Others were recruits long needed. Even a great mission like Foochow had no more evangelistic missionaries in 1918 than it had ten years before.

E. The Building Program. . . . The appropriations, however, have made very little provision for building operations.

F. Loss on Exchange. . . . Up to November 15, 1920, the Board had paid $353,-034.41 to make up this loss on the 1920 appropriations to China. . . .

G. Developing the Centenary as a movement in China. . . . The Centenary as a contagious, spiritual, visionful movement is coming to China. . . . Under the blessings of Him who called us unto the Centenary, [the appropriations of 1920] are pumping lifeblood into the Methodist Episcopal Church in China and into the race over there.

18

Correspondence and actions with reference to the holding of property by the Methodist Episcopal Church, South, in China, 1886-87

GEN. J. D. KENNEDY
U. S. CONSUL-GENERAL
SHANGHAI

SIR:

The undersigned having been appointed by the China Mission Conference of the Methodist Episcopal Church, South, held in Shanghai, November 17, 1886, hereby submit to you the following enquiries, upon which we ask your decision:

1. Can a Board of Trustees elected by the China Mission Conference above mentioned legally hold property in China?

2. If so, what steps are necessary to be taken in order to transfer property now held by power of attorney of the Board of Missions of the Methodist Episcopal Church, South, to said Board of Trustees?

3. What steps are necessary to secure to said Board of Trustees property held in the interior of China by individual members of the Methodist Episcopal Church, South? The deeds to said property are made out in due form according to Chinese

law, and registered in the District Magistrate's office. Some of the deeds are made absolute and in fee simple to inidividuals. Others of said deeds state that the property is held in trust for the Church.

> Y. J. ALLEN
> C. F. REID
> A. P. PARKER
> *Committee*

The decision

To your second: .... By the power delegated to him, or his agent, he has certain defined rights which he must strictly pursue to validate his acts; and while there is, after enumerating his various powers, an omnibus clause which apparently gives him, or his agent, the right to transfer, yet, on construing the instrument as a whole, the maxim of *expressio unius exclusio alterius* would apply, and every power being defined but that to transfer, I advise that deed be made. It might hold water, and no question ever raised, especially as in all church relations the presumption is that the principle of "Behold, how good and pleasant it is for brethren to dwell together in unity" is followed; but, as history shows that *brethren* do sometimes fall out, it is better to do things legally, *strictissimo jure*. The attorney of the Board need have no apprehension of acting without authority of his principals, for by the action of your General Conference, page 4, *Daily Advocate*, May 20, 1886 (which resolutions, I take it, are an exact copy of the original), it is the express mandate of that body that, on its organization, the China Conference should hold and *control all church property here*. And as the master is superior to the servant, the Board of Missions *eo instanti*, according to these resolutions on the organization of the China Conference, become *functi officio* so far as property here is concerned, and all power delegated to their attorney, when that event was consummated, ceased. But as the legal seizen is in the Board of Missions per its attorney, it is better to have titles vested in your Trustees to make the legal form complete.

As to the third inquiry: I suggest that the individuals in whose names property is held in the interior execute titles to your Board of Trustees. ...

> J. D. KENNEDY

Shanghai, China
Nov. 20, 1886

Committee recommendations to the conference

1. That this Conference elect a Board of Trustees, to consist of three members, who shall hold all property of the Board of Missions of the Methodist Episcopal Church, South, within the bounds of the China Mission Conference, in trust for the Methodist Episcopal Church, South.

2. That this Conference instruct the attorney for the Board of Missions, or his agent, to transfer by deed to said Board of Trustees all property now held by him for said Board of Missions.

3. That this Conference instruct those persons now holding property in their individual names for the Methodist Episcopal Church, South, to transfer by deed all such property to said Board of Trustees.

APPENDIXES

Report of the Board of Trustees, 1887

1. We have carried out the instructions of this Conference at its last session in reference to the titles to Church property in Shanghai, all of which property has been regularly transferred to this Board and registered in due form.

2. The instructions in reference to Church property in the interior have not been carried out, for the following reasons: (1) The titles to property now held in the interior are, in our opinion, valid and secure. (2) To attempt any further change in reference to them would certainly involve us in a considerable expense, and should any difficulty arise with the Chinese officials, might endanger the tenure of some of our property. We therefore deem it inexpedient to take any further action in the matter.

19

Action of March 29, 1937, by the Eastern Asia Central Conference, to create a Board of Trustees to hold property of the Methodist Episcopal Church in China

[Voted to] elect a Board of Trustees consisting of thirteen members, which Board of Trustees shall have in trust the property of the Methodist Episcopal Church in China.

This Board of Trustees shall be constituted as follows: (1) The delegation of each Annual Conference shall nominate one member. (2) The Nominating Committee of the Eastern Asia Central Conference shall nominate five members at large. (3) These thirteen names shall then be presented to the Eastern Asia Central Conference for election.

Hereafter Annual Conference representation on this Board of Trustees shall be elected by the united sessions of the Annual and Lay Conferences.

A CHRONOLOGY OF THE CENTURY

1835 Wesleyan Missionary Lyceum voted that the Methodist Episcopal Church should open work in China. Missionary Society of the Methodist Episcopal Church voted to ask the bishops to select missionaries for China.

1845 Judson Collins graduated at University of Michigan and asked to be sent to China.

1846 Vermont Conference raised money to start a China Mission. Missionary Society made an appropriation to open a mission in China. Adams and Collins appointed as missionaries to China. Committee on Foreign Missions of the Methodist Episcopal Church, South, recommended the establishment of a mission to China, and the General Conference concurred.

1847 Foochow selected as the location of the Methodist Episcopal Mission in China. The Rev. and Mrs. Moses C. White and the Rev. Judson D. Collins sailed from Boston on April 15, and landed in Foochow on September 7.

1848 First reinforcements arrived in Foochow. The Rev. Charles Taylor and the Rev. B. Jenkins, and their families, sailed from Boston April 24, and the Taylor family arrived in Shanghai on September 20. Collins opened a school for boys in Foochow. First Sunday school session held in Foochow March 5. Mrs. White died and was buried in Foochow. Mission concluded on November 28 that its financial condition was desperate.

1849 The Rev. B. Jenkins and family arrived in Shanghai in May.

1850 First formal religious service was held in the chapel in Shanghai. Miss Sperry arrived in Foochow to become the wife of the Rev. R. S. Maclay. Girls' school opened in Foochow.

1851 The Gospel of Matthew published in Foochow colloquial. A special gift was authorized by the Board in New York for the erection of a church in Foochow. Ellen Henrietta Maclay born in Foochow.

1852 Liew Tsoh-Sung and his wife baptized in the Methodist Episcopal Church, South, in Shanghai.

1853 Foochow Mission reduced to only Dr. and Mrs. I. W. Wiley. Shanghai Mission reduced to only the Rev. and Mrs. W. G. E. Cunnyngham.

1854 Appropriation of $30,000 for the Shanghai Mission to provide for a church, press, and school.

1855 Board of Missions in New York favored securing permanent leases on property in China. Room rented in the Chong-seng ward in Foochow for a chapel. First quarterly conference of the Methodist Episcopal Church, South, organized in Shanghai.

1856 Cing Sing Dong and Tieng Ang Dong dedicated in Foochow. A small chapel erected in Shanghai. The Boys' Boarding School in Foochow opened.

APPENDIXES

1857 Ting Ang baptized in Tieng Ang Dong, Foochow, June 14.

1858 First quarterly conference of the Methodist Episcopal Church organized in Foochow.

1859 All male schools in Shanghai dismissed for lack of funds. First child baptized in the Methodist Episcopal Church, South, in Shanghai. The Misses Woolston and Miss Potter arrived in Foochow. Waugh Female Seminary opened in Foochow. A chapel room rented in Foochow city, and preaching began at other points. Persecution occurred at To-cheng.

1860 Soochow selected by the Shanghai Mission as a station. Riots compelled missionaries to move out of Foochow city. Hu Bo-Mi admitted to the Wyoming Conference.

1861 Members at Goi-hung contributed toward the cost of a church building at that place.

1862 Foochow Mission Press opened. Hu Sing-Eng baptized in the Girls' School. The Rev. Nathan Sites and family moved to Ngu-kang.

1863 Yenping appears as a point on the Nantai Circuit, Foochow.

1864 Hu Yong-Mi admitted to the Wyoming Conference.

1865 Bishop Edward Thompson made the first episcopal visit to Foochow.

1866 A large character New Testament in colloquial character published in Foochow.

1867 Virgil C. Hart and E. S. Todd entered Kiukiang on December 1, and commenced work there for the Methodist Episcopal Church.

1868 Foochow Mission decided to open a Peking Circuit. Effort made to secure locally the entire support ($72) of the pastor of Cing Sing Dong.

1869 The Rev. L. N. Wheeler and the Rev. H. H. Lowry commenced work in Peking. Peking and Kiukiang separated from the Foochow Mission. Bishop Kingsley ordained "The Seven Golden Candlesticks" in Foochow. Foochow Boys' Boarding School became a school for ministerial training but within the year was temporarily suspended.

1870 A boys' school opened in Soochow. Sia Sek-Ong renounced all claim to mission funds for his personal support.

1871 First public service held in Peking, first probationers admitted, first property secured. The Woolston sisters became missionaries of the Woman's Foreign Missionary Society, which also appointed Maria Brown and Mary Porter to Peking. The Rev. R. S. Maclay left Foochow, to be transferred to open work in Japan. Hinghwa District organized.

1872 First session of the Peking Annual Meeting held. Peking Girls' School opened. Appropriation of $10,000 by the Board of Missions of the Methodist Episcopal Church to open work in Canton.

1873 Kiukiang Female Boarding School opened. Wang Jui-Fu, of Anchiachuang, Shantung, baptized. Yungchung made a new appointment. Bishop Harris appointed four Chinese as presiding elders in Foochow. Dr. Lucinda Combs sent to Peking; Misses Gertrude Howe and Lucy Hoag to Kiukiang.

1874 Dr. Trask arrived in Foochow; Dr. Lettie Mason in Kiukiang. The first Chinese *Zion's Herald* published in Foochow.

1875 The presiding elder of the Foochow District entirely supported by the Chinese. First hospital for women and children in Peking opened. China Agency of the American Bible Society opened in Shanghai.

1876 Bishop Marvin ordained four deacons and two elders in the Methodist Episcopal Church, South, in Shanghai.

1877 A woman's hospital opened in Foochow. A Methodist Society organized in Tientsin. Dr. W. R. Lambuth opened medical work for the Methodist Episcopal Church, South. Foochow Annual Conference organized, Bishop I. W. Wiley presiding.

1878 Yungchun separated from the Hinghwa District. First Methodist hymnal issued.

1879 A lay delegate elected to General Conference by the Foochow Conference.

1880 The Rev. S. L. Baldwin attended the General Conference of the Methodist Episcopal Church, as the first delegate from China. Pleasant College for Girls opened at Nant-ziang. Central China appointed a superintendent for all its schools.

1881 The Central China Mission divided into five districts; land bought at Wuhu; Chinkiang opened as a mission station. Appropriation made for the opening of a mission in West China. Anglo-Chinese colleges in Foochow and Shanghai and "Fowler University" in Kiukiang started. Dr. Young J. Allen appointed superintendent of the China Mission of the Methodist Episcopal Church, South. Woman's work begun in Soochow. Isabella Fisher Hospital for women opened in Tientsin.

1882 Hospital work in Soochow begun. The Rev. and Mrs. L. N. Wheeler and the Rev. and Mrs. Spencer Lewis arrived in Chungking to open the West China Mission.

1883 Chinkiang Girls' Boarding School opened. The Woolston sisters resigned in protest against educational policies. Hu King-Eng asked for a medical education in the United States.

1884 First preaching service was held in Chungking; the girls' boarding school opened. Medical school opened in connection with Soochow Hospital. Missionaries of the Women's Foreign Missionary Society placed under the direction of the Conferences by action of the General Conference of the Methodist Episcopal Church. Bishop Isaac W. Wiley died in Foochow.

1885 In Asbury Church, Peking, the church stewards collected the pastor's salary. Effort made in Hinghwa to adapt hymns to Chinese music.

1886 China Mission Conference organized by Bishop A. W. Wilson. China Mission Conference organized a property-holding board of trustees. Property purchased three miles out from Chungking. Riots forced missionaries to evacuate Chungking. The Foochow Woman's Conference organized.

1887 Board of trustees of the China Mission Conference took over church property. The Rev. Virgil C. Hart sent to reopen the West China work. Men's and women's hospitals in Soochow united.

1888 First class graduated from the Foochow Girls' School. Nanking University started.

1889 *Foochow Union Hymn and Tune Book* published.

1890 First annual meeting held in West China. Ding Maing-Ing became the first graduate of the Anglo-Chinese College, Foochow. Nanking Theological School was being erected.

1891 Board of Trustees organized for Wiley Institute, Peking. Chengtu opened as a mission station. Foochow Woman's Conference became a delegated body. The Bible in Foochow colloquial completed.

1892 McTyeire School formally opened in March. Wiley Institute, Peking, had five graduates.

1893 North China Annual Conference organized. Chungking Hospital and the church in Shanghai became fully selfsupporting. Knowles and Hitt Bible Schools, and the "Special Gift Day Schools" in Foochow started. Woman's Foreign Missionary Society resumed work in West China.

1894 Chinkiang Institute, the first kindergarten in Peking, and Woolston Hospital, Foochow, opened. Ingchung became a mission station.

1895 Buffington Institute made a part of the Anglo-Chinese College, Shanghai. Dr. Hu King-Eng arrived from the United States.

1896 Hinghwa Mission Conference constituted by the General Conference. The Rev. C. F. Reid appointed presiding elder of the Korea District. Bishop I. W. Joyce assigned to China—the first bishop assigned to a two-year term.

1897 Jubilee held in Foochow. Bishop Joyce visited West China. China Central Conference organized in Shanghai.

1898 Fukien *Christian Advocate* became the *Chinese Christian Advocate*. Taian opened as a mission station.

1899 Two women opened work for the Methodist Protestant Church in Hunan. The women of the Hokchiang District made a "thank offering."

1900 Shanghai made an episcopal residence by the General Conference of the Methodist Episcopal Church.

1901 Attempt made to withdraw from the Ingchung field. William Nast College came into being.

1902 Iongbing opened as a mission station.

1903 A China-wide board of education authorized by the Central Conference. Central Conference asked for the undertaking of work in Shanghai by the Methodist Episcopal Church. The Methodist Publishing House opened in Shanghai.

1904 China made an Episcopal Area of the Methodist Episcopal Church; Bishop J. W. Bashford assigned. Hinghwa Mission Conference became an annual conference. A tentative organization made for Hwa Nan College.

1905 The Union School for Nurses started in Peking.

1906 Peking Women's Medical College proposed. Yungan became a missionary residence. Yungchung became a self-supporting circuit.

1907 Central China became a mission conference. Korea separated from the China Conference. West China appointed two missionaries to Tibet.

1908 Bishop W. S. Lewis appointed to China; Peking and Foochow made episcopal residences. West China Mission Conference organized. Miss Lydia Trimble appointed president of Hwa Nan College.

1909 The Rev. C. S. Heininger sent by the Woman's Foreign Missionary Society of the Methodist Protestant Church to open work in Kalgan. Central China Mission Conference became an annual conference. West China Union University started.

1910 Quadrennial episcopal administration of its China work commenced by the Methodist Episcopal Church, South. Union of Nanking University accomplished. Nurses training schools organized in Foochow and Soochow. Union Kindergarten Training School, Foochow, started.

1911 The Methodist Episcopal Church in Canton purchased land. The Anglo-Chinese College in Shanghai became a part of Soochow University. Overtures received from the Presbyterian Church for union in publishing.

1912 The Kiangsi Mission Conference organized. Methodists commenced cooperating in the Anglican Medical College, Foochow.

1913 *China Christian Advocate* started. China Forward Movement launched. West China became an annual conference. Financial aid by the Congregationalists to the Kalgan Mission discontinued. Woman's Missionary Society organized in Foochow. A Prayer Service for the Chinese Republic held in Asbury Church.

1914 Shanhaikwan opened as a mission station. Two girls graduated from the Peking Women's Medical College. The Chengtu Union Women's Normal School received its first pupils.

1915 The Mission Press, Foochow, disposed of. Central Treasurer's Office opened in Shanghai. Comparative Law School of China was opened in Shanghai. Ming-ngie School opened on a co-operative basis in Futsing.

1916 Stewart Fund made available. Fukien Construction Bureau organized. Yenping Annual Conference organized. Fuchow, Kiangsi, became a missionary station. The hospital in Taian opened in charge of Chinese.

1917 Kiangsi Mission Conference became an annual conference. Woman's Missionary Society organized in the China Conference.

1918 The Board of Missions of the Methodist Protestant Church took over the men's work at Kalgan. The final proof of the new Mandarin Bible read. West China became an annual conference. College work discontinued at William Nast.

1919 A church in Chufu became a reality. The China Mission Conference of the Methodist Protestant Church organized and its first ministers ordained.

1920 The Rev. R. Y. Lo appointed as general editor. Miss Geraldine Townsend sent to China as general secretary of the Epworth League. Cram and Ryang sent from Korea to open work for the Methodist Episcopal Church, South, in Manchuria. Program Statement Conference was held in Peking. China given three bishops by the General Conference of the Methodist Episcopal Church.

1921   Syracuse Hospital Unit arrived in Chungking. First class graduated from Hwa Nan College.

1922   Yungchun Mission Conference organized. China Mission Conference decided to send a mission to the Chinese in Manchuria. Wufenshi congregation decided to support the church by cotton spinning.

1923   The Methodist Publishing House liquidated. All-China Finance Committee authorized. Miss Ethel Li sent to Yungang by the Woman's Missionary Society of the Foochow Conference. Miss Janet Ho licensed as a local preacher.

1924   West China Conference divided. Three missionaries from the China Mission Conference went to Harbin.

1925   Shangtung Conference organized. South Fukien Mission Conference became an annual conference.

1926   Yenching Women's College combined with the men's college.

1927   Most schools came under Chinese administrators. Lincoln Chang and Spencer Lewis jointly presided over the West China Conference. West China Conference Minutes kept in Chinese only.

1928   Mrs. W. T. Hobart killed by a bullet in Taian-fu. Foochow temporarily discontinued as an episcopal residence. Women admitted to Soochow University.

1929   First meeting held of the China Central Council in the China Conference of the Methodist Episcopal Church, South. West China Conference had three presiding officers.

1930   John Gowdy and Wang Chih-Ping elected bishops by the Central Conference.

1931   South Fukien Conference voted to unite with the Church of Christ in China.

1932   Fukien Christian University inaugurated co-education.

1933   Hwa Nan College registered with the government. Youth Conference held on Pootoo.

1934   Bishop Wang Chih-Ping resigned. National secretaries of religious education appointed. Central Conference ordered a commission for taking over church property, approved of laymen in annual conference, and recommended the dedication of infants.

1935   Joint Commission on Unity of the Methodist Episcopal Church and the Methodist Episcopal Church, South, met in Shanghai. Women in West China organized a society to send the gospel to the Miaos. Woman's Foreign Missionary Society withdrew from Shantung.

1936   *Hymns of Universal Praise* published. General Conference equalized assessments for the episcopal fund.

1937   Ralph A. Ward elected a bishop. West China Conferences reunited. Central Conference voted to create a board of trustees. Board of Founders of Nanking Theological School organized.

1938   North China Conference held its 1937 session. The Revs. Zau Tsong-Foh and Mau Myung-Zo went to Kungming.

1939   The Methodist Episcopal, Methodist Episcopal, South, and Methodist Protestant churches united by joint action at Kansas City.

1940   The Kiangsi Conference, after four years without a meeting, met in Shanghai. Episcopal salaries fixed by a General Conference committee.

1941   Z. T. Kaung, W. Y. Chen, and Carleton Lacy elected bishops. The eight-year term for bishops reaffirmed. Central Conference authorized the organization of a property-holding body.

1942   Japanese forced a re-organization of religious bodies in North China. "Pastor's tax" in Futsing changed to a thank offering basis.

1943   Five-Year Program of Church Advance adopted.

1944   General Conference universalized the basis for episcopal salaries.

1945   Bishop Ward released from imprisonment after the Japanese surrender.

1946   Many missionaries returned to China.

1947   Centennial celebration in Foochow in November.

APPENDIX C
METHODIST BISHOPS IN CHINA

BISHOPS OF THE METHODIST EPISCOPAL CHURCH, SOUTH

E. M. Marvin, 1876
A. W. Wilson, 1886-91
Joseph S. Key, 1892-93
C. B. Galloway, 1894
E. R. Hendrix, 1895
A. W. Wilson, 1898-1900
C. B. Galloway, 1902-04
W. A. Candler, 1906
A. W. Wilson, 1907
Seth Ward, 1908
E. E. Hoss, 1910

W. B. Murrah, 1911-13
James Atkins, 1914
E. E. Hoss, 1915
John C. Kilgo, 1917
W. F. McMurray, 1918
W. R. Lambuth, 1919-20
S. R. Hay, 1922
H. A. Boaz, 1923-25
William N. Ainsworth, 1926-29
Paul B. Kern, 1930-33
Arthur J. Moore, 1934-38

BISHOPS OF THE METHODIST EPISCOPAL CHURCH

Edward Thomson, 1865
Colvin Kingsley, 1869
W. L. Harris, 1873
Isaac W. Wiley, 1877
Thomas Bowman, 1881
Stephen M. Merrill, 1883
Isaac W. Wiley, 1884
H. W. Warren, 1887
C. H. Fowler, 1888
E. G. Andrews, 1889
D. A. Goodsell, 1891
W. F. Mallalieu, 1892
R. S. Foster, 1893
W. X. Ninde, 1894
J. M. Walden, 1895

Isaac W. Joyce, 1896-97
Earl Cranston, 1898-99
David H. Moore, 1900-03
J. W. Bashford, 1904-10
W. S. Lewis, 1908-21
Herbert Welch, 1918
L. J. Birney, 1920-31
F. T. Keeney, 1920-23
G. R. Grose, 1924-29
W. E. Brown, 1924-27
John Gowdy, 1930-39
Wang Chih-Ping, 1930-33
Herbert Welch, 1932-35
Ralph A. Ward, 1934-39
W. E. Hammaker, 1936-38

BISHOPS OF THE METHODIST CHURCH

Arthur J. Moore, 1939-40
John Gowdy, 1939-41
Ralph A. Ward, 1939—

Z. T. Kaung, 1941—
W. Y. Chen, 1941—
Carleton Lacy, 1941—

APPENDIX D
GEOGRAPHICAL NAMES WITH VARIANT SPELLINGS

Ankechuang—Anchiachuang
Bingtang—Haitang
Chang-chau—Changchow
Chufu—Chu-fu; Chu-fuh-hsien
Foochow—Fuhchau; Fuh Chau; Hok-chue
Futsing—Hokchiang
Haitang—Bingtang
Hok-chue—Foochow
Hokchiang—Futsing
Ing-ang—Yungang
Ing-chung—Yung-chun; Yungchun
Iong-bing—Nanping; Yenping
Kiang-nan—Kiangsu
Kutien—Kucheng

Kwan-san—Quinsan
Lek-du—Lutu
Lungtien—Ngucheng
Mingchiang—Mintsing
Nantziang—Nant-ziang
Quinsan—Kwan-san
Shanhaikuan—Shan-hai-Kuan
Taian—Tai-an; Taian-fu
Taik-hwa—Tehwa
Tsun-hua—Tsunghwa
Yek-iong—Yekiong
Yenping—Iongbing; Nanping
Yungan—Ingang
Yungchun—Yung-chun; Ingchung

REFERENCES

CHAPTER I: THE DAY OF MARCH HAS COME

1. Luccock and Hutchinson, *The Story of Methodism* (New York: Methodist Book Concern, 1926), p. 310.
2. *Ibid.*, p. 338.
3. *The Great Wall Crumbles* (New York: The Macmillan Co., 1935), p. 188.
4. *Ibid.* p. 194.
5. Hosea Ballou Morse and Harley Farnsworth MacNair, *Far Eastern International Relations* (Boston: Houghton, Mifflin Co., 1931), p. 60.
6. *The Middle Kingdom* (New York: Scribners and Sons, 1895), p. 511.
7. *A History of Christian Missions in China* (New York: The Macmillan Co., 1929), p. 229.
8. D. Macgillivray, *A Century of Protestant Missions in China* (Shanghai: Presbyterian Mission Press, 1907), p. 2.
9. Records of the Missionary Board, Vol. IV, pp. 475-77.
10. *Ibid.*, minutes, July 30, 1846.
11. The original of this letter is pasted in the journal of Moses C. White.
12. Reid and Gracey, *Missions and Missionary Society of the Methodist Episcopal Church* (New York: Phillips and Hunt, 1882), p. 415.
13. Moses C. White, *op. cit.*, p. 83.
14. Records of the Missionary Board.
15. R. S. Maclay, *Life Among the Chinese* (New York: Carleton and Porter, 1861), pp. 142-43.
16. From the special meeting minutes of the board of managers of the Board of Missions of the Methodist Episcopal Church, March 26, 1847.
17. *Ibid.*
18. *Ibid.*
19. Richard Angell, Chairman of Committee on Foreign Missions, 1st M. E. Ch. So., Miss. Soc., 1846, p. 54.
20. 3rd M. E. Ch. So., Miss. Soc., p. 72-73.

CHAPTER II: A FOUNDATION IS LAID

1. 3rd M. E. Ch. So., Miss. Soc., p. 76, 78.
2. From a letter quoted in 32nd M. E. Miss. Soc.
3. Quoted in 30th M. E. Miss. Soc.
4. Minutes of the China Committee, M. E. Miss. Soc., May 14, 1855.
5. *The Central Conference of the Methodist Episcopal Church* (Foochow: Christian Herald Press, 1940), p. 36.
6. From correspondence on file in the Board of Missions, 150 Fifth Ave., New York.
7. F. T. Cartwright, *Notes on Early Foochow History;* an unpublished manuscript, 1923.
8. Frank Mason North, a manuscript in the library of the Division of Foreign Missions, New York, quoted from the *Missionary Advocate,* 1849.
9. Manuscript in the library of the Division of Foreign Missions, New York.
10. 32nd M. E. Miss. Soc.
11. I. W. Wiley, *The Missionary Cemetery and the Fallen Missionaries of Fuh Chau, China* (New York: Carleton & Porter, 1858), p. 71, 79.
12. 35th M. E. Miss. Soc.
13. 16th M. E. Ch. So., Miss. Soc., p. 100.
14. 5th M. E. Ch. So., Miss. Soc., p. 66.
15. B. Jenkins, 16th M. E. Ch. So., Miss. Soc., p. 97.
16. 5th M. E. Ch. So., Miss. Soc., p. 67.
17. 12th M. E. Ch. So., Miss. Soc., p. 90.
18. 12th M. E. Ch. So., Miss. Soc., p. 92.
19. 15th M. E. Ch. So., Miss. Soc., p. 98.
20. 16th M. E. Ch. So., Miss. Soc., p. 94.
21. Nashville: Cokesbury Press, 1926, pp. 99-100.

22. F. T. Cartwright, *Notes on Early Foo-chow History.*

23. *Missionary Advocate*, March, 1859.

24. Worley, *op. cit.*, p. 83.

25. *Missionary Advocate*, November 1861.

26. 40th M. E. Miss. Soc.

CHAPTER III: IT SPREADS AND GROWS

1. *Life Among the Chinese* (New York: Carleton and Porter, 1861), p. 153.

2. New York: The Macmillan Co., 1927, p. 277.

3. *China and Methodism* (Cincinnati: Methodist Book Concern, 1906), p. 58

4. 53rd M. E. Miss. Soc.

5. A. H. Tuttle, *Mary Porter Gamewell and her Story of the Siege of Peking* (New York: Methodist Book Concern, 1907) p. 13.

6. *Ibid.* p. 39.

7. *Missionary Advocate*, March 15, 1870.

8. L. N. Wheeler in 54th M. E. Miss. Soc.

9. 65th M. E. Miss. Soc., p. 80.

10. Manuscript, "Pionering in West China."

11. Tuttle, *op. cit.*

12. 68th M. E. Miss. Soc., p. 99.

13. E. I. Hart, *Virgil C. Hart: Missionary Statesman;* (New York: Doran, 1917), p. 149.

14. *Zion's Herald*, May 4, 1887.

15. 71st M. E. Miss. Soc., p. 105.

16. 72nd M. E. Miss. Soc., p. 105.

17. 34th M. E. Wom. Fgn. Miss. Soc., Mary E. Holt, p. 137.

18. M. E. Bd. Fgn. Miss., 1914. G. W. Verity, p. 154.

19. M. E. Bd. Fgn. Miss., 1919. Henry S. Leitzel, p. 106.

20. M. E. Bd. Fgn. Miss., 1917, p. 234.

21. 82nd M. E. Miss. Soc., p. 146.

22. M. E. Bd. Fgn. Miss., 1911. Ding Cih-Sing, p. 97.

23. 85th M. E. Miss. Soc., p. 131.

24. 1st Cent. Conf. E. Asia, 1915, p. 8.

25. 2nd Cent. Conf. E. Asia, 1920, Episcopal Address, p. 71.

26. 3rd Cent. Conf. E. Asia, 1923, p. 150.

27. *Journal*, minutes of the Foochow Annual Conference, Dec. 10, 1938.

28. Letter to author.

29. Horace S. Williams, official *Journals* of the Kalgan Mission Conference of The Methodist Church, Memorial Number, 1939, pp. 49-50.

CHAPTER IV: UPWARD AND ONWARD

1. J. M. Reid, *Missions and Missionary Society of the Methodist Episcopal Church* (New York: Phillips and Hunt, 1882), I, 407.

2. *Journal*, first session, Foochow Annual Conference, 1877, minutes for the first day, December, 20, 1877.

3. 61st M. E. Miss. Soc., p. 49.

4. Reid, *op. cit.* p. 407

5. *Ibid.*, p. 408.

6. A. P. Parker, M. E. Ch. So., Bd. Miss. 1881. p. 40.

7. Elmer T. Clark, *The Chiangs of China* (Nashville: Methodist Publishing House, 1943), p. 25.

8. From a "Statement of Facts," taken from the *Journals* of the North Carolina Conference of the Methodist Episcopal Church, South, for the years 1885-1887, furnished the author by the Rev. E. H. Nease, secretary of the Western North Carolina Conference.

9. Reid, *op cit.*, I, 380.

10. Perry O. Hanson, manuscript "History of the Shantung Annual Conference," in library of Division of Foreign Missions, New York.

11. 5th China Cent. Conf., 1911, Report of Committee on Memorials, p. 40.

12. 3rd Cent. Conf. E. Asia, 1923, pp. 149-50.

13. 32nd M. E. Wom. Fgn. Miss. Soc., p. 153.

14. M. E. Bd. Fgn. Miss., 1915, p. 208.

15. 2nd China Cent. Conf., 1899, constitutional amendments, p. 53.

16. H. W. Worley, *Central Conference of*

the Methodist Episcopal Church (Foochow: Christian Herald Press, 1940), p. 247.

17. M. E. Bd. Fgn. Miss., 1926, F. M. Pyke, p. 78.

18. Miss Young in "History of Shangtung Annual Conference," a manuscript in the library of Division of Foreign Missions, New York, p. 48.

19. M. E. Bd. Fgn. Miss., 1923; p. 78.

CHAPTER V: MEN OF GOOD STANDING IN CHARGE

1. Worley, *op. cit.*, pp. 60, 62.
2. 3rd China Cent. Conf., 1903, p. 37.
3. Worley, *op. cit.*, pp. 239, 241.
4. 4th China Cent. Conf., 1907, p. 24.
5. Ida Belle Lewis, *Bishop Wilson Seeley Lewis* (Sioux City: Morningside College, 1929), pp. 106-07.
6. 6th China Cent. Conf., 1915, p. 76.
7. I. G. John, *Handbook of Methodist Missions* (Nashville, 1893), p. 201.
8. 68th M. E. Ch. So. Bd. Miss., p. 99.
9. 72nd M. E. Ch. So. Bd. Miss., p. 104.
10. Letter from F. D. Gamewell to Mrs. John Gowdy.
11. *Ibid.*

12. Worley, *op. cit.*, p. 275.
13. Worley, *op. cit.*, p. 276.
14. Letter from Carleton Lacy to the author.
15. *Journal*, p. 5.
16. O. E. Goddard, secretary of Foreign Department, in Missionary Yearbook, Methodist Episcopal Church, South, 1930; Board of Missions, Nashville, p. 17.
17. Worley, *op. cit.*, p. 298.
18. Carleton Lacy, "The Central Conference Question Box," *China Christian Advocate*, December, 1940.
19. Worley, *op. cit.*, p. 297.

CHAPTER VI: EARTHQUAKE SHOCKS THREATEN

1. From quotations from early letters quoted by F. T. Cartwright in *Notes on Early Foochow History*, from records in the Board of Foreign Missions, New York.
2. Spencer Lewis, "Pioneering in West China," a manuscript.
3. *Ibid.*
4. 32nd M. E. Wom. Fgn. Miss. Soc., L. A. Alderman, p. 157.
5. 83rd M. E. Miss. Soc., W. T. Hobart, p. 112.
6. Fletcher S. Brockman, *I Discover the Orient* (New York: Harper & Bros., 1935), p. 53.
7. 82nd M. E. Miss. Soc., p. 129.
8. K. S. Latourette, *A History of Christian Missions in China* (New York: The Macmillan Co., 1929), p. 478.
9. *Zion's Herald*, January 9, 1924.
10. M. E. Bd. Fgn. Miss., 1912, p. 77.
11. M. E. Bd. Fgn. Miss., 1913, p. 206.
12. M. E. Bd. Fgn. Miss., 1921, G. L. Davis, p. 142.
13. M. E. Bd. Fgn. Miss., 1926, p. 85.
14. *A Record of the Decade* 1919-1929.

The yearbook of the M. E. Wom. Fgn. Miss. Soc., being the 60th Annual Report, 1929. p. 26.
15. Report of the executive secretary of the Division of Foreign Missions to the 3rd annual meeting of the Board of Missions, December 6-12, 1942. p. 62.
16. *China Christian Advocate*, September, 1938.
17. Reported to the 3rd Annual Meeting of the Board of Missions, December 6-12, 1942.
18. Carleton Lacy, *The Great Migration and the Church in West China* (Shanghai, 1940), p. 36-37.
19. *Ibid.* p. 1.
20. *Ibid.*, pp. 80-82.
21. Letter to friends.
22. *China Christian Advocate*, April 1940.
23. Report of the executive secretary of The Division of Foreign Missions to the 3rd annual meeting of the Board of Missions, December 6-12, 1942. pp. 45-46.

CHAPTER VII: INFORM THE MIND

1. Herbert Welch, *Men of the Outposts* (Abingdon Press, New York, 1937), p. 105.

2. 39th M. E. Miss. Soc.

3. 51st M. E. Miss. Soc.

4. 63rd M. E. Miss. Soc., p. 65.

5. *Our Oriental Missions* (Cincinnati: Methodist Book Concern, 1870), I, 253-54.

6. 14th M. E. Wom. Fgn. Miss. Soc., p. 25.

7. *Ibid.* p. 24.

8. *The Missionary Reporter*, February 1890.

9. 60th M. E. Ch. So. Bd. Miss., p. 32.

10. 66th M. E. Ch. So. Bd. Miss., p. 84.

11. 62nd M. E. Miss. Soc., V. C. Hart, p. 60.

12. 63rd M. E. Miss. Soc., V. C. Hart, p. 75.

13. 79th M. E. Miss. Soc., pp. 120-21.

14. 79th M. E. Miss. Soc., W. C. Longden, p. 120.

15. Ford, *History of the Educational Work of the Methodist Episcopal Church in China* (Foochow: Christian Herald Press, 1938), p. 53.

16. 72nd M. E. Miss. Soc., p. 107.

17. A. H. Tuttle, *Mary Porter Gamewell* (New York: Methodist Book Concern, 1907), pp. 61-63.

18. 76th M. E. Miss. Soc., Alice M. Stanton, p. 69.

19. 76th M. E. Miss. Soc., p. 78.

20. Tuttle, *op. cit.*, p. 55.

21. 76th M. E. Miss. Soc., p. 44.

22. 77th M. E. Miss. Soc., p. 50.

23. 3rd China Cent. Conf., 1903, p. 52.

24. 5th China Cent. Conf., 1911, p. 46.

25. 84th M. E. Miss. Soc., p. 170.

26. 36th M. E. Wom. Fgn. Miss. Soc., 1904-05, p. 164.

27. 39th M. E. Wom. Fgn. Miss. Soc., p. 142.

28. 40th M. E. Wom. Fgn. Miss. Soc., 1909, p. 141.

29. M. E. Bd. Fgn. Miss., 1912, p. 119.

30. M. E. Bd. Fgn. Miss., 1920, p. 88.

31. *Zion's Herald*, January 9, 1924.

32. M. E. Bd. Fgn. Miss., 1918, p. 192.

33. M. E. Bd. Fgn. Miss., 1914, J. M. Yard, p. 158.

34. 3rd. Cent. Conf. E. Asia, 1923, p. 74.

35. Ford, *op. cit.*, p. 243.

36. Ford, *op. cit.*, p. 276.

37. *Valorous Ventures* (Boston: Women's Foreign Missionary Society, 1936) p. 233.

38. M. E. Bd. Fgn. Miss., 1926, F. T. Cartwright, p. 63.

39. "Pioneering in West China," a manuscript.

40. The *Christian Advocate* (Chicago), September 9, 1943.

41. M. E. Bd. Fgn. Miss., 1937; from the report of the corresponding secretaries, p. 72.

42. From "A Summary of the Episcopal Address" to the Central Conference of Eastern Asia, *China Christian Advocate*, April 1937.

43. Quoted in the report of the executive secretary of the Division of Foreign Missions, December 1942.

44. Special Cent. Conf. E. Asia, 1930. From the Episcopal Address.

45. 7th Cent. Conf. E. Asia, 1937. From the Episcopal Address.

46. 3rd Cent. Conf. E. Asia, 1923. Report of Committee on Sunday Schools and Epworth League, adopted at the morning session, November 24.

47. 7th Cent. Conf. E. Asia, from the Episcopal Address.

48. Irma Highbaugh in *China Christian Advocate*, March 1940.

49. From the Episcopal Address to the Central Conference of East Asia, 1937.

50. *China Christian Advocate*, May, 1937.

CHAPTER VIII: THEY HEAL

1. 11th M. E. Wom. Fgn. Miss. Soc., 1879-80, p. 32.

2. 12th M. E. Wom. Fgn. Miss. Soc., 1880-81, p. 38.

REFERENCES

3. 78th M. E. Miss. Soc., p. 48.
4. 68th M. E. Miss. Soc., p. 77.
5. M. E. Bd. Fgn. Miss., 1919, p. 40.
6. 40th M. E. Wom. Fgn. Miss. Soc., 1909, p. 166.
7. "Medical Work of the M. E. Church in Peking, China." A memorandum written for the author.
8. 3rd Cent. Conf. E. Asia, 1923, pp. 79-80.
9. "History of Shantung Annual Confer-

ence." A Manuscript in the library of the Division of Foreign Missions, New York.
10. *China Christian Advocate*, December, 1937.
11. *Ibid.*
12. Quoted in the report of the executive secretary of the Division of Foreign Missions to the 3rd Annual Meeting, 1942, pp. 56-57.

CHAPTER IX: PUBLISH GLAD TIDINGS

1. Minutes of the China Committee, M. E. Miss. Soc. November 2, 1859.
2. 44th M. E. Miss. Soc.
3. *Methodist Review of Missions*, June, 1895.
4. 2nd China Cent. Conf., 1899.
5. 85th M. E. Miss. Soc., p. 127.
6. M. E. Bd. Fgn. Miss., 1915.
7. 3rd Cent. Conf. E. Asia, from the Episcopal Address.
8. *Methodist Review of Missions*, May, 1894.

9. M. E. Bd. Fgn. Miss., 1918; p. 209.
10. "Pioneering in West China," a manuscript.
11. 6th Cent. Conf. E. Asia, 1934; from the Episcopal Address.
12. From an article "Hymnology in Foreign Missions," in *Julian's Dictionary of Hymnology*.
13. 7th Cent. Conf. E. Asia, 1937, p. 43.
14. James Burke, *My Father in China* (New York: Farrar and Rinehart, Inc., 1942.)

CHAPTER X: WE GIVE THEE

1. 60th M. E. Miss. Soc., N. Sites, p. 56.
2. Cokesbury Press, Nashville, pp. 65-66.
3. Reid and Gracey, *Missions and Missionary Society of the Methodist Episcopal Church* (New York: Phillips and Hunt), pp. 743-44.
4. *Missionary Advocate*, May 16, 1871.
5. 56th M. E. Miss. Soc., p. 56.
6. 68th M. E. Miss. Soc., p. 89.
7. 57th M. E. Miss. Soc., N. J. Plumb, p. 54.
8. 72nd M. E. Miss. Soc., p. 83.
9. *Missionary Advocate*, April 5, 1873, p. 55.
10. 57th M. E. Miss. Soc., p. 51.
11. 64th M. E. Miss. Soc., H. H. Lowry, pp. 68-69.
12. 72nd M. E. Miss. Soc., W. H. Lacy, p. 54.
13. 78th M. E. Miss. Soc., J. H. Worley, p. 28.
14. M. E. Bd. Fgn. Miss., 1918, pp. 216-17.
15. 69th M. E. Ch. So. Bd. Miss., 1915. Report of J. L. Hendry.

16. 3rd China Cent. Conf., 1903. Report of Committee on State of the Church, p. 30.
17. Ida Belle Lewis: *Bishop Wilson Seeley Lewis* (Morningside College, Sioux City, 1929).
18. M. E. Bd. Fgn. Miss., 1919, p. 132.
19. Ida Belle Lewis, *op. cit.*
20. Wesley M. Smith, personal letter, July 3, 1943.
21. M. E. Bd. Fgn. Miss., 1924, p. 43.
22. *Ibid.*, p. 51.
23. *Ibid.*, p. 45.
24. M. E. Bd. Fgn. Miss., 1925, J. W. Hawley, p. 68.
25. H. V. Lacy "Can You Beat It?" *Zion's Herald*, March 13, 1929.
26. 5th Cent. Conf. E. Asia, 1934, the Episcopal Address, p. 36.
27. M. E. Bd. Fgn. Miss., 1929, W. R. Johnson, p. 110.
28. 5th Cent. Conf. E. Asia, 1934, p. 39.
29. Special Cent. Conf. E. Asia, 1930, the Episcopal Address, p. 96.

30. 5th Cent. Conf. E. Asia, 1934, p. 40.
31. Mary Culler White, "The Story of the Years," *China Christian Advocate*, December 1935.
32. W. S. Bissonnette, "The Church Is on the March," *China Christian Advocate*, January 1939.
33. Ortha M. Lane, "Harvest Festival at the Ankechuang Methodist Church" *China Christian Advocate*, November 1940.
34. Mary Sing-Gieu Carleton, personal letter to the author, June 7, 1943.
35. Carleton Lacy, *The Great Migration and the Church in West China* (Shanghai, 1940), p. 45.

CHAPTER XI: BOUNTIES RECEIVE

1. M. E. Bd. Fgn. Miss., 1910, p. 41.
2. M. E. Bd. Fgn. Miss., 1920, corresponding secretaries' report, p. 17.
3. M. E. Bd. Fgn. Miss., 1919, p. 67.
4. M. E. Bd. Fgn. Miss., 1919, p. 87.
5. M. E. Bd. Fgn. Miss., 1921, corresponding secretary's report, p. 28.
6. 3rd Cent. Conf. E. Asia, 1923, Episcopal Address, p. 10.
7. W. W. Pinson, *Walter Russell Lambuth* (Nashville: Cokesbury Press, 1924), pp. 194-95.

CHAPTER XII: WOMEN ACT LIKE THAT

1. A. H. Tuttle, *Mary Porter Gamewell* (New York: Methodist Book Concern), pp. 63-64.
2. Tuttle *op. cit.*, p. 102.
3. *Ibid.*
4. *Ibid.*, pp. 102-3.
5. M. E. Bd. Fgn. Miss., 1925, p. 107.
6. China Bulletin No. 11, August 24, 1938, issued by the corresponding secretaries of the Board of Foreign Missions of the Methodist Episcopal Church.

CHAPTER XIII: NEW OCCASIONS TEACH NEW DUTIES

1. 82nd M. E. Miss. Soc., p. 136.
2. 5th Cent. China Conf., 1911, p. 58.
3. 5th Cent. Conf. E. Asia, p. 60.
4. Special Cent. Conf. E. Asia, 1930, p. 27.
5. M. E. Bd. Fgn. Miss., 1915, p. 182.
6. 6th China Cent. Conf., 1915, p. 73.
7. 68th M. E. Miss. Soc., p. 75.
8. 2nd Cent. Conf. E. Asia, 1920, p. 13.
9. M. E. Bd. Fgn. Miss., 1911; p. 156.
10. M. E. Bd. Fgn. Miss., 1921, p. 215.

CHAPTER XIV: ALL ONE BODY

1. 4th China Cent. Conf., 1907, p. 67.
2. 5th China Cent. Conf., 1911, p. 58.
3. Luccock and Hutchinson, *The Story of Methodism* (New York: Methodist Book Concern, 1926), p. 494.
4. Carleton Lacy, *China Christian Advocate*, November 1940.
5. *China Christian Advocate*, November 1940.
6. *China Christian Advocate*, November 1938.
7. "The Methodist Church in Eastern Central China." Quoted in the report of the executive secretary of the Division of Foreign Missions to the 3rd Annual Meeting, 1942, p. 125.
8. M. E. Bd. Fgn. Miss., 1911, Carl A. Felt, p. 131.
9. M. E. Bd. Fgn. Miss., 1913, Frederick Brown, p. 278.
10. *The Central Conference of the Methodist Episcopal Church* (Foochow: Christian Herald Press, 1940), p. 191.
11. 3rd Cent. Conf. E. Asia, 1923, from the Episcopal Address.
12. *Ibid*, p. 173.
13. Report on Special Mission to China to the China Committee, April 23-26, 1946, p. 10.
14. Special Cent. Conf. E. Asia, 1930, from the Episcopal Address.

REFERENCES

15. *China Christian Advocate*, November, 1940.
16. *Christian Advocate*, Chicago, April 27, 1944.
17. Special Cent. Conf. E. Asia, 1930, memorial from Yenping Conference, p. 40.
18. *China Christian Advocate*, February 1937.
19. *China Christian Advocate*, February 1937.
20. *Christian Advocate*, Chicago, January 27, 1944.
21. Board of Missions and Church Extension, New York, 1942. p. 125.
22. *Ibid.*, p. 118.
Luccock and Hutchinson, *op. cit.*, *p.* 491.

CHAPTER XV: THE NOBLE HOST

1. 84th M. E. Miss. Soc., p. 136.
2. 72nd M. E. Miss. Soc., W. F. Walker, p. 87.
3. 80th M. E. Miss. Soc., W. T. Hobart, p. 144.
4. 85th M. E. Miss. Soc., p. 162.
5. 51st M. E. Wom. Fgn. Miss. Soc., yearbook, 1920, p. 64.
6. M. E. Bd. Fgn. Miss., 1921, p. 85.
7. M. E. Bd. Fgn. Miss., 1921, p. 95.
8. M. E. Bd. Fgn. Miss., 1915, p. 189.
9. M. E. Bd. Fgn. Miss., 1913, p. 267.
10. M. E. Bd. Fgn. Miss., 1923, p. 92.
11. M. E. Bd. Fgn. Miss., 1913, pp. 274-5.
12. M. E. Bd. Fgn. Miss., 1927, W. R. Johnson, p. 128.
13. M. E. Bd. Fgn. Miss., *The Imperishable Message, the Story of 1930 and 1931*, pp. 34-35.
14. Richard T. Baker, *Methodism in China The War Years* (New York: Board of Missions and Church Extension, 1946), pp 5-6.
15. *Ibid.* p. 7.
16. Elmer T. Clark, *The Chiangs of China* (New York & Nashville: Abingdon-Cokesbury Press, 1943), p. 79.
17. *Ibid.* p. 84.
18. James Burke, *My Father in China* (New York: Farrar and Rinehart, Inc., 1942), p. 347.
19. 7th Cent. Conf. E. Asia, 1937, address by Chiang Kai-shek, pp. 46-48.
20. Roy L. Smith in the *Christian Advocate*; quoted by the *China Christian Advocate*, November 1939.
21. M. E. Bd. Fgn. Miss., 1925, p. 98.

CHAPTER XIV: WE ARE ABLE

1. By permission of Earl Marlatt.
2. *Fighting Angel—Portrait of a Soul* (New York: Reynal and Hitchcock, 1936), pp. 75, 128. By permission.
3. *Zion's Herald*, January 9, 1924.
4. 72nd M. E. Miss. Soc., James Jackson, p. 86.
5. M. E. Ch. So., Bd. Miss., 1929, p. 251.
6. M. E. Bd. Fgn. Miss., *The Imperishable Message—The Story of 1930 and 1931*, p. 38.
7. M. E. Wom. Fgn. Miss. Soc., 1929, yearbook. A record of the decade 1919-1929; p. 27.
8. M. E. Ch. So., Bd. Miss., 1888; p. 71.
9. M. E. Bd. Fgn. Miss., 1927; Report of the Committee on China, p. 72.
10. *Ibid.* 1934.
11. 5th Cent. Conf. E. Asia, from the Commission on Organization, p. 57.
12. *China Christian Advocate*, April 1937.
13. F. T. Cartwright, in a memorandum sent the author.
14. *Daily Christian Advocate*, May 2, 1944.
15. "The Work of Moore Memorial Church as presented to the First China Central Conference of the Methodist Church, Shanghai, March 31, 1941," a bulletin.
16. Mary Carleton in *China Christian Advocate*, February 1940.
17. M. E. Ch. So. Bd. Miss., 1917-18, annual report of Miss Esther Case, p. 84.
18. Edith Simester in a mimeographed letter September 5, 1942.

CHAPTER XVII: THE CHURCH WILL REMAIN

1. Fletcher Brockman, *I Discover the Orient* (New York: Harper & Bros., 1935), p. 199.
2. Report of executive secretary of the Division of Foreign Missions, 3rd Annual Meeting, 1942.
3. *A History of Christian Missions in China* (New York: The Macmillan Co., 1929), p. 43.
4. Harry W. Worley, *The Central Conference of the Methodist Episcopal Church* (Foochow: Christian Herald Press, 1940), p. 177.
5. The Rev. W. S. Walsh, quoted in *China and the Far East*. Clark University Lectures edited by George H. Blakeslee (New York: Thomas Y. Crowell & Co., 1910), p. 250.
6. Commercial Press, Shanghai, 1926, p. 226.
7. W. Reginald Wheeler, *John E. Williams of Nanking* (New York: Fleming H. Revell Co., 1937), p. 85.
8. *Daily Christian Advocate*, May 2, 1944.
9. *The United Church Record and Missionary Review*, Toronto, November 1938.
10. Latourette, *op. cit.*, p. 801.

APPENDIX A

1. Records of the Missionary Board, Vol. II, May 20, 1835. In files of Board of Foreign Missions of The Methodist Church, New York.
4. 3rd M. E. Ch., So. Miss. Soc., 1848, pp. 69-70.
5. Minutes, special meeting, Board of Managers of the Missionary Society of the Methodist Episcopal Church.
6. In files of the Division of Foreign Missions of The Methodist Church, New York.
7. (a) 6th M. E. Ch. So. Miss. Soc., p. 88. (b) 7th M. E. Ch. So. Miss. Soc., p. 102.
8. 15th M. E. Ch. So. Miss. Soc., 1860, p. 94.
9. In files of Board of Foreign Missions, New York.
10. 45th M. E. Miss. Soc.
11. In files of Board of Foreign Missions, New York.
12. Carleton Lacy: *The Great Migration and the Church in West China* (Shanghai, 1940), pp. 19, 23, 58, 72, 37.
13. Exhibit F, M. E. Bd. Fgn. Miss., 1937, p. 141.
14. 63rd M. E. Miss. Soc., pp. 64-65.
15. *China Christian Advocate*, August, 1940.
16. A report written for this book in which the writer modestly omits his own large share in this work.
17. M. E. Bd. Fgn. Miss., 1920, pp. 17-21.
18. (a) 41st M. E. Ch. So. Miss. Bd., 1887; pp. 85-86.
    (b) *Ibid.* pp. 86-87.
    (c) *Ibid.* p. 87.
    (d) 42nd M. E. Ch. So. Miss. Bd., 1888. p. 71.
19. 7th Cent. Conf. E. Asia, 1937; p. 31.

INDEX

INDEX

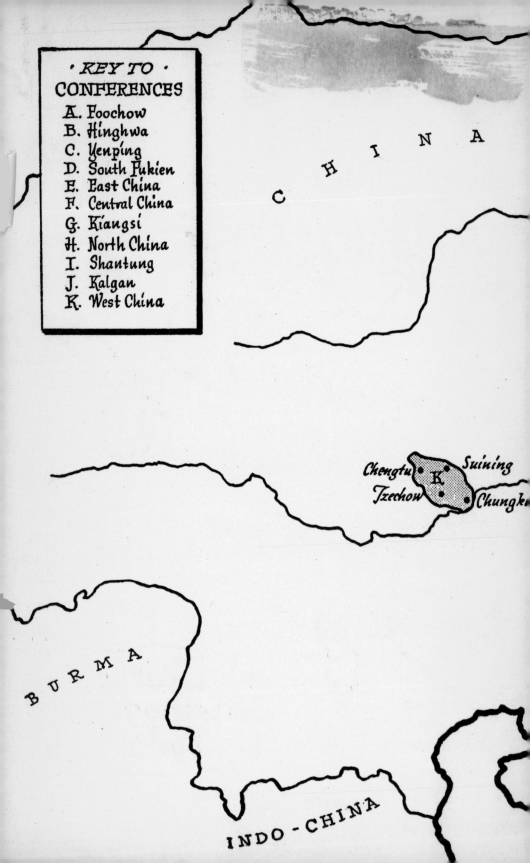

KEY TO
CONFERENCES
A. Foochow
B. Hinghwa
C. Yenping
D. South Fukien
E. East China
F. Central China
G. Kiangsi
H. North China
I. Shantung
J. Kalgan
K. West China

CHINA

Chengtu   Suining
K
Tzechow   Chungk

BURMA

INDO-CHINA